Commonsense Talent Management

Commonsense Talent Management

USING STRATEGIC HUMAN RESOURCES TO IMPROVE COMPANY PERFORMANCE

Steven T. Hunt

WILEY

Published by Wiley
One Montgomery Street, Suite 1200, San Francisco, CA 94104-4594—www.wiley.com

Cover image: IStockphoto and Thinkstock
Cover design: JPuda

For additional copies or bulk purchases of this book or to learn more about Wiley's Workplace Learning offerings, please contact us toll free at 1-866-888-5159 or by email at workplacelearning@wiley.com.

Wiley also publishes its books in a variety of electronic formats and by print-on-demand. Some material included with standard print versions of this book may not be included in e-books or in print-on-demand. If the version of this book that you purchased references media such as a CD or DVD that was not included in your purchase, you may download this material at http://booksupport.wiley.com. For more information about Wiley products, visit www.wiley.com.

Library of Congress Cataloging-in-Publication Data has been applied for and is on file with the Library of Congress.

ISBN 978-0-470-44241-8 (pbk); ISBN 978-1-118-23392-4 (ebk); ISBN 978-1-118-22023-8 (ebk)

FIRST EDITION

PB Printing   10 9 8 7 6 5 4 3 2 1

CONTENTS

TABLES, FIGURES, AND DISCUSSIONS

TABLES

FIGURES

DISCUSSIONS

This book is dedicated to the memory of Alan James Hunt

If I have seen further it is by standing on the shoulders of giants.

—Isaac Newton

Other than health and family, few things are more important to happiness than having meaningful and fulfilling work. Creating high-quality work environments positively influences the lives of employees, their families, their managers, their customers, and the broader society. Higher-quality work environments create better world environments.

Despite the value of high-quality work environments, our society is plagued by examples of poorly run companies. Workplaces are so frequently mismanaged that there is even a genre of humor solely devoted to making fun of office life (*Dilbert* and *The Office* come readily to mind). I often find this humor enjoyable, but I also find it somewhat sad, and even tragic. It is sad because it is based on real problems that financially and emotionally hurt employees, managers, customers, and their families. It is tragic because we have the knowledge to avoid most of these problems, but many organizations do not use this knowledge.

This book is titled *Commonsense Talent Management* because the concepts it explains are based on fundamental psychological principles about employee behavior. These principles are well established and for the most part fairly straightforward. They make basic sense provided you are aware of them. But they are also overlooked by many managers and companies. As an example, consider the importance of working with employees to set clearly defined job goals and providing employees with constructive behavioral feedback and coaching. Setting goals and providing feedback are basic management techniques that have a significant impact on workforce productivity, but many companies do not do either of these things consistently or effectively. Why is this? If we all know we should do it, why don't we? This book addresses these sorts of questions by examining how to get leaders, managers, employees, and human resource specialists to carry out commonsense activities necessary to create highly productive work environments.

I often say that creating a healthy workplace is like living a healthy lifestyle. Everyone knows that losing weight requires changing one's diet and exercising more. It is not a matter of knowing what to do; it is doing it on a regular basis. As you will see in this book, the same thing can often be said for workforce management. We know what to do yet struggle to do it consistently. However, it is not hard to do provided we focus on basic guidelines and principles.

This book provides guidance on how to create more productive, healthy, efficient, and sustainable work environments through the effective use of human resource processes. The book is specifically written for human resource professionals because those are the people whose responsibility typically includes increasing workforce productivity and creating higher-quality work environments. The topics in the book are also relevant to all business leaders concerned with creating an efficient, productive, and sustainable workforce.

Commonsense Talent Management

Why Read This Book?

The Good, the Great, and the Stupidus Maximus Award

In 2001 a book called *Good to Great* was published that profiled companies that were considered to have exemplary business practices.[1] One of those companies was the electronics retail company Circuit City. Less than ten years after *Good to Great* was published, Circuit City was bankrupt, and its stock was delisted. How did such a high-performing company go so quickly from good to great to gone?

Many things contributed to the demise of Circuit City, but one action that stands out was the decision in 2007 to fire their most experienced employees and replace them with less-expensive newly hired staff. This move provided immediate financial benefits but created lasting and permanent damage to Circuit City's performance. It even led to the creation of an award to recognize colossally bad management actions: the Stupidus Maximus Award. The award observed, "It doesn't take a genius to know that getting rid of your most experienced and productive workers is not only a terribly shortsighted strategy, but incredibly dumb."[2]

It would be nice if stories such as this one from Circuit City were rare. They are not. We all have stories of apparently stupid things we have seen managers do. Bad management seems to be something we simply expect and accept as something we just have to live with, much like bad weather. What leads to all these bad management decisions? Most people who get promoted to management positions have had to demonstrate that they possess at least a reasonable level of intelligence and have shown that they can be trusted at some basic level to support and help others. Very few managers are particularly unintelligent, cruel, or unethical. Circuit City's decisions were almost certainly done by extremely bright and highly successful executives. These executives may have earned the Stupidus Maximus award, but they were not stupid people. The reality is that all of us are capable of making stupid management decisions. Many of us, although it may be painful to admit, have already done so. The challenge is that companies do not learn that their management decisions were stupid or ineffective until after they have been made.

The reason companies make bad workforce management decisions is usually the same reason people make other bad decisions: they fail to think through the consequences of their actions or overlook crucial pieces of information. Poor management decisions are often the result of not appreciating what actually drives employee performance. More often than not, this comes from looking at decisions from the perspective of the organization without thinking about these decisions from the perspective of employees. A decision that makes sense in terms of a company's financial models may not make sense if you look beyond these numbers at the psychological factors that underlie employee actions that drive company profits. Employees do not do things because their company wants them to. They do things because they want to do them, have the capabilities to do them, and have confidence that solely they can succeed.

Successful companies are not built solely on the things leader and managers do themselves. Successful companies result from what leaders and managers are able to get their employees to do. This requires understanding work from the perspective of others and knowing how to predict and change employee behavior to align with business needs. That's ultimately what this book is about.

This book is a guide to using strategic human resources (HR) to increase business performance. Strategic HR encompasses a variety of processes, including staffing, talent management, performance management, compensation, succession, development, and training. The term *strategic HR* is used to distinguish these processes from other HR processes that are more administrative in nature.

Strategic HR focuses on processes used to align the workforce to deliver business results. It is often described as getting the right people in the right jobs doing the right things and doing it in a way that supports the right development for what we want people to do tomorrow. Administrative HR focuses on administrative and legal processes associated with the employment of people: managing payroll, providing health care benefits, and handling the administrative and legal details associated with establishing and terminating employment contracts, for example.

Strategic HR is critical to achieving business objectives consistently and effectively. It has a major impact on the profit, growth, and long-term sustainability of organizations. Administrative HR is critical to organizational functioning but is not a strong source of business advantage. For example, although it is difficult to motivate employees if their paychecks don't show up, paying people on time is not going to give a company competitive advantage. In this sense, administrative HR is similar to other crucial support services such as processing expense reports, maintaining e-mail systems, and managing building facilities. Administrative HR gets little attention from most business leaders unless it fails to work. Business leaders rarely ask administrative HR questions such as, "How do I ensure people get paid on time?" But they often ask strategic HR questions such as, "How can I get the employees I need to support this project?" or, "How do I get people aligned around the company's strategic goals?"

There is a symbiotic relationship between strategic HR processes and administrative HR processes. Although there is a tendency to discuss these two sides of HR as though one were more important than the other, the reality is that we need both. Administrative HR is needed to employ people. Strategic HR is necessary for ensuring that people are doing what we have employed them to do. Strategic HR is where companies gain the most competitive advantage because it is about increasing workforce productivity and not just maintaining standard corporate infrastructure. If HR professionals want to increase the impact they have on their company's strategic initiatives and business operations, then being good at strategic HR is how they will get it (see the discussion: "Strategic HR: Leadership: What It Does and Does Not Look Like").

STRATEGIC HR LEADERSHIP: WHAT IT DOES AND DOES NOT LOOK LIKE

If HR is going to influence business strategies, then its leaders must show how HR methods can improve business results. These leaders must be willing to advance bold recommendations on how HR processes can support business operations and back up these claims with decisive action. People in HR often speak about "getting a seat at the leadership table," but HR leaders must also play a vocal role in the conversation at this table if they wish to keep this seat. My experience is that not all HR leaders are comfortable taking such a highly visible role. The following two stories illustrate the difference between strategic HR leaders and HR leaders who may be at the leadership table but seem reluctant to speak up.

The first story illustrates what strategic HR leadership looks like. A major manufacturing company suffered a severe downturn in business due to the 2008 recession. It hired a new CEO who realized the company would go bankrupt unless it radically changed its strategic focus. This meant getting a tradition-bound company to adopt difficult and highly challenging goals quickly. HR leaders in the organization spoke up and said that improving the HR processes used to manage employee goals could play a central role in this turnaround. They then committed to implementing HR technology that allowed the organization to set and track goals across more than twenty thousand employees in over fifteen countries. They agreed to do it in less than four months. This was an extremely ambitious HR initiative, and it played a central role in the company's turnaround strategy. Rather than shy away from this high-profile and risky engagement, the HR leaders committed to making it happen. Two years later, this company had completed an extremely successful business turnaround, and the HR organization had played a highly visible role in making it happen.

Compare the previous story of strategic HR leadership to the following one illustrating a different type of HR leader. A product marketing company was about to launch a new technology-enabled process to set and track employee goals. Two weeks before the goal management process was to be launched, the HR leadership team learned that the company had made a massive acquisition. Business leaders wanted to align the two workforces as quickly as possible around a common set of strategic objectives. The immediate reaction among some members of the team overseeing the goal management process was, "This is perfect timing because goal management is central to workforce alignment." Yet the HR leadership team did not appear to see it this way.

Traditionally at this company, goals had mainly been used as a way to justify compensation decisions. They thought of goals only as a tool for personnel administration, not as a means to support strategic communication and alignment. Rather than seize this opportunity to demonstrate how this HR process could support a critical business need, the HR department chose to delay the goal management process launch until the acquisition settled down.

The difference between these two stories was the difference in the willingness of HR leaders to play a central, high-profile role in supporting a mission-critical business need. If HR leaders want to have strategic impact, they need to be willing to take on projects that put HR in the spotlight. Such projects are likely to be high stress and high risk, but such things are necessary to becoming highly relevant to business strategies. It is not enough to have a seat at the leadership table; you need to influence the conversation.

This book explains the major design questions that underlie effective strategic HR processes. It does not prescribe using certain specific strategic HR processes or give advice that assumes there is one best way to manage people. There isn't one best way to manage people in general. However, there is a best way to manage the people in your organization, taking into account your company's particular workforce characteristics, business needs, and resource constraints. This book helps you think about strategic HR process design and deployment so you can uncover the practices that are truly best for your company. It will also help you recognize and avoid particularly bad practices, such as firing your most skilled and experienced employees to save short-term costs!

This book is based on psychological research studying factors important to workforce productivity, combined with my experience working with companies of all sizes around the globe.[3] The more than twenty years I have worked with companies seeking to improve workforce productivity that have hammered three fundamental beliefs into my brain. First, there are very few true best practices. What works in one company may not work in another (see the discussion: "The Problem with HR Case Studies"). In fact, what works in one company may actually hurt performance in another. Second, although there are no true best practices, there are necessary practices that influence the design of many HR processes. These practices may not provide competitive advantage, but HR processes will not work if you do not address them. Third, the reason HR often fails to be effective is that companies did not fully think through key design questions when building and deploying HR processes. In particular, they did not consider how these processes must interact with employee psychology to create the behavioral changes they are intended to achieve.

THE PROBLEM WITH HR CASE STUDIES

This book contains many stories of effective and ineffective HR practices drawn from work I have done with hundreds of organizations. I intentionally do not share the names of these companies for several reasons. Foremost, which companies these are is not the point. The point is what we can learn from their experiences. Furthermore, not all of these stories portray companies in a positive light. Finally, I do not want to perpetuate a tendency in the HR field to copy other organizations' HR practices based on the name of the company instead of the nature of the practice.

The field of HR has a history of idolizing companies based more on their current financial performance than on the quality of their workforce management methods. It is common to see books or case studies written about HR methods used by companies that have achieved financial success. These usually include an explicit or implicit admonition that other companies should use the same HR methods. There are two problems with this approach. First, HR processes that work in other organizations may not work or even be feasible in your own. Second, just because a practice worked for a company in the past does not mean it will continue to work in the future. Companies need to adjust their HR methods to meet the shifting nature of labor markets, technological resources, business models, and economies.

The value of strategic HR methods depends on your company's business needs, its culture, characteristics of its employees, its resources, and a range of other variables. This point was succinctly made by a colleague of mine in the 1990s when General Electric (GE) was doing exceptionally well under the leadership of its famous CEO, Jack Welch. Many books were written about HR methods at GE under Welch as examples of HR best practices. During that time, an HR professional asked my friend, "What does our company need to copy the HR practices used at GE?" to which he replied, "100 years of history, 100,000 global employees, and hundreds of millions of dollars' worth of financial capital." His response was somewhat flippant, but the point is valid. GE's practices worked extremely well for GE at that time in history. But that does not mean they will work equally well for another company or at another time.

This book contains dozens of examples of HR methods drawn from scores of different companies. Only three of these companies are mentioned by name: GE, Circuit City, and Enron (in chapter 6). GE is an example of a company whose HR practices have significantly changed over the years to adapt to shifting business needs. Many HR practices that GE was famous for in the 1990s such as forced ranking are no longer used by GE today. Circuit City and Enron are examples of companies that were once extremely successful and were lauded for having highly effective strategic HR practices. Both also experienced colossal business failures that were caused in part by flaws in their approaches to strategic HR and a failure to effectively change their HR methods to meet changing business demands. The lesson to be learned is to never implement a strategic HR practice just because someone else is doing it. Study what other companies are doing as a source of ideas and insight, but do not implement an HR practice until you critically examine whether it makes sense for your company's unique situation.

This book takes a comprehensive look across all of the major strategic HR processes used to hire, motivate, develop, and retain employees throughout the employment life cycle. It addresses design issues affecting specific strategic HR processes and explains issues related to integrating multiple processes to address different types of business needs. Unlike many other HR books, this book does not prescribe how HR processes should be designed. Instead it walks through the major considerations to ensure the processes you create are the right ones for your business. This book is not an instructional manual that presumes to tell you how to manage your workforce. It is a guide through the major questions, concepts, and issues to consider when building and deploying strategic HR processes to support the unique business needs and culture of your company.

The book summarizes years of experience and knowledge into a set of frameworks, key questions, and diagnostic tools that will help you create a healthier, more productive work environment for employees, managers, and customers alike. I do not pretend that this book has all the answers. But it does provide solutions and concepts that have been effectively leveraged across a huge variety of companies. Some of the topics discussed are a bit complex as a result of the topic area. As is commonly said, if this problem was easy to fix, someone would have figured out the solution long ago and we'd all be using it. Nevertheless, many of the concepts in this book can be effectively learned and applied to your company's strategic HR processes in a matter of weeks. If you want to understand how to think through HR at a more strategic level, how to articulate its value to others, and how to design processes that positively change employee behavior, this book is for you.

1.1 HOW THIS BOOK IS STRUCTURED

Chapter 2 provides clarity on what strategic HR is, why it is important, and why it is often difficult. The chapter also explains the four fundamental strategic HR processes of right people, right things, right way, and right development.

Chapter 3 introduces the concept of business execution, explains why understanding a company's business execution drivers is fundamental to the design of effective strategic HR processes, and describes the link between the six key business execution drivers and the four fundamental strategic HR processes.

Chapters 4 through 7 discuss critical design questions underlying each of the four fundamental strategic HR processes: right people, right things, right way, and right development. These chapters discuss how to build and deploy processes associated with staffing, goal management, performance management, succession management, development, and other forms of strategic HR.

Chapter 8 looks at methods for integrating and aligning different areas of strategic HR to create an overall strategic HR road map. This chapter could be read either before or after chapters 4 through 7. I placed it later in the book because I believe it is often easier to develop strategies if you have a solid understanding of the methods that will be used to execute them.

Chapter 9 discusses methods for deploying integrated strategic HR initiatives. This includes techniques to get employees, managers, and leaders to adopt and effectively use HR processes.

Appendix 1 contains a detailed competency library and associated structured interview questions that can be used to implement many of the concepts discussed in the book. Appendix 2 discusses how many of the principles in the book can be applied to build out a comprehensive succession management program. This provides an example of what is involved in building a truly integrated strategic HR process.

This book can be read as a complete document or as a reference guide where you read individual sections by themselves. The Contents provides a fairly detailed guide to the topics covered in the chapters, and the index can be consulted for looking up specific topics. Each chapter also includes discussions that address particular concepts and methods related to strategic HR. A glossary at the end of the book defines common strategic HR words and phrases.

1.2   THE ROLE OF HR TECHNOLOGY IN STRATEGIC HR

The term *HR technology* refers to specialized computer systems designed to support HR processes. This is not a book about HR technology. The concepts discussed in this book can be applied independent of using any particular type of technology. Nevertheless, many of the processes discussed in this book are difficult, if not impossible, to implement in large organizations without the use of effective HR technology (see "How Technology Is Transforming HR: The Death of the Paper Binder").

HOW TECHNOLOGY IS TRANSFORMING HR: THE DEATH OF THE PAPER BINDER

Until recently, strategic HR processes such as performance management, career development, goal setting, compensation, and succession management were conducted using paper forms, slide presentations, and spreadsheets often filled with half-completed, manually entered employee reviews and profiles. HR departments spent months pulling together data needed to support compensation decisions and succession planning, for example. Much of this information was obsolete by the time it was assembled. This left HR in the unenviable position of trying to engage leaders in strategic talent conversations using clumsy paper binders full of questionable information.

Thanks to advances in technology systems, we are finally seeing the death of the HR paper binder. HR is shifting from manually created spreadsheets and documents to dynamic online, web-based systems that make clumsy processes much more efficient and easy to use. One company I worked with set coordinated goals across more than ten thousand employees worldwide in less than sixty days. Another global company achieved the following in one year across over thirty countries:

- Set 1,787,465 performance objectives aligned to the company's overall business strategy
- Completed 253,465 performance reviews using a single consistent process
- Conducted close to 6,000 talent review and calibration meetings

With a single mouse click, this company can instantaneously generate online reports providing immediate visibility into what people are doing across the company and how well they are doing it. These sorts of processes would be impossible to implement or support without the use of specialized strategic HR technology.

Advances in HR technology have provided companies with many new capabilities they did not previously have, such as the ability to quickly record and post training videos on company intranet sites or the ability to instantaneously search across the entire workforce to find employees who possess specialized skills. But much of the value of HR technology also comes from enabling managers to take advantage of strategic HR data and processes that have long been available but were historically difficult to use. In this sense, the impact that technology has on HR can be likened to the impact that GPS technology has had on the use of street maps. These technological systems take existing information and knowledge out of documents where it was rarely accessed and put it in the hands of decision makers when they need it in a format they can readily use.

Major advances have been made over the past twenty years in the development of HR technology to support strategic HR processes—for example:

- Staffing systems used to post job openings on the Internet, find qualified candidates through searching through Internet sites, automatically screen and select candidates using online assessments, and transition new employees into the organization
- Management systems used to communicate and set employee goals, measure and track employee performance, and develop and measure employee skills
- Reporting systems that integrate data on employee accomplishments, qualifications, and pay levels to guide compensation and internal staffing and promotion decisions
- Learning systems that provide employees with online access to training and knowledge resources necessary to perform their jobs
- Social communication tools that allow employees to share ideas, feedback, and suggestions with each other through online forums

HR technology enables companies to achieve results that would be impossible to achieve without the use of technology. An example is tracking the performance, potential, and career goals of employees across a company and then conducting real-time searches to match existing employees to new job opportunities in the organization. Another is providing tools so employees in one part of an organization can record and share instructional videos with employees elsewhere in the company.

Using HR technology does not lead to positive results unless the technology is used correctly. But failing to leverage advances in technology limits a company's ability to use strategic HR methods. Many examples of poorly designed strategic HR processes are based in part on reliance on inadequate HR technology. Consider the example of the performance review. The traditional performance reviews that many companies use ask managers to fill out a form once a year rating employee performance.[4] Managers are supposed to share these forms with employees in a way that inspires the employees to increase their performance. These annual performance reviews rarely work as intended, however. Many managers do not think about the review until a few weeks before it is due, and as a result they often do not know what to write on the reviews. Their reviews frequently contain vague notes based on what they can remember from the few months immediately prior to the review and may ignore the first half of the year entirely. Not surprisingly, employees often find the review process to be demeaning and generally unpleasant. And many companies never use the results of the reviews for anything at all. The forms go into a file, never to be seen again. Yet these types of reviews were (and still are) used by lots and lots of companies. How did we ever get to this point?

Technology constraints provide one explanation for the creation of ineffective annual performance review processes. At some point in the past, business leaders decided they wanted to consistently measure performance of employees so they could reward high performers and address problems caused by underperformers. Paper forms were the best technology available at that time. The only performance management process that could be effectively implemented using paper was the annual review form. If companies had access to the online tools that currently exist for measuring employee performance, it seems unlikely anyone would have created the traditional paper-based annual performance review process. For example, technology now provides tools that capture customer and coworker comments about employee performance on an ongoing basis, allow managers to go back and review employee performance against goals and projects assigned to them over the course of the year, and provide databases of content to help managers provide effective behaviorally based feedback. If these tools were around fifty years ago the traditional paper-based performance review would probably not exist today.

An analogy can be made to traditional HR methods such as the annual performance review form and the QWERTY keyboard (QWERTY refers to how the keys are ordered, starting with the upper left of the keyboard). The QWERTY keyboard was created because of a technology constraint. It was designed to slow down typing speed because early typewriters jammed if people typed too fast. If computers had been available when keyboards were invented, the QWERTY keyboard would never have been created. We use QWERTY keyboards not because they work well with modern technology but because they worked well with technology available 120 years ago. We continue to use them because they are familiar even though other keyboard designs would significantly increase our typing speed and accuracy.

The same is true for many traditional strategic HR processes. These processes were not adopted because they were highly effective. They were adopted because they worked with the technology available at the time they were created. There are many examples of this, such as using labor-intensive and inaccurate manual reviews of résumés as the main process for screening candidates, trying to align employee goals with corporate strategies using PowerPoint presentations and Excel spreadsheets, and attempting to develop complex capabilities like global team leadership primarily using classroom training. We finally have the technology needed to replace or augment these obsolete practices with methods that are far more effective. It is time to make this change.

Most of the strategic HR methods discussed in this book are based on well-established and rigorously tested theories of employee psychology that are not particularly new. But until we had better HR technology, we couldn't effectively use them on a widespread basis. HR technology has radically improved and gets more powerful every year. This technology makes it possible to apply knowledge gained from decades of scientific research on employee performance to radically improve business results. It is just a matter of using this knowledge and technology correctly.

HR technology also decreases administrative burdens associated with managing talent, which frees HR professionals to focus on addressing business-relevant issues. Instead of spending time asking people to "please fill out their talent forms," HR can use technology to gain insights and drive strategic discussions around information contained in those forms. Technology systems enable HR departments to shift their focus from administering processes to working with business leaders to ensure these processes are supporting business needs.

Technology also allows HR to provide data and job aids to managers that help them make better decisions about people. These tools help managers more accurately evaluate employee performance and provide constructive, behaviorally based feedback to assist with employee development. Another benefit of HR technology is the visibility it provides into whether managers are carrying out basic management tasks such as setting employee goals and providing employee feedback. One client told me that until her company implemented strategic HR technology, it had no way to effectively measure whether managers were talking to employees about performance at all, let alone whether they were doing it well. The implementation of technology-based strategic HR processes made it possible to measure whether managers were practicing the most basic tasks associated with managing employees: setting expectations, evaluating performance against expectations, and providing feedback.

Strategic HR technology allows organizations to create processes that profoundly improve how line managers run their businesses. This technology enables HR leaders to change the role they play within companies. Thanks to innovations in talent management technology, HR has now, perhaps for the first time in its history, both the knowledge and the tools needed to play a true leadership role in driving the execution of business strategies. The next step is for HR leaders to take ownership of this role. We have the tools and knowledge; we just need the courage and conviction to use them.

1.3 WHY THIS BOOK MATTERS

Work matters a lot. Where we work, our success at work, whom we work with, how we work with them, whom we manage, and how we are managed by others all have major impacts on our health, happiness, and financial success. When used appropriately, HR processes improve both business performance and employee satisfaction. This benefits everyone: employees, managers, leaders, HR professionals, customers, and shareholders. Strategic HR processes can and should play a central role in building better workplaces and, through this, creating a better world overall. But it is up to us to use these processes in a way that matters.

NOTES

1. Collins, J. (2001). *Good to great.* New York: HarperBusiness.

2. *Workforce Management* (2008, April 7), p. 34.

3. Citations are included for passages where readers may wish more information or research evidence beyond what is provided in the book itself.

4. Garr, S. S. (2013). *The state of performance management: Performance appraisal process benchmarks.* Deloitte Development LLC.

Strategic HR

What It Is, Why It Is Important, and Why It Is Often Difficult

*T*he War for Talent was an influential book published in 2001 that emphasized the growing impact that workforce quality has on business performance. The book noted that "in 1900 only 17 percent of jobs required knowledge workers, now over 60 percent do. . . As the economy becomes more knowledge based, the differential value of highly talented people continues to mount."[1] Since that book appeared, the importance of attracting, hiring, developing, using, and retaining high-quality talent has steadily grown. Business success is becoming less about having better business strategies and more about having the talent to execute these strategies effectively. Winning does not just come from knowing what to do; it comes from doing it faster and better than everyone else.

A company that does not have employees who can support its strategies will fail, no matter how good its strategies are. This realization that people are very often the most important competitive differentiator is forcing organizations to excel in three ways:

- *Increasing employee performance.* As skilled labor becomes scarcer, the cost of qualified employees increases. Labor now accounts for more than

60 percent of the operating cost in most companies.[2] Companies must realize a high level of return on the sizable investment that they make in people. This means maximizing employee performance.

- *Attracting, developing, and retaining high-performing employees.* It is often said that employees are a company's most valuable asset. This is true if you are talking about high-performing employees. These employees typically generate three times or more revenue than average employees.[3] But the things that make employees high performers also make them a retention risk (e.g., achievement orientation, marketable skills). Companies must be able to both hire and keep high-performing talent to compete in the labor market.

- *Identifying and addressing low-performing employees.* High-performing employees may be a company's most valuable asset, but low-performing employees can be a company's most expensive liability. Low performers damage the revenue stream, decrease the productivity of coworkers, and drive away high-performing employees. Tolerating low performance drags down company profitability, business growth, and employee morale.

The only way to meet these challenges is to ensure managers are:

1. *Employing the right people:* They hire employees who can effectively perform their jobs and will stay with the company long enough to justify the cost of hiring them.

2. *Focusing people on the right things:* They make sure that employees are working on things that support strategic business priorities and do not spend time on activities that do not align with company needs.

3. *Ensuring people do things the right way:* They take steps so that high performance is recognized and encouraged and poor performance is identified and addressed.

4. *Giving people the right development:* They provide employees with development opportunities that enable them to perform their current roles more effectively and progress into future roles that support the company's long-term business needs.

The purpose of strategic HR is to provide organizations with tools, knowledge, and guidance that ensure these four things are being done in an effective and consistent manner. I refer to these as the 4Rs of strategic HR: hire the right people, focus them on the right things, ensure they are doing things the right way, and foster the right development.

2.1 THE FUNDAMENTAL PROCESSES OF STRATEGIC HR

Strategic HR is ultimately about maximizing workforce productivity. Workforce productivity requires making sure a company has the employees it needs to support its business strategies and that these employees are performing their jobs in a manner that supports the business needs of the organization. Strategic HR increases workforce productivity by providing methods that help companies find and place people in jobs where they will be effective (e.g., staffing, succession management), improve employees' current job performance (e.g., by performance management or training), and retain and develop employees over time (e.g., through compensation and career development). The one thing that links all strategic HR methods is a focus on predicting and increasing job performance to ensure people are placed in roles where they will succeed, improve productivity in current roles, and build capabilities needed for future roles.

Figure 2.1 illustrates the basic components of job performance and the fundamental strategic HR processes used to influence them. Increasing job performance ultimately depends on managing three things:

- *Goals* that define the business outcomes associated with an employee's job (e.g., achieving sales quotas, minimizing accidents, maintaining productivity levels, processing documents). Goals define the reason that a job exists. People are employed to do something; goals clarify what they are employed to do.

- *Competencies* that describe behaviors that employees are expected to display on the job—building relationships, planning and organizing, solving problems, and other activities that influence success or reflect important cultural values of the company. People often distinguish goals from competencies using the concept of "what versus how." Goals define what a person is supposed to do in the job, and competencies describe how they are expected to do it.

- *Attributes* are characteristics of employees that are associated with job success. They include qualifications (e.g., job experience, education, certifications), aptitudes (e.g., personality and ability traits), and interests (e.g., career aspirations, salary preferences, work schedule expectations). Attributes define

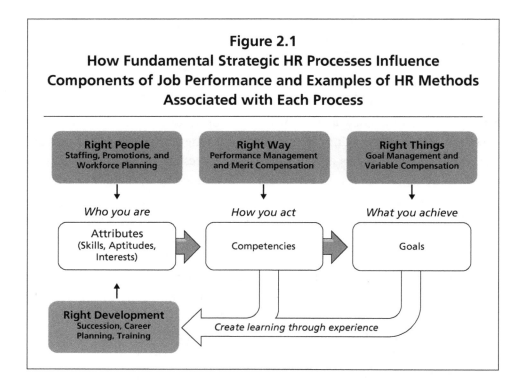

Figure 2.1
How Fundamental Strategic HR Processes Influence Components of Job Performance and Examples of HR Methods Associated with Each Process

who employees are in terms of their knowledge, skills, and abilities. The attributes employees possess influence the competencies they display, which determine the goals they can achieve.

The relationship of attributes, competencies, and goals can be summed up as, "Who you are (*attributes*) influences how you act (*competencies*), which determines what you achieve (*goals*)." Any effort to increase workforce productivity must ultimately influence employee attributes, competencies, or goals to be successful. All processes that increase employee performance, engagement, retention, or any other variable associated with the productivity of individual employees will at some point focus on aligning, clarifying, or developing employee attributes, competencies, and goals.

There are four basic ways to influence employee attributes, competencies, and goals, and they correspond to the 4Rs of strategic HR:

1. Hire the *right people*. Staff positions with employees whose personal attributes match the competencies and goals associated with their jobs. This is

the primary focus of recruiting, workforce planning, and certain aspects of succession management and compensation.

2. Focus employees on the *right things*. Clearly identify and communicate the goals you want employees to achieve, and measure and reward employees against these goals. This is the focus of goal management, goal-based compensation, and variable pay.

3. Make sure people are doing their job the *right way*. Define the competencies employees must display to achieve their job goals or support the desired company culture, and provide feedback and other resources that encourage them to demonstrate these competencies. This is the primary focus of performance management and merit-based compensation.

4. Provide job experiences and resources that drive the *right development*. Create a work environment that helps employees develop the attributes that influence competency performance and goal accomplishment. Put people in jobs, assign them goals, and provide them with training and learning resources that build their capabilities to more effectively perform their current role and progress into future job roles. This is the primary focus of career development and certain aspects of succession management.

Right people, right things, right way, and right development: these are the fundamental processes that define strategic HR. They roughly correspond with the traditional talent management processes of staffing, goal management, performance management, and succession management and career development.[4] However, the 4R model is not based on human resources. It is based on the psychology of employee behavior. These four processes reflect basic psychological mechanisms that influence human performance: matching individual differences to task demands (right people), focusing motivation and attention (right things), providing feedback on behavior (right way), and enabling learning through experience (right development). These mechanisms reflect elemental methods for predicting and changing people's behavior.

Because the 4R model is based on well-established psychological principles, it can be used to define strategic HR methods for any company as long as it employs people (and I've yet to encounter a company that does not employ at least one or two humans). The relative importance of the four factors will change depending on a company's business needs, but the basic structure of the 4R model remains consistent across industries, cultures, and workforces. Furthermore, the 4R model will be just as relevant for defining strategic HR fifty years from now as it is today. Even if the concept of strategic HR disappears, these four fundamental processes will continue to represent the basic mechanisms for improving workforce productivity. This is because the 4R model is rooted in basic human psychology. As I like to say, "People don't evolve at the same pace that business fads come and go."

2.2 WHY DO WE NEED STRATEGIC HR DEPARTMENTS?

The 4R processes are given the label of "strategic HR" because they are typically managed by HR departments. However, these processes must be used by line managers and employees to be effective. The role of strategic HR departments is to provide tools and methods that help leaders, managers, and employees increase their productivity. The reason we need strategic HR departments is that many managers struggle to manage people. Ideally, managers would excel at hiring the right people, focusing them on the right things, and giving them the right development without any help from a centralized HR function. But the world is not ideal. Strategic HR departments play an important role in business performance by designing and deploying processes to help managers do an effective job hiring, evaluating, rewarding, motivating, and developing the people they manage.

The reasons we need strategic HR departments are similar to the reasons we need financial departments. One could ask, "Why do we need finance and accounting?" or "Why do companies force managers to keep track of budgets and money under the guidance of a centralized finance department?" People are likely to respond to these questions with two observations:

- Finance is a specialized area of expertise, and it is unrealistic to expect managers to create effective accounting and budgeting processes on their own.
- Financial resources aren't owned by managers; they are owned by the company, and managers are allowed to use them. As such, the organization needs to create processes to ensure managers are allocating and using these resources appropriately.

These are the same reasons that companies need strategic HR departments. Strategic HR is a specialized area of expertise. Most managers do not fully understand how to effectively hire, evaluate, motivate, and develop employees. Nor do managers "own" the talent in their departments. Employees are far too costly a resource to risk being mishandled by managers who lack knowledge and expertise in strategic HR methods.

2.3 WHAT MAKES STRATEGIC HR DIFFICULT

The goal of strategic HR is to help leaders and managers get the right people in the right jobs doing the right things to make a business succeed. This goal may sound straightforward, but it is often difficult to achieve. This is because it involves helping managers master the often subtle art and science of predicting and improving job performance. It also requires building processes that have a powerful but often complex and indirect relationship to business outcomes.

One of the things that makes strategic HR challenging is that it requires forecasting and changing the day-to-day behavior of individual employees—for example, predicting what someone is likely to do if she is put in a new job or helping employees change their focus in order to support a new business strategy. Predicting and influencing human behavior is difficult.[5] The divorce rate and weight-loss industries provide some sense of how hard it is for people to predict and change their own behavior even when their personal health and happiness are clearly at stake.

Being effective at strategic HR requires helping managers understand how employees' motives, abilities, and behaviors interact to influence business results. Managers often ask themselves, "Why is that employee acting that way?" A manager's success is tied to the performance of his or her employees, so managers want their employees to be productive. Even extremely incompetent managers usually think that what they are doing is going to help increase employee performance. The abusive manager who insults employees often thinks that this will make people work harder.[6] A major part of strategic HR is helping managers learn how to effectively influence employee behavior and avoid practices that decrease productivity, and make sure that people who lack the talent needed to effectively manage employees are not allowed to hold managerial positions. To achieve this goal, companies need to evaluate managers based on how their actions affect the employees they manage. This involves doing things like rewarding managers who attract and promote high-performing employees into the organization and confronting managers whose behavior causes employees to quit the company.

Another challenge to strategic HR is its often indirect relationship to business results. Strategic HR practices, whether focused on staffing, compensation, performance management, or career development, all share the same goal of getting managers and employees to do things that support the company's business strategies and objectives. But HR practices do not affect employee behavior directly. Employee behaviors are directly determined by attributes of the employees themselves—their knowledge, attitudes, motives, and so on. These attributes are a result of employees' personalities, abilities, and values, combined with aspects of their work environment such as incentives, resources, and their coworkers. This is where strategic HR processes come into play. Strategic HR processes support the hiring of certain kinds of employees and the creation of certain kinds of work environments. This increases the probability that employees will display behaviors that support the company's strategic direction. Over time, these behaviors lead to improved business results.

Aligning employee behaviors with a company's business needs is where the rubber meets the road in terms of strategic HR. But the indirect relationship between strategic HR practices and business results increases the risk of creating strategic HR programs that sound good in principle but fail to effectively influence employee behaviors. For example, a 360-degree survey feedback process that works well in a company with a historically supportive and open culture might have negative consequences if used in a company with a less-trusting, more cynical workforce.[7] Or consider the example of pay for performance, a philosophy that employees should receive different amounts of compensation based on their level of job performance. It is rooted in a belief the people will be more productive if they are paid for their results. But implementing a pay-for-performance compensation structure does not directly lead to improved business results.[8] What it does is provide managers with tools to reward employees based on goals that support the company's strategy. This is done with the assumption that employees will be motivated to display behaviors associated with achieving these goals. But this assumption may not be true. Pay for performance will work only if (1) employees understand their goals, (2) employees see the rewards as adequate incentive for pursuing these goals, (3) employees feel they are capable of achieving the goals, and (4) the methods employees use to achieve these goals support the needs of the business. If these conditions are not met, then pay-for-performance programs may actually decrease workforce productivity by demotivating employees or encouraging counterproductive behaviors (see the discussion: "Why Paying Employees to Be Safe Can Be Unhealthy"). A well-designed pay-for-performance process must take these factors into account to ensure it motivates rather than alienates employees.

WHY PAYING EMPLOYEES TO BE SAFE CAN BE UNHEALTHY

Pay-for-performance programs motivate employees by providing financial rewards based on achieving specific goals or outcomes. If used correctly, these programs have been shown to significantly increase employee productivity.[a] However, they can create significant problems for organizations if they are not carefully thought through. One example comes from efforts to use pay for performance to reduce workplace accidents and injuries.

To encourage safe behavior, some manufacturing plants have given employees bonuses if there were no accidents or injuries during a certain period of time—for example, paying a bonus to employees for every week that passed without any accidents. When companies used this approach, they discovered that accident rates did not necessarily go down; what did decrease was employees' willingness to report accidents. Rather than reporting accidents, employees would hide them so they could achieve their bonuses. Plant managers have told me about employees who continued to work with severe injuries, even a broken leg, because they did not want to file an accident report. The employees did not feel they could effectively control accident rates, so they found another way to achieve the rewards.

The lesson to be learned is you often get what you pay for, but what you pay for may not actually be what you want.

[a]Peterson, S. J., & Luthan, F. (2006). The impact of financial and nonfinancial incentives on business-unit outcomes over time. *Journal of Applied Psychology, 91,* 156–165.

The ability to influence employee behavior makes strategic HR a highly effective method for driving business results. Small changes in employee behavior can have massive impacts on business performance.[9] But the behavior of employees can be difficult to understand, and the factors that underlie employee behavior are rarely simple. As a result, it can be difficult to determine exactly how well a strategic HR process is likely to work. Care is needed to ensure that strategic HR processes are designed and deployed in a manner that will have the desired effect on employee behavior.

2.4 CONCLUSION

Being effective at strategic HR processes requires understanding the basic factors that influence employee performance, designing HR processes based on how employees truly behave, and recognizing and accepting that this may be quite different from how we might wish they would behave. It requires looking at strategic HR methods from the combined perspective of the business, the HR field, and the field of employee psychology. Strategic HR demands an appreciation of employee psychology beyond what it is reasonable to expect most managers to have. At the same time, it requires creating processes that enable managers to effectively predict and change employee behavior within their work environment, reward managers who do this well, and address managers whose actions have a negative impact on overall workforce productivity.

What makes strategic HR difficult is the need to think through all of these factors when designing and deploying strategic HR methods. This may seem like a lot. But as we will see, it is not overly complicated provided you understand and work through some basic steps and concepts before implementing new strategic HR methods in your organization.

NOTES

1. Michaels, E., Hanfield-Jones, H., & Axelrod, B. (2001). *The war for talent*. Boston: Harvard Business School Press, p. 1.

2. Huselid, M. A., Becker, B. E., & Beatty, R. W. (2005). *The workforce scorecard: Managing human capital to execute strategy*. Boston: Harvard Business School Press.

3. Boudreau, J. W. (1991). Utility analysis in human resource management decisions. In M. D. Dunnette & L. M. Hough (Eds.), *Handbook of industrial and organizational psychology* (2nd ed., Vol. 2, pp. 621–745). Palo Alto, CA: Consulting Psychologists Press. Fitz-Enz, J. (2000). *The ROI of human capital: Measuring the economic value of employee performance*. New York: AMACOM.

4. You might wonder where processes focused on increasing performance of teams or changing organizational cultures fit into these four processes. Each of these four processes can be implemented with a focus on groups instead of individuals. For example, team-building exercises can be considered group-oriented approaches associated with "doing things the right way" and "giving employees the right development." There are certainly differences in how processes are designed when they are focused on groups. But since groups are made up of individuals, most things that influence individual behavior have parallels to things that influence group behavior (e.g., member goals, member attributes, behavioral feedback).

5. Ackerman, P. L., & Humphreys, L. G. (1990). Individual differences theory in industrial and organizational psychology. In M. D. Dunnette & L. M. Hough (Eds.), *Handbook of industrial and organizational psychology* (pp. 223–282). Palo Alto, CA: Consulting Psychologists Press. Hunt, S. T. (2007). *Hiring success: The art and science of staffing assessment and employee selection.* San Francisco: Jossey-Bass.

6. Sutton, R. I. (2007). *The no asshole rule: Building a civilized workplace and surviving one that isn't.* New York: Business Plus.

7. Morgeson, F. P., Mumford, T. V., & Campion, M. A. (2005). Coming full circle: Using research and practice to address 27 questions about 360-degree feedback programs. *Consulting Psychology Journal: Practice and Research, 57*(3), 196–209.

8. Schaubroeck, J., Shaw, J. D., Duffy, M. K., & Mitra, A. (2008). An under-met and over-met expectations model of employee reactions to merit raises. *Journal of Applied Psychology, 93*(2), 424–434.

9. Hunt, S. T. (2007). *Hiring success: The art and science of staffing assessment and employee selection.* San Francisco: Pfeiffer.

Business Execution and Strategic HR

The purpose of strategic HR is to get employees to do what the company needs them to do to achieve its business objectives. The term used to describe this is *business execution*. This chapter discusses how to use strategic HR to drive business execution. Section 3.1 discusses the role business execution plays in company performance and how it ties to strategic HR at a general level. Section 3.2 explains how to assess a company's business execution capability and requirements. Sections 3.3 and 3.4 discuss how to link business execution needs to strategic HR processes and how to use different strategic HR processes to support a company's specific business execution needs. Sections 3.5 and 3.6 address key concepts related to increasing strategic HR process maturity and building integrated strategic HR processes tied to business execution requirements.

3.1 DEFINING BUSINESS EXECUTION

Running a business requires doing three things:

1. *Defining strategy*. Figuring out what you need to do to succeed

2. *Managing assets.* Securing the capital and resources required to support the strategy

3. *Driving business execution.* Building and managing the workforce so you effectively leverage company assets to deliver strategic objectives

Defining strategies is about determining your business objectives and developing plans to achieve them. Managing assets is about getting the tools, money, materials, technology, and other resources needed to carry out your plans. Business execution is about actually carrying out the plan to achieve your goals. An analogy can be made to weight loss that helps illustrate these three things. My strategy is to lose ten pounds before December by exercising more and eating right. My assets include a membership to a health club and joining a vegetable co-op. Business execution in this case is about actually exercising at the gym and eating more vegetables in order to lose the weight. Which of these three is the hardest?

The CEO typically has a lead role in defining strategy with considerable support from business operations, product development, and marketing. Managing assets is often owned by finance and supply chain. Driving business execution is ultimately the responsibility of line leaders, but because it is about having the right people doing the right things, it is directly supported by HR. Due to advances in HR technology, HR leaders now have both the knowledge and tools to play a central role in driving business execution. The next step is for HR leaders to take ownership of this role, which often includes convincing other business leaders of the value of strategic HR.

Many business leaders have historically viewed HR as an administrative function that is necessary but relatively uninteresting to business operations. HR processes in some companies might be likened to electrical wiring in a house. A house without good electrical wiring is unsafe, inefficient, and potentially unlivable, but most people don't buy houses because they have superior electrical wiring. The same might be said about the way many companies use strategic HR processes such as performance management, staffing, or learning and development. Operations leaders appreciate the importance of these processes for running a stable company, but they do not see them as tools for increasing business execution.

When operations leaders tell me, "I don't care a lot about HR processes," my response is, "Do you care about people doing what you need them to do to support your business strategies?" If their answer is yes, then they do care about strategic HR. The problem is they do not appreciate the impact that strategic HR has on business execution and do not know how to use strategic HR processes to drive business results. Many business leaders also do not appreciate how advances in HR technology make it possible to use strategic HR processes far more effectively now compared to how they have been used in the past (see the discussion: "Technology and the Evolution of Strategic HR"). These misperceptions must be addressed in order to effectively use strategic HR methods in an organization. This is done by clearly articulating how different HR methods can help the company achieve its business objectives.

TECHNOLOGY AND THE EVOLUTION OF STRATEGIC HR

An HR department needs two things in order to use strategic HR processes to drive business execution:

- *Expertise.* The HR department must have expertise in methods for predicting and changing employee behavior. For example, understanding how to use goals to motivate employee performance, or being able to measure employee performance in a manner that enables the company to predict an employee's future potential.

- *Implementation.* The HR organization must be able to efficiently deploy its business execution expertise across the organization. It does not matter if the HR department knows how to increase employee performance if it cannot effectively share this knowledge with the line leaders who actually manage employees.

Technology plays a pivotal role in enabling HR to support business execution. Its impact has been twofold. First, by increasing administrative efficiency, technology has enabled HR professionals to focus more time on building methods for increasing workforce productivity. Second, technology provides a medium for getting HR expertise into the hands of managers so it can be applied across the organization. To illustrate how technology has affected the role of HR, let's take a look at four different generations of HR that have emerged over the past twenty or so years:

- *Pre-1990: Generation "personnel administration."* Prior to 1990, many HR organizations were almost entirely focused on personnel administration. This was due in part to the sheer amount of time required to manually administer HR processes before the widespread use of computers. Prior to 1990, many HR organizations were not even called "human resources." Instead, they had titles such as Office of Personnel Administration or Personnel Department. The main focus of HR in this generation was how to process employee paperwork efficiently.

- *1990 to 2000: Generation "human resources."* Two things happened in the 1990s that led to personnel management being redefined as "human resources." First, implementation of HR process automation technology significantly reduced the time needed to perform administrative HR tasks, which freed up HR organizations to focus more on topics related to strategic HR. This led to significant advances in the expertise found within HR related to predicting and changing employee behavior. Many of the talent management techniques that are now widely used were largely developed in the 1990s (e.g., competency models, structured interviews, goal setting). Second, the widespread adoption of personal computers made it possible for HR organizations to use more sophisticated techniques to support key talent decisions related to hiring, promotions, and pay (e.g., using computer-based tools to evaluate employee performance and assess job candidates). Throughout the 1990s, the focus of HR shifted beyond simple personnel management to include processes designed to improve the quality of workforce decisions (e.g., selecting high-performing employees, proactively managing employee turnover, and using job goals to drive employee development).

- *2001 to 2010: Generation "talent management."* Widespread adoption of Internet systems in the 2000s allowed HR organization to share data across what had previously been independent HR processes— for example, automatically importing data collected during the hiring process into systems used to support ongoing employee development. Greater access to data enabled HR to shift from focusing on specific employee decisions to creating more integrated methods to increase workforce productivity. No longer was HR limited to being a series of isolated silos focusing on staffing, training, compensation, and succession. Now HR could function as a set of integrated processes designed to ensure a steady supply of high-performing talent in critical job roles.

- *2011–. Generation "business execution."* As companies adopt more efficient and easy-to-use computing applications, HR organizations are spending less time administering HR processes and more time figuring out how to use these processes to increase workforce productivity. HR is focusing less on simply keeping track of who employees are and more on ensuring that these employees are being used effectively to support the company's short- and long-term business strategies.

Improvements in HR technology over the past twenty years have enabled the role of HR to move beyond providing administrative support to enabling execution of business strategies. The result is HR departments are now in a position where they can significantly improve how line-of-business leaders manage their workforces.

3.2   ASSESSING BUSINESS EXECUTION NEEDS

To be successful, a company must identify the right strategies to achieve its business goals and then execute these strategies better, faster, and more efficiently than the competition can. There can be little doubt about the value of good strategies, but execution makes the difference between having good strategies and achieving great results. As the pace of market change increases, it is even more critical to evaluate and manage a company's ability to rapidly execute business strategies to meet unforeseen opportunities and challenges.

Business execution is defined as the ability to use company assets to achieve business results (see figure 3.1). Because employees represent the largest asset cost for most companies, the major issue affecting business execution capability is utilization of talent. Despite the importance of business execution, most companies have little insight into their ability to meet business execution needs. This includes their ability to redeploy their assets to meet future business challenges. Many companies have elaborate systems to define strategies and monitor assets, but few put equal emphasis into the methods used to manage and measure business execution capability.

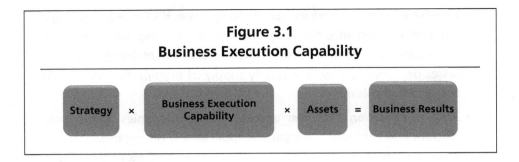

Figure 3.1
Business Execution Capability

Strategy × Business Execution Capability × Assets = Business Results

No single process or set of metrics fully captures the concept of business execution. Companies must develop multiple processes to support different types of business execution needs. These needs can be broken into six general categories of business execution drivers: alignment, productivity, efficiency, sustainability, scalability, and governance. These drivers were identified through examining the underlying business challenges that led companies to make significant investments in strategic HR processes:[1]

- *Alignment: Are people focusing on the things that matter for delivering our strategy?* Alignment requires the ability to rapidly and systematically communicate business goals to employees throughout the organization so they see the connection between high-level strategies and how they spend their time at work. Does everyone in your company know what goals they are expected to accomplish? Do they understand why their goals are important to the company's overall strategy? Achieving alignment requires effective communication between senior leaders and employees about the company's strategy and what each individual employee can do to support it. I once saw a great example of increasing alignment in a global manufacturing company. This company was facing bankruptcy unless it radically shifted its focus to more profitable projects. It used strategic HR processes centered on goal setting and performance management to ensure that employees across the organization were working on projects that could be tied directly back to key strategic initiatives. The increased visibility and accountability created by these processes motivated employees to do what was necessary to return the organization to profitability.

- *Productivity: Are people doing what we asked them to do?* It is important to differentiate between alignment and productivity in any examination of business execution. Alignment is fundamentally about strategic communication. Productivity is about defining, evaluating, and improving performance. The difference between alignment and productivity is the difference between knowing what you should do and actually doing it. Productivity depends on leaders' holding employees accountable for results and employees being given the incentives and resources required to create these results. I once worked with a technology company that used strategic HR processes to increase the productivity of its research and development divisions. It was critical that the company develop and get new products to market as fast as possible, and that depended on the performance of highly expensive engineers. The company could not afford to lose good engineers, but it could not afford to employ engineers who were not pulling their weight. The company turned to strategic HR methods to evaluate the performance of engineers on a regular basis and held senior leaders accountable for rewarding and retaining high-performing engineers and developing or managing out engineers who were performing poorly.

• *Efficiency: Are we efficiently using the people in our company?* It is one thing to achieve results. It is another to achieve these results using the minimal possible resources. Efficiency comes from having people with the right skills in the right positions, recognizing and retaining superior performers, appropriately managing poor performers, and allocating rewards and resources in a way that maximizes productivity. I have worked with many companies that have increased efficiency by using strategic HR methods that ensure compensation is allocated to employees based on how much they contribute to the organization. By creating a tighter link between pay and performance, these companies were able to increase the retention of high-performing employees, and some even decreased the total amount spent on compensation because they no longer gave the same increase across the entire employee population. Another example of increasing efficiency comes from a sales organization that studied relationships between manager span of control and sales performance.[2] They discovered that managers whose teams had more than ten employees performed more poorly due to the inability of the manager to provide effective coaching to all the team members. They also found that teams with fewer than five employees performed at about the same level as teams with six to ten employees, so there was no value paying for two managers from a team of ten when one manager would be just as effective. The most efficient span of control came from having teams with six to ten employees.

• *Sustainability: Are we able to maintain stable, consistent performance over time?* One of the biggest threats to business execution is the unplanned loss of critical talent required to achieve key strategic goals. Managing this risk requires developing processes to manage employee turnover and knowledge transfer effectively. Ensuring a company's results are sustainable over time also requires understanding whether key people in the company are engaged and fully committed to the organization. An energy company I worked with addressed sustainability issues by using strategic HR methods to forecast the number of skilled line workers predicted to retire over the next fifteen years. They then built highly focused recruitment and development programs to ensure they had employees available to quickly fill these future vacancies as they occurred. Their goal was not to reduce turnover overall but to eliminate unexpected and unmanaged turnover.

• *Scalability: Do we have processes in place to ensure a steady supply of the talent needed to execute our strategies?* Scalability is a key element of business execution when companies are in growth mode. It is also important for being able to efficiently reduce or reallocate the workforce based on shifting business needs. Businesses must be able to scale their workforces to manage changes in business demands and strategic focus. This requires creating processes to attract, develop, and retain the people needed to support the company's evolving business needs. It also means having methods to reduce or reallocate head count in an efficient, fair, and productive manner. A US-based financial company used strategic HR methods to address its ability to scale operations in Asia. The company forecast the level and number of skilled employees needed to support its Asian business growth targets. It then developed an integrated set of staffing, development, and succession management programs to ensure having the talent needed to support its Asian growth plans.

• *Governance (security, compliance, and risk management): Is anyone in the company doing something that could create significant liabilities for our business?* There are many stories of highly successful companies that suffered significant financial losses or even ruination due to inappropriate behavior by a few employees. Governance is about creating methods that reduce the likelihood that employees will do something that will put the company at significant risk or long-term disadvantage. This includes creating processes to reduce the risk of excluding certain demographic groups of employees from career benefits and opportunities, achieving short-term results through inappropriate methods, or tolerating negligent, unethical, or unsafe behavior. A global retail organization I worked with faced issues of governance when it discovered that store managers in certain regions were favoring men over women when making promotion decisions. To address this issue, the leaders implemented strategic HR processes to ensure promotion decisions were made using consistent, transparent, and job-relevant criteria. This both decreased bias in promotions overall and made it more apparent if certain managers were making decisions based on factors that were not job relevant.

The relative importance of these six business execution drivers changes depending on a company's strategy, external market demands, current workforce capabilities, and existing talent management practices. The most important drivers for companies undergoing rapid growth are likely to be quite different from companies whose growth is relatively slow or even declining. The drivers that matter the most to technology companies might be different from those that matter most to health care organizations. (See the discussion: "Six Questions for Assessing Business Execution Capability" for a simple diagnostic way to evaluate your organization's current business execution drivers.)

SIX QUESTIONS FOR ASSESSING BUSINESS EXECUTION CAPABILITY

Business execution capability is defined as a company's ability to align and use its assets to achieve strategic objectives. In most companies, the most expensive asset is its workforce. Salary, benefits, and other employee-related expenses represent over 60 percent of the operating costs for most organizations. For this reason, business execution capability depends heavily on a company's ability to optimize the productivity of its workforce.

The following six questions can be used to estimate your company's business execution capability. Discuss these with your operations leaders to assess the relative strengths and weaknesses of business execution in your company. Ask leaders to respond to each question using a 1 to 5 scale, where 1 means, "No, I have little confidence in our ability to do this if required," and 5 means, "Yes, I am extremely confident we could do this if required."

Question 1: Alignment. Can our company significantly change its strategic direction in nine months or less? This is the sort of change many companies faced during the peak of the 2008 recession. Quite a few companies have discovered too late that they were not up to the challenge. Could you refocus your workforce around a new set of goals quickly? This requires more than just communicating the change. It requires ensuring that employees understand their individual role in the change and that they know what activities they need to stop doing and what things they need to start doing that they were not doing before. Answering a confident yes to this question requires having methods that allow you to quickly clarify how changes in the overall company strategy affect the individual goals and job responsibilities of each employee across the organization.

Question 2: Productivity. Can our company agree on who the top 20 percent performing employees are, and explain this to the other 80 percent in a way that doesn't make them feel that they should be pursuing opportunities elsewhere? One of the common traits found across high-performance work environments is a clear understanding of what success and failure look like. Employees in a high-performance environment do not have to ask someone whether they are doing well. Constant feedback allows them to self-evaluate whether they are performing above or below expected levels. They also trust that performance evaluations are consistently and fairly applied. Even if their performance is below average this year, they know what they need to do to become a top performer next year. There is no guesswork around the question, "What does it take to succeed here?" Performance is not a function of who you know or work for; it is a function of what you do and accomplish. Answering a confident yes to this question requires having processes that clearly define, communicate, and consistently measure the performance expectations set for employees.

Question 3: Efficiency. Can our company determine the return on investment we receive from investing in employees' salary, bonus, and development? It is appropriate and intelligent for companies to invest more resources in the employees who make the greatest contributions to organizational profit and growth. This includes pay, promotions, and access to career development resources and opportunities. Companies invest resources in employees with the assumption that this will lead to increased revenue and decreased operating costs. Yet few companies rigorously test to ensure they are investing resources in the employees who provide the greatest returns to the company. Many do not even know if they have hired an optimal number of people in different roles, or if they are under- or overstaffing positions. Achieving peak efficiency requires having processes that establish clear links between operational profitability and growth, workforce head count, employee performance, and costs associated with employee pay and development. Answering a confident "yes" to this question requires having data that enable you to determine how investments in the workforce affect company performance and having processes to shift workforce resources so they provide the greatest returns with the least costs.

Question 4: Sustainability. Can our company effectively sustain our current level of performance over the next three years? It is one thing to achieve performance goals in the short term. It is another to consistently achieve performance targets year after year. Sustained performance is one of the differences between good companies and great ones. When it comes to business execution, the biggest risk to sustainability is unexpected and unmanaged employee turnover. At some point, every employee who works for you will leave your company. What processes do you have to avoid preventable turnover, manage unpreventable turnover, and ensure consistent operations in the face of workforce change? Answering a confident yes to this question requires having clear strategies and methods for predicting and managing turnover, maintaining employee engagement levels, and transferring knowledge across different segments of the workforce.

Question 5: Scalability: Can our company adapt the size of its workforce to meet projected business growth demands over the next three years? Companies often hope for aggressive growth, but many struggle with the demands it creates. If necessary, could you increase the size of your workforce by 50 percent in under twelve months to support increased market demand for your products and services? This kind of explosive growth is happening in emerging markets, but few companies can manage it effectively. Conversely, if you were hit by a sudden drop in business revenue, are you well equipped to respond? Could you reduce workforce costs by 20 percent and still maintain critical productivity, quality, and customer service levels? It is one thing to grow efficiently, but quite another to scale back operations gracefully when necessary. Answering a confident yes to this question requires having methods to accurately project future workforce requirements and processes to smoothly increase, decrease, or reallocate the workforce based on changing business needs.

Question 6: Governance (security and compliance). Can our company ensure no one is creating inappropriate levels of legal or financial risk for the organization? The CEO of one of the largest companies in the world once told me, "In a company this big, there is probably somebody somewhere doing something they should not be doing." He then said that although there is no way to absolutely prevent employees from engaging in inappropriate, illegal, or unethical activities, companies can create processes that reinforce norms and beliefs around legal and ethical behavior. Establishing hiring, promotion, pay, and performance processes that reinforce consistent beliefs around appropriate behavior significantly reduces the chance of hiring and tolerating employees who intentionally or inadvertently put a company at significant risk. Companies can also collect measures to determine whether people in the company are intentionally or unintentionally making decisions around pay, promotions, and hiring that might unfairly disadvantage certain employee populations. It is difficult to ever answer a totally confident "yes" to this particular question, but a reasonable level of confidence can be obtained by instituting clear hiring, performance, pay, and promotion processes that reinforce a commitment to core company values and tracking data to ensure these processes are being followed across the organization.

3.3 USING STRATEGIC HR PROCESSES TO SUPPORT BUSINESS EXECUTION

Strategic HR processes support business execution by changing the workforce either through bringing new employees into the organization or getting existing employees to do things in the future that they were not doing in the past.[3] The challenge to HR professionals is figuring out what workforce changes are most relevant to the company's strategic needs. To be strategic, HR leaders must understand which business execution drivers (alignment, productivity, efficiency, sustainability, scalability, or governance) are most critical to business leaders and build HR processes that link to these drivers. Linking business strategies to specific HR processes is basically a three-step process.

Step 1. Understand the company's business strategy. What must the company achieve to fulfill the commitments it has made to its shareholders?

Step 2. Define what business execution drivers are most critical to achieving this strategy. Engage line leaders in a discussion around two questions: "What do we need employees to do in the future?" and, "What people do we need to add to the workforce?" Answering these questions will determine which of the six business execution drivers are most critical to achieving the company's business strategy. It can also be useful to ask business leaders to rank-order the six business execution drivers based on criticality to the business. Asking line leaders to explain why certain drivers are more important than others provides significant insight into where to focus strategic HR efforts.

Step 3. Implement appropriate strategic HR processes to support key business execution drivers. All of the 4R strategic HR processes have some effect on each of the six business execution drivers. But certain processes will be more relevant to business operations depending on which business execution drivers are most critical to achieving a company's strategic objectives.

To illustrate how this three-step process works, consider this hypothetical conversation between a chief human resource officer (CHRO) and a CEO:

CEO: I just got back from our annual board meeting.

CHRO: What are our really big strategic commitments for next year? [Step 1]

CEO: There are several, but the most challenging is to achieve 25 percent market growth in the Asia-Pacific region. It is a highly competitive market.

CHRO: I can imagine there must be a lot of business challenges associated with this strategy. What about the people aspect? Do you think we can do this with our existing workforce and how it is structured? [Step 2]

CEO: To be honest, I hadn't thought about it from that perspective. But I don't see how we can achieve 25 percent growth unless we hire a lot more sales and services people and help our leadership team in the region keep them focused on these aggressive growth targets.

CHRO: So we need to focus on scaling the talent in that region and aligning them around these growth goals? [The alignment and scalability business execution drivers]

CEO: Yes, although I'm not sure how we're going to do that in less than twelve months.

CHRO: This seems as if it is largely a matter of getting the right people in the right jobs and focusing them on the right things. The HR department has a lot of expertise and some pretty powerful tools in this area. Would you like me to set up a meeting next week to provide you with a road map setting out actions to build the Asia-Pacific team you need to meet these growth targets? [Step 3]

CEO: That would be great! I look forward to seeing what your team puts together.

It will probably take a bit more than a short conversation to define your company's strategic HR needs, but the logic you use should still follow these same three basic steps because they establish a link between HR processes and specific business needs. Failure to define business execution drivers can result in focusing on less valuable HR processes and may leave line leaders confused about the business relevance of HR activities.

Finally, remember that the relative importance of business execution drivers often changes over time and within companies. For example, scalability is critical when a company is growing, but as it matures, emphasis may shift to efficiency and sustainability. Different drivers may also be more or less important for certain parts of the company depending on their size, business goals, and the nature of their workforces. This can create challenges for HR departments tasked with supporting multiple functions. As an example, I once worked with a global manufacturing company that had a wide range of products. One of the more mature product divisions was completely focused on efficiency and increasing margins. In contrast, a new product area was struggling with scaling to meet growth demands.

The first department wanted HR to build processes to increase performance and productivity of existing employees, while the second department cared only about building processes to hire and train new employees. The challenge the HR department had to solve was how to balance the needs of both areas.

3.4 LINKING SPECIFIC BUSINESS EXECUTION DRIVERS TO DIFFERENT HR PROCESSES

The business value of different HR processes depends on which business execution drivers are most critical to achieving a company's strategic goals. Figure 3.2 illustrates how the six business execution drivers of alignment, productivity, efficiency, sustainability, scalability, and governance link to the 4R strategic HR processes of right people, right things, right way, and right development. The typical relationships between business execution drivers and HR processes are described below. The most relevant HR processes are listed in parentheses in the rough order of their influence on each business execution driver:

Figure 3.2
Relationship of Strategic HR Processes to Business Execution Drivers

	Right People	Right Way	Right Things	Right Development
Alignment		✓	✓✓	
Productivity	✓	✓✓	✓✓	✓✓
Efficiency	✓✓	✓✓	✓	✓
Sustainability	✓✓			✓✓
Scalability	✓✓	✓		✓✓
Governance	✓	✓✓		

1. *Creating alignment (right things, right way).* Alignment is primarily about employees knowing what goals they should focus on and why these are important to the company's overall strategy. The best way to increase alignment is to implement goal management processes that ensure employees are focusing on the right things. This includes making sure employees understand how their actions influence the success of the organization as a whole. Performance management processes that evaluate whether employees are doing things the right way may also be relevant for alignment. This is particularly true if a company is focusing on aligning employees around cultural behaviors and values as opposed to specific tactical goals.

2. *Increasing productivity (right way, right things, right people, right development).* Productivity is directly influenced by performance management processes that communicate, encourage, and hold employees accountable for meeting performance expectations (doing the right things the right way). It is also indirectly influenced by ensuring that employees are placed in jobs that leverage their strengths and are given tools and resources to increase their performance levels.

3. *Improving efficiency (right people, right things, right way, right development).* A variety of methods can increase efficiency. First, ensure the company has optimal staffing levels in all jobs. Nothing undermines efficiency more than under- or overstaffing positions. Second, ensure people are working in the most productive manner possible. This requires focusing people on goals that are critical to business success and consistently measuring and improving their performance. Efficiency can also be improved by increasing internal hiring and promotion of existing employees and avoiding costs associated with external staffing.

4. *Ensuring sustainability (right development, right people).* Sustainability is primarily about managing turnover in key positions through effective staffing, workforce planning, and succession management. The ability to forecast and plan for turnover is particularly critical to sustaining consistent performance. This includes hiring and developing people to manage job transitions, as well as managing current employees in a manner that decreases the risk of unplanned, regrettable turnover.

5. *Creating scalability (right people, right development, right way).* There are two basic types of scalability: growth to support expanding business demands and cutting back the workforce to manage shifts in business needs. Scaling to support growth requires having methods to rapidly recruit external talent and get them up to speed to take on new roles. Scaling to meet shifts in business needs requires having methods to reallocate staff based on changing workforce requirements and, if necessary, having tools to guide intelligent downsizing decisions that take into account employee performance contributions.

6. *Governance (right way, right people).* There are two primary types of governance: governance focused on complying with government or contractual laws and regulations and governance focused on discouraging employees from taking excessive risks or engaging in counterproductive activities. The former tends to emphasize the use of fair and appropriate methods for staffing positions and evaluating performance. The latter tends to emphasize methods to communicate and measure core performance expectations and standards.

The relationship between business execution drivers and strategic HR processes is more complex than how it is illustrated in figure 3.2. But having a general sense of the relationship between strategic HR processes and the business execution drivers they have an impact on is critical to effective design and deployment of strategic HR methods. Experience shows that many HR organizations fail to clearly articulate the business execution reasons for implementing HR methods. Many HR practitioners do not fully understand how the processes they support bear on their company's business strategies. Even if the links between HR processes and business drivers are well understood in HR, they may not be apparent to non-HR line leaders. If the relationship between HR processes and business needs is not identified and communicated, then these processes are likely to be viewed as administrative activities with little relevance to day-to-day business operations.

3.5 INCREASING STRATEGIC HR PROCESS MATURITY

Using HR to drive business execution begins with understanding which business execution drivers are most critical to supporting business needs. The next action is to build HR processes to support these drivers. Figure 3.3 illustrates five levels of maturity associated with the four core strategic HR processes of right people, right things, right way, and right development. Higher levels of maturity increase business execution capability but also require more resources and effort to achieve. Companies do not need or necessarily want to be at the highest levels of maturity for each of the 4R strategic HR processes. Understanding a company's current maturity levels and how these relate to its business execution provides a framework for prioritizing the development and integration of HR methods.

3.5.1 Right People Maturity Levels

Ensuring you have the right people begins with creating processes to efficiently fill open positions. Level 2 focuses on building assessments to ensure you are hiring high performers. Level 3 shifts the emphasis from screening candidates to building internal and external talent pools of qualified applicants. Level 4 moves from building general talent pools to making specific forecasts around the number of people you need to hire to fill different positions and when you will need them. This sets the stage for level 5: building talent pipelines to efficiently and effectively put the right people in the right jobs at the right time.

Figure 3.3
Levels of Strategic HR Process Maturity

Level 5	Building talent pipelines	Operational	Influential	Maintaining talent pipelines
Level 4	Forecasting future talent needs	Coordinated effort	Calibrated	Carreer growth
Level 3	Building talent pools	Meaningful goals	High impact	Business-driven development
Level 2	Selecting high performers	Aligned goals	Well defined	Targeted development
Level 1	Filling open positions	Tangible goals	Consistent	Individual development planning
	Right People	Right Things	Right Way	Right Development

3.5.2   Right Things Maturity Levels

Making sure employees are focused on the right things begins with ensuring that employees have well-defined goals. Do not underestimate the business value of achieving this level. Simply getting managers to sit down with their employees and map out clear goals and expectations is a major leap forward for many organizations. Level 2 focuses on ensuring that employees' goals are aligned with the company's overall strategy. This is typically done through some form of goal-cascading process. Level 3 shifts the focus from setting goals that are important to the company to setting goals that are meaningful to employees. This requires using methods to ensure that employees see goals as relevant to their personal career aspirations. Level 4 focuses on building collaboration within the company around common types of goals. It is about breaking down silos and coordinating efforts across peers and departments. Level 5 emphasizes getting business leaders to use goal processes as tools for running and managing the business. As one operations leader put it, "You are using goal management correctly when it ceases to become a tool for personnel administration and becomes a tool for strategy communication."

3.5.3   Right Way Maturity Levels

Ensuring employees are doing things the right way requires defining, communicating, and measuring their performance. Performance evaluations are then used to inform development discussions and staffing and pay decisions. The basis of accurate measurement is consistency, the lowest level of maturity. It requires making sure employee performance is evaluated using consistent, standardized methods. Level 2 emphasizes creating clear performance definitions, competency models, and goal criteria to guide performance evaluations. Level 3 focuses on using performance data so it affects decisions related to employee pay, development, and staffing. Level 4 emphasizes the use of calibration processes that get managers across the organization to agree on common levels of performance expectations and employee evaluations. At level 5, business leaders leverage performance management data to gain insight into the workforce itself—for example, determining what competencies are most relevant to success in different roles, assessing the overall strengths and weaknesses of the workforce, and identifying actions that can be used to increase overall workforce productivity.

3.5.4 Right Development

Right development emphasizes the use of career and succession management to build the overall capabilities of the workforce. The lowest level is simply making sure employees have discussed development needs with their managers and have some form of development plan. Level 2 focuses on guiding employee development to build specific organizational capabilities or prepare employees for certain job roles. This requires guiding employee development based on future business needs. Level 3 emphasizes having managers staff jobs and assign goals in a way that stretches employees to develop new skills and capabilities. Level 4 shifts the time horizon into the future by providing employees with guidance on identifying and achieving long-term career objectives within the organization. Level 5 is about actively integrating employee development with workforce planning and staffing to maintain a steady supply of high-performing talent in key jobs across the company.

Organizations do not necessarily need to master lower levels of maturity to achieve higher levels. But maturity levels do tend to build on one another somewhat like the stories of a building. The stronger the foundation of the lower stories is, the more stable the higher levels will be. For example, it is difficult to make influential decisions using performance management data (level 5 of "right way") if your company does not have well-defined performance definitions and consistent processes for evaluating employee performance (levels 1 and 2).

3.6 INTEGRATING STRATEGIC HR PROCESSES

I have now explained the fundamental 4R strategic HR processes and discussed their relationship to business execution drivers. I have also outlined different levels of HR process maturity that companies may strive for based on their business execution needs. But I have not specifically addressed the issue of HR process integration. The phrase *integrated HR* is often bandied about as something every company should aspire for, but it is rarely defined.

Integrated HR requires coordinating the 4R processes of right people, right things, right way, and right development. Examples include blending right things and right development by assigning employees business goals that enable them to develop new capabilities or blending right people and right way by using performance management evaluations to guide internal staffing decisions. Integrating HR processes is important for at least three reasons:

- *Optimization.* Increasing the maturity level of one HR process often requires leveraging techniques or data from other HR processes. You cannot fully optimize any of the four strategic HR process without incorporating elements from other processes. For example, level 3 of right development is called "business-driven development." This level is achieved by using business goals (right things) and job assignments (right people) to support employee development.

- *Coordination.* Employees become frustrated when they experience uncoordinated HR processes within the same company. As one vice president of operations memorably told me, "The only thing that integrates our HR processes is the poor victim, I mean employee, subjected to them." Different strategic HR processes should use common tools, models, and terminology so managers and employees can transfer knowledge learned from one process to another—for example, using the same competency model to support staffing, performance management, and succession management.

- *Efficiency.* Integrating HR processes enables companies to be more efficient in collecting talent management data, developing and supporting HR technology, and training employees. It allows companies to reuse elements of one process to support other processes. Examples are having goal management data (right things) feed into the processes used for performance management (right way) and succession management (right people and right development), or using the same technology platform to support setting goals, evaluating performance, rewarding and compensating employees, and creating development plans.

Figures 3.4 and 3.5 illustrate how the four core strategic HR processes integrate with one another. Figure 3.4 uses a pyramid to illustrate that as talent management processes become more mature, they also become more integrated. You cannot get to the top of a pyramid by building just one side. Similarly, you cannot achieve the highest levels of strategic HR process maturity by focusing on a single process. This is why it is important to draw on multiple strategic HR functions when developing long-term HR strategies. For example, if you are focusing on increasing staffing effectiveness maturity (right people), be sure to include the people who manage development and succession management (right development) because the work they do will either enable or constrain the ability of the company to attract high-quality candidates and build talent pools.

Figure 3.5 illustrates the notion of process integration in more detail by comparing the maturity levels associated with right people and right development. At the lowest level of maturity, these two processes are independent. Methods used to ensure that employees have individual development plans may have little to do with the methods used to efficiently fill open positions. This changes as process maturity increases. At level 2, both processes focus on hiring or developing people based on well-defined job performance requirements. Level 3 for right people and right development emphasizes building talent pools within the organization to support future business needs. Level 4 requires the development of long-term models that forecast future workforce needs and career opportunities. And at level 5, the two processes blend into a single process that orchestrates staffing and development activities to maintain a steady supply of high-performing talent in critical job roles.

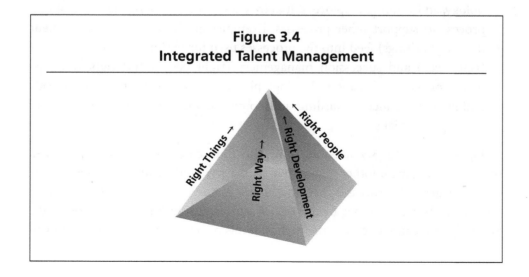

Figure 3.4
Integrated Talent Management

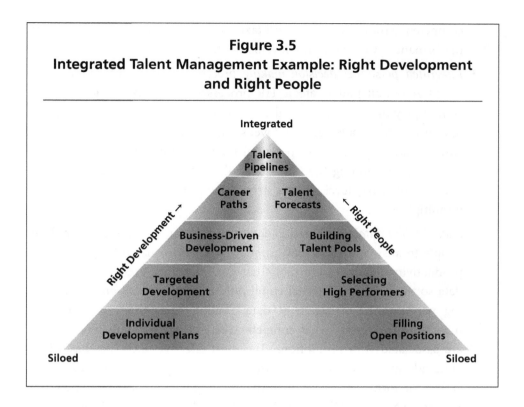

Figure 3.5
Integrated Talent Management Example: Right Development and Right People

Integrated

Talent Pipelines

Career Paths • Talent Forecasts

Right Development → • ← Right People

Business-Driven Development • Building Talent Pools

Targeted Development • Selecting High Performers

Individual Development Plans • Filling Open Positions

Siloed ⋯ Siloed

When building a strategic HR road map or vision, it is important to think about long-term structural integration points between different HR processes. Otherwise you can inadvertently create incompatible processes that prevent achieving higher levels of HR maturity. Following are six critical integration points to consider when developing a strategic HR road map. These are certainly not the only points of integration, but they are major ones to keep in mind:

1. *A single system for employee record keeping.* As you build out HR systems, focus on creating a single system that incorporates data from each of the 4R strategic HR processes. This will make it much easier to collect data in one process and then use these data to support other processes.

2. *Common definitions of job performance.* Build job descriptions, competency models, and goal plans that can effectively support multiple strategic HR functions. Think how job performance data will be used to provide employees with developmental feedback, determine pay increases, and guide staffing and promotion decisions. Emphasize the use of standard

competency frameworks and skill taxonomies that can be used for staffing, performance evaluation, and development.

3. *Integrated personnel decision-making processes.* Review information collected across all four strategic HR processes and think about the role it should play in pay, staffing, and development decisions. For example, you may want to consider an employee's past record of career development when evaluating his or her potential for future job roles. Similarly, there is value in examining the kinds of goals employees have achieved when deciding their pay level. Always strive to collect information once and use it multiple ways.

4. *Shared talent databases.* Develop databases that can be accessed by multiple people to answer a variety of questions related to maximizing workforce productivity. Examples are tools that give recruiters access to succession data so they can find internal employees to fill open positions or combining performance management data, staffing data, and career development data to identify what competencies and development interventions are associated with promotions. The most effective talent databases integrate administrative HR data with strategic HR data (see the discussion: "HRIS Platforms and Workforce Analytic Applications: The Gas and Oil of Integrated Strategic HR Technology"). When building these databases, it is also important to develop guidelines around data access and security.

HRIS PLATFORMS AND WORKFORCE ANALYTIC APPLICATIONS: THE GAS AND OIL OF INTEGRATED STRATEGIC HR TECHNOLOGY

Strategic HR involves developing processes to ensure a company hires the right people, gets them doing the right things the right way, and provides them with the right development. Each of these processes benefits from using different types of specialized HR technology—for example:

- *Right people:* Search engines and staffing tools that help companies find and hire employees with the attributes needed to succeed in different jobs

- *Right things:* Goal management systems that allow companies to quickly communicate and coordinate job objectives across the organization to ensure people are focused on the right things

- *Right way:* Performance management systems that enable managers to accurately evaluate employees and provide feedback and rewards to increase their effectiveness

- *Right development:* Learning management and development systems that help employees acquire the knowledge, skills, and experiences to perform their jobs and advance to positions with increasing levels of responsibility

These four core areas of strategic HR can be thought of as the sides of a pyramid. At low levels of process maturity, the processes are relatively independent. But at high levels these processes become highly intertwined. Figure 3.6 illustrates this concept.

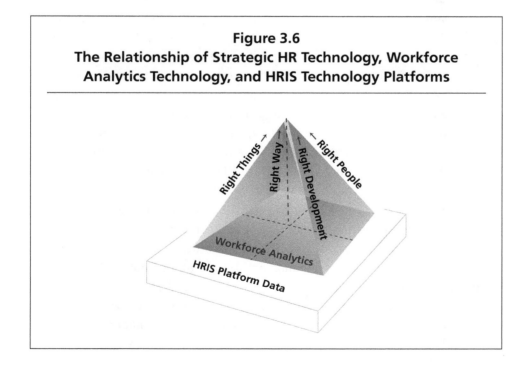

Figure 3.6
The Relationship of Strategic HR Technology, Workforce Analytics Technology, and HRIS Technology Platforms

Strategic HR technology plays a crucial role integrating different HR processes as they reach higher levels of maturity. For example, HR technology makes it possible to enroll newly hired employees automatically into training programs needed to perform their jobs. The technology also makes it possible to link performance management assessments to career development systems so employees are directed to specific learning resources based on their performance strengths and weaknesses. These data can then be fed into succession management systems used to identify and track potential future leaders within the organization.

Figure 3.6 also shows how two additional technology systems, HRIS (human resource information system) platforms and workforce analytics systems, affect the four main areas of strategic HR. These additional systems are not always focused on strategic HR, but they have an influence on strategic HR processes similar to how gas and oil influence the performance of an engine.

HRIS platforms are a form of computer technology used to support administrative HR tasks such as processing compensation, storing employee records (e.g., name, address), and tracking organizational data about employees such as job title and reporting relationships. These systems contain critical information—employee names, job titles, and salaries, for example—but tend to contain little information about what these employees actually do, how effectively they do it, or what potential they have to do other things in the future.

Because HRISs are tied to ongoing operations such as payroll and benefits, many of the data in these systems undergo considerable quality control to ensure they are accurate. HRISs usually contain the most up-to-date information about who is working in the company, where they live, and how much they are paid. But these data are relatively uninteresting in terms of telling us about employee productivity or potential. In contrast, strategic HR systems contain significant information about employee performance and potential. But data in strategic HR technology systems tends to be less current and accurate than data in HRISs. This is because most strategic HR processes like performance management occur less frequently and do not have the near-term operational impact of administrative HR tasks like payroll processing.

Historically, HRIS and strategic HR systems operated independently with limited data transfer. But companies are increasingly using technology platforms that support both HRIS and strategic HR functions. This is helping to create the best of both worlds by giving companies detailed workforce data that are administratively accurate and strategically informative.

Workforce analytics systems are technology applications that access, manipulate, and analyze data about employees to gain insights into workforce productivity, staffing levels, and other factors affecting workforce quality. These applications act as pipelines and dashboards that integrate data from several locations to create different pictures of an organization. Workforce analytics systems, for example, integrate HRIS and strategic HR data to generate reports showing level of turnover based on job function, employee performance, and salary or run models that show projected future staffing demands based on historic turnover rates taking into account the depth of internal talent pools and talent levels found in external labor markets.

Many of the data used by workforce analytics applications come from strategic HR technology and HRIS. Linking workforce analytics applications, HRIS and strategic HR technology allow companies to fully leverage the insights that can be gained from analyzing HR data. This increases the value, visibility, and use of strategic HR processes overall. For example, imagine a company used workforce analytics applications to track turnover levels of high-performing employees participating in high-potential development programs. If the company discovered that participation decreased turnover, they could leverage the strategic HR processes that provided these data to enroll more employees in the programs.

HRIS data can be thought of as the gas that fuels strategic HR processes by providing more complete and up-to-date information about employees. Workforce analytics applications can be thought of as the oil that makes strategic HR methods run in more efficient and integrated fashion. Linking these three types of systems together creates a sum that is greater than its parts.

5. *Single operational dashboards.* Determine what sort of HR data will provide the most value to business leaders and present them on a single data display or dashboard. HR data are usually more interesting when presented in combination with financial or operational data. Think through what data will be most interesting to business leaders and how to display them so they lead to meaningful insights. This is critical to achieving the highest levels of talent management maturity. Having this end in mind is also important for ensuring that you collect the necessary data in the right format. For example, rather than showing overall turnover rate or the percentage of employees rated as high performers, it is more informative to show the turnover rate of employees who are rated as high performers. Rather than showing average performance ratings in different divisions, present a comparison of the financial performance of divisions with average performance ratings in each division.

6. *Integrated compensation and staffing strategies.* The most visible actions companies make related to workforce management are those around hiring, promotions, terminations, and pay (see the discussion: "Pay and Promotions: The Ultimate Expression of Company Values"). Think about how your company makes pay and staffing decisions. Is it about being in the right job, achieving the right things, doing things the right way, focusing on the right development, or some balance of all four? Does it balance elements of what jobs people are in, what they have accomplished, how they act, and what they are doing to develop their capabilities? Or does it disproportionately emphasize one of the four aspects of strategic HR? For example, some companies base promotions almost entirely on past performance with little emphasis on using staffing to support employee development. Many companies base pay primarily on goal accomplishment, with much less attention paid to how these goals were achieved. Overly emphasizing some elements of talent management while underemphasizing others is not necessarily bad. In fact, it may make sense for many jobs. But whether good or bad, the highly visible nature of compensation and staffing decisions will either reinforce or undermine a company's commitment to integrating different elements of strategic HR for building and rewarding the workforce.

Paying attention to these integration points reduces the risk of creating HR processes that are overly siloed and potentially incompatible or that contradict one another. Always ask, "How could the process I'm designing influence or benefit from integrating with other processes?" Creating an integrated HR steering committee and establishing a single strategic HR coordinator can also help to create processes that employees and operations leaders will see as seamless, well-coordinated, and coherent.

PAY AND PROMOTIONS: THE ULTIMATE EXPRESSION OF COMPANY VALUES

Nothing says more about what a company truly values than the decisions it makes around hiring, promoting, and financially rewarding. These represent concrete actions to invest in some people over others based on their perceived value to the company. When a company promotes or compensates an employee, it is implicitly saying, "We value this person so much that we have decided to give him more money, responsibility, and power regardless of what shortcomings he may have." Ideally promotions and pay are based on a systematic and careful review of what the person has accomplished, how he acts within the company, and his progress against business objectives. In these cases, promotions and pay underscore the company's commitment toward its stated values and strategies. But all too often promotion and pay decisions are made hastily, focus on short-term operational needs, or are used to prevent people from quitting rather than rewarding their contributions to the company. Frequently they overemphasize one aspect of performance while ignoring others. Promotions and pay decisions made in these situations often result in sending a message to employees that the company may say it values certain behaviors but what it truly rewards is something else entirely.

Promotion decisions probably have the most impact because they are highly visible to everyone in the organization. When employees see one of their peers get promoted, they immediately draw conclusions about why this person was rewarded. They will view it as an implied endorsement that all of the things this person did, both good and bad, are valued, accepted, or tolerated by the company. It does not matter if these conclusions are accurate because perception is reality.

Nothing says more about what a company truly cares about than pay and promotion decisions. What systems does your company have in place to ensure these decisions reflect its stated values? Do people understand how pay and promotion decisions are made? Is the process transparent, or are employees left to make up their own reasons for why some people were rewarded while others went unrecognized? Are you certain that your company is honestly putting its money where its mouth is?

3.7 CONCLUSION

Companies are most likely to achieve their business objectives when they do the following things well:

- *Get the right people in the right jobs.* Staff positions with employees whose attributes match the demands and requirements associated with job goals and competencies. This is the primary focus of recruiting and succession planning.

- *Focus them on the right things.* Clearly identify and communicate the goals they want employees to achieve; then measure and reward employees against these goals. This is the focus of goal management and variable pay.

- *Ensure they do things the right way.* Define the competencies employees must have to achieve their job goals and evaluate and reward employees based on the degree to which they demonstrate these competencies. This is the primary focus of performance management and merit pay.

- *Provide them with the right development.* Create a work environment that helps employees develop attributes that support the competencies that drive goal accomplishment. This is the primary focus of career development and succession management.

Effective strategic HR develops these four fundamental processes to support the company's most important business execution drivers, basically a three-step process:

1. *Understand your company's business objectives.* What are the most critical commitments the company must fulfill to meet the expectations of its

shareholders? The only way to answer this question is to spend time talking with operations leaders about what business goals are top of mind for them.

2. *Define how these business objectives tie back to key business execution drivers.* Engage line leaders in a discussion around the following questions: "To achieve our business objectives, what sort of employees do we need, and what must they accomplish?" and, "What do we need people to do tomorrow that they are not doing today?" How will the company need to change its workforce in order to meet its strategic commitments? What will people need to do in the future that they are not doing now? Will the company need to add talent to the workforce that it does not currently have? Answering these questions will help determine which of the six business execution drivers are most critical to achieving the company's business strategy.

3. *Implement the appropriate strategic HR processes to support the key business execution drivers.* Determine which of the 4R processes will have the most impact on the business execution drivers that are critical to your company. Assess the current maturity level of these processes, and determine what improvements will have the greatest influence on your company's ability to execute its strategies. Do not be afraid to drive change, but limit change to things that will make a significant difference to the company's strategic success. Emphasize the use of integrated, efficient processes and technology to ensure you achieve the maximum value with the least disruption to ongoing business operations. Finally, communicate the business reasons for adopting more effective strategic HR processes. Make sure HR processes are viewed as tools to drive business execution and are not merely seen as additional administrative tasks.

The remainder of this book discusses critical design questions related to using the four fundamental HR processes to support your company's unique business execution needs. The emphasis is on using HR processes as tools for business execution as opposed to administrative compliance. We have the knowledge and tools needed to use strategic HR processes to drive business execution. It is up to us to make it happen.

NOTES

1. Starting in 2008, SuccessFactors began investigating the underlying business reasons that led to decisions to invest in strategic HR technology. This involved asking companies to explain what had led them to invest time, money, and other resources to deploy technology-enabled strategic HR processes. This work led to the identification of the six business execution drivers presented here.

2. *Span of control* refers to the number of employees reporting in to a manager. A manager who has five employees reporting to her has a span of control of five.

3. This includes continuing to work for the company. Increasing retention and managing turnover are major issues related to business execution, particularly the business execution drivers productivity, sustainability, and scalability.

Right People

Designing Recruiting and Staffing Processes

Running a successful business depends on having the right people in the right roles to effectively execute its strategies. The most important decision a company makes about its employees is to hire them. Every other action made about employees is a direct result of that initial decision to bring them into the organization.

Despite the strategic importance of hiring, many companies have treated recruiting as a largely administrative process.[1] Rather than focusing on the business value associated with hiring, recruiters often focus on increasing the number of job requisitions processed, with little emphasis on how the newly hired people perform after they join the company. As one person put it, "HR departments that focus on number of hires instead of quality of hires might as well measure effectiveness by the kilos of people they've employed." Fortunately, the growing influence of strategic HR is steadily changing the focus from quantity to quality of hiring. This is the result of several factors:

- *Scarcity of skilled talent.* Experienced recruiters know there is always a limited supply of qualified high performers available to fill skilled jobs at the salary companies want to pay them. This skill shortage is growing due to the increasing complexity of jobs, decreasing birth rates in many countries, and more intensive competition for talent around the globe.[2] Do not be fooled by overall unemployment statistics. There may be more people available in the job market in general, but that does not mean they are people who have the skills and competencies needed to support your company's strategies.

- *Cost of labor.* As the supply of skilled labor decreases, its cost increases. Companies cannot afford to make hiring mistakes given how much it costs to bring people into the organization. There is also the insidious problem of hiring marginal performers and having them stay. In many countries, it is both difficult and costly to fire someone for underperformance.

- *Importance of human capital.* The past thirty years have seen a steady shift from a resource-based to a knowledge- and service-based economy. In today's market, competitive advantage depends less on what companies own and more on whom they employ. Your company's ability to hire skilled, high-performing employees simultaneously supports the goals of your business while depriving your competitors of the talent they may need to compete against you.

Recruiting was once seen as a back-office function that was often outsourced as a commodity service. It is now becoming a key differentiator in the emerging war for talent. Winning this war requires rethinking key questions around what makes a good recruiting process.

This chapter is organized into three sections. Section 4.1 discusses fundamental changes in how companies are thinking about recruiting and the growing emphasis on creating more collaborative, quality-focused recruiting processes that balance hiring quality with hiring efficiency. Section 4.2 discusses nine key questions to ask when designing a recruiting process. There is no one best way to do recruiting, but the best recruiting processes all address these questions thoroughly. Section 4.3 discusses different levels of recruiting process maturity that can be used to guide the creation of a long-term road map for achieving recruiting excellence.

4.1 RECRUITING TO SUPPORT BUSINESS EXECUTION

From a strategic perspective, the goal of recruiting is not simply to hire people into the organization. Rather, it is to efficiently place and retain the right people in the right roles to effectively support the company's business strategies. This is a significant change from how some recruiting departments traditionally viewed their role (see the discussion: "From Processing Candidates to Hiring Performers: The Changing Role of Recruiting"). Organizations that approach recruiting with a strategic mindset are distinguished by the emphasis they place on five key topics: quality of hire, quality of sourcing, networking and relationships, hiring manager involvement, and integrated talent management.

FROM PROCESSING CANDIDATES TO HIRING PERFORMERS: THE CHANGING ROLE OF RECRUITING

The past thirty years have seen significant changes in the field of recruiting. Prior to the advent of the Internet, much of what recruiters did was associated with the basic identification and processing of candidates. Recruiting tended to be an administrative function focused on placing want ads, processing and sorting job applications, and setting up candidate interviews. Some companies also tasked recruiters with handling the paperwork for new employees. The Internet freed recruiting departments from much of this administrative burden and allowed them to streamline the recruiting function significantly. But recruiting still tended to be judged on process metrics such as time to fill and number of people hired. Staffing departments were rarely held accountable for the performance of new employees. Nor were they expected to challenge managers on whether it made more sense to fill positions internally or externally.

The growing importance of strategic HR is shifting recruiting from a focus on hiring efficiency to a focus on staffing effectiveness. Recruiting departments are still held accountable for efficiently processing and rapidly placing candidates. But the difference between administrative recruiting departments and strategic ones lies in the ability to fill positions with the best-performing candidates at the lowest cost. This requires recruiters to collaborate with hiring managers to ensure they accurately define job requirements, tapping into the social networks of hiring managers and other employees to find the best candidates, using rigorous candidate selection methods that validly predict future job performance, and extending recruiting beyond the hiring decision to accelerate and track job performance after employees have been hired.

4.1.1 Quality of Hiring Decisions

Even slight improvements in the quality of hiring can have a massive financial impact on organizational performance.[3] For example, by changing its hiring methods, a call center company was able to increase retention of call center agents by about one week. This may not seem like a lot, but given the costs of hiring and the fact that the company hired more than one thousand agents every year, this small increase in retention added up to millions of dollars in savings. Quality of hiring can also make or break companies when it comes to staffing critical leadership and technical positions. For example, consider the financial benefits associated with hiring the right merchandise buyers in a retail company or the costs associated with putting the wrong person in charge of quality control in a manufacturing plant.

Strategic HR organizations know the value of the quality of hiring and constantly emphasize it to line-of-business leaders (see "Getting Hiring Managers to Take Recruiting Seriously"). They review every step in the recruiting process based on how it will affect the company's ability to attract and select the best performers. Recruiters are evaluated not just on time to fill positions but on the performance and retention of employees they help bring into the company. A quick way to assess whether an organization has a mind-set based on quality of hiring is to ask recruiters, "How do you know if you effectively filled a position?" A quality-oriented recruiter will focus on measuring how candidates perform after they are hired and will not simply review metrics related to sourcing and screening candidates.

GETTING HIRING MANAGERS TO TAKE RECRUITING SERIOUSLY

You might think that hiring managers would be obsessive about hiring the best employees possible. After all, they are the ones who directly benefit or suffer from a good- or bad-quality hiring decision. However, this is not always true. Many managers only think about recruiting when they have open positions on their teams. And when this happens, they often think about filling the position as fast as possible without thinking too much about whether the person they are hiring is truly the best candidate available. In essence, they view recruiting more as an operational inconvenience than as a valuable opportunity to improve the quality of the people on their teams. These managers often resist investing more time than is absolutely necessary to define job requirements, source and select candidates, and onboard new employees.

The best way to shift hiring managers' mind-sets toward recruiting is to make sure they are fully aware of the costs and benefits associated with hiring decisions. Before beginning the recruiting process, ask managers these questions:

- *What is the minimum financial impact this position will have on your department and the company overall?* The typical assumption is that employees will contribute revenue to the company that is at least equal to twice their cost in salary and benefits. In other words, we pay people with the assumption that the value they provide to the company is greater than what we pay them. So how much is this position worth? Remember to take into account that we probably expect this person to stay in this position for at least a few years so his or her annual financial contributions will be multiplied by his or her expected tenure.

- *What is the maximum financial impact of this position if we hire a top performer?* Studies show that top-performing employees often generate three or more times the revenue of average performers. How much financial value would come from hiring the absolutely best candidate into this role?

- *What is the cost of poor performance?* People sometimes say employees are our most valuable assets, but employees who perform poorly can be an expensive liability. How much damage could realistically be caused by making a poor hiring decision?

- *Taking all this into account, how much financial value is associated with this hiring decision?* What is the difference in the value of a good decision versus the cost of a poor one? To put this in perspective, think about the last time you invested this much money to purchase equipment, acquire materials, or enter into a service contract agreement with a vendor. How much time did you spend defining the specifications for this investment, reviewing proposals, and making the purchasing decision? Doesn't it make sense to spend an equal amount of time on the recruiting process to ensure you hire the best employee possible?

I have had this sort of discussion with many line-of-business leaders. Almost every conversation ended with leaders expressing a sense of surprise and appreciation about the importance of hiring the best people possible. The exceptions were leaders who already understood that one of the most important business decisions they ever made was deciding who to bring onto their teams. In either case, the result is greater willingness to collaborate with HR departments to build and deploy more effective recruiting processes.

4.1.2   Quality of Sourcing

The quality of the people you hire for a job is constrained by the quality of who applies. The field of candidate sourcing has been radically changed by the Internet. Companies can now easily and quickly source candidates from hundreds of online job sites and social networking systems. Companies with integrated strategic HR technology systems can also source internal candidates by scanning databases of current employees. This ready access to so many candidates is a mixed blessing, however. On the positive side, companies can find qualified candidates for jobs regardless of where they are located around the globe. On the negative side, companies can be inundated with thousands of applications from unqualified candidates.

Sourcing is much less about the number of candidates and much more about their quality. Sourcing has become so important that there is now a specialized field of recruiting marketing that uses sophisticated web tools to attract candidates and rapidly sort through applicants and workforce data to find sources that yield the best candidates with the least cost. The specialized technology and workforce analytics applications associated with recruiting marketing enable companies to find, attract, and engage high-quality candidates with the minimal investment possible.

4.1.3   Relationships and Networking

Recruiters use a variety of methods for finding job candidates, but often they find the best-quality candidates through networking. Networking is particularly valuable when hiring for positions that require specialized experience. These positions tend to be filled by people who have extensive networks of professional colleagues. As one recruiter explained, "When hiring for a skilled position, the ideal candidate is probably a person whom either the hiring manager or one of the manager's colleagues already knows. Hiring managers are rarely more than two degrees of separation from the best candidate."

Networking is effective for several reasons. First, managers and employees are likely to recommend better-quality candidates since they don't want to work with people whom they view as incompetent or unmotivated. Second, the best candidates tend to be currently employed elsewhere. These so-called passive candidates already have jobs and may not take notice of job postings, but they may respond to an inquiry about a job opportunity from someone they know. A third benefit of networking is that it does not cost a lot of money, unlike job postings, which can be associated with hefty fees.

Strategic HR organizations embrace networking for finding and attracting the best candidates. They invest in tools to help recruiters build and maintain pools of qualified candidates they can leverage for future hiring. They instruct recruiters on how to leverage the networks of line-of-business managers and employees. They also provide employees with tools and rewards that encourage everyone in the organization to play a part in finding high-quality talent. This includes making use of internal and external social networking technology and sites—for example, providing employees with tools that allow them to share job openings with people they may know through public social networking sites such as Facebook or LinkedIn.

4.1.4 Hiring Manager Involvement

A common problem in recruiting is a tendency for hiring managers to distance themselves from the actual recruiting process. Rather than collaborating with recruiters, some hiring managers assume they can give the recruiter a job requisition and that two weeks later they will be presented with the perfect candidate. Strategic HR organizations stress the need to keep hiring managers and other line employees actively engaged throughout the recruiting process. They use collaboration tools that give managers visibility into the types of candidates being sourced and selected. For example, online databases make it easy for recruiters to share potential candidates with hiring managers and allow hiring managers to make comments and suggestions to the recruiters about candidate qualifications.

These tools help managers compare candidates, get a sense of the quality in the available talent pool, and exchange thoughts and opinions with other members of the recruiting team. This allows managers and recruiters to jointly determine if they should expand, reduce, or otherwise redefine the scope of the job or candidate search based on the talent available. Emphasis is also placed on using interview processes that allow multiple stakeholders to evaluate candidates (e.g., allowing coworkers to participate in the interview process).

Actively involving hiring managers and other employees in the sourcing and selection process improves the quality of applicants and ensures that line leadership feels a sense of ownership around the final hiring decision. Involving multiple employees in the hiring process also helps with bringing new employees into the organization because they have already met and established a connection with many of their future coworkers. Of course, there is an efficiency trade-off in terms of the time required for more people to participate in the hiring process. But in general, few hiring decisions should be made by a single person acting without involvement from their colleagues.

4.1.5 Integrated Talent Management

Recruiting is something people often think about only when there is a job vacancy in their group. Hiring is thus treated as an isolated event that lives outside the ongoing talent management process. The most effective strategic HR organizations campaign against this limited view of recruiting. They view recruiting not just about filling positions but as a key part of a broader set of strategic HR processes. It is about creating talent flows within the organization through integrating staffing, employee development, succession management, and career planning. Recruiting may not be something that's done every day, but it is something that needs to be kept constantly in mind, especially during times of large-scale company growth or change.

Two concepts are particularly important to consider when viewing recruiting as part of an integrated strategic HR framework:

- *Balancing internal versus external hiring.* Recruiting activities that are integrated into a broader strategic HR framework actively balance the relative merits of internal versus external hiring. Staffing is used to support internal employee career development and succession management and to bring new talent into the company. Managers and recruiters discuss whether open positions should be used to build the capabilities of existing employees or to bring in new skills from outside.

- *Workforce planning and job design.* The best time to source talent is before you need it. Recruiters should not passively wait for line managers to come to them with open requisitions and then go out looking for candidates. Strategic HR organizations create ongoing discussions between recruiters and line managers about the company's business strategies and future hiring needs necessary to support them. This includes anticipating the need to fill potential vacancies for existing jobs and forecasting the need to staff new types of jobs to support ongoing business growth.

The five themes of hiring quality, sourcing quality, relationship recruiting, manager involvement, and integrated talent management should be reinforced throughout the design of recruiting processes. Keeping these themes in mind will decrease the risk of creating recruiting processes that may be efficient but provide questionable value when it comes to supporting business execution.

4.2 CRITICAL RECRUITING DESIGN QUESTIONS

There is no one best way to do recruiting. What works extremely well for a regional health care organization may be disastrous for a multinational software company. The processes that are appropriate for hiring new college graduates are much different from those used to hire senior executives. But companies that have the most successful recruiting processes typically have one thing in common: they have carefully thought through the following recruitment design questions:

1. What types of jobs are we hiring for?
2. How many people will we need to hire, and when will we need them?
3. What sort of people do we need to hire? What attributes do candidates need to possess to become effective employees?
4. What roles will hiring managers, recruiters, coworkers, and candidates play in the hiring process?
5. How will we source candidates?

6. How will we select candidates?

7. How will we get newly hired employees up to full productivity?

8. How will we retain employees after they are hired?

9. How will we measure recruiting success and improve our processes over time?

The answers to these questions will vary from organization to organization. But failure to adequately address any of them will almost always result in a flawed recruiting process.

4.2.1 What Types of Jobs Are We Hiring For?

When it comes to recruiting, not all jobs are created equal. The methods needed to effectively fill jobs vary widely depending on the job type. Table 4.1 provides a description of four broad categories of jobs and discusses how each one influences recruiting process design:

- *Pivotal* jobs are positions where differences in performance have huge impacts on business performance. Recruiting for these jobs places a strong emphasis on hiring the best candidates possible.

- *Critical* jobs are crucial for business operations and require specialized skills and capabilities. Recruiting for these jobs depends heavily on having effective sourcing strategies.

- *High-volume* jobs are positions where companies hire hundreds or even thousands of employees a year. These positions require automated recruiting processes that can efficiently source and screen large numbers of candidates without overwhelming recruiters or hiring managers.

- *Operational* jobs are positions that are necessary to keep the organization running, but that are not particularly pivotal or critical. These tend to be filled intermittently and require recruiting processes that can be quickly scaled up or down based on current hiring needs.

Some jobs cut across several of these categories, and most large organizations have jobs falling into all four categories. What is important is to recognize that the ideal recruiting process will change depending on the type of job. Many companies need several distinct recruiting processes to support the variety of jobs they must fill.

Table 4.1
Job Categories and Related Recruiting Processes

Type of Job	Examples	Typical Emphases of Recruiting Processes for These Types of Jobs
Pivotal jobs, where differences in performance have a significant impact on company profitability	Strategic leadership roles such as CEO or other senior executive Key operational roles such as manufacturing plant managers or technical experts in software companies	Aggressive strategies for sourcing talent In-depth processes for screening and selecting the best candidates Leveraging internal talent through succession management
Critical jobs, which are necessary for maintaining company operations and where there is a significant shortage of talent	Jobs requiring specialized skills such as nurses in health care or maintenance specialists in utility companies	Identifying and building relationships with potential candidates early in their educational career, often years before they are qualified to be hired Creating strong employee value propositions to attract qualified candidates (i.e., showing why the company is a highly desirable place to work) Using career development and training to build internal talent pools
High-volume jobs, where the company hires large numbers of employees each year	Hourly frontline retail jobs Entry-level college graduate jobs such as engineers in a large aerospace company	Creating broad sourcing strategies to attract large numbers of candidates Automated methods for screening employees Sophisticated selection tools to increase the quality of those hired Automated onboarding processes

(Continued)

Type of Job	Examples	Typical Emphases of Recruiting Processes for These Types of Jobs
Operational jobs, which are necessary for maintaining company operations but are not a key source of competitive differentiation for the organization	Shared services jobs such as administration, security, or facilities management	Recruiting processes that can be quickly scaled up or down since the company hires these positions only intermittently Workforce planning to forecast shortages so recruiting processes can be ramped up in advance

4.2.2 How Many People Will We Need to Hire, and When Will We Need Them?

Recruiting organizations can often be characterized by how they engage with line leaders. *Reactive* recruiting organizations can be thought of as support departments that respond to staffing requests from hiring managers as quickly as possible. *Proactive* recruiting organizations actively reach out and engage with hiring managers to forecast future job needs and ensure talent is available when needed. Proactive recruiting is about building and sourcing talent pools before they are needed. It is usually more effective to adopt a proactive than a reactive stance, particularly if the company is trying to staff hard-to-fill jobs with high-performing talent (see the discussion: "The Differences among Time-to-Hire, Time-to-Fill, and Time-to-Start, and Why This Matters").

THE DIFFERENCES AMONG TIME-TO-HIRE, TIME-TO-FILL, AND TIME-TO-START, AND WHY THIS MATTERS

Time-to-hire is one of the most frequently used metrics for evaluating recruiting performance. Usually measured in days, time-to-hire refers to the total elapsed time required to staff an open position. Despite its wide use, time-to-hire is among the most poorly understood metrics in the field of staffing.

The first thing to realize about time-to-hire is that it is primarily a measure of process speed. It is not necessarily associated with candidate quality. Because there is little value in making bad hiring decisions quickly, the emphasis that time-to-hire places on time over quality significantly limits its value as a measure of staffing performance. The second issue with time-to-hire is it suffers from poor definition. Some organizations measure time-to-hire starting with the initial approval of a requisition, and others do not start measuring it until a requisition has been assigned to a recruiter or posted to a career site. Another critical difference in time-to-hire definitions is whether to stop measuring when an offer is secured from an approved candidate or to include time that elapses after a candidate accepts an offer but before actually starting the job.

Because time-to-hire is poorly defined, it is better to replace it with two other metrics, time-to-fill and time-to-start, that have more precise definitions.

Time-to-fill: the elapsed time between the initial approval or posting of a requisition and the final acceptance of a job offer from an approved candidate

Time-to-start: the elapsed time between the initial approval or posting of a requisition and the actual day when the new employee begins working in the position

Time-to-start is usually longer than time-to-fill since candidates must accept a job offer before they start that job. But many factors that affect time-to-start do not affect time-to-fill. For example, company policies restricting employees from moving into a new internal position until a replacement is found for their current role may radically lengthen time-to-start but could have little effect on time-to-fill. There are also situations where a company may intentionally increase time-to-fill while simultaneously taking steps to decrease time-to-start. Although such staffing strategies may seem contradictory, they make sense when time-to-fill and time-to-start are analyzed independently instead of being lumped into a single time-to-hire metric.

We first look at increasing time-to-fill to increase the chances of a better candidate applying. A few years ago, I worked with a company that analyzed the impact that hiring strategies had on its ability to hire star candidates with certain rare qualifications.[a] These star candidates generated extraordinary levels of revenue for the company, but there were rarely enough available at any given time to meet the company's operational staffing needs. This company determined that in some situations, it was advantageous to purposefully increase average time-to-fill to increase the likelihood of hiring more star candidates. To understand this finding, remember that star candidates are by definition rare, so receiving applications from star candidates is a relatively infrequent event. If the company focused on minimizing time-to-fill, it was likely to hire fewer nonstar candidates because it did not wait long enough for a star candidate to apply.

So how long should companies wait for star candidates to apply before they decide to close a requisition? The answer depends on the job and the labor market. In this study, the organization leaders determined that if they intentionally waited five days before filling positions, they would receive an additional $300,000 per year by hiring better-quality candidates. Of course, these gains had to be offset against costs associated with leaving positions unfilled for five days. Whether this trade-off is worth it depends on other factors. But the potential to make $300,000 simply by waiting a few days before making a hiring decision certainly seems worth exploring.

Now we look at decreasing time-to-start to zero without affecting time-to-fill. Companies that recognize the difference between time-to-fill and time-to-start can develop staffing strategies to ensure that time-to-start remains near zero. These strategies allow the company to avoid disruptions in company operations caused by vacancies while avoiding the risk of lowering hiring standards just to fill a position. For example, the staffing department in one retail organization made a commitment to keep store manager jobs 100 percent staffed at all times. This meant having no open management positions by reducing time-to-start to less than a day.

To achieve this goal, the company decoupled the process used for hiring new store managers from the process used to place newly hired managers into specific store positions. It then intentionally overhired so that within a given region, there were always slightly more store managers than store manager positions. After their initial training, newly hired store managers were provided with additional in-store training until a vacancy occurred in their region. They were then immediately transferred into the vacant position to minimize any discontinuity in store operations.

In addition to increasing operational continuity, these changes led to improvements in the process used to hire new store managers. Although recruiters feel constant pressure to keep the pipeline filled with good candidates, they are no longer under the gun to staff a specific position in a specific store as fast as possible. They can hire in a more systematic and measured fashion, focusing on candidate quality instead of responding to the hiring crisis of the moment. They are not pressured to lower their hiring standards just to get someone in the door and can scrutinize candidates without worrying about the added pressure to staff an existing vacancy.

Decoupling the concept of time-to-fill from time-to-start represents an innovative approach toward staffing. These examples illustrate what can happen when staffing leaders take the time to critically analyze staffing metrics and processes. What gets measured is what gets managed, so it makes sense to understand exactly what you are measuring.

[a]Hunt, S. (2004). *Understanding time to hire metrics.* Electronic Recruiting Exchange.

Shifting from a reactive to proactive recruiting stance requires making a commitment to workforce planning, which involves HR and business managers working together to anticipate the company's future staffing needs. It is beyond the scope of this chapter to fully discuss what is involved in effective workforce planning. But at a minimum it requires creating structured processes and collecting data to accomplish the following:

- *Agreeing on likely business growth scenarios extending at least three years into the future.* Looking more than three years out is important because the labor market trends that are felt in recruiting unfold over years, not quarters.

- *Determining what sort of talent will be required to support different business growth scenarios.* This involves analyzing the kinds of jobs required to support various business strategies and growth expectations and then determining the skills and experience that candidates will need to perform these jobs.

- *Analyzing the skills and experience of the current workforce and forecasting the likelihood of losing employees with particular skill sets due to turnover, retirement, or movement within the organization.* It can be particularly insightful to talk about predicted employee turnover in terms of "years of experience lost" instead of "number of employees leaving." For example, imagine that a company expects to lose ten engineers in the next three years due to retirement. Assume the average tenure of these engineers is thirty years. There is a big difference between "we expect to lose ten engineers over the next three years" and "we expect to lose three hundred years of experience in the next three years." It may also be worthwhile to examine the value of experience. For example, in many manufacturing, health care, and computer programming jobs, there is a strong, positive relationship of years of experience, employee productivity, and work quality.

- *Calculating gaps between the employees currently in the organization and the ones likely to be needed over the next several years, and then designing staffing strategies to ensure the company will have the talent it needs when it needs it.* The staffing strategies should integrate external hiring, internal employee development, succession planning, the use of contingent workers, or a mixture of all of these. The possibility of addressing workforce shortages by increasing the productivity of current employees should also be considered.

Moving to proactive recruiting shifts recruiters from an administrative orientation focused on responding to hiring managers' requests to a strategic orientation of actively working with business leaders to figure out what sort of people the company should be hiring and how to get them.

4.2.3 What Sort of Employees Do We Need to Hire? What Attributes Do Candidates Need to Possess to Become Effective Employees?

The main objective of strategic recruiting is to hire employees who will deliver effective levels of job performance. To achieve this objective, it is critical to clearly define job performance and understand how it relates to different candidate attributes. What specific business outcomes does the company want to achieve by recruiting new employees? Is the goal to improve employee retention, increase productivity, provide better customer service, achieve higher sales revenue, or have an impact on some other outcome? Is this a pivotal position where it is crucial to spend the time and resources necessary to find and hire the best possible candidate? Or is this more of an operational role where hiring solid but not necessarily outstanding employees will suffice?

There is a cost to hiring the best talent available. Not all roles need to be filled with the most qualified candidates, who also tend to be the most expensive and hardest to find. The importance of hiring the "absolutely best" candidates available varies depending on the job. Some jobs in a company are more pivotal than others in terms of their impact on overall business performance.[4] Pivotal jobs are ones where differences in performance have major impacts on business outcomes. This includes senior leadership roles such as the CEO, but can also include critical operational and technical roles (e.g., frontline customer service staff in a luxury hotel or software architects in a technology company). These are the jobs where you want to hire the best-quality talent available. Yet there are also jobs where having solid, reliable performance may be as valuable as having the best performance possible, and maybe even more valuable. For example, many service support functions and long-term operational roles do not need to be staffed by the most experienced people available. For these roles, hiring people who are good, efficient, and consistent may be more valuable than hiring people who are outstanding but often also more costly and demanding.

Every staffing process should start by asking hiring managers to clarify the business goals they want to support through hiring new employees. This necessitates making decisions that emphasize certain outcomes over others because employee attributes that have a positive impact on some outcomes often have a negative impact on others (see "No One Is Good at Everything"). For example, a common trade-off when evaluating candidates is whether to focus on productivity versus stability. The most highly productive employees are often the first to leave to pursue new opportunities.[5] These employees are usually driven by a desire to move to increasingly challenging positions, are more likely to have job opportunities elsewhere, and may quickly tire of jobs after they master them. While there is value in having highly productive employees, there is also value in having a stable workforce. The financial value of maximizing productivity versus maximizing retention varies depending on a company's business model. Discussing the relative value of different business outcomes such as these is an important part of designing a recruiting strategy that will deliver the best results.

Effective recruiting requires making choices on the relative importance of different candidate attributes. It is hard to envision a candidate attribute that is always desirable regardless of the job. Attributes that are strengths in some jobs are weaknesses in others. For example, being highly agreeable may be a desirable trait when applied to things like fostering teamwork and getting along with others but can be a weakness for jobs that require taking a firm stance on an issue or holding others accountable for their behavior. Candidates with the strongest levels of experience and technical capability typically cost the most to employ. Extremely detail-oriented individuals may struggle with high levels of change.

Hiring requires balancing relative strengths and weaknesses to find candidates who are the optimal fit given the job demands. When talking about candidate qualifications, keep in mind there is probably no candidate that will be a perfect fit with every demand of the job. Candidates who excel at some aspects of a job will invariably be less effective in others. It is important to work with hiring managers to determine which attributes are the most important for job success and agree on areas where it may be necessary to make certain trade-offs. Hiring managers and recruiters who insist on finding candidates who excel at everything are likely to end up looking for candidates who don't exist.

Developing a clear understanding of what drives job performance in a certain role can be difficult. When managers are asked, "What makes a great employee?" they tend to answer in vague generalities about passion, dedication, and a "can-do" attitude. These characteristics sound good, but they reveal next to nothing about what makes high-performing employees noticeably different from average or poor ones. This is why it is important to use job analysis techniques to define the employee behaviors and characteristics that drive job performance.

Job analysis is not an overly complex discipline to master, and there are many books available that cover different job analysis methods.[6] Any worthwhile job analysis method will require the involvement of hiring managers, current employees, and other subject matter experts familiar with the job being staffed. Most methods require subject matter experts to clarify specific tasks performed on the job and provide examples of things current or former employees have done on the job that illustrate effective or ineffective behavior (for an example of one job analysis method, see the discussion: "A Simple Job Analysis Technique").

A SIMPLE JOB ANALYSIS TECHNIQUE

It is not possible to hire the best candidates unless you know what they are expected to do in the job after they are hired. However, hiring managers frequently struggle when asked to describe what candidates will need to do to be successful in a job. Rather than defining what behaviors are critical for job success, they rattle off generic platitudes about good performance, such as "being a service-oriented team player." These things sound good but reveal little about what people actually need to do to be successful on the job.

The following steps outline a simple job analysis method that walks hiring managers through defining what skills and competencies candidates need to be successful in a job. These steps are not intended to replace more rigorous and specific job analysis techniques, but they can be effective for quickly clarifying what criteria to use when assessing candidates:

Step 1: Define the job goals. Ask the hiring manager to list the five to ten things employees must accomplish in this job to be successful. These should be tangible accomplishments, results, or outcomes that employees must achieve. As I sometimes put it, "If we built a machine to do this job instead of hiring people, what would this machine have to create?" Or I might say, "If we hired someone and you never actually saw her work after she was hired, what things would she have to accomplish in order to provide evidence that she performed the job successfully?"

Step 2: Define the work environment in terms of challenges and enablers. Start by asking the hiring manager to list three to six challenges about the work environment that employees must overcome, manage, or simply learn to accept in order to be successful in the job. These are typically related to things like resource constraints, the culture of the company, the nature of the competition, or the nature of the job tasks themselves. What about the environment might make this job hard for some people? Next, ask the manager to list three to six enablers found in the work environment. What technology, tools, support, or other resources will employees have to use to be successful in this job? What about the culture of the company, the nature of the job opportunity, or the job tasks themselves make this a desirable position?

Step 3: Identify key job competencies. Define five to ten types of behavior that employees need to display to be successful in this job, taking into account the job goals and environmental challenges and enablers. What do high-performing employees do differently from average employees? What do employees struggle with? Encourage the hiring manager to provide examples of what previous employees did that illustrate the difference between effective and ineffective performance in this job. It may be useful to ask hiring managers to review a competency library like the one contained in appendix A and select the five to ten competencies that best describe the characteristics that differentiate great employees from good ones and average employees from unsuccessful performers. Emphasize that what is important is not to identify every behavior people need to display to be successful, but to highlight the competencies that will have the greatest impact on distinguishing effective from ineffective candidates.

Step 4: Identify critical candidate attributes. Look at the information identified in steps 1, 2, and 3. Do any of these require employees to possess specific skills, certifications, or experiences? Stress the difference between necessary skills and qualification employees must possess in order to be eligible to hold the job (e.g., formal licensing requirements) and the skills and experiences that are desirable but not necessary (e.g., having three years of job-relevant experience instead of two). Remind the manager that increasing the number of skill requirements placed on jobs can significantly increase the difficulty and cost of staffing them.

These four steps can be completed in as little as forty-five minutes when working with individual hiring managers, although it is often more effective to conduct them with multiple hiring managers and subject matter experts in a longer workshop setting. These steps can be used as the foundation of a highly rigorous job analysis process. They can also be used as an efficient way to help hiring managers articulate the job requirements for a position they may be filling only once.

A well-conducted job analysis provides a clear picture of the functions fulfilled on the job and the employee attributes required to perform the job successfully. This includes having clear definitions of the job components:

- *Job title.* If possible, use job titles that external candidates will understand so they can tell whether they are interested in and potentially qualified for the job.

- *Job tasks, responsibilities, and objectives.* These describe the kinds of goals people in the job are expected to accomplish or the tasks they will need to perform (e.g., maintaining customer service levels, building new products, achieving sales quotas).

- *Job requirements.* Credentials or licenses candidates must possess to be eligible to hold the job regardless of their other qualifications (e.g., US citizenship, licensed degrees).

- *Relevant qualifications.* Skills and experience that candidates are expected to possess to be considered qualified for the position (e.g., years of experience, job-relevant training, and course work).

- *Job competencies.* Behaviors people are expected to display on the job (e.g., supporting team members, planning and organizing, thinking analytically).

- *Conditions of employment.* Things people must accept in order to perform the job (e.g., work hours, job location, physical job requirements or Americans with Disabilities Act requirements, travel schedule, pay).

Clearly defining these categories will provide clarity and focus for subsequent decisions concerning what sort of candidates to source, how to select among different job applicants, and what actions will be required to bring newly hired employees up to speed. This information can also be used to create performance management and career development processes to maximize the productivity of employees after they are hired.

4.2.4   What Roles Will Hiring Managers, Recruiters, Coworkers, and Candidates Play in the Hiring Process?

Finding, selecting, hiring, and onboarding employees is a cooperative effort. It goes beyond the role of any one individual or department. In the design of recruiting processes, attention should be placed on determining the involvement of four particularly key stakeholder groups at different stages of the recruiting cycle:

1. *Recruiters or human resources (or both).* Individuals who are formally tasked with managing processes to support sourcing, selecting, and onboarding new employees

2. *Hiring managers.* The person or people responsible for overseeing the budget and salary associated with the new person—the ultimate decision maker on whether to hire a candidate

3. *Coworkers.* People other than the hiring manager who will have input into the hiring decision—typically coworkers or managers from other departments who will work with the candidate if hired

4. *Candidates.* Individuals being considered for the job—external applicants or internal employees seeking a position

Table 4.2 provides an example of how these four stakeholder groups might be involved in different steps of the recruiting process. The table calls out specific responsibilities that recruiters, hiring managers, coworkers, and candidates have related to defining job requirements, sourcing and hiring candidates, and onboarding candidates after they are hired. Note that almost every role has some level of involvement in each step. It is particularly important to emphasize the role that hiring managers play in each of the steps.

The responsibility for hiring high-performing talent into a company ultimately lies with hiring managers, not recruiters. Recruiters are there to guide and support hiring managers. Staffing processes that allow hiring managers to shift responsibility for making good hiring decisions from themselves to the recruiting function are doomed to disappointment and failure. Most experienced recruiters can tell stories about being blamed for not being able to fill a position when the real problem was that the hiring manager never fully defined what constituted a top candidate or was unresponsive when asked to review and meet with candidates whom the recruiter recommended. To maximize the effectiveness of recruiting processes and minimize risks of finger pointing over recruiting problems, it is sometimes useful to document the role the hiring manager plays during the hiring process through a service-level agreement or similar formal statement of responsibilities.

Table 4.2
Recruiting Roles

Stage	Recruiter Role	Hiring Manager Role	Coworker Role	Candidate Role
Defining job requirements and candidate qualifications	Provide tools to define job competencies, skills, and qualifications.	Work with recruiter to define job demands, requirements, and candidate qualifications.	Input into job demands, requirements, and qualifications.	Typically none unless the job is created to fit the capabilities of a specific person.
Sourcing candidates	Provide tools and guidance to hiring managers and employees on using social relationships to find candidates. Maintain talent pools with potential candidates. Use job postings, search tools, and other methods to find candidates.	Leverage personal social networks to find candidates. Recommend potential talent sources to recruiters.	Leverage personal social networks to find candidates. Recommend potential talent sources to recruiters.	Respond to job opportunities.
Screening candidates	Screen out clearly unqualified candidates. Recommend qualified candidates to hiring manager for review.	Review qualified candidates for suitability. Provide feedback to recruiter on why certain candidates were or were not selected.	May have input into the screening process.	Provide necessary information required to evaluate qualifications.

(Continued)

Stage	Recruiter Role	Hiring Manager Role	Coworker Role	Candidate Role
Selecting candidates	Provide interview guides to hiring managers and employees. If relevant, administer and interpret advanced selection tools. Communicate to candidates why and how selection tools are used; answer candidate questions.	Conduct interviews and other assessments to evaluate candidates. Provide information on the quality of candidates.	Conduct interviews and other assessments to evaluate candidates. Provide information on quality of candidates.	Complete necessary assessments and interviews.
"Selling" candidates on the job	Engage qualified candidates to keep them interested in the job. Sell candidates on the benefits of the company as an employer.	Communicate the opportunities provided by the job to candidates. Treat candidates with appropriate respect and courtesy.	Communicate the opportunities provided by the job to candidates. Treat candidates with appropriate respect and courtesy.	Ask questions about the job and express career preferences.
Make the hiring decision	Provide advice on strengths and weaknesses of candidates.	Take ownership for the final hiring decision. Explain to recruiters why candidates were or were not considered acceptable.	Provide advice on strengths and weaknesses of candidates.	Accept or decline the offer.

Stage	Recruiter Role	Hiring Manager Role	Coworker Role	Candidate Role
Onboarding newly hired employees	Provide guidance to candidates and hiring managers on steps required to bring a new employee on-board. Optional: Manage certain administrative tasks for recently hired employees.	Ensure steps are taken so new employees can quickly get up to speed.	Engage new employees; make them feel welcome.	Participate in onboarding process.
Tracking performance after hiring	Collect data on performance and retention of candidates after they have been hired. Evaluate the effectiveness of recruiting methods based on performance and retention of newly hired employees.	Provide data on the performance of newly hired employees.	May provide input into the performance of new employees.	Provide feedback on the quality of the hiring and onboarding process.

4.2.5 How Will We Source Candidates?

Sourcing candidates is one of the key differentiators of a highly effective recruiting process. You cannot hire the best candidates for a job if they never apply in the first place. Companies that excel at finding and attracting the best candidate not only improve the productivity of their own workforce, they also deprive their competition from hiring top-quality talent.

There are a variety of approaches for sourcing candidates. Table 4.3 lists several of these approaches and their relative strengths and weaknesses.

Table 4.3
Sourcing Methods

Sourcing Method	Strengths	Weaknesses	When It Tends to Be Most Effective
Employer branding	Has impacts on large numbers of candidates. Attracts candidates the company might not otherwise reach. Can integrate with and support other company branding efforts.	Takes a long time. Marketing costs can be significant. Impact is hard to track; does not tie to hiring specific individuals. May attract large numbers of poorly qualified candidates.	Hiring large numbers of candidates over many years. Seeking to create awareness among certain candidate pools.
Building talent pools	Critical for creating talent pipelines and shortening time to hire. Builds strong relationships with key groups of candidates (internal or external).	Expensive to maintain relationships over time. May be difficult to prequalify candidates for inclusion in talent pools. Can be a challenge to maintain the quality of talent pools.	A tendency or preference for hiring candidates from the same sources exists. There is a strategic focus on hiring candidates with certain common characteristics (e.g., demographics, educational credentials).
Job posting	Quick and easy way to reach a large number of candidates. Jobs can be posted on sites visited by specific types of candidates.	Often some of the best candidates are already employed and do not look at job postings. Can be expensive depending on the site. May attract large numbers of poorly qualified candidates.	Hiring for jobs with very clearly defined qualifications and hiring criteria. Hiring for jobs in a certain specialized area where there are career-specific, technical job sites.

Sourcing Method	Strengths	Weaknesses	When It Tends to Be Most Effective
Professional recruiting	Leverages seasoned professionals who may have extensive networks of candidates and strong recruiting skills.	Expensive. Outside recruiters may be more focused on filling positions than hiring high-quality employees.	Hiring for specialized technical and leadership positions where candidates tend to be scarce or already employed elsewhere.
Social networking	Taps into professional networks maintained by current employees. Attractive because best applicants often come from employee referrals. Relatively inexpensive.	Works only if existing employees have contact with the kinds of candidates desired. Can be time-consuming.	Hiring for technical or industry-specific positions where the best candidates are probably one or two degrees of separation from existing employees.
Career pathing	Creates a talent flow within the organization. Usually less expensive and more successful than hiring externally. Increases retention within the company.	Best candidates may not necessarily be current employees. Creates vacancies within the organization due to moving talent. Requires investing time and resources into developing internal talent.	Hiring for positions where there are clear career paths within the company. Hiring for positions where familiarity with the company is critical to job success.

Employer branding uses marketing techniques to build a company's reputation as a good place to work among segments of potential candidates. For example, companies interested in hiring engineers might sponsor events at university engineering schools or place ads in engineering trade journals that reinforce the benefits of working for the organization. There are many techniques for building an employer brand, but the most successful employer branding campaigns tend to have two things in common:

- The company has clearly defined the brand message it wants to convey based on the kinds of candidates it wants to attract. A good employer brand uniquely differentiates why it is better to work for the company compared to other organizations that hire for the same types of jobs.

- Careful thought has gone into which candidates to target with the branding message. The goal is not to encourage all job candidates to apply. It is to encourage qualified candidates with certain characteristics to apply, while perhaps even actively discouraging candidates who are not likely to be a good fit with the company.

I once worked with a company in the environmental science industry that developed an employment brand that effectively met both of these criteria. This company lacked the funds to pay geosciences engineers as much as other companies hiring candidates with similar degrees. To address this issue, the company built an employment brand emphasizing it as a place where engineers can work on solving major environmental problems. This company could not pay as much as other organizations, but it could entice engineers who were willing to sacrifice their earnings potential in order to work on what the company called "save the planet" projects.

Building talent pools involves maintaining relationships with groups of potential candidates for future jobs. Talent pools may consist of students, job seekers, and current employees who possess certain skills or experience desired by the company. These pools serve as a source of candidates when there is an opening. One of the major factors to consider when building talent pools is how much focus to place on internal versus external candidates. Many companies overlook their existing employee population when sourcing talent, although internal employees are often the best source of qualified candidates.

Job postings are advertisements that communicate job opportunities using online job boards, websites, or newspapers. There is usually a fee for posting jobs on specific sites. Traditionally job posting was probably the most common method used to advertise job openings. However, social networking sites are increasingly displacing job postings as the main way to market job openings.

Professional recruiting refers to using professional recruiters to seek out potential candidates. Professional recruiting may be supported by in-house recruiters or external, contingency-based recruiting organizations. Professional recruiters can be very effective for staffing hard-to-fill positions, but tend to be far more expensive compared to other sourcing methods.

Social networking means finding candidates by leveraging people's personal relationships. It increasingly uses technology such as LinkedIn, Twitter, Facebook, and other sites to communicate job opportunities to potential candidates. This technology is becoming a dominant method for sourcing candidates. There are several advantages to social networking. First, many people in professional or specialized roles are hired based on personal referrals. Second, networking results in the hiring of individuals who are already known by people in the company. This helps create a stronger social bond within the company and tends to decrease turnover, since people like to work with people whom they also consider to be friends. Many companies are also using social networking technology to create and maintain employee "alumni" groups that encourage past employees to recommend candidates for jobs within the company and encourage former employees to rejoin the organization.

Career pathing refers to methods that help existing employees move into new jobs within the company. It thus integrates training, succession management, mentoring, and other career development methods that help employees identify future roles in the company and acquire the skills and experiences needed to qualify for them. The goal of career pathing is to get employees to look beyond their current role and take a longer-term perspective toward pursuing future job opportunities within the organization. This is critical for moving staffing from a process for filling open positions to a process used to maintain a steady supply of high-performing talent for critical roles across the company.

The sourcing strategies that make the most sense vary depending on the jobs being filled, the size and location of the hiring organization, and the depth of available recruiting resources. The most effective recruiting processes leverage a mixture of sourcing methods to maximize the probability that the right candidate will apply for the right job at the right time. It is also important to consider the preferred communication medium of the candidates who are being targeted, which may differ significantly based on candidate demographics (see the discussion: "Generational Differences and Recruiting: Saying the Same Things Differently"). Also consider how much emphasis to place on filling positions with internal versus external candidates.

It can be very beneficial to use recruiting marketing methods to monitor the value of different sourcing strategies. Recruiting marketing uses data analytics to determine which sources generate the most successful candidates at the least cost. Effective collection and analysis of sourcing data is important because the value of sources changes based on job type and over time. For example, employee referrals may be an excellent source of candidates for certain jobs but yield poor results for others. And Internet job sites that yielded successful candidates in the past may quickly become outdated given how rapidly Internet preferences and habits shift from one year to the next.

GENERATIONAL DIFFERENCES AND RECRUITING: SAYING THE SAME THINGS DIFFERENTLY

As long as there have been adults and children, one group has been emphasizing how different they are from the other. But there are significant research challenges to figuring out whether generations really are different. This is particularly true when trying to determine if different generations have different career expectations. Apparent generational differences may simply be due to differences in the lifestyles people have at different ages. What people want from work when they are twenty and single tends to be different from what they want when they are forty and married with two kids. Apparent generational differences can also be due to changing economic conditions. Employees currently in their twenties may act differently from how older workers acted when they were in their twenties because when older workers were in their twenties, the labor market and the economy were much different.

Some of the more rigorous research on generational differences and employee attitudes suggests that what people fundamentally want from a job has not changed much over the years.[a] Regardless of generation, most workers are looking for jobs that provide some sense of challenge and career growth, fair compensation, a reasonable level of work-life balance, and some degree of stability. What does appear to change across generations is how people communicate. In particular, there are big differences in candidates' preferences and expectations for using the telephone, e-mail, social media, and other methods to interact with employers. In sum, when it comes to recruiting across different generations, the issue is not so much what you say but the methods you use to say it. A company's recruiting message should probably remain relatively constant across candidates from different generations to avoid accusations of age discrimination. But the way that message is communicated may change depending on what generation you are targeting.

[a]Deal, J. (2006). *Retiring the generation gap: How employees young and old can find common ground.* San Francisco: Jossey-Bass. Meister, J. C., & Willyerd, K. (2010). *The 2020 workplace: How innovative companies attract, develop, and keep tomorrow's employees today.* New York: HarperCollins.

4.2.6 How Will We Select Candidates?

After you have identified and contacted candidates and they have applied, you have to decide which candidate to extend an offer to. Effective staffing assessment methods are critical to increasing the quality of hiring. Even small investments spent to improve the accuracy of selection decisions can often significantly increase the productivity and retention of employees.

Table 4.4 lists a variety of tools used for candidate selection. It can be difficult to determine which selection methods to use given the number available. The best methods vary depending on the nature of the job and the depth of the company's resources. However, there is one selection method used in virtually every recruiting process: candidate interviews. Given the prevalence of interviewing, companies can reap significant benefits by maximizing the efficiency and effectiveness of the interview process. There are many ways to do this, ranging from designing preset interview questions to providing manager training on how to conduct an effective interview. Two of the simplest ways to significantly improve interviewing are structured interview guides and coordinating multiple interviews:

- *Structured interview guides.* Considerable research has shown that interview results do not accurately predict job performance unless the interviewer follows a structured process of asking every candidate the same set of interview questions tied to specific job requirements.[7] It is extremely important to create structured interview tools that ensure interviewers are asking the right questions about the right topics. There are many forms of structured interviews, but one of the easiest and most effective is behavioral-based interviewing. Appendix A contains an example of common job competencies and associated behavioral interview questions, as well as a simple guide for conducting structured interviews. Consider using this or similar content to build structured interview guides to support your company's hiring needs.

- *Coordinating multiple interviews.* Candidates for most jobs will be interviewed by several people within the organization during the hiring process. It is important to ensure that these interviews are coordinated so that candidates are not asked the same questions multiple times by multiple people. There should also be an efficient way to collect and collate interview results to ensure a fully informed final hiring decision. The easiest way to do this in a large organization is to use technology systems that provide tools for coordinating, conducting, and collating results from interviews.

The last area to be addressed when designing selection methods is determining what data will be used to evaluate the accuracy of selection tools over time. Many recruiters act as though the hiring process ends shortly after an employee accepts a job. A better practice is to extend the hiring process to include tracking employee performance and retention for a year or more after hiring. If an employee is fired or quits within the first year, it is probably the result of hiring someone who never should have been given the job in the first place. The only way to truly fix this sort of problem is to evaluate and improve prehire selection methods based on posthire performance data gathered after hiring. It can be particularly useful to examine why certain new employees did not meet expectations. For example, if employees quit in the first year on the job, try to determine why they left and use these findings to inform future sourcing and selection strategies.

Table 4.4 Types of Staffing Assessment Tools	
Physical exams	
Drug screens	Use medical screening procedures to detect whether candidates have used illegal or controlled substances (e.g., urinalysis, analysis of hair samples).
Physical ability tests	Require candidates to perform physical tasks such as lifting weights, completing cardiovascular exercises, or demonstrating flexibility.

Background investigations

Criminal record checks	Search public records and private databases to determine if applicants have any prior criminal convictions.
Social security verification	Search online databases to ensure that a candidate's social security number is valid.
Reference checks	Collect information from former employers or academic institutions to verify previous employment status (and possibly job performance) as well as educational credentials.
Credit reports	Contact credit reporting agencies to obtain information about a candidate's financial history.

Résumé screens

Electronic recruiting agents	Search the web for qualified candidates based on keywords found in résumés posted on internal or external career boards.
Résumé capture and reviews	Evaluate candidates based on the content of résumés they submit directly to the company or résumés posted to web-based job boards.

Interviews

Unstructured interviews	Evaluate candidates by having a discussion with them about topics that seem relevant to the job.
Structured interviews: Motivational questions	Evaluate candidates by asking predefined questions about interests, career goals, and plans.
Structured interviews: Situational questions	Evaluate candidates by asking how they would respond to hypothetical situations similar to those they may encounter on the job.
Structured interviews: Behavioral questions	Evaluate candidates by asking them to describe experiences and accomplishments that relate to things they will have to do on the job.

(Continued)

Self-report measures

Prescreening questionnaires, weighted application blanks	Ask very direct questions to candidates to determine if they possess specific skills, experiences, or credentials needed to perform a job (e.g., "Are you willing to work weekends?" or "Have you ever used MS Excel?").
Personality questionnaires	Ask candidates a series of self-descriptive questions about their likes, preferences, behaviors, and experiences that reflect personality traits associated with job performance.
Integrity and reliability tests	Ask candidates about beliefs, preferences, and experiences that reflect a propensity for counterproductive behavior.
Biodata inventories	Ask questions about previous life experiences and accomplishments that show statistical relationships to job performance.
Culture and work environment fit inventories	Ask questions about job preferences, values, beliefs, and desired work environment to predict organizational commitment and job satisfaction with a specific job or company.

Knowledge; skill and ability tests bad simulations

Ability tests and measures of problem-solving aptitude	Predict ability to solve problems and interpret information by asking applicants to solve questions that require processing information to arrive at logically based conclusions.
Knowledge and skills tests and measures of past learning achievement	Assess familiarity of and mastery with regard to specific types of information or tasks (e.g., knowledge of accounting rules, ability to use certain software programs, typing skills).
Job simulations, assessment centers, and work samples	Use audio, video, computer simulations, or human actors to recreate actual job situations and then assess how candidates react to these scenarios.

Source: Hunt, S. T. (2007). *Hiring success: The art and science of staffing assessment and employee selection.* San Francisco: Jossey-Bass.

4.2.7 How Will We Get Newly Hired Employees Up to Full Productivity?

Companies lose money on newly hired employees until these employees reach a basic level of on-the-job competence. It can take several months before newly hired employees know the ropes well enough to make a real contribution. They are not adding value when they are spending most of their time figuring out where to sit, who their team members are, or how to fill out their health care benefit plan forms. High-performing employees tend to find this onboarding phase frustrating. They want to get up to speed and contribute to the company as fast as possible. They may even quit if they feel it is taking too long to become productive. This is why it is important to make employee onboarding as quick and efficient as possible.

There are three basic categories of onboarding for new employees:[8]

- *Administrative onboarding* focuses on the tactical details associated with establishing new employees in a company's payroll structure, benefit plans, office environment, and computer systems. Although these actions are purely administrative, they can be a source of considerable frustration and inefficiency if they are not done well. Linking staffing systems to the systems used to manage and track employee payroll, benefits, performance, and logistics can significantly reduce the time and effort spent on administrative onboarding.

- *Technical onboarding* focuses on ensuring employees have the training, knowledge, and tools needed to perform their job. Depending on the job, technical onboarding may take less than a day or more than a year. Companies that have extensive technical onboarding requirements may want to link their recruiting technology to career development and learning management system technology.

- *Social onboarding* focuses on welcoming employees into the corporate community so they feel part of the broader corporate culture. It helps new employees get to know the people they work with in terms of their interests, experiences, and history. This aspect of onboarding is often overlooked, but it is very important for several reasons.[9] Strong social ties with work colleagues play a role in driving employee engagement and retention. Social networks also form a foundation for enabling effective teamwork. Fortunately, technology tools now exist to help companies support social onboarding in a consistent, scalable fashion.

Best-in-class staffing organizations recognize that the hiring process is not finished until the new employee is fully up to speed as a contributing member of the organization. Technology plays a major role in this step as it allow companies to automatically transfer data collected during the staffing process into the systems and processes used to manage and support employees after they are hired.

4.2.8 How Will We Retain Employees after They Are Hired?

It is extremely expensive for organizations to go through the process of hiring candidates only to have the new employees quit early into their tenure. Candidate turnover within the first year should be considered a failure in the staffing process for most jobs, since something about the job and candidate clearly did not match. Retention after the first year is more a function of how employees are managed and the career opportunities they see within the organization. Nevertheless, staffing organizations might also want to pay attention to reasons that employees leave later in their careers and see if there are ways to help longer-term retention levels through changes in the hiring process. High-performing employees are of special importance in this regard. Among the main reasons they quit are these:

- Perceived lack of career growth opportunities within the company
- A sense of inequity around pay, promotion, and staffing decisions
- A general sense of misfit between their personal interests or work preferences and the characteristics of their manager, job, or company culture

Staffing organizations should actively work with the leaders of other strategic HR processes such as compensation, employee development, performance management, and leadership development to ensure that the employer brand being promised to candidates during the recruiting process is fulfilled in the treatment of candidates after they are hired. Tracking data across the employee life cycle is central to this effort. This requires having workforce analytical systems that support the collection and integration of data on recruiting, performance, compensation, succession and development, and internal job transfers.

4.2.9 How Will We Measure Recruiting Success and Improve Our Processes over Time?

It is impossible to know if a hiring process is truly effective unless the criteria that will be used to measure staffing success have been defined. How do we know if we made a good hiring decision? How can we tell if our hiring process is efficient over the long term? Answering these questions lies at the heart of creating a staffing process that is truly focused on business execution.

Table 4.5 lists several metrics to measure staffing effectiveness. (The metrics that are most important from a business execution standpoint are shown in italics.) All of these reflect how staffing programs affect workforce productivity. Time-to-fill, although it has its limitations, is a critical metric for ensuring that staffing processes are minimizing disruptions to business operations caused by vacancies in key roles. Measures of productive and counterproductive performance and employee retention are central to evaluating whether the company is hiring high-quality candidates whose capabilities and interests match the demands of the job. Time-to-competence is critical to ensuring the effectiveness of onboarding methods. Examining data on internal promotions and job

---

Table 4.5
Staffing Metrics

Prehiring Metrics	Posthiring Metrics
Number of hires	*Productive performance*
Applicant volume	*Counterproductive performance*
Applicant source	*Tenure*
Time to hire	Time and attendance
Time-to-fill	Hiring manager attitudes
Cost per hire	Employee attitudes
Applicant quality	Rating performance/*time to competence*
Applicant-to-hire ratio	Turnover costs
Offer-to-acceptance ratio	Employee demographics and EEO statistics
Applicant Demographics and Equal Employment Opportunity statistics	*Internal promotions and transfers*
Applicant reactions	Turnover reasons

Note: The entries in italics are the most important metrics from a business execution standpoint.

Source: Hunt, S. T. (2006). Using metrics to guide staffing strategies across dispersed workforces. *Journal of Corporate Recruiting Leadership, 2,* 3–17.

transfers is key to shifting the focus of staffing from a process that concentrates on filling near-term vacancies to one used to create long-term talent pipelines. The metrics in table 4.5 should be reviewed with stakeholders associated with the staffing process to decide which are most important, how the data will be collected, and what actions will be taken based on the results.

4.3 RECRUITING PROCESS MATURITY

Developing a high-performing recruiting process is not a short-term undertaking. Creating effective employer brands and developing large talent pools of qualified candidates can take months or even years. It is important to approach the creation of a recruiting process as a continuous improvement journey rather than a one-time event. This means adopting a deliberate, systematic long-term approach toward process design.

Figure 4.1 illustrates the maturity phases organizations go through as they develop their recruiting processes. These phases reflect a shift from a reactive "filling-of-positions" approach to a more proactive approach of maintaining a steady supply of high-performing talent.

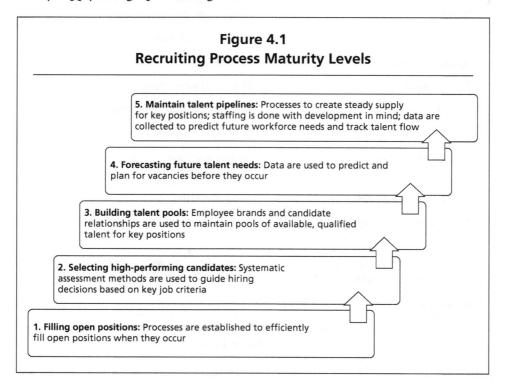

Figure 4.1
Recruiting Process Maturity Levels

5. Maintain talent pipelines: Processes to create steady supply for key positions; staffing is done with development in mind; data are collected to predict future workforce needs and track talent flow

4. Forecasting future talent needs: Data are used to predict and plan for vacancies before they occur

3. Building talent pools: Employee brands and candidate relationships are used to maintain pools of available, qualified talent for key positions

2. Selecting high-performing candidates: Systematic assessment methods are used to guide hiring decisions based on key job criteria

1. Filling open positions: Processes are established to efficiently fill open positions when they occur

The first level of maturity is to establish efficient methods for filling open positions. This involves establishing methods to create and track job requisitions and efficiently process candidates as they move through the hiring process. Achieving level 1 provides a stable platform to support the next levels.

Level 2 focuses on implementing tools to improve the accuracy of hiring decisions. This may include integrating more sophisticated selection tools into the hiring process. At a minimum, it should emphasize more effective interview processes. Level 2 forces companies to define what kinds of candidates they wish to hire, a requirement for getting to level 3, building talent pools.

Level 3 focuses on creating internal and external pools of candidates that can be used to fill future positions. A key part of achieving level 3 is creating tools to provide the staffing organization with visibility into internal talent along with external talent pools. While level 3 provides a general sense of the amount of talent available to fill different types of jobs, level 4 focuses on defining the gap between the talent that exists within the company and the talent that will be needed in the future. This is where workforce planning becomes critical. Level 5 represents a fundamental shift from staffing to fill positions to staffing as a means to create and maintain ongoing talent pipelines. At this level, companies are able to consistently and quickly fill positions with high-performing employees by proactively forecasting talent needs and preidentifying qualified candidates. This is where staffing becomes a major competitive differentiator for driving strategic success.

Higher levels of process maturity provide greater levels of business value. At the same time, there is a cost to achieving higher maturity levels, and it may not make sense to be at the highest level possible for all jobs. This is particularly true for many operational positions where the focus of hiring may be more tactical than strategic. What is important is to consider what level of maturity makes sense for your organization given your current business execution drivers and long-term strategic needs.

4.4 CONCLUSION

Companies get to make an initial hiring decision only once for every employee. Ensuring managers are hiring the right people into the organization is probably the single most important outcome of effective strategic HR methods. All other strategic HR methods are going to be either enhanced or constrained by the quality of this initial decision. For this reason, it is vital to do everything you can to make sure this decision is the right one.

There is no one best way to hire employees. Different jobs require different recruiting processes. What is important is to build out processes that make the most sense for the jobs you are filling. This means actively involving managers in defining job requirements, working with managers and employees to source and select talent, developing and rigorously applying effective selection methods, and extending the hiring process beyond the hiring decision to include onboarding and posthiring performance. No matter how much time and work you put into designing your organization's recruiting process, there will always be another next step for driving further improvement. No company ever achieves the perfect recruiting process. But with a little effort and consideration given to some of the issues presented in this chapter, every company can create recruiting and staffing processes that are far better than the ones they are currently using.

NOTES

1. The terms *staffing* and *recruiting* are used interchangeably. One could make a distinction that recruiting is more about finding talent and staffing is more about hiring people into jobs. But these two functions have become so intertwined that most companies tend to view them as the same general process. For consistency, I tend to use the term *recruiting* more often than *staffing* because it connotes both sourcing and hiring talent.

2. Hunt, E. B. (1996). *Will we be smart enough: A cognitive analysis of the coming workforce.* New York: Russell Sage. Barnow, B. S., Trutko, J., & Piatak, J. S. (2013). *Occupational labor shortages: Concepts, causes, consequences, and cures.* Kalamazoo, MI: Upjohn Institute.

3. Hunt, S. T. (2007). *Hiring success: The art and science of staffing assessment and employee selection.* San Francisco: Jossey-Bass.

4. Boudreau, J. W., & Ramstad, P. M. (2007). *Beyond HR: The new science of human capital.* Boston: Harvard Business School Press.

5. Hom, P. W., & Salamin, A. (2005). In search of the elusive U-shaped performance-tenure relationship: Are high performing Swiss bankers more liable to quit? *Journal of Applied Psychology, 90,* 1204–1216.

6. Brannick, M. T., & Levine, E. L. (2002). *Job analysis: Methods, research, and applications for human resource management in the new millennium.*

Thousand Oaks, CA: Sage. Gael, S. (1988). *Handbook of job analysis for business, industry, and government.* New York: Wiley.

7. Schmidt, F. L., & Hunter, J. E. (1998). The validity and utility of selection methods in personnel psychology: Practical and theoretical implications of 85 years of research findings. *Psychological Bulletin, 124,* 262–274.

8. Bauer, T. N., Bodner, T., Erdogan, B., Truxillo, D. M., & Tucker, J. S. (2007). Newcomer adjustment during organizational socialization: A meta-analytic review of antecedents, outcomes and methods. *Journal of Applied Psychology, 92,* 707–721.

9. Smith, L.G.E., Amiot, C. E., Smith, J. R., Callan, V. J., & Terry, D. J. (2013). A longitudinal test: The social validation and coping model of organizational identity development. *Journal of Management, 39,* 1952–1978.

Doing the Right Things
Becoming a Goal-Driven Organization

Focusing people on the right things is basically about good goal management, which is among the most powerful methods companies have to execute business strategies. Hundreds of studies have examined the impact of goal management on workforce productivity (see the discussion: "Goal-Setting Theory and Research: A Three-Hundred-Word Summary of More Than One Thousand Empirical Research Articles"). The common finding from this research is this: *Employees assigned specific, difficult, yet achievable goals consistently outperform employees who are given no goals or nonspecific goals encouraging them to "do their best."*

GOAL-SETTING THEORY AND RESEARCH: A THREE-HUNDRED-WORD SUMMARY OF MORE THAN ONE THOUSAND EMPIRICAL RESEARCH ARTICLES

There are relatively few widely accepted truths in the field of industrial-organizational psychology. But one finding that is almost universally agreed on is that employees who are assigned specific, difficult, yet achievable goals consistently outperform employees who are given no goals or nonspecific goals encouraging them to "do their best." This finding was not arrived at without considerable controversy and empirical investigation. More than one thousand empirical, peer-reviewed research articles have been published on the topic of goal management and its impact on employee performance. People have examined almost every aspect of goal setting, ranging from the optimal number of goals employees should have to whether the value of goals varies depending on an employee's personality traits. Hundreds of studies have been conducted to test the boundaries of goal setting and find places where goals may not work well. This research has identified goal-setting techniques that enable or limit goal effectiveness and certain situations that mediate the value of goals, but the fundamental premise of goal-setting theory has remained intact: if you want to maximize employee performance, invest time in setting clear employee goals.

Following are some of the more influential publications in the field of goal-setting research—just the tip of the iceberg when it comes to this research topic:

Kanfer, R., Chen, G., & Pritchard, R. D. (2008). *Work motivation: Past, present, and future*. London: Routledge.

Kernan, M. C., & Lord, R. G. (1990). Effects of valence, expectancies, and goal-performance discrepancies in single and multiple goal environments. *Journal of Applied Psychology, 75*, 194–203.

Klein, H. J. (1991). Further evidence on the relationship between goal setting and expectancy theories. *Organizational Behavior and Human Decision Processes, 49*, 230–257.

Latham, G. P. (2004). The motivational benefits of goal-setting. *Academy of Management Executive, 18*, 126–129.

Locke, E. A., Chah, D. O., Harrison, S., & Lustgarten, N. (1989). Separating the effects of goal specificity from goal level. *Organizational Behavior and Human Decision Processes, 43*, 270–287.

Locke, E. A., & Latham, G. P. (1990). *A theory of goal setting and task performance*. Englewood Cliffs, NJ: Prentice Hall.

Manderlink, G., & Harackiewicz, J. M. (1984). Proximal versus distal goal setting and intrinsic motivation. *Journal of Personality and Social Psychology, 47*, 918–928.

Seijts, G. H., & Latham, G. P. (2005). Learning versus performance goals: When should each be used? *Academy of Management Executive, 19*, 124–131.

Shaw, K. N. (2004). Changing the goal-setting process at Microsoft. *Academy of Management Executive, 18*, 139–142.

Tubbs, M. E., Boehne, D. M., & Dahl, J. G. (1993). Expectancy, valence, and motivational force functions in goal-setting research: An empirical test. *Journal of Applied Psychology, 78*, 361–373.

The basic concept of goal setting is so straightforward it almost seems silly: employees are much more likely to do what you want them to do if they (1) know exactly what it is you want them to do, (2) believe they can do it, and (c) are motivated to do it. Yet virtually every employee can tell stories about jobs where they were not sure exactly what they were supposed to do or why it mattered.

The effective use of goals can increase performance levels by 25 percent or more.[1] The financial value of goal management is staggering given the relatively low cost associated with implementing goal management methods. Because the value of goals is tied to fundamental psychological principles of employee behavior, the benefits of goal management do not depend on being in a certain industry or market. Every company that employs people benefits from goal management. Effective use of goals provides a means for:

- *Setting direction.* Goals clearly define what employees are expected to accomplish. When used correctly, they create clarity around the role and importance of a person's job. They let employees know what it is they are supposed to be doing and why that work is important to the company.

- *Providing feedback.* Goals allow employees to track their own progress. If employees have clear goals and access to metrics that measure these goals, they can accurately assess their performance without asking for feedback from their managers, peers, or customers. This allows employees to self-manage performance more effectively.

- *Creating intrinsic motivation.* Simply having a goal can motivate people to accomplish it. People often draw satisfaction merely from knowing they completed a goal, that is, achieving the goal is its own reward. Goals that have this property are said to provide "intrinsic motivation."[2]

- *Creating extrinsic motivation.* Goals provide a means to link work accomplishments to other rewards, such as pay and promotions. Tying goal achievement to external rewards is referred to as increasing the level of extrinsic motivation associated with a goal. Goals are particularly important for creating pay-for-performance processes because they provide a clear set of agreed-on standards for determining compensation decisions.

- *Building confidence.* A manager who assigns an important goal to an employee is sending an implicit signal that the manager believes the employee is capable of achieving the goal. This creates higher levels of self-confidence for that employee, which leads that person to stronger levels of performance.[3]

Companies with well-designed goal management processes execute business strategies quickly and efficiently by aligning employees around the things that matter. Goal management also helps companies adapt to changing market conditions by providing a means to refocus employees on new sets of priorities. Goal management can also increase employee engagement and retention by creating a link between employees' jobs and the broader mission and strategy of the organization.

The question is not whether goal management methods should be implemented at a company but how to best implement them. This chapter provides guidance on using goal management to drive business execution. It also highlights common problems that can undermine goal management effectiveness. Goal management is more complex than simply telling people what to do. Effective use of goals increases employee productivity, engagement, and motivation. Ineffective use of goals can have the opposite effect.

Section 5.1 starts the chapter by discussing what it means to be a goal-driven organization. Section 5.2 discusses how goal management fits into an integrated talent management process and explains the relationships between goals and other factors that drive employee performance such as skills and competencies. Section 5.3 reviews eight critical design questions that should be addressed when designing and implementing goal management processes in an organization. Section 5.4 describes five levels of goal management maturity and discusses methods for achieving each level.

5.1 WHAT IT MEANS TO BE A "GOAL-DRIVEN" ORGANIZATION

Being a goal-driven organization means ensuring that all employees are focused on achieving clearly defined goals supporting the business needs of the company.

This is not simply a matter of communicating the company strategy to every employee. The personal interests of individual employees should be clearly linked to the success of the entire organization. Being goal driven requires engaging employees at all levels of the company in meaningful discussion to identify what they can achieve that will help execute the company's business strategy, tying these to their personal job interests, and then holding them accountable for the commitments they make to support the business's overall strategic mission.

The following characteristics are found in organizations that effectively leverage goal setting to drive business execution:

- *All employees have clearly defined goals tailored to their specific job and linked to the overall strategy of the company.* When asked, employees can say exactly what their goals are, when they need to be achieved, how they will be measured, and why they are important to the company's strategy and mission.

- *Managers are held accountable for setting effective goals with their direct reports and ensuring these goals are met.* The performance of managers is evaluated based on the quality of the goals assigned to the people they manage and whether they achieve these goals. Managers whose employees have poorly defined goals or consistently fail to achieve the goals assigned to them are considered to be poor managers and are treated accordingly.

- *Clearly defined processes are used to align strategic goals with operational goals.* Consistent methods are used to translate strategic goals related to company profit, growth, and other business outcomes into tactical goals that specific departments and employees must achieve to deliver on longer-term strategic commitments.

- *Performance against goals is reviewed regularly to guide operational decisions.* Goals are reviewed on an ongoing basis throughout the year to guide decisions about business strategies, resource allocation, and project coordination. Data on goal accomplishment are used to gain insight into the operational performance of the company. This does not mean micromanaging employees against their goals. It does mean checking in with employees to ensure they are on track to succeed and understand what is needed to get them back on track if they are starting to fall behind.

- *Goal plans are adjusted throughout the year to reflect changes in business strategies or operational tactics.* Goals are updated, redefined, and recommunicated in response to changes in business strategy that may occur throughout the year. If the company decides to modify its direction or approach, these modifications are captured in individual goal plans. Companies should also monitor how frequently goals are changed to avoid confusion and inefficiency caused by constantly changing direction or shifting priorities.

- *Goal performance data are used to guide personnel decisions.* Decisions regarding pay, promotion, and staffing are based in part on employees' performance against past goals and discussing the relationships between people's past goal accomplishments and the sorts of goals they will be assigned in the future.

A quick way to evaluate whether a company has a goal-driven culture is to ask employees to describe the link between the business strategies of the organization and their day-to-day jobs (see the discussion: "Goal-Driven Cultures and Employee Engagement"). Employees in goal-driven organizations know what they are supposed to be working on and why it matters to the business. They know why their job is important. You can walk up to any employee and ask, "What are the major things you have to get done this year to be successful in your job, and how does this tie to the company's overall strategy?" and that person can give you a quick, precise answer. Employees in goal-driven cultures see a direct relationship between how they are evaluated and the impact they have on the success of the company as a whole. They feel connected to the strategies set by top business leaders and know that their success and the company's success are closely intertwined.

GOAL-DRIVEN CULTURES AND EMPLOYEE ENGAGEMENT

The following five statements can be used to measure whether a company has a goal-driven culture. Asking employees whether they agree with these statements provides a quick sense of the degree to which an organization has a strong goal orientation:

1. I know exactly what goals I am expected to accomplish in my job.

2. The work that I do is well aligned with my company's strategy.

3. Decisions about my pay and career opportunities depend in part on how well I perform against a formal goal plan that my manager and I agree on.

4. The company takes steps to ensure my goals are accurate and appropriate.

5. My manager and I review and update my goals throughout the year to ensure they are aligned with changes in company needs and strategy.

These five statements are similar to survey questions frequently used to assess employee engagement. This is because one of the primary ways to increase employee engagement is to ensure employees have a clear sense of purpose in their jobs and know why their work matters.[a] Goals play a critical role in clarifying why employees' jobs are meaningful and important.

Effective use of goals increases the performance levels of employees and also plays a key role in increasing employee satisfaction and retention. After implementing more effective goal management, one company saw its employee engagement survey scores increase by 16 percent in a single year. The impact that goals had on this increase was reflected in survey comments such as "I finally understand how I fit in with the larger organization."

[a]Buckingham, M., & Coffman, C. (1999). *First break all the rules: What the world's greatest managers do differently.* New York: Simon & Schuster.

5.2 THE ROLE OF GOALS IN AN INTEGRATED STRATEGIC HR SYSTEM

Goal management plays a pivotal role in converting business strategies from lofty, long-term aspirations communicated by senior leaders into tangible commitments and deliverables owned by employees at all levels of the organization. But companies often fail to maximize the value of goal management by allowing it to become subsumed within other strategic HR processes such as performance management or career development. This tends to occur when companies confuse the management of goals with the management of learning objectives and competencies.

To understand how goals fit into the broader field of strategic HR, let's revisit the three basic components of job performance introduced in chapter 2. Increasing job performance ultimately depends on managing three things:

- *Goals* describe the business outcomes employees are expected to support or accomplish (e.g., achieving sales quotas, minimizing accidents, maintaining productivity levels, processing documents). In essence, goals define the reason that a job exists. People are employed to deliver, create, complete, produce, or otherwise accomplish specific things. Goals clarify these things.

- *Competencies* describe the behaviors employees are expected to display on the job—for example, building relationships, planning and organizing, solving problems, and other activities that influence success or reflect the company's cultural values. People often distinguish goals from competencies using the concept of "what versus how." Goals define what a person is supposed to do in the job, and competencies describe how he or she is expected to do it.

- *Attributes* are characteristics of employees that are associated with job success. They include qualifications (e.g., job experience, education, certifications), aptitudes (e.g., personality and ability traits), and interests (e.g., career aspirations, salary preferences, work schedule expectations). Attributes define who employees are in terms of their knowledge, skills, and abilities. The attributes employees possess influence the competencies they display, which determine the goals they can achieve.

The relationship of attributes, competencies, and goals can be summed up as, "What you achieve [goals] depends on how you act [competencies], which is largely determined by who you are [attributes]." Attributes, competencies, and goals are managed using four fundamental types of HR processes broadly focused on right people (staffing), right things (goal management), right way (performance management), and right development (career management). Of these four processes, goal management is among the most critical for driving business alignment, productivity, and efficiency.

Goals define what employees need to accomplish for the company to be successful. Managing employees without defining job goals is like asking someone to enter a foot race without telling the person where the finish line is. He or she may get there eventually but is likely to waste a lot of time and energy along the way. Staffing, performance management, and career development make sure you have the right people in the race and are giving them effective guidance and motivation along the way. But goal management defines what they actually need to accomplish to win the race.

Goal management, performance management, and career development methods should complement one another but should not be treated as the same thing. Goal management processes are used to define business goals. They should be kept distinct from career development and performance management processes that emphasize employee learning objectives and job competencies. An employee's goal plan should define what the employee needs to accomplish to support the company's business strategies. Things related to competencies or career learning objectives should be managed as part of performance management and career development, not goal management.

Employees frequently make the mistake of putting their learning objectives on their goal plans. Goals define what employees must achieve in their job to be successful. Learning objectives describe what they are doing to build their personal attributes and capabilities to improve their performance or advance their careers (e.g., knowledge, skills, and experience). Learning objectives are the focus of career development processes and should not be placed on job goal plans. At the same time, learning objectives can support the accomplishment of job goals. Consider an example. Imagine an employee's job requires her to achieve the goal of "report accurate customer satisfaction scores on a monthly basis." In order to do this more effectively, the employee decides she needs to "learn how to use Excel." The job goal in this example is "report accurate customer satisfaction scores." "Learning to use Excel" is a learning objective because it focuses on building the employee's knowledge. From a business perspective, it is reporting the customer satisfaction scores that ultimately matters, not whether the employee did or did not learn how to use Excel. In sum, learning objectives often define things employees must develop to be effective in their roles, but they are different from job goals, which describe what employees must accomplish to support the company's strategies.

It is also important to distinguish job goals from competencies. Competencies define behaviors that employees are expected to display in a job. Goals define what people are expected to achieve as a result of displaying these behaviors. Competencies play a critical role in driving workforce productivity, employee development, and company culture. But it is ultimately the accomplishment of goals that determines whether a company achieves its strategic business objectives. Creating performance management processes that clearly define and evaluate job competencies ensures that people accomplish goals in a manner that is efficient and supports the company's norms and values. But competencies are not the same as goals and should not be included in goal management processes.

Goal management processes should be treated as distinct from processes used to manage competencies and learning objectives, but there is a logical connection among goals, competencies, and learning objectives. When a company assigns goals to employees, invariably some employees will struggle to achieve them. Companies can then use performance management methods to give employees feedback on the competencies they need to display to accomplish their goals. This helps employees identify what behaviors they need to change in order to succeed. Sometimes an employee's inability to display certain competencies will be due to a lack of skills or knowledge. In these cases, companies can use career development programs to help employees build the attributes needed to display the competencies that drive goal accomplishment. For example, imagine a salesperson was given the goal of "selling 100 units in Q1." A month into this assignment, the manager realizes the salesperson is not on track to achieve this goal. Upon observing the employee, the manager realizes the employee is struggling because he is not effectively displaying the competency "addressing customer needs." After a conversation with the employee, the manager learns that the employee does not know enough about the product to answer customer questions effectively. As a result of this conversation, the employee sets a learning objective of "complete product training," which will help him display the competency "addressing customer needs," which will enable him to accomplish their job goal of "selling 100 units in Q1."

Goals, competencies, and learning objectives have related but very distinct roles for increasing employee performance. The most effective strategic HR processes are designed with a clear understanding of these different roles. The methods used to define, measure, and manage goals, competencies, and learning objectives are significantly different from one another. Goal management, performance management, and career development processes should be built and managed as integrated but distinct activities. The rigor of keeping these three somewhat related concepts distinct may seem somewhat trivial, but it pays off by reducing confusion and process inefficiency. Over time, managers and employees will understand and appreciate the value of differentiating among goals, competencies, and learning objectives.

5.3 GOAL MANAGEMENT CRITICAL DESIGN QUESTIONS

All companies use some form of goal setting to direct people's efforts on the job. The question is not whether to set goals but how to do it effectively. To truly leverage the power of goals, companies must put thought into designing goal management processes that make the most sense for their particular jobs and business needs. The following design questions are central to building fully effective goal management processes:

1. How will you ensure employees have well-defined goal plans?

2. What are you doing to ensure employees feel a sense of commitment and ownership toward the goals they are assigned?

3. What methods are used to align employees' goals with company business strategies?

4. How is employee goal accomplishment measured?

5. What is the relationship between goal accomplishment and employee pay, promotions, and recognition?

6. How are goals used to support employee development and career growth?

7. How does the organization coordinate goals across different employees to foster communication and collaboration?

8. How are goals used to guide business execution on an ongoing basis?

The answers to these questions depend on your company's business strategies, the nature of its workforce, and its talent management processes. The correct answer to each question can vary considerably from organization to organization. Failure to address any of the questions can result in a suboptimal goal management process.

5.3.1 How Will You Ensure Employees Have Well-Defined Goal Plans?

Research has shown that employees often struggle to understand exactly what it is they are expected to do when they show up on the job.[4] This lack of goal definition decreases employee productivity and retention, increases anxiety around role clarity and value, and raises the potential for internal conflict and organizational politics around responsibilities and accountability. In fact, the survey question, "I know what is expected of me at work," strongly correlates with employee engagement and employee turnover. The most direct way to address problems caused by lack of clear goals is to ensure employees and their managers sit down on a regular basis to define the goals employee are expected to accomplish.

The simple action of requiring managers to meet with employees to establish goal plans drives tremendous value for business execution. It forces managers to engage with employees around what actions and accomplishments should take priority in their jobs. By establishing clear expectations, goals increase productivity in the near term and set the foundation for fairer and more effective conversations and decisions related to talent management later (e.g., on compensation and promotions). Tracking whether employees have goal plans also provides a metric for evaluating if managers are performing the most basic part of their job: talking with employees about what they should be doing. In fact, there is a positive correlation between the frequency with which managers work with their employees to maintain goal plans and financial metrics reflecting overall company performance.[5]

Two things need to be considered when designing processes to ensure employees have well-defined goal plans. First, managers and employees should be given clear guidelines on what a well-defined goal plan looks like. Second, managers and employees need to set goals in a manner that gives employees a sense of ownership and accountability toward achieving them.

Creating a Well-Defined Goal Plan Many employees do not think of work in terms of discrete, well-defined goals. Even highly experienced employees can find it difficult to summarize their roles in terms of a short list of succinct, well-defined, and measurable objectives. Fortunately, there are at least three ways to help employees create well-defined goal plans: (1) provide goal libraries, (2) communicate criteria for creating and evaluating goal plans, and (3) train employees on goal setting methodologies.

Goal libraries are databases containing common goals and goal plans associated with different types of jobs. An example from a goal library is provided in figure 5.1. Goal libraries can be an effective starting point for crafting goals, although library goals often need to be modified to fit an employee's specific job or role. The challenge to using goal libraries is they can take considerable effort to create and can be difficult to maintain over time.

Figure 5.1
Example of Contents from a Goal Library

What is your goal?

Category: Financial ▾

Decr ✎

Decrease amount of money spent on office supplies by $___ by ordering in bulk and e ▲
Negotiate contracts with outside vendors that decreases printing costs by __ (%)
Decrease return rates __% by (date)
Decrease abandonment rate of calls in queue to __% by (date)
Decrease number of rings until answered to __(#) rings by (date)
Decrease time to reach qualified representative __% by (date)
Decrease average cost per hire __% by (date)
Decrease defect rate __% by (date)
Decrease cost to serve __% by (date)
Decrease abandonment rate of calls in queue to __% by (date)
Decrease number of rings until answered to __(#) rings by (date)
Decrease time to reach qualified representative __% by (date) ▾

Source: SuccessFactors, an SAP Company, used with permission.

Another method for creating well-defined goals is to provide employees and managers with clear criteria and frameworks for creating and evaluating goal plans. Table 5.1 provides a set of criteria for developing goal plans and addresses common problems found in employee goal plans. Providing simple sets of rules and recommendations like those in table 5.1 leads to the creation of more consistent goal plans across the company and helps employees to develop and critique their goals without having to rely on extensive input from others.

Most of the criteria in table 5.1 are relatively uncontroversial, but there is one possible exception that warrants a bit more discussion. This is the guideline to "have at least five goals and no more than ten." Empirical research suggests the optimal number of goals on an employee goal plan is around eight.[6] My own experience suggests that most jobs cannot be adequately described in fewer than five goals. When people try to describe a job in fewer than five, they either leave out important aspects of their work or combine different goals into less clearly defined, broad categories of "general things they have to do." Employees who have more than ten goals may be focusing on too many things. The purpose of goal plans is to describe what employees need to keep in mind as they go about

Table 5.1
Some Simple Goal-Setting Guidelines

Have at least five goals and no more than ten,

- Do not oversimplify what you actually do; get credit for your contributions!
- Focus on what matters the most; don't try to catalogue everything you do.
- You should be able to quickly list all the goals on your goal plan from memory.

Goals define the things you are here to do; they explain why your job exists and why it is important.

- Even if someone never actually saw you work, he or she should be able to use your goals as evidence of the contributions you make to the company.

Define goals to be independent of each other.

- It should be possible to achieve one goal without achieving another.

Do not list personal learning objectives in your goal plan.

- Goals can (and should) drive personal development, but they must reflect business needs.
- Example: instead of listing a goal like, "Learn to use Microsoft Excel," write the business needs driving this learning objective, such as, "Support project X, which will require learning Microsoft Excel."

Personalize cascaded goals to your job.

- Change the names of cascaded goals; make them relevant to your role.
- Tasks or deliverables associated with the goals cascaded to you by your supervisor may become your actual goals.
- You may create several different goals on your goal plan to support a single goal cascaded to you by your supervisor.

performing and planning their day-to-day work. They should be able to easily recite all their goals from memory. And a well-known finding from psychology is the number of items on a list that people can easily commit to memory is between five and nine (often referred to as the "7 plus or minus 2" rule in introductory psychology classes).[7]

Some employees resist reducing their goal plans to fewer than ten goals. I have seen goal plans with over thirty different goals listed for a single employee! When this happens, it is usually because the employee has confused goals with tasks. *Goals* are outcomes, accomplishments, or responsibilities people need to fulfill to be effective in their jobs. *Tasks* are activities they perform to achieve these goals. For example, a goal might be, "Install a new heating system." Tasks for this goal might include things like "create a list of system specifications" and "review proposals from vendors." Some employees list all the tasks they intend to perform as separate goals, which can lead to the creation of very lengthy goal plans. Although it may be useful to describe the tasks a person plans to accomplish to achieve a goal, tasks are not what the company truly cares about. Tasks are a means to an end but not the end unto itself. To use a sports analogy, the difference between tasks and goals is like the difference between executing plays in football and scoring points. At the end of the day, achieving points is what matters, not the number of plays run.

A third method for establishing effective goal plans is to provide employees with a framework for writing and structuring goals. The most common framework is to teach employees how to set goals that are SMART: Specific, Measurable, Achievable, Relevant, and Time-Bound (see the discussion: "Making a Goal Plan SMART").

MAKING A GOAL PLAN SMART

The acronym SMART describes a method for ensuring that goals agreed on by managers and employees are well defined and clearly understood. To be SMART, a goal must be:

Specific: The details of the goal are defined so that its achievement can be objectively determined. Whether a goal is accomplished should not depend on someone's subjective evaluation; it should be based on tangible, observable facts and outcomes. Goals should be defined at a specific enough level so that there will be little debate about whether the goal was or was not achieved.

Measurable: The definition of the goal includes a list of one or more metrics or criteria that can be used to evaluate if the person is on track to accomplish the goal. Ideally, metrics are quantifiable measures such as percentages or numbers, for example, "achieve 95 percent uptime on service delivery" or "closed five new contracts in my region." But they can also be qualitative indicators of goal achievement, for example, "installed a new software system" or "completed a training course."

Attainable: The goal can realistically be accomplished. The skills, resources, and tools needed to achieve the goal are available to the employee, and it is reasonable to expect the employee to achieve the goal successfully. This does *not* mean the goal will be easy to accomplish, but that it is realistic to expect that the employee can accomplish it.

Relevant: The goal should support the overall strategy and mission of the company. It reflects things the person is expected to do as part of their job.

Time-bound: The goal definition should include specific milestones and deadlines for its accomplishment. Specific dates are agreed on for determining whether the goal has or has not been achieved.

The following story illustrates how the SMART criteria can guide the creation of goals. Imagine that a retail store manager asked a frontline clerk to set a goal for the coming year. The employee responded with a goal "to improve my performance." This goal does not meet any of the SMART criteria. So the manager and employee reviewed the following questions to make the goal SMART:

- Is it *specific?* "Improve my performance" is not a specific enough goal to be verifiable. Whether the employee's performance has improved will depend on what is meant by performance. Is improving performance a matter of better attendance, sales, customer service, attention to detail, or something else? To make the goal more specific, let's assume that the manager and employee rewrote the goal as, "Improve my performance delivering service to store customers."

- Is it *measurable?* The goal "improve my performance delivering service to store customers" is reasonably specific, but does not define how to measure achievement of the goal. To address this, the manager and employee expanded the goal to, "Improve my performance delivering service to store customers as demonstrated by a significant increase in customer survey scores collected during my shift."

- Is it *achievable?* Determining whether a goal is achievable requires the manager and employee to reach agreement between what is desired by the business and what the employee thinks is possible. Employees should be encouraged to strive for goals that they view as difficult but achievable. These types of goals have been shown to create the highest levels of performance. For example, the manager may want customer satisfaction survey scores to increase by 10 percent, but the employee may feel that such an increase depends on too many factors they cannot control. The employee may argue for a 1 percent increase, but the manager may view this as too easy to achieve. For the purpose of this illustration, let's assume the manager and employee agree on setting the goal as a 5 percent increase in customer survey scores because this number is felt to be difficult but realistic to attain by both the manager and employee.

- Is it *relevant?* This means making sure the goal is associated with the employee's job duties and the company's overall business strategy. Improving customer service is relevant to the job in this example. But it might not be considered relevant if the employee worked in a noncustomer-facing role in a distribution center.

- Is it *time-bound?* This means making sure there is a specific date when the goal is expected to be completed. The manager and employee need to agree on a date when they will formally review the goal to see if it has been achieved. This can be done by expanding the goal to this: "Improve my performance delivering service to store customers, demonstrated by achieving a 5 percent increase in customer survey scores collected during my shift by the end of Q4 of this year."

When a goal lacks any of the five SMART criteria, employees are at risk of not fully understanding what it is they are expected to do or how their success will be evaluated. By going through a process of discussion, the manager and employee in this example were able to translate the non-SMART goal of "improve my performance" to a difficult but achievable SMART goal of "improve my performance delivering service to store customers demonstrated by achieving a 5 percent increase in customer survey scores collected during my shift by the end of Q4 of this year."

Although the SMART framework is probably the most widely used, I have found it to be less effective than another framework called the COD model: Commitments, Outcomes, and Deliverables (see the discussion: "Commitment, Outcome, Deliverable (COD) Goal Methodology"). All of the major concepts associated with the SMART framework are incorporated into the COD model. But they are presented in a way that is simpler and reflects how employees and managers actually discuss goals. Managers are encouraged to talk with employees about what *commitments* they can make to support business initiatives, the *deliverables* they will meet to fulfill each commitment, and the business *outcomes* this will create.

The discussion provides guidance for using the COD method to set goals. An additional advantage of the COD framework is how well it supports the concept of goal cascading, which will be discussed later in the chapter. People are instructed that a deliverable at one level in the organization may be reframed as a commitment at the next level down. This has proven to be useful in helping people better understand how to leverage goal processes to communicate and align employees around new business initiatives.

The most important point is not whether you use goal libraries, SMART goals, COD goals, or some other goal-setting framework. What is important is to provide employees and managers with some method to ensure they are setting well-defined and appropriate goals.

Goal setting is somewhat like riding a bike. It is not hard to learn, but if you don't do it correctly, you can hurt yourself. Furthermore, if you ask managers and employees if they know how to set goals they will probably say yes. But this does not mean they know how to do it well. The following are examples of actual goals I have seen on goal plans created by managers and employees who purported to know how to set goals: "to lose ten pounds by December," "to get along with others," "to hit our revenue targets," or "to increase my performance." With the exception of losing ten pounds, none of these goals meets the criteria of being well defined. And the only one that was well defined was not job relevant (at least not for the job this employee held). The lesson is that it is very important to provide managers and employees with clear criteria and methods for setting goals or people will waste a lot of time writing goals that are not well defined, job relevant, or motivational.

COMMITMENT, OUTCOME, DELIVERABLE (COD) GOAL METHODOLOGY

Your goal plan, which defines what you are responsible for doing within the organization to support the company's business needs, should consist of five to ten specific commitments you have made to support the strategic needs of the organization. Each commitment will be associated with a variety of specific outcomes and deliverables. The following guidelines will help in building out your goal plans.

Commitment: What I'm Doing

- Develop a short phrase that describes what you are doing and why it is relevant to the business.

- Customize commitments to your particular role; they should define what you specifically do in the company.

- Identify five to ten different commitments, each associated with one or more outcomes and deliverables.

- Link all commitments to commitments on your manager's or other people's goal plans so they directly or indirectly roll up to the CEO's goal plan.

Outcomes: Why I'm Doing It

- Identify the results you will create by achieving this commitment, that is, the evidence that will demonstrate you were successful.

- Try to have no more than four outcomes per commitment. A single outcome may be adequate for some commitments.

- You can tie several commitments to the same general outcomes. This is very common when one outcome is dependent on a variety of commitments being met (e.g., "increase corporate profitability by 5 percent").

Deliverables: How I Will Do It

- Identify the actions you will complete to meet the commitment, that is, the tactical strategy you are taking to drive the outcomes.

- Try to have no more than five deliverables per commitment.

- Deliverables at one level of the company often become commitments for people at the next level; you may cascade certain deliverables as commitments for your direct reports

The following is an example of a goal written using the COD format:

Commitment: Improve customer service levels in the stores I manage to increase return customer traffic and sales

Outcomes: Scores of 90 percent or better on in-store customer surveys; Increase year on year store sales by 5 percent

Deliverables: Provide customer service training to all store employees by the end of the first quarter; review customer survey results with team on the first week of each month; implement customer suggestion program by June of this year

---

5.3.2 What Are You Doing to Ensure Employees Feel a Sense of Commitment and Ownership toward the Goals They Are Assigned?

Goals will not have an impact on performance if employees feel little sense of commitment toward achieving them. Managers must remember that goal setting is not about telling people what to do. It is about working with people to clarify what needs to be done in a manner that builds commitment toward goal accomplishment. There are many ways to increase the motivational power of goals. The best and least expensive way is to ensure managers pay attention to three concepts when they work with employees to create goal plans: participative goal setting, managing goal difficulty, and addressing goal-setting anxiety.

Participative Goal Setting One effective way to build goal commitment is to use participative goal setting. This technique requires managers to meet with employees to discuss what goals make the most sense given their capabilities and the organization's business needs. Participative goal setting gives employees a sense of influence and buy-in over the goals that are assigned to them. The opposite of participative goal setting is to simply assign goals to employees without their participation. When it comes to motivation, there is a big difference between telling people what to do compared with talking with them about what they should be doing.

The simplest participative goal-setting techniques involve some variation of the following steps:

Step 1. Managers ask employees to list the goals they plan to accomplish over the coming work period to support the organization.

Step 2. Managers create their own set of proposed goals they want employees to achieve.

Step 3. Managers and employees discuss the two sets of goals to find a mutually acceptable set of final goals.

Step 1 is often the most difficult step in this process. Employees may struggle to identify possible goals. When this happens, managers need to be careful not to simply tell employees what the manager thinks their goals should be. Instead, they should use one or more of the following techniques to help employees identify goals:

- Have employees list things they created, accomplished, or influenced over the past month, quarter, or year that contributed to the company's success. These can be used as a source of inspiration for creating future goals for the next time period.

- Have the manager share his or her goals with the employee and ask what things the employee can accomplish to support these goals. This reflects a method called goal cascading, which I discuss later in this chapter.

- Challenge employees to list the things they do that justify why their job exists. In other words, what does the company pay them to produce? This method focuses employees on the importance of being able to define and articulate the goals of their job. But it can be quite threatening if done poorly and should be used with caution.

There are certain jobs where a lot of participative goal setting is neither necessary nor expected. These tend to be jobs where roles are well defined or responsibilities are determined based on collective bargaining or other contract agreements. For example, someone hired to clean tables in a restaurant does not need to spend a lot of time talking with the manager to determine whether his or her goals involve keeping the tables clean. However, it might make sense to use participative goal setting to determine how many tables an employee can realistically clean on a busy night. Employees who work in highly well-defined roles appreciate being consulted on whether their job goals are realistic and obtainable. These employees may not expect to have a lot of influence in the goal-setting process, but simply knowing that they are allowed to voice their opinions increases their engagement and job satisfaction.[8]

Another advantage of participative goal setting is that it lessens the risk that employees will accept goals that are illogical, overly risky, or even downright counterproductive. There are many examples of situations where employees accepted goals that did not make sense because they did not feel empowered to question their manager. Some tragic examples can be found in the transportation and manufacturing industries where employees were given goals focused on "minimizing costs" or "maximizing revenue" that ultimately led to accidents caused by mechanical problems. After these accidents, employees stated that they knew the goals were putting the machinery at risk, but they didn't feel they had permission or authority to question the goals they had been assigned.

Managing Goal Difficulty   Goals have the strongest impact on productivity when they are difficult but achievable. Managers should challenge employees to set ambitious goals where a successful outcome is possible but not certain. But managers also need to be sensitive to stress caused by having too many challenging goals. Goal plans ideally include a mixture of difficult goals along with goals that are important but not as challenging. The less difficult goals provide employees with a sense of balance and confidence that they will be able to meet their job expectations. Managers must also be careful about pushing employees too hard month after month. Most people are capable of putting in high levels of effort when required to accomplish critical goals. But over time, they will stop putting effort into goals if they feel the goals have become unrealistic, unreasonable, or unsustainable.

Addressing Goal-Setting Anxiety   If employees are not used to setting goals, they may have concerns about how the goals will be used. The best way to address this is to clearly communicate why the organization is implementing more rigorous goal management methods and how these methods will help employees to be more successful. The following are several benefits to help employees understand the value they personally gain from adopting goal management processes in their organization.

Improving Strategic Communication   Well-defined goal plans clarify what people are working on and how it relates to the company's business strategy. Goals establish priorities for employees. They also help employees communicate to their peers and leaders what they are doing to support the company's strategies. To reinforce this message, let employees know who will be looking at their goal plans and how this information will be used to guide company decisions.

Fairly Evaluating Performance   Goals provide a clear and transparent method for evaluating employee contributions to the organization. They reduce reliance on subjective opinions or ill-defined criteria when making decisions about pay, promotions, or job assignments. To emphasize this point, let employees know how goal accomplishment will be used to guide pay and promotion decisions.

Managing Workloads   Rigorous use of goals protects employees when there are changes in the business. Having clearly defined goal plans reduces the risk that managers will ask employees to take on additional responsibilities without discussing how this has an impact on their existing commitments. To emphasize this, establish guidelines for updating employee goal plans during the year to reflect shifting organizational priorities. For example, restrict goal plans to a maximum of ten goals and inform managers that they must work with their employees to remove or readjust their existing goals before they can ask them to take on a significant new assignment. Some caution is needed when setting these sorts of guidelines lest employees become too caught up on whether something is or is not on their formal goal plan. But there is usually value in encouraging employees and managers to carefully think about priorities before committing to taking on new work.

Providing Credit for Contributions   Most employees have experienced situations where they have been asked to work on one objective, only to be told later to stop working on that activity and pursue another objective. By tracking goals, companies give employees credit for work they have done on an initiative even if the larger project may not have been completed due to changes in the overall business strategy. Let employees know how goal data will be reviewed and what methods will be put in place to ensure people are recognized for past contributions.

Balance the Use of Goals as a Tool for Communication versus Evaluation   Another potential way to reduce goal anxiety is to use goals solely as a communication tool until people become comfortable with them. After people become comfortable with the goal-setting process, goals can move beyond strategy communication to include supporting pay and promotion decisions. However, employees in some jobs may view goals as relevant only if they have a direct impact on their pay. In these cases, it may be important to tie goal achievement to pay and personnel decisions so people take the process seriously. How much you emphasize goals as tools for communication versus tools to guide personnel evaluation will affect how employees react to them. Put thought into what makes sense for your organization. The approach that makes the most sense will vary depending on the situation.

5.3.3   What Methods Are Used to Align Employees' Goals with Company Business Strategies?

Goal management is not just about making sure employees have well-defined goal plans. It is also about making sure these plans align with the overall objectives of the company. This requires ensuring that goal conversations between managers and employees incorporate information about company strategy. There are three primary methods for doing this: establishing goal categories, using prepopulated goal plans, or implementing goal cascading. Each has its own strengths and weaknesses. Establishing goal categories is the easiest but least effective. Creating prepopulated goal plans provides the most clarity to employees but is the most difficult to maintain. Goal cascading is the most effective, but it requires managers to invest the most time by talking with employees about how to develop appropriate goal plans.

Goal Categories   This method starts with identifying broad categories of goals that the company needs to address to support its business strategies (e.g., financial performance, customer service, safety). Employees are then instructed to set goals that fit into some or all of these categories.

The most common example of goal categories comes from the balanced scorecard management theory.[9] This approach argues that every company should focus on four categories of goals: (1) providing customer service; (2) increasing operational efficiency and quality; (3) attracting, retaining, and developing employees; and (4) achieving financial targets. Balanced scorecard categories are fairly effective for ensuring that employees are setting goals that support key elements of company performance. There may also be value in creating additional goal categories that reflect a company's particular business strategy, market, or industry—for example, a manufacturing company might create a goal category called "workplace safety" to ensure employees are actively thinking about ways to reduce injuries and accidents, and a technology company that emphasizes innovation might create a goal category called "new product development" to reinforce the importance of setting goals that drive creativity and exploration. But companies should avoid creating too many categories lest employees become confused or overwhelmed. It is also important to remind employees that certain categories may be more or less relevant to their particular jobs. Some employees might put most or all of their goals under a single category.

The value of goal categories is their ability to get employees to think about the company's overall strategic needs when setting goals. Rather than starting the goal-setting process by having employees ask themselves, "What do I need to get done in my job?" goal categories encourage employees to think about setting goals from a different perspective: "What does the company need me to support through my work?" Goal categories also make it possible to track goals based on common strategic themes. This allows companies to analyze goals to make sure they adequately support different strategic initiatives. For example, goal data might be used to diagnose if the company is on track to achieve its customer service objectives but at risk of not meeting financial objectives.

Predefined Goal Plans Predefined goal plans are preset combinations of goals developed for specific jobs or groups of jobs based on company strategy. Employees are assigned predefined goal plans based on their role in the organization. For example, all customer service representatives in a company might be given a predefined goal plan with five core goals:

1. Achieve an average customer satisfaction score of x percent.
2. Become certified to support at least x additional product lines.
3. Reduce the time to resolve customer problems by x percent.
4. Sell at least $x of additional products and services.
5. Maintain a customer renewal rate of at least x percent.

Every customer service representative would be assigned these same five goals, although the numerical targets associated with the goals might change from one employee to the next based on experience level, job location, or some other variables.

Predefined goal plans provide detailed guidance to employees and managers on what things are important to the company. They also significantly reduce the time needed to establish goals since employees are working from a preset template. Predefined goal plans can be highly effective when setting goals for jobs with large numbers of employees or for jobs where the basic responsibilities and tasks do not change that much from one year to the next (e.g., hourly retail jobs, certain jobs in health care, many frontline sales jobs). The disadvantage is it takes time to develop predefined goal plans, particularly if you are trying to set goals for a wide range of job types. Predefined goal plans also do not work well for jobs where the goals employees have can change significantly based on shifting company needs and strategies.

Cascading Goals Goal cascading is a method for communicating business strategies so all employees in the company understand the role they play in strategy execution. The goal-cascading process starts when senior leaders set their goal plans based on company strategy. Leaders share their goal plans with their direct reports, who in turn set goals that align with and support those of their supervisor. By doing this, companies can ensure that employees at all levels are working on goals that link back to the organization's overall strategic initiatives.

Figure 5.2 provides an illustration of goal cascading drawn from the health care industry. In this example, the CEO of a hospital sets a goal to "decrease annual operating costs by $5 million by the end of Q4." This goal is cascaded to the chief operating officer (COO) of the hospital, who proposes that one way to reduce operating costs is to "decrease the rate of illnesses acquired by patients while in the hospital by 10 percent by the end of Q4." The COO then cascades this goal to her director of facilities, who determines that the best way his area can reduce patient-acquired illness is to "implement health and safety programs by the end of Q2 in all the departments managed by facilities." This is cascaded to

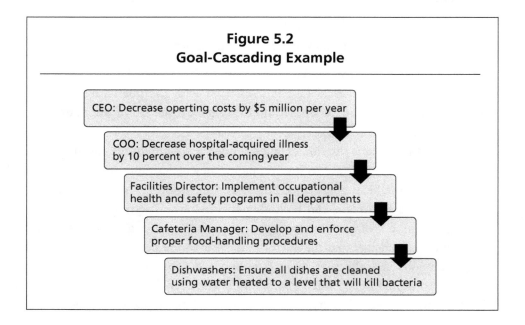

Figure 5.2
Goal-Cascading Example

CEO: Decrease operting costs by $5 million per year

COO: Decrease hospital-acquired illness by 10 percent over the coming year

Facilities Director: Implement occupational health and safety programs in all departments

Cafeteria Manager: Develop and enforce proper food-handling procedures

Dishwashers: Ensure all dishes are cleaned using water heated to a level that will kill bacteria

the cafeteria manager, who suggests that the most appropriate health and safety programs in her area are to "develop and enforce proper food-handling procedures for all cafeteria positions by the end of Q1." The cafeteria manager's goal is cascaded to the dishwashing supervisor, who interprets this as setting a goal for his team to "ensure all dishes are cleaned in water heated to an appropriate level to kill bacteria."

The power of goal cascading is its ability to get everyone in the organization aligned around the same strategic objectives in a way that makes sense given their particular jobs in the organization. Consider how the example in figure 5.2 illustrates the link between a high-level strategic objective of "save $5 million" and a seemingly minor tactical task like "wash dishes using water heated at an appropriate level."

Goal cascading also makes employees' goals more meaningful by linking them to the overall mission and strategy of the organization. Consider how the dishwashing employee in this example might have reacted if his supervisor simply said, "You need to wash the dishes in hotter water." He might have resented being told to do something that made his work more difficult. Compare this to the supervisor who says, "You need to wash the dishes in hotter water to kill the bacteria that cause patient illnesses, which directly affects the mission and financial stability of the hospital." Now the dishwashing employee understands the rationale for the request and why changing how he does his job is important to the overall success of the hospital.

When done well, goal cascading is much more than a method for communicating what the company's strategic objectives are. It is a method to help employees identify what they can do to support those objectives. The key to effective goal cascading is to approach it as a process for translating high-level strategic objectives into actionable goals that employees can directly influence. This can be done by encouraging leaders and managers to clarify the relationships of three types of goals:

• *Outcomes are goals that result indirectly from actions taken by employees.* This includes things such as "increase sales by 10 percent," "grow market share by 25 percent," or "reduce operating costs by $5 million." Companies cannot directly increase outcome goals such as sales volumes or market share. Instead, they take actions that lead to these outcomes. For example, the accomplishment of launching a new marketing plan may result in customers' buying more of the company's products, which creates the outcomes of increased sales or market share.

The advantage of outcome goals is they can be tied directly to critical indicators of company performance. Outcome goals are frequently associated with senior leadership roles as well as certain roles in sales and marketing where people are comfortable being held accountable for results they may only indirectly influence. The disadvantage of outcome goals is that employees often find them to be confusing or demotivating because they cannot directly control them. Many things influence outcome goals besides the actions of employees (e.g., changes in the broader market and economy). Outcome goals are only indirectly influenced by what employees actually do. This may reduce employees' sense that they can directly affect these goals, and many employees do not find these goals to be highly meaningful. This was illustrated in a meeting I attended where a CEO boldly proclaimed that the company's goal was to become the first billion-dollar company in their industry niche. One of the company's engineers replied, "That's great, but it doesn't mean anything to me. What do you actually want me to build?"

• *Accomplishment* goals describe things employees can directly achieve or create—for example, "develop three new products," "implement a new technology system," or "deploy a new purchasing process." Accomplishments describe things employees do to create outcomes. They indicate the actions and deliverables a company is going to undertake to drive its strategic objectives. Accomplishment goals tend to be associated with professional positions where people are responsible for creating, building, or developing new products and services.

• *Responsibilities* are goals that describe ongoing performance levels employees are expected to maintain. Employees must support certain responsibilities if the company is to achieve certain outcomes. Examples of responsibility goals include "process 100 calls per day," "keep the error rate to less than 1 per 1,000," and "score 95 percent on monthly safety audits." These types of goals are commonly associated with administrative, manufacturing, and customer service positions where the focus is mainly on supporting existing operations.

Goal cascading connects high-level strategic outcome goals with accomplishment and responsibility goals that are meaningful to employees in different functions and levels across the organization. Figure 5.2 shows how an outcome goal of "reduce operating cost by $5 million" was connected to an accomplishment goal, "implement health and safety programs," which in turn was connected to a specific responsibility goal of "wash the dishes in water heated to an appropriate temperature." Imagine how the cafeteria workers in this example might have reacted if they were simply given the original outcome goal: "reduce operating cost by $5 million." At best they might have seen the goal as irrelevant to their jobs and something they could not have a direct impact on. They might also find the goal to be threatening and even intimidating because it is clearly something they cannot achieve by themselves. At worst, giving them this goal could lead the employees do doing the wrong things for the right reasons, such as deciding to wash the dishes in cold water to save money on heating costs.

Goal cascading starts with the creation of well-defined goals at the highest levels of the organization. It is not possible to implement goal cascading without considerable involvement of senior leadership, who must set well-defined goals that can be effectively cascaded to their direct reports. In most cases, the quality of employees' goal plans directly reflects the quality of their supervisors' goal plans. Leaders who create and cascade goals provide visible role models of how to use goals to drive business execution. But the opposite is true as well: if leaders do not invest energy into setting and communicating well-defined goals, it is folly to expect that their direct reports will invest the time necessary to create effective goal plans. Leaders must also discuss how their goals can be linked to the goals of their direct reports. The best and perhaps only way to implement goal cascading effectively is to have senior leaders set and cascade their goals and then follow up with people in the company, asking them, "What are you doing to support the goals I cascaded?"

Implementing goal cascading also requires that managers know how to engage their direct reports in goal-cascading conversations. The COD method of goal setting discussed earlier is particularly well suited to goal cascading. This is because it is based on how business leaders naturally go about communicating and managing business strategies. When using the COD method, leaders are instructed that a "deliverable" at one level in the organization may be reframed as a "commitment" at the next level down. Leaders are encouraged to meet with their direct reports to discuss how their commitments and deliverables align with commitments, outcomes, and deliverables of individual people in the group. This approach helps align employees around higher-level business initiatives. Figure 5.3 provides an example of how this works. A manager cascades a broader commitment to one of her direct reports. The direct report then creates two new commitments that support certain deliverables associated with the managers' higher-level commitment, but also reflect the nature of the employee's particular role on the manager's team.

Figure 5.3
Goal Cascading Using the Commitments, Outcomes, Deliverables Methodology

1. Manager cascades a commitment to an employee on their team that has multiple deliverables

Manager's Goal plan

Commitment
- Improve product quality and reduce costs created by re-work

Outcomes
- Decrease product defect rate to less than 1 per 10,000 units
- Lower cost per unit manufacturing costs by 5%

Deliverables
- Re-engineer product inspection process
- Hire a process maintenance engineer
- Implement alpha quality training across the manufacturing team
- Re-negotiate vendor contracts to obtain higher quality raw materials

2. The employee translates this into two commitments based on those deliverables that are relevent to his role

Employee's Goal plan

Commitment 1
- Re-engineer product inspection process

Outcomes
- Decrease product defect rate to less than 1 per 10,000 units
- Shorten product inspection time by 5%

Deliverables
- Conduct kaizen workshop with manufacturing team during Q1
- Document and train supervisors on new process by end of Q2

Commitment 2
- Implement alpha quality training across the manufacturing team

Outcomes
- Decrease product defect rate to less than 1 per 10,000 units
- 100% certification of manufacturing team on Alpha quality process

Deliverables
- Develop quality training curriculum
- Arrange for training department to deliver training for all employees by Q2

It often makes sense to use different goal alignment strategies for different parts of the company, for example, using goal cascading with senior leaders, directors. and managers and switching to goal categories or predefined goal plans for lower-level frontline jobs. What is important is to have some method in place to make sure employee goal plans are supporting company strategic initiatives and critical business outcomes. This includes making sure the goals of senior leaders align with the goals of their direct reports' direct reports. In most companies, it is the people two levels or more down from the senior-most leader who comprise the bulk of the employee population. From an execution standpoint, it is not the CEO's strategic goals that matter as much as the goals of people further down in the organization who are ultimately responsible for executing the strategy.

5.3.4 How Is Employee Goal Accomplishment Measured?

If goals were perfectly defined, there would be no reason to discuss measurement of goal accomplishment. Goal accomplishment would be self-evident because you could simply examine a goal and determine whether it was or was not achieved. But the reality is that most goals are not so well defined. For example, if someone had a goal to sell $10,000 worth of product and sold only $9,000, did he totally fail to achieve his goal? Should he be evaluated as performing at the same level as someone who sold only $5,000? Many goals are also associated with less tangible concepts related to quality or performance. For example, if an author has a goal to "complete a three-hundred-page book by September," can we evaluate whether she achieved that goal solely based on the number of pages she wrote? Or should the evaluation include some attempt to assess the quality of what she wrote in addition to examining the absolute number of pages?

Goal-setting methods like SMART and COD help make goals easier to measure and evaluate. This reduces subjectivity when evaluating employees' goal accomplishments. These methods also help employees understand why they received certain evaluations and what they need to do differently to change the evaluation in the future. But there is almost always some subjectivity inherent in judging employee performance as it pertains to goal accomplishment. How goals are evaluated can become a particularly significant point of contention if goals are used to guide pay or promotion decisions. For this reason, a decision should be made early on whether goals can and should be evaluated solely on tangible, objective metrics or whether goal accomplishment will be determined based on some overall rating agreed on by an employee and his or her manager.

Some goals lend themselves to more objective evaluation because they can be easily measured using available metrics—for example, sales goals associated with hitting specific financial targets or manufacturing goals associated with producing specific numbers of products. But goals for many jobs are difficult to measure objectively due to the nature of goals themselves or because an inordinate level of effort would be required to collect truly objective goal data. In these cases, it is good to agree on a standard goal accomplishment rating scale such as the following:

1 = Very poor performance: Failed to meet most or all goal expectations

2 = Poor performance: Met some goal expectations but not all

3 = Effective performance: Met all goal expectations

4 = Exceptional performance: Exceeded goal expectations

Employees should meet with their managers to review their goals and, if possible, reach consensus on the goal accomplishment rating. If agreement cannot be reached, then it is usually the manager who gets to make the final rating. If possible, it is also beneficial to have the manager's evaluation reviewed by his or her supervisor or peers, or both, through some form of performance assessment calibration process.

It is important to set expectations around the goal accomplishment levels most employees will achieve. For example, if the example of the scale above was used to evaluate goal accomplishment, the expectation should be set that most employees will receive 3s assuming they are generally solid performers. The rating of 4 is reserved for employees whose performance truly went above and beyond goal expectations. This will encourage employees to strive for difficult goals without overly punishing them if they fail to accomplish everything they set out to achieve. If someone always succeeds at achieving every goal, then it is questionable whether this person is truly challenging himself or herself.

People are not setting truly difficult goals if they consistently exceed their goal expectations year after year. Yet many companies develop cultures where anything less than 100 percent goal completion is viewed as failure. Companies with cultures like this are unable to differentiate between high-performing employees who set and achieve difficult goals and mediocre employees who set and achieve relatively simple goals. For example, a large consulting company had an unwritten policy where the only way to be promoted was to be rated as having had perfect goal accomplishment. The best way to succeed in this company was to set easy goals and avoid any assignment where success was not almost certain. Employees who set ambitious goals and failed to achieve them might as well leave the organization. Methods for addressing this type of rating inflation are discussed in chapter 6.

It is also useful to set expectations around how frequently employees should update progress against goals. Emphasize to managers that if their employees fail to achieve their goals, then the manager is probably going to struggle to achieve his or her goals as well. If a goal is at risk of not being achieved, it is in the manager's and employee's best interest to discuss it early enough so something can be done to get it back on track before it is due. Employees and managers should update and review goal progress on a fairly regular basis throughout the year. How often this should happen varies depending on the type of job. It requires balancing the manager's need to stay informed with the employee's desire for a sense of autonomy. For hourly sales jobs, this might be something done daily or weekly. For pharmaceutical research positions, this might be done quarterly. Whatever time frame is chosen, you will know the process is working when neither managers nor employees feel any sense of surprise when they meet to discuss whether the employee's goals were achieved.

5.3.5 What Is the Relationship between Goal Accomplishment and Employee Pay, Promotions, and Recognition?

Goals define what people are expected to do in their jobs, so goal accomplishment should naturally play a central role in decisions related to compensation, promotion, and other forms of recognition used to reward and retain employees. Linking pay and promotions to goal accomplishment increases the meaningfulness of goals, reinforces organizational priorities, and creates a more consistent, transparent, and fair process for making personnel decisions. But some risks are associated with tying financial incentives and other tangible rewards to goal accomplishment. The following design principles help reduce these risks when developing pay-for-performance strategies built around goals:

• *Balance goals versus competencies.* Performance can be defined in terms of two dimensions: what you accomplish and how you accomplish it. What you accomplish is measured by goal achievement. How you accomplish it is typically measured through competency evaluations or other ratings of employee job behavior. Pay-for-performance systems should balance goals and competencies when allocating pay decisions. Overemphasizing goals can lead to an unhealthy "ends always justify the means" approach to performance. Employees should not be rewarded for achieving goals if the methods used to achieve them violated company values or involved ethically questionable practices. To manage this risk, many pay-for-performance processes use a roughly equal weighting of goals versus competencies when calculating overall performance levels.

- *Protect the intrinsic motivational value of goals.* Research shows that the goals people pursue voluntarily can become less enjoyable when they are paid to accomplish them. This reflects the difference between doing something because you want to do it and doing something because someone expects you to do it (e.g., the difference between playing music for fun versus playing professionally). This issue tends to be less of a concern in a job setting, since employees naturally expect to be paid for what they do. But if employees are accomplishing certain goals without any specific financial incentives, then attaching financial rewards to these goals might actually decrease their motivation toward achieving them.

- *Define the link between goal accomplishment and pay.* When employees feel that pay decisions are based on clearly defined and consistently applied procedures, they are more likely to accept pay outcomes as fair, even if the decisions do not benefit them personally. This is referred to as procedural justice.[10] The key to creating procedurally just pay strategies is to make sure that goals are clearly measurable and well understood. If employees understand the measures used to determine pay, they are much more likely to accept the results of pay decisions.

- *Encourage challenging goals.* One problem that can result when goals are linked to pay decisions is the potential for employees to avoid setting demanding goals where the outcome is uncertain since they know this could hurt their pay. Pay strategies should support employees who take on challenging goals, even if it means they may not always achieve the goals they set. Do not punish people who are willing to challenge themselves with difficult goals and reward those who play it safe by committing only to easier goals.

- *Encourage teamwork and collaboration.* Using goals to drive pay may encourage some employees to focus on activities that support their personal goals with little concern for the broader goals of their team or organization. It is a good idea to base pay on a mix of individual goals and broader team- or organization-based goals. This helps to create a balance between "what is good for me" versus "what is good for the group."

- *Balance the value placed on financial stability versus financial opportunity.* People differ widely in their preference and tolerance for financial uncertainty. Employees in sales jobs tend to be more comfortable with linking some or all of their pay to goal accomplishment because they are willing to trade the financial stability of a regular salary for the opportunity to make considerably more money by hitting all of their goals. In contrast, many service employees want a more stable source of revenue. They will trade the opportunity to make more money through a goal-based bonus plan for the greater financial stability associated with receiving a fixed salary. It is important to think about the stability preferences of employees before implementing a pay-for-performance strategy. Some association between pay and performance is almost always desirable. But whether the percentage of pay tied to goal attainment should be 5 percent, 50 percent, 100 percent, or some other variable will change from one job to the next. Also remember that what motivates people in leadership roles when it comes to pay may not be the same thing that motivates the people they lead (see the discussion: "Different Types of Goals for Different Types of Roles—We Don't All Want the Same Thing").

- *Emphasize that goals are about a lot more than pay.* If compensation and promotion decisions are communicated as the main reason for goal management, then employees and managers may view goal management solely as a method for evaluating employee performance as opposed to executing business strategies. Managers may look at employee goals only once a year, when it is time to make compensation decisions. And employees may be overly conservative when they set goals if they view them solely as a tool to determine pay or promotion opportunities. If this is happening, you might consider downplaying the link between goal accomplishment and pay and promotion. This does not mean getting rid of the association between goals and personnel decisions completely. Just be clear that people view goal management first and foremost as a tool for driving business strategies and secondarily as a tool to guide and justify compensation and staffing decisions.

DIFFERENT TYPES OF GOALS FOR DIFFERENT TYPES OF ROLES—WE DON'T ALL WANT THE SAME THING

Goals are one of the most powerful methods companies can use to motivate and align employees around strategic initiatives. However, what makes goals meaningful and motivating varies significantly across different types of employees.[a] Each of the following types of goal orientation reflects characteristics that make certain goals more or less motivational for different kinds of people:

- *Purpose driven.* Purpose-driven people value goals that make them feel part of a larger team or mission. They are motivated by goals that illustrate how their work contributes to a greater strategy or vision. They tend to appreciate goals that give them a sense of "being part of something bigger than myself." Health care, environmental, charity, and volunteer organizations tend to be effective at using purpose-driven goals.

- *Mastery driven*. Mastery-driven individuals are motivated by goals that challenge them to develop and test their capabilities. They get satisfaction from proving to themselves and others that they can accomplish difficult goals. Artists, scientists, doctors, and engineers are often strongly motivated by mastery goals that require developing elegant creations and innovative solutions to difficult problems.

- *Competitively driven*. Competitively driven individuals enjoy goals that allow them to compete against other individuals, teams, or organizations. They measure success in part by how well they perform relative to others. Competitive goals are often particularly strong motivators for many athletes, salespeople, and business leaders.

- *Transactionally driven*. Transactionally driven employees focus on goals that are tied to clear benefits and rewards. Most often these are financial bonuses, prizes, promotions, or other rewards with clear monetary value. These people evaluate goals based on the rewards tied to their accomplishment rather than the goal itself. Many people in sales and financial investment positions are strongly transactionally driven.

- *Security driven*. Security-driven individuals value goals that provide them with a sense of role clarity and job stability. They value goals that give them a sense of control and ownership over their future employment prospects ("If I achieve these things, then I can count on future employment and access to certain career opportunities"). Public sector, manufacturing, and certain service industries often attract people who place a lot of value on security-driven goals.

There are positives and negatives to each type of goal orientation. Any one of them taken to an extreme is likely to have negative consequences. For example, overemphasizing transactional goals over mastery goals can lead to focusing solely on money without paying attention to quality. Conversely, overly focusing on mastery goals without value purpose-driven goals can lead to investing time in projects that are intellectually impressive but of little relevance to the overall mission of the organization. Furthermore, no person is solely motivated by any single type of goal. The goals people value can vary depending on the context. For example, a person might be heavily focused on transactional goals at work, but put more emphasis on mastery-driven goals when pursuing personal hobbies.

People who strongly favor one type of goal often seem to mock or scorn people who focus on other goal types. For example, purpose-driven individuals may look down on people who are focused on transactional goals, making comments like, "They care only about cash." Conversely, transactionally driven people may mock purpose-driven or mastery-driven employees by making comments like, "Mission and visions don't pay the bills. Show me the money!" A common mistake of business leaders is to assume that the things that make goals meaningful to managers are the same things that make goals meaningful to their employees.

I believe that no single goal type is inherently better than another. They can all be valuable forms of motivation. What is important is to recognize that a goal's motivation value may be different for different people. Just because a goal is motivating to one employee does not mean it will be equally motivating to another. Part of the art of goal setting is balancing the use of different types of goals in way that maximizes overall workforce productivity.

[a]Button, S. B., Mathieu, J. E., & Zajac, D. M. (1996). Goal orientation in organizational research: A conceptual and empirical foundation. *Organizational Behavior and Human Decision Processes, 67*, 26–48.

Linking goal accomplishment to pay and promotion decisions is critical to maximizing workforce productivity, alignment, and efficiency. But it needs to be done with caution, or it can create unintended and potentially damaging consequences. It is probably not possible to create a perfect pay-for-performance process. But by paying attention to the factors listed above, you can create one that does far more good than harm.

5.3.6 How Are Goals Used to Support Employee Development and Career Growth?

Effective goal setting requires striking a balance between what the company needs to accomplish, what employees can do, and what employees want to get out of their jobs. Pay and promotions are part of this equation. But another powerful and often overlooked way to increase the motivational value of goals is to link them to an employee's career objectives.

One effective method for linking goals to employee career growth is to have managers and employees evaluate goals in terms of organizational value and developmental value. *Organizational value* reflects how important a goal is to the company in terms of key strategic objectives or job requirements. Goals that are low in organizational value may be nice to accomplish but are not critical to the organization. Goals high in organizational value are critical to the organization and may be considered to be the most important part of the person's job.

Developmental value reflects how much a goal requires the employee to learn new things or exposes this person to unfamiliar work environments, problems, or business situations. Goals that have little developmental value are usually things that an employee has done before. They may be mentally complex or time-consuming, but the employee "knows what he or she is doing." Goals with low development value can also be unfamiliar but easy to master. Goals high in development value typically involve things that are unfamiliar to employees and that require them to develop additional skills, acquire new experiences, or work in new areas. This does not mean the employees lack confidence in achieving the goal; rather, in order to achieve it, they will have to acquire new knowledge, skills, and experiences. For example, an employee interested in developing cross-cultural leadership skills might be given a job assignment that requires her to work with customers in different parts of the world. This goal is high in development value because it means working in other countries, which will require this person to build cross-cultural skills.

Figure 5.4 provides an example of a person's work goals plotted based on organizational value and developmental value. The goals are divided into four quadrants: business-driven development, functional, self-focused development, and underutilization.

Business-driven development goals are high in organizational value and high in development value. These are things that employees have to do for work that will require them to gain new experiences and develop new skills. These goals tend to be highly meaningful to employees because they are both important to the company and help them build capabilities to advance their careers. The downside of these goals is that they tend to be mentally demanding. They require learning how to do the work while getting the work done at the same time. People who have too many business-driven development goals risk becoming overwhelmed or burning out:

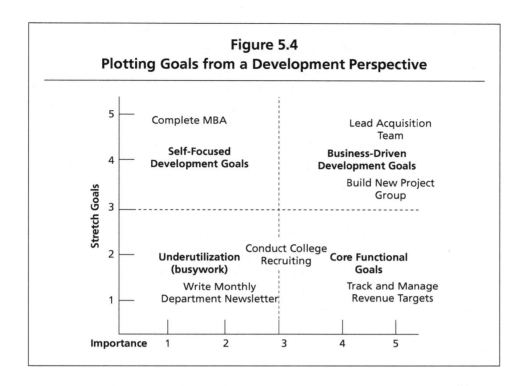

Figure 5.4
Plotting Goals from a Development Perspective

- *Functional goals* are high in organizational value but low in development value. These are things that employees know how to do and have typically done before. They are not necessarily easy, but they are familiar. The advantage of functional goals is they allow employees to contribute to the organization by focusing on important but familiar tasks. The disadvantage is they do not push employees to grow and develop new capabilities. People who have too many functional goals may feel as if they are stuck in a rut, doing the same things over and over.

- *Self-focused development goals* are low in organizational value but high in development value. The advantage of these goals is they allow employees to take developmental risks since failure will not have a major negative impact on the business. The disadvantage is that employees may never get around to these goals since they are not important to the organization. This quadrant is sometimes referred to as the "books I want to read" or "classes I keep hoping to take" section of someone's goal plan.

- *Underutilization goals* are low in both organizational value and developmental value. These may be goals that used to have more value but have become less important or less challenging over time. Underutilization goals provide little value to the company or the employee and should be removed from an employee's goal plan if possible. It may make sense to reassign these goals to other employees who will gain more developmental value from performing them. What may be a relatively unimportant and low-development-value goal for a more tenured employee might be a challenging and important goal for a less-experienced employee.

Based on my experience working with clients, the optimal mix of goals is approximately 40 to 50 percent business-driven development, 40 to 50 percent functional, 10 to 20 percent personal development, and 0 percent underutilization. Assigning goals using this career development mind-set makes goal plans more meaningful to employees because they support their career aspirations. It also avoids motivational problems that can occur when employees feel overwhelmed by too many business-driven development goals, feel stuck in a dead-end job due to too many functional goals, or feel undervalued due to too many self-focused or underutilization goals. Perhaps most important, this goal-setting approach allows the organization to build the capabilities it will need tomorrow through changing how it accomplishes business goals today.

It is important to encourage managers to assign goals with development in mind. Operationally focused managers tend to assign goals to the people they know can achieve them. These managers assign goals based on people's prior experience achieving similar goals. In other words, people are asked to do something because they have done it before. While this makes sense for achieving short-term results, it undermines the power of using goals to drive long-term employee development. Employees grow weary of being asked to perform the same old tasks over and over without being given a chance to demonstrate their ability to do something new.

To maximize the motivational value of goals, managers need to approach goals as a tool for engaging and developing employees, not just for getting work done. Managers should be trained on the concept of mapping employee goals based on organizational value and development value. They should be encouraged to use goal assignments to balance the company's short-term operational needs with employees' longer-term career objectives. The organization might also give managers goals that encourage them to provide their direct reports with developmentally meaningful job assignments (e.g., rewarding managers for building the capabilities of their teams, increasing internal promotion rates, and improving employee engagement and retention).

5.3.7 How Does the Organization Coordinate Goals across Different Employees to Foster Communication and Collaboration?

It is quite common to find that two people in the same organization are working on almost exactly the same goal totally unbeknown to one another. This situation leads to wasted resources, missed opportunities to collaborate, and possible conflicts over "whose work is best." The best way to avoid this problem is to promote communication and collaboration between groups with similar goals by increasing goal visibility, sharing and linking goals, and creating common interest groups and communities.

Increasing Goal Visibility   The most basic step for improving goal coordination is to give employees insight into the goals of other people they work with—for example, by listing employee goal plans on a publicly available intranet system in the company. Employees should be actively encouraged to share and discuss their goals with others so they can benefit from the support and advice of those around them. Employee goal plans should be public unless there is a very clear business or legal reason for keeping them private. Employees should not treat their goals as secrets to be kept from their coworkers.

Even business confidential goals can be shared in a way that does not disclose sensitive information. For example, an employee could share goals related to increasing sales revenue without showing actual revenue targets. This could be done by stating something like, "Hit revenue targets outlined in the strategic operations plan," where the operations plan is a confidential document. Similarly, a vice president of business development could share a goal of "growing market share through successfully completing acquisitions agreed to by the board" without including detailed information about what acquisitions are planned.

Sharing and Linking Goals   Another method to encourage collaboration is to assign one goal to multiple employees or link one employee's goals to the goals of other employees. This encourages employees to work together to achieve goals reflecting common interests. Linked and shared goals can be powerful tools for encouraging collaboration, but they must also be carefully managed or they may create internal tension and resentment among employee groups. Shared and linked goals can pose risks if clear guidelines are not established around how goal performance will be evaluated. For example, how will the organization assign responsibility for failure to achieve a shared goal? Will responsibility be shared equally across all employees, or will some employees be given more responsibility than others?

Creating Common Interest Groups and Communities The development of social technology makes it much easier for companies to bring together groups of employees who share the same or similar sets of goals. For example, I have seen companies create online groups and discussion forums where employees discuss how to achieve goals related to improving customer service, developing new products, or building the companies[1] brand in the market. The employees joining these groups do not share the same exact goals, but are working on different goals tied together by common themes such as customer service, product innovation, or brand awareness. Creating online common interest groups encourages employees to communicate ideas, resources, and advice on how to achieve similar goals. It also creates a sense of camaraderie among employees who are wrestling with the same types of challenges. This approach avoids many of the issues that can arise from shared and linked goals since no assumptions are made around shared goal responsibility. Common interest groups can be particularly powerful in geographically distributed or virtual workforces where employees do not physically work together. By having a group of compatriots to turn to for advice, employees feel a greater sense of support and connection to the company. Organizations may even provide formal rewards and recognition to employees based on the contributions they make to supporting their broader community of colleagues who share common goals.

5.3.8 How Are Goals Used to Guide Business Execution on an Ongoing Basis?

Many organizations view goal setting as an annual or quarterly event. Goals in these companies are typically set at the beginning of the quarter or year and are reviewed only at the end of that time period to make personnel decisions associated with pay and promotions. Goals are rarely reviewed or updated during the year. Such infrequent use of goals significantly limits their value for driving business execution.

To maximize the value of goal management, companies must shift goal management from an administrative process used solely for evaluating employee performance to an operational process used to guide decisions about business execution. This involves creating processes and norms that ensure goals are frequently discussed, reviewed, and updated. Four things are particularly important for making this shift: focus on goal accomplishment instead of employee performance, establish goal-based operational reviews, regularly update goals, and link goals to other business metrics. How these are implemented can vary significantly depending on the type of job and organization. For example, operational reviews typically occur much less frequently in a biomedical research organization than in a call center sales organization. But both organizations need some form of goal-based operational review process if they are to maximize the strategic value of goal management.

Focus on Goal Accomplishment Instead of Employee Performance   Using goals operationally requires shifting the focus of goals from being "something an employee is expected to do" to "something the organization needs to accomplish." Goals should be treated primarily as metrics for measuring company performance and secondarily as measures of employee success. If an employee says, "I'm behind on one of my goals," it should not be immediately interpreted as a sign that the employee is failing to do his or her job. It should be seen as a sign that the company may need to shift resources to get the goal back on track.

Employees will not be comfortable calling attention to goals they are struggling to achieve if they see goals as something that is mainly used to evaluate their personal performance. When an employee says he is not achieving a goal, the initial response from his manager should be, "What can the company do differently to help you succeed?" as opposed to, "What are you failing to do?" This does not mean that goal accomplishment will not affect compensation and promotion status, but compensation and promotion decisions are not the primary reason for using goals. One way to test whether your company is using goals for business execution and not just personnel administration is to ask, "Would goal setting still be important and worthwhile if the company was forced to freeze pay for a year?"

Establish Goal-Based Operation Reviews   The purpose of goals is to define what individual people across the company need to do to execute the organization's overall strategies. Goals should be discussed on an ongoing basis. Operations meetings should include reviewing the goals the group or company needs to achieve, discussing whether they are on track, and exploring how to achieve them more effectively. Goals should also be used to guide decisions about the allocation of scarce organizational resources. If managers want additional resources in terms of finances, technology, head count, or training, they should justify their request by linking it to specific organizational and employee goals.

The simplest way to incorporate goals into operations discussions is to leverage people's goal plans as a tool for guiding operation review meetings. For example, I knew a manager who used weekly operations meetings as an opportunity to publicly discuss the goal plans of direct reports. Each week a different person on the team shared his or her goal plan and reviewed the progress he or she made on different goals. When people know their goals are going to be discussed and reviewed in an open setting on a regular basis, they will put more effort into keeping goal plans updated and ensuring that their performance against goals is on track. The open discussion of goals also keeps the goal management process focused on relationships between people's goals and business needs as opposed to using goals as a way to evaluate each person's individual performance.

Regularly Update Goals   One way to see if a company is using goals to drive business execution is to evaluate how frequently people review and update their goals. Company strategies usually shift somewhat over the course of a year. Most companies modify the tactics they use to accomplish strategies on a quarterly basis, if not more often. If goals are updated only once or twice a year, then it is unlikely they are being used to guide ongoing operational decisions. Similarly, it is important to encourage employees to update and modify goals over the year to reflect changes in their roles, business tactics, or market conditions. Few jobs stay exactly the same over a course of twelve months, and employees should be expected to regularly update and occasionally even change their goals throughout the year. It is important to put some guidelines and review processes in place to ensure people don't game the system by lowering or changing their goals to ensure they have 100 percent goal achievement. But goals should not be seen as something set in stone that can be updated only annually or quarterly. If the company changes its strategy or tactics or an employee changes his or her job role, then these changes should be reflected in people's formal goal plans.

Link Goals to Other Business Metrics   There should be a clear relationship between employees' goals and operational metrics such as profit and loss (P&L)

statements, customer service measures, financial forecasts, and productivity charts. Creating links between goals and operational metrics calls attention to the role that goals play in driving the success of the company. This allows people to see the impact that goal accomplishment has on overall company performance. It also allows leaders to diagnose issues that are affecting performance against key operational metrics. For example, if a company is failing to achieve its revenue targets, is it because the company has not effectively executed its strategy or because the strategy itself is incorrect? In other words, have people failed to accomplish the goals associated with the strategy, or did the goals they set fail to drive the business outcomes the company was expecting?

Goals define what the company has to achieve to be successful. As such, they should be reviewed regularly, discussed openly, tied to key business metrics, and updated throughout the year to reflect shifts in company strategies and tactics. Leveraging goal management as a tool to drive business execution requires making the review and discussion of goals integral to day-to-day actions and decisions taking place within the company. This requires treating goals as important to business operations, and not just as things employees have to do to get a raise or be promoted.

5.4   GOAL MANAGEMENT PROCESS MATURITY

It is remarkable how quickly companies can implement goal management processes when goals are made a priority by senior leadership. I have seen companies go from no standardized goal management process to the implementation of goal plans across over ten thousand employees in less than four months. But creation of goal plans is only the first step toward creating a world-class goal management process. Additional time is required to develop the internal skills and processes required to efficiently cascade and set well-defined goals, effectively manage and update goals throughout the year, and coordinate activities across the company to align efforts to accomplish shared goals. Improving goal management methods can quickly produce rewards associated with increased employee engagement, productivity, and retention. But fully realizing the business execution value of goal management methods requires ongoing efforts lasting multiple years.

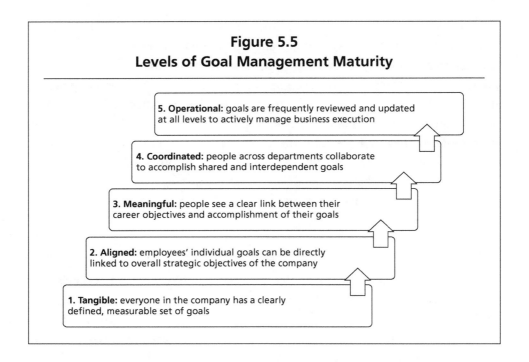

Figure 5.5
Levels of Goal Management Maturity

5. Operational: goals are frequently reviewed and updated at all levels to actively manage business execution

4. Coordinated: people across departments collaborate to accomplish shared and interdependent goals

3. Meaningful: people see a clear link between their career objectives and accomplishment of their goals

2. Aligned: employees' individual goals can be directly linked to overall strategic objectives of the company

1. Tangible: everyone in the company has a clearly defined, measurable set of goals

Figure 5.5 lists five general maturity levels that companies go through as they develop their goal-setting processes. The levels begin with simply having goals and progresses up to using goals as a strategic tool to communicate, monitor, and manage the execution of business strategies.

The first level of maturity focuses on making sure employees have well-defined goals. Do not underestimate the business value of achieving this level. Simply getting managers to sit down with their employees and map out a clear set of goals and expectations is a major leap forward for many organizations. The value of achieving this level was memorably captured in a comment an employee made on an engagement survey conducted shortly after implementation of a new goal management process in a large multinational company: "For the first time in the fourteen years I have been with this company, I actually know what I am supposed to be doing in my job."

Level 2 focuses on ensuring that employees' goals are aligned with the company's overall strategy. This is typically done through some form of goal-cascading process. It can also be achieved through the use of goal categories or standardized goal plans. It is important to focus on creating alignment early in the goal-setting process or the company risks focusing employees on activities that may not fully support the company's overall strategic objectives. Level 3 shifts the focus from setting goals that are important to the company to setting goals that are also meaningful to employees. This involves using methods to ensure that employees see goals as being relevant to their personal career aspirations. The best way to do this is to establish goal plans that integrate business needs and employee development and to tie goal accomplishments to pay and promotion decisions.

Level 4 focuses on building collaboration within the company around common types of goals. It is about breaking down silos and coordinating common efforts across peers and departments. This level is achieved through making goals visible across the organization and providing employees with tools that promote collaboration among employees with similar or common goals.

Level 5 emphasizes getting business leaders to use goal processes as tools for running and managing the business. As one COO put it, "You are using goal management correctly when it ceases to be just a tool for personnel administration and becomes a tool for communicating and evaluating strategies." This level is achieved by reviewing goal progress through the year, using goal metrics to diagnose how well the organization is executing on its strategic objectives, and leveraging goal management processes as a means to quickly update company direction and align the workforce around shifting strategic initiatives.

You do not necessarily need to master lower levels of goal management maturity to reach some of the higher levels. But maturity levels do tend to build on one another somewhat like the stories of a building. The stronger the foundation of the lower stories is, the more stable the higher levels will be. For example, it is difficult to make operational use of goals unless employee goals are tangible and well defined.

Companies also do not need to place equal emphasis on all five maturity levels across all parts of the organization. For example, goal coordination may be more important for some jobs than others. Companies may also differ from one department to the next in terms of the emphasis placed on using formal processes to ensure goal alignment. What is important is to consider what level of goal maturity is most critical to driving business success given a particular organization's business strategies, workforce characteristics, and operational challenges, and then to stay focused on steadily developing and improving goal management methods until that level is achieved.

5.5 CONCLUSION

Goal management is one of the most powerful and most underused tools for driving business execution. This chapter has explained why goals are critical for business execution and provided guidelines for answering critical questions that underlie the design of effective goal management processes. All companies use some form of goal management, but few do it extremely well. Companies that make a concerted effort to fully leverage the value of goals to guide and motivate employee performance tend to outperform and outlast their competition.

NOTES

1. Kleingeld, A., Mierlo, H., & Arends, L. (2013). The Effect of goal setting on group performance: A meta-analysis. *Journal of Applied Psychology*, *96*, 1289–1304.

2. Lee, F. K., Sheldon, K. M., & Turban, D. B. (2003). Personality and the goal striving process: The influence of achievement goal patterns, goal level, and mental focus on performance and enjoyment. *Journal of Applied Psychology*, *88*, 256–265.

3. Gist, M. E. (1986). Self-efficacy: Implications for organizational behavior and human resource management. *Academy of Management Review*, *12*, 472–485.

4. Buckingham, M., & Coffman, C. (1999). *First break all the rules: What the world's greatest managers do differently*. New York: Simon & Schuster.

5. Becker, B. E., & Huselid, M. A. (1998). High performance work systems and firm performance: A synthesis of research and managerial implications. *Personnel and Human Resources Management*, *16*, 53–101. Berggren, E., & Strezo, M. (2011). *How companies leverage business execution software to drive excess shareholder return*. SuccessFactors Research white paper, www.successfactors.com. Bloom, N., & Van Reenen, J. (2007). Measuring and explaining management practices across firms and countries. *Quarterly Journal of Economics*, *122*, 1341–1408.

6. Berggren, E., & Messick, K. (2008). *Moving mountains*. SuccessFactors Research white paper, www.successfactors.com.

7. Crowder, R. G. (1976). *Principles of learning and memory*. San Francisco: W. H. Freeman.

8. Spencer, D. G. (1986). Employee voice and employee retention. *Academy of Management Journal, 29*, 488–502. Wood, S. J., & Wall, T. D. (2007). Work enrichment and employee voice in human resource management-performance studies. *International Journal of Human Resource Management, 18*, 1335–1372.

9. Kaplan R. S., and Norton D. P. (1992, January–February). The balanced scorecard: Measures that drive performance. *Harvard Business Review*, 71–80.

10. Colquitt, J. A. (2001). On the dimensionality of organizational justice: A construct validation of a measure. *Journal of Applied Psychology, 86*(3), 386–400. Colquitt, J. A., Conlon, D. E., Wesson, M. J., Poster, C.O.L., & Ng, K. Y. (2001). Justice at the millennium: A meta-analytic review of 25 years of organizational justice research. *Journal of Applied Psychology, 86*, 425–445.

Doing Things the Right Way

SIX

Using Performance Management to Increase Business Execution

E nsuring that employees are doing the right things the right way is central to driving business execution. This is the primary purpose of performance management, although many performance management processes fail to fulfill this purpose. *Performance management* refers to processes used to communicate job expectations to employees, evaluate employees against those expectations, and use these evaluations to guide talent management decisions related to compensation, staffing, and development. Performance management encompasses a variety of activities, including talent reviews, calibration sessions, pay-for-performance plans, performance feedback, and other methods that measure employees based on the degree to which their actions and accomplishments align with the company's expectations and objectives.

This chapter discusses how to use performance management to increase workforce productivity. There is a reason this chapter is the longest one in this book: designing and deploying effective performance management processes is not easy. It requires addressing highly sensitive topics related to measuring the contributions of individual employees and making decisions about their pay, promotions, and employment. Creating a successful performance management

151

program requires attending to several big picture strategic issues and myriad specific details to ensure that the processes fit the culture and needs of your company.

There is no such thing as a neutral performance management process. People will either like it or dislike it. Many performance management processes are criticized as lacking business impact, creating unnecessary administrative overhead, and negatively affecting employee attitudes. But if done correctly, performance management is a powerful method for creating highly engaged, efficient, and productive workforces. The key to creating an effective performance management process lies in thinking through the questions discussed in this chapter and designing a process that makes the most sense for your company.

The chapter is organized into five sections. Section 6.1 addresses the reasons that performance management is difficult to do well. Section 6.2 discusses the impact of performance management on business performance. Section 6.3 examines how to balance the often conflicting goals of performance management. Section 6.4 addresses seven fundamental questions to consider when designing performance management processes. Section 6.5 explains different levels of performance management process maturity and how to increase performance management effectiveness over time.

6.1 WHY IS PERFORMANCE MANAGEMENT SO DIFFICULT?

Performance management is not a new concept. There are references to it in the Old Testament, and the government of China used documented performance management processes as early as the third century AD.[1] Despite or perhaps because of its longstanding use, performance management is frequently criticized as a process that is neither enjoyable nor effective. A recent Google search on "problems with performance management" returned over 21 million (!) separate entries. Many criticisms level particularly harsh accusations at performance appraisals, the portion of performance management focused on evaluating individual employee contributions. Some critics urge companies to abolish performance appraisals and scrap performance management altogether.

Most extreme condemnations of performance management are misguided (for more discussion, see the discussion: "Why Claims to Abolish Performance Appraisals Are Wrong and Dangerous"). Nevertheless, it is reasonable to ask why people have such negative attitudes toward performance management. It has been around for thousands of years and almost every company uses it. You'd think that by now, we would have figured out how to do it well.

WHY CLAIMS TO ABOLISH PERFORMANCE EVALUATIONS ARE WRONG AND DANGEROUS

Most attempts to achieve weight loss through dieting fail. Does that mean dieting is an ineffective way to lose weight? Should people ignore their diet and just focus on exercise? No, of course not. Many people struggle to follow healthy diets. But just because it's difficult to manage what we eat does not mean we should ignore our diet altogether. This analogy applies to claims that performance evaluations do not work and should be completely eliminated or replaced by processes that rely solely on performance coaching.

Do Performance Evaluation Processes Improve Organizational Performance?

Rigorous empirical research shows that performance evaluation processes work when they are appropriately designed and deployed. Following is a small sample of evidence from researchers who have studied this topic. With the exception of the passage by Eichinger et al., these are from academics who to my knowledge have no financial interest in what sort of talent management process a company chooses to use. Some excerpts are taken from peer review journals and have somewhat confusing language and terminology. But it is important to present these quotes verbatim to emphasize that these are research findings, not my personal opinions.

> A performance management system can make the following important contributions: motivation to perform is increased, self-esteem is increased, managers gain insight about subordinates, the definitions of job and criteria are clarified, self-insight and development are enhanced, administrative actions are fair and appropriate, organizational goals are made clear, employees become more competent, there is better protection from lawsuits, better and

more timely differentiation between good and poor performers, supervisors' view of performance are communicated more clearly, organizational change is facilitated. (Aguinis, 2007 p. 4)

Researchers have begun to try to determine the return on investment of . . . using better selection methods, better training and development, and better performance management applications . . . At this time, the order from most to least is rigorous performance management, then training and development, then selection . . . So the fastest way to improve performance of any unit is to set rigorous performance standards and get rid of those who do not measure up. (Eichinger, Lombardo, & Ulrich, 2006, p. 208)

Results suggested that forced distribution rating systems of the type we simulated could improve the performance potential of the typical organization's workforce and that the great majority of improvement should be expected to occur during the first several years. (Scullen, Bergey, & Aiman-Smith, 2005, p. 24)

The practice evaluation tool [measures the use of] eighteen key management practices . . . The monitoring section focuses on the tracking of performance of individuals, reviewing performance (e.g., through regular appraisals and job plans), and consequence management (e.g., making sure that plans are kept and appropriate sanctions and rewards are in place) . . . Better management practices are strongly associated with superior firm performance in terms of productivity, profitability, Tobin's Q, sales growth, and survival. (Bloom & Van Reenen, 2007, pp. 1361, 1391)

Research shows that a well-designed and well-implemented performance evaluation process is a key part of a high-performance organization. But research also shows that performance evaluation is a double-edged sword:

Some negative consequences associated with low-quality and poorly implemented systems [include] increased turnover, use of misleading information, lowered self-esteem, wasted time and money, damaged relationships, decreased motivation to perform, employee burnout and job dissatisfaction, increased risk of litigation, unjustified demands on managers' resources, varying and unfair standards and ratings, emerging biases, unclear ratings system. (Aguinis, 2007, p. 7)

A well-designed performance evaluation process significantly improves workforce productivity, and a poor process can severely hurt productivity. The key question is not whether to do performance appraisals, but how to do them effectively.

Should We Stop Doing Performance Evaluations Because People Don't Like Them?

Claims that we should do away with performance evaluations because people don't like them are misguided. First, it is misleading to say that people hate performance evaluations. To the contrary, many employees express frustration when their company delays or fails to conduct their performance review. What is more accurate is that people don't like poor performance evaluation processes. This is not the same as not liking any performance evaluation process. Second, just because some people may not like something is not adequate reason to stop doing it. Most people I know don't particularly like going through the financial budgeting process, but that doesn't mean we should stop creating budgets. Whether people like it or not, having a consistent performance evaluation process is critical to effective, efficient, and fair workforce management.

Should Companies Replace Performance Evaluations with Performance Coaching?

Performance evaluations are an important component of an effective performance management system, but they are only one component. Another equally critical component is performance coaching. Companies need both accurate evaluations and effective feedback and development to maximize workforce productivity. Just as you need to focus on both diet and exercise to maximize your health, performance evaluation and performance coaching are two separate but interdependent processes that contribute to workforce productivity. Evaluation gives people feedback on what they need to improve, and coaching provides them with guidance on how to improve it. For example, a manager might give an employee evaluative feedback that his or her e-mail messages are too long and as a result people struggle to interpret them, and then provide coaching suggestions on how to write more succinctly. Each is valuable in different ways, and one should not be used to replace the other. The best results are achieved through using both in a coordinated fashion.

Can performance evaluations be improved? Absolutely! Are many of the performance evaluation processes currently used by companies causing more harm than good? Probably! Should companies invest more energy into creating better performance coaching and dialogue? Without a doubt! But this doesn't mean performance evaluations don't work. Recommendations to eliminate performance evaluations are misguided and harmful. Performance evaluations add tremendous value when they are appropriately designed and implemented. The focus should not be on abolishing them. The focus should be on how to improve their design, use, and impact.

Sources: Aguinis, H. (2007). *Performance management.* Upper Saddle River, NJ: Pearson Prentice Hall. Eichinger, R. W., Lombardo, M. M., & Ulrich, D. (2006). *100 things you need to know: Best people practices for managers and HR.* Minneapolis: Lominger. Scullen, S. E., Bergey, P. K., & Aiman-Smith, L. (2005). Forced distribution rating systems and the improvement of workforce potential. *Personnel Psychology, 58,* 1–32. Bloom, N., & Van Reenen, J. (2007). Measuring and explaining management practices across firms and countries. *Quarterly Journal of Economics, 122,* 1341–1408

Performance management is difficult for two reasons. The first challenge has to do with the basic purpose of performance management. To be effective, performance management must differentiate between more and less effective employees. Deciding whether someone is doing his or her job the right way is an extremely sensitive topic. Rather than explaining the psychological reasons for this, let us do a quick self-reflective exercise. Imagine you were given the following feedback by your boss (for the record, I am not advocating these statements as examples of effectively worded feedback):

a. "You are not getting the job you wanted because we are giving it to a person who is better qualified."

b. "You are not focusing on the things that matter most to this company."

c. "You are not performing your job as well as your coworkers and that's why you are getting paid less than them."

d. "You need to start acting differently if you want to get what you want."

Of these statements, which one would you least like to hear from your supervisor? My guess is they all felt somewhat unpleasant because they all focus on performance weaknesses. Yet all four statements reflect the kinds of comments that may arise from the use of rigorous performance management.

Effective performance management requires dealing with the reality that some employees perform at a higher level than others. Performance management would be easy if everyone performed at the same level, if people never felt insulted or threatened by critical performance reviews, or if they never acted overly entitled because they received a high performance rating. But people do not perform at the same level, and it is important to differentiate employees based on their relative contributions. Similarly, people do react emotionally to performance evaluations, and it is important to ensure that employees do not feel they are losers just because they received a lower performance rating than some of their peers. Performance management requires balancing behavioral feedback with motivational support. People need to understand what they are doing ineffectively in order to change their behavior to do things the right way. They also need to be given recognition, rewards, and respect that instill the desire and confidence needed to build on past successes to achieve even higher levels of performance. This requires providing a mixture of critical yet supportive feedback on past performance, constructive suggestions for increasing future performance, and clarifying consequences and rewards associated with long-term performance accomplishments.

The second major challenge to performance management is that it is expected to do many different things that do not always align well with one another. Performance management programs often mix multiple, conflicting objectives related to coaching, evaluation, compensation, staffing, and development together into a single process. This can lead to processes that don't do any one of those things particularly well. A key to designing effective performance management processes is to clarify exactly what the process is expected to accomplish. Only then can you make appropriate design decisions to ensure that your performance management process does what it is intended to do.

6.2 WHY DO WE NEED PERFORMANCE MANAGEMENT?

Performance management is used to ensure people are performing their jobs in the right way. Every company practices performance management, even if it does not have an official performance management process. Without some form of performance management, a company would simply be hiring people and hoping they did their jobs effectively. The question is not whether your company uses performance management; it is whether your performance management methods are appropriately designed, clearly defined, consistently applied, and effectively used to increase workforce productivity and support business needs.

Research has shown that companies that use rigorous, well-defined performance management processes to evaluate and make decisions about employees tend to be more successful (see the discussion: "Why Claims to Abolish Performance Appraisals Are Both Wrong and Dangerous"). The value of performance management is rooted in one of the most basic laws of psychology: to increase performance, people need feedback on how well their behaviors and accomplishments match the needs of and expectations of the organization. There are many methods for collecting and delivering performance feedback, some more effective than others, depending on the situation. But the overriding principle is that some form of feedback is essential to improving performance.

There are significant risks associated with not having well-designed performance management processes. Companies that lack effective performance management lose top talent because they fail to recognize and reward high-performing employees. They are likely to suffer financial losses resulting from allowing people to perform their jobs in an incompetent or counterproductive manner. In addition, companies that do not use standardized performance management methods to guide pay, promotion, and termination decisions often place themselves at considerable legal risk.[2] Many countries have strict laws governing processes used to hire, pay, promote, and terminate employees. These laws are based on the belief that it is unfair to deny someone his or her economic livelihood without evidence that such action is warranted. Just as many people believe it is unfair to evict someone from his or her home without due cause, many people believe it is unfair to deny someone employment opportunities without justification. Performance management plays a key role in providing the evidence companies need to justify personnel decisions should they be challenged in a court of law.

In sum, performance management helps maximize workforce productivity, minimize costs associated with employee underperformance, and manage risks associated with fair and consistent personnel decisions. Companies need performance management to:

- Increase productivity by ensuring employees are given feedback and incentives that help them learn from experience and motivate them to increase their effectiveness

- Identify and address employee behaviors that may be limiting or damaging organizational productivity and draining organizational resources

- Attract and retain high-performing employees through encouraging, recognizing, and rewarding performance contributions

- Provide a clear, consistent, and defensible set of standards for making decisions that have an impact on employee welfare such as pay and termination

- Comply with legal requirements and cultural expectations related to fair and consistent evaluation of employee contributions

Achieving these results depends on appropriately designed and deployed performance management methods.

6.3 BALANCING THE CONFLICTING GOALS OF PERFORMANCE MANAGEMENT

The single biggest challenge to designing a performance management program is the need to support different activities that don't necessarily align well with each other. These include:

- *Evaluating performance.* This is about accurate measurement of employee behavior and contributions. It requires using well-structured, consistently defined methods to rate employees based on their performance levels. The most accurate performance evaluations are done by people other than the person being evaluated. Most of us simply aren't good at objectively and accurately evaluating our own effectiveness, particularly when it means comparing ourselves to others. This is the reason most companies do not allow employees to evaluate their own performance without some form of manager review.

- *Providing performance feedback* so employees know how well they are performing and understand the gaps they must address to increase their effectiveness.

- *Coaching employees* to increase workforce alignment and productivity. Coaching involves creating dialogue and discussion between managers, employees, and their coworkers. It is best done on an ongoing basis and does not require any formal performance evaluation or rating.

- *Talent management decisions* about staffing, promotions, pay, and terminations that are based in part on employee performance. Companies should invest more in employees who contribute the most to the company's success. Linking pay and staffing decisions to performance strengthens a company's overall workforce. Allocating resources based on performance increases the engagement and retention of high-performing employees, inspires average-performing employees to strive for higher levels of performance, and drives low-performing employees out of the organization.

Supporting all four of these activities through a single performance management process is difficult because it requires balancing competing interests. The most challenging is creating a performance management process that accurately identifies high and low performers while simultaneously giving employees a positive, constructive coaching experience. The goal of sharing performance feedback and coaching employees can directly conflict with the goal of evaluating performance. In fact, the accuracy of manager evaluations of performance often improves if the evaluations are never shared with employees.[3]

A recurring theme in this chapter is finding ways to balance the need to have accurate measures of performance that compare employees against one another with the desire to create nonthreatening coaching dialogues between employees and managers that emphasizes development over evaluation. The best way to do this is to approach performance management as a series of interconnected subprocesses. One subprocess focuses on evaluating employees as accurately as possible, while another focuses on providing employees with performance coaching and feedback to support development. A third part focuses on using performance data to guide how the company invests its financial resources in terms of staffing and compensation decisions. The methods used to support employee coaching and feedback should not be totally independent of methods used to guide employee evaluation, pay, and staffing decisions. But there are times when steps supporting one performance management objective should be clearly and intentionally conducted separately from steps supporting a different objective.

6.4 CRITICAL PERFORMANCE MANAGEMENT DESIGN QUESTIONS

There is no one best way to do performance management. What works well for a regional health care organization might be inefficient for a multinational software company. Processes appropriate for frontline hourly retail employees would be totally ineffective for senior executives. Organizations with rapidly growing workforces and expanding markets may need different methods from organizations with aging workforces or shrinking profit margins. Fully leveraging the power of performance management requires designing a process that makes the most sense given your particular business needs, organizational culture, employee population, and resource constraints. The reason many companies struggle with performance management is they haven't put enough time in critically thinking through key process design questions. Creating the right performance management process requires spending time thinking about what "right" looks like for your company.

The following questions are central to the design of effective performance management processes:

1. What are the primary objectives of your performance management process?

2. How do you define effective performance?

3. How will you evaluate performance?

4. How will you calibrate performance?

5. How are data from performance evaluations used? What is the relationship of performance evaluations, pay, promotions, development, and workforce management?

6. How frequently do you measure performance? How does performance management fit into your broader business cycle?

7. What training and incentives do managers and employees need to effectively use performance management processes?

The answers to these questions depend on your company's particular business strategies, the nature of its workforce, and its current talent management processes. The answers vary considerably from organization to organization. Failure to adequately address any of the questions can result in a suboptimal performance management process. With that in mind, let's take a more detailed look at each question.

6.4.1 What Are the Primary Objectives of Your Performance Management Process?

Developing an effective performance management process requires balancing different and potentially conflicting objectives (see the discussion: "Evaluating Performance for Classification versus Development"). Methods that strongly emphasize identifying high and low performers can hurt efforts to support the development of individual employees. Performance management processes designed solely to comply with legal regulations associated with pay, promotion, and termination decisions may have little impact on employee behavior or development. Performance management processes that provide rich, behaviorally descriptive data to support performance coaching can have little value for guiding pay for performance decisions.

EVALUATING PERFORMANCE FOR CLASSIFICATION VERSUS DEVELOPMENT

Figure 6.1 illustrates a conflict that is central to performance management design. This conflict is rooted in the desire to use performance management processes for two related but somewhat conflicting goals:

- *Classification:* Assessing employee performance to support decisions about where to invest scarce resources such as pay, promotions, or limited development opportunities (e.g., job assignments, expensive training courses)

- *Development:* Assessing employee performance to provide coaching feedback and advice to increase effectiveness

Both objectives require evaluating employee job performance. But how employees should be evaluated is different depending on whether

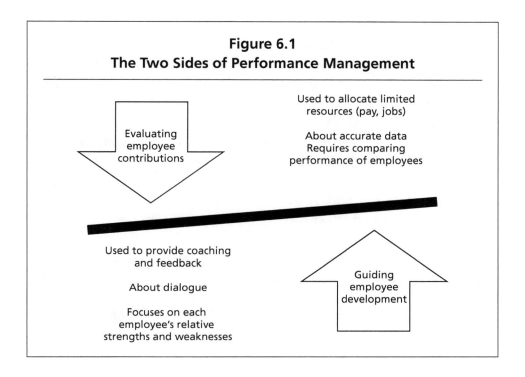

Figure 6.1
The Two Sides of Performance Management

Evaluating employee contributions

Used to allocate limited resources (pay, jobs)

About accurate data
Requires comparing performance of employees

Used to provide coaching and feedback

About dialogue

Focuses on each employee's relative strengths and weaknesses

Guiding employee development

the focus is on classification or development. Classification decisions compare employees against one another to determine which employees deserve higher pay raises, development resources, or promotion opportunities. This requires recognizing that certain employees perform at a higher level than others. Performance evaluation methods that are effective for classifying employees use ratings, calibration, and expected performance distributions to identify differences in performance levels among employees.

Developmental assessments are about letting employees know what they can do to be more successful. Performance evaluations used for development focus on helping employees understand their personal strengths and weaknesses to determine the best way to increase their individual effectiveness. Rather than comparing employees to identify the "best performer," these evaluations emphasize differences within each employee. They may provide descriptions of employee behaviors with no overall evaluative information at all (e.g., "You have bias for action but may not spend enough time on planning"). These assessments are useful for development but provide no information about whether one employee is better than another. For example, knowing that the weakest part of my golf game is driving and the weakest part of my colleague's golf game is putting does not tell you whether I am a better golfer than my colleague. But it does tell both of us how we can get better at the game.

Performance management methods that stress development tend to avoid normative evaluations like ratings and rankings that directly compare people to one another. There is evidence that normative evaluations of performance can actually hurt development.[a] They may cause some employees to give up rather than try to compete against their peers, create infighting among coworkers, and lead to a sense of entitlement for employees who are identified as the best. But purely descriptive, developmental evaluations will not help companies that are seeking to create fair, consistent, and accurate methods to categorize high or low performers for the purpose of compensation, development, or staffing.

It does not make sense to argue whether classification is more or less important than development. Companies must both evaluate and develop employees to create a high-performance culture. The key is to build a performance management process that effectively balances both needs. This can be illustrated using an example from coaching youth sports. Imagine you are coaching a basketball team of twelve-year-old kids. During practice, you constantly evaluate the performance of the players to provide encouragement on what they are doing well and give tips on how they could improve their game—for example, "You're doing a great job running down the court, but you need to use the backboard when shooting the ball."

Good coaching feedback is highly descriptive and focuses on each person's strengths and weaknesses relative to his or her own performance. It also downplays or completely avoids comparing players to one another. A good youth basketball coach is unlikely to tell a player, "You're the worst shooter on the team." Even if it is true, such a statement is not going to help the child become a better player. In fact, it is more likely to make him or her give up completely.

Now imagine you are asked to select your five best players for an all-star team. Your player evaluations will shift from a focus on development to a focus on classification. You want to identify the best players. You may start talking with your fellow coaches about who is the best shot, who is fastest, and who is the best all-around athlete. If you are a good coach, you will not share these evaluations with the players. If a player who did not make the all-star team asks why, you might tell him or her specific things needed to improve, but you are not going to tell this player that he or she was the worst player to try out. It is one thing to tell a player, "The best way to make the team next year is to work on your speed." It is quite another to say, "You are slower than your teammates so that's why we didn't pick you."

This example illustrates a fundamental dilemma of performance management. How can you create a process that supports coaching players while also providing the data needed to make accurate decisions around who should be on the all-star team? Start with an understanding that there are two basic types of performance assessments: assessments for classification and assessments for development. Managers use both types of assessments to evaluate performance, but there is a time to use one and a time for another. Success lies in knowing when and how to use them.

[a]Dweck, C. S. (1990). Self-theories and goals: Their roles in motivation, personality, and development. In *The Nebraska Symposium on Motivation, 1990* (pp. 199–235). Lincoln: University of Nebraska Press. Roch, S. G., Sternburgh, A. M., & Caputo, P. M. (2007). Absolute vs. relative performance rating formats: Implications for fairness and organizational justice. *International Journal of Selection and Assessment, 15,* 302–316.

There are two keys to balancing the elements of performance management design:

1. Prioritize the objectives you want to support through the process, and make process decisions with these objectives in mind.

2. Recognize that processes that support one objective may have a negative impact on another, and modify your process design decisions accordingly.

Table 6.1 illustrates trade-offs associated with performance management process design. No performance management process can support every objective in the table equally well. If you want to increase alignment, you need to sacrifice efficiency. If you want to maximize efficiency, you need to make sacrifices to productivity, alignment, or scalability. The art of performance management design lies in balancing these trade-offs based on your organization's business needs. This starts by ordering the goals of your performance management process from most to least important. Is the purpose of performance management to improve identification of high performers, support pay decisions, guide staffing and succession decisions, create coaching dialogue, support career development, ensure legal compliance, or something else entirely? How you answer this question will influence how you answer more-detailed performance management design questions.

Table 6.1
Performance Management Process Objectives, Elements, and Trade-Offs

Business Execution Driver: "If you want to increase . . . "	Element: " . . . then emphasize . . ."	Trade-off: " . . . but this may have a negative impact on . . ."
Alignment around common goals and strategies	Processes for setting, cascading, and aligning goals Highly detailed competency models that provide clear behavioral definitions of performance for different roles	Process efficiency by adding time to the goal-setting process and increasing the complexity of performance appraisals
Productivity by maximizing individual performance	Rigorously evaluating employees against well-defined standards Calibration methods that compare employees to one another Differentiating high from average and low performers through pay, promotion, staffing, and development decisions Rigorous use of performance improvement processes to manage out underperformers	Process efficiency by adding time to the evaluation process Scalability and sustainability unless care is taken to also collect developmentally valuable performance data Governance by increasing risk of complaints about unfair pay and performance decisions

Business Execution Driver: "If you want to increase . . . "	Element: " . . . then emphasize . . ."	Trade-off: ". . . but this may have a negative impact on . . ."
Efficiency by streamlining processes	Short, targeted definitions of performance Minimal use of second-level reviews and peer input Eliminating requirements related to ongoing evaluations or providing developmental feedback	Alignment by decreasing the information contained in performance definitions Productivity by decreasing the rigor and accuracy of performance evaluations Scalability and sustainability by removing developmental content and activities from the process
Scalability and sustainability by retaining and developing employees	Behaviorally descriptive competency models that define different levels of performance Assigning business goals to employees based in part on developmental needs Collection of qualitative, descriptive performance data Extensive opportunities to create employee-manager dialogue	Process efficiency by adding length and complexity to the performance management process Productivity unless efforts are made to also collect rigorous evaluations that compare performance across employees
Governance by instituting standardized evaluation processes	Simple, standardized, and easy-to-follow performance methods Clear definitions of effective and ineffective performance Clear links between performance management data and pay and promotion decisions	Scalability and sustainability by decreasing the emphasis on collecting qualitative behavioral performance data Productivity if managers are not allowed to significantly differentiate between employee pay and promotion decisions based on performance

6.4.2 How Do You Define Effective Performance?

Performance is often treated like "socially appropriate humor": everyone assumes we know what it is, but each person defines it in his or her own way, and we often have vastly different concepts of what it looks like. For the purposes of this chapter, performance will be broadly defined as "the degree to which an employee meets or exceeds the expectations of the organization given his or her role in the company." Most companies would accept this as a reasonable definition of performance, but it still leaves a lot of ambiguity around what employees must actually do to display effective performance.

Good performance management processes create a clear definition of effective performance across the company. This is a hallmark of high-performance cultures. In a high-performance culture, no one has to ask if someone's performance is effective: the criteria are clear and obvious to everyone. Consider environments like the Olympics or Navy SEAL training. People in these environments know what they are expected to do. There are few arguments over whether a person succeeded or failed to meet expectations. Performance in most organizations cannot be defined with the level of clarity that can be found in sporting events or military training, but companies can vastly improve performance clarity through more effective performance management.

Defining Performance Based on Goals, Competencies, and Skills Most companies define performance using some combination of the following criteria:

- Achieving goals: whether people accomplished the objectives assigned to them

- Demonstrating competencies: whether people display behaviors expected of those in their role

- Building skills: acquisition of knowledge, experience, and expertise associated with their role

These three criteria correspond to the core elements of an integrated strategic HR system: what you accomplish on the job (goals) is a function of how you act (competencies), which depends in part on who you are (skills and other attributes). Creating clear definitions of performance starts with ensuring that managers understand the differences between goals, competencies, and skills. Most managers are fairly good at identifying goals, but it is common to confuse the difference between skills and competencies. Part of performance management includes training managers and employees to understand why it is important to treat skills and competencies as related but separate concepts (see the discussion: "The Importance of Clear Performance Definitions: Comparing Competencies and Skills").

THE IMPORTANCE OF CLEAR PERFORMANCE DEFINITIONS: COMPARING COMPETENCIES AND SKILLS

People often discuss employee performance using very vague terms like "passion," "team spirit," or "a player." Many of these terms sound emotionally powerful but lack any common, agreed-on meaning. Managers who discuss performance using these sorts of terms are likely to frustrate employees. There is nothing motivating about being told to "work smarter, not harder" or "give 110 percent." All it does is tell people that they are doing something wrong without giving them any insight into what they should be doing instead.

Effective performance management requires that managers and employees talk about performance using clear, well-defined language. This includes understanding the differences between employee competencies and employee skills. Table 6.2 lists ways that competencies and skills differ from one another. Skills reflect knowledge and capabilities that people acquire through formal education or on-the-job training and experience. Skills determine what you know how to do. Competencies reflect how you use that knowledge to get things done. Competencies describe categories of employee behavior that drive success within a job or work environment. Competencies, like behavior, are not something employees "have." They are things an employee displays or has displayed. The concept of competencies calls attention to the influence that employee behavior has on job success. It reinforces the fact that job performance is a result of many behaviors, and there are many ways to succeed and fail in a job.

One way to test if you are talking about a competency versus a skill is to consider if someone would ever say, "I don't know how to do that." People are willing to admit to not having different skills. In

Table 6.2
Comparing Skills and Competencies

Skills	Competencies
Knowledge and experience required for jobs such as "HTML programming," "employment law," or "postmerger integration"	Behavioral categories that influence job performance such as "building relationships," "managing stress," or "planning and organizing"
People know or don't know skills	People are effective or ineffective at competencies
Over 1,000 skills are needed to describe the jobs in most large companies	Fewer than one hundred competencies can describe the jobs in most large companies
Skills needed for jobs can change significantly as new ones are created and others become outdated	Competencies associated with jobs tend to stay the same over time; they do not change much
Skills are developed through a mix of formal training, education, and experience	Competencies are primarily developed as a result of on-the-job learning
People can assess their own skills if given clear definitions for proficiency levels	People struggle to assess their own effectiveness with regard to competencies

contrast, they may admit to being less effective at different competencies, but it is unlikely for someone to say that he or she simply does not have the knowledge or experience a competency requires. For example, you can imagine someone saying, "I don't know how to use Excel," but it is hard to imagine someone saying, "I don't know how to build relationships."

The distinction between competencies and skills is important because methods used to assess and develop competencies are much different from methods used to assess and develop skills. Employees may have skills associated with certain competencies, but you can never know if an employee will actually display a competency until you observe that person in a job. Skills can be evaluated to some degree by observing on-the-job behavior, but they can also be evaluated using standardized tests or job simulation exercises. Competencies are primarily developed through providing people with job experiences that increase their self-awareness and self-management with regard to behaviors related to the competency. In contrast, skills can be effectively developed through providing people with formal training, instruction, and education. Training methods that effectively develop employee skills often fail when used to develop employee competencies.

Making managers and employees aware of the difference between competencies and skills can significantly improve the quality of performance conversations. Managers will be able to more accurately evaluate employee performance and provide more meaningful coaching advice to employees. Employees will better understand what is required to act on this advice.

When designing a performance management process, it is necessary to decide how much emphasis to place on goals, competencies, and skills when evaluating employees. Most companies define performance as a balance of goals and competencies and do not put any direct emphasis on skills. For example, 50 percent of an employee's overall performance evaluation will depend on whether he or she has achieved his or her goals and 50 percent on the degree to which he or she has displayed key job competencies. This ensures that people are evaluated based on what they accomplished (goals) and how they accomplished it (competencies). By balancing these two concepts, companies seek to ensure that performance is about doing the right things the right way.

Some companies place more emphasis on goals than competencies since results are felt to be more valuable than behaviors (e.g., 70 percent weighting of goals versus 30 percent weighting of competencies). The decision to emphasize goals more than competencies can reflect the company culture and the nature of the job. For example, many sales and manufacturing jobs strongly emphasize goals because these jobs can be linked to clear and measurable outcomes. Some companies believe that employee performance should be based more on goals since they have a more direct impact on business results. Even if goals are weighted more heavily than competencies, it is useful to always put some weight on competencies to ensure that employees carry out their jobs in a way that supports the company's norms and values.

Companies have developed performance management processes that base employee evaluations entirely on goal accomplishment. But this is risky because it can create a culture that rewards employees for "doing the right things the wrong way." One of the most famous examples of this comes from the energy trading company Enron, one of the fastest-growing companies in the late 1990s. The company built a culture based on hiring ambitious and intellectually talented individuals, giving them challenging goals tied to significant financial rewards, and then evaluating and promoting them almost solely on their ability to achieve these goals. Over time the company developed a culture where the only thing that mattered was hitting financial targets, regardless of whether the methods used to achieve them might be ethically questionable. A famous example was a recording of Enron employees intentionally causing power shortages in California in order to boost up the cost of energy. This focus on "hit the numbers and nothing else matters" worked for many years but eventually led to major scandals, criminal investigations, bankruptcy, and the dissolution of the organization.

Another benefit of using competencies for evaluating performance is they tend to be relatively consistent across situations and over time. Competencies that are important for one job are usually important for other jobs as well. If a competency is important this year, it will probably be important several years from now. For example, if a competency like "planning and organizing" is important in one job, then it is probably important in other jobs and is likely to continue to be important over time. This makes competencies useful for predicting long-term employee performance and assessing employee potential to perform other roles. In contrast, goals change considerably from one job to another and from one year to the next. If a goal was important this year or in this job, that does not mean it will be important next year or in another job. Another advantage of including competencies in performance management is the role they play in employee development by providing language to support effective coaching conversations (see the discussion: "The Role of Competencies in Performance Management").

Most companies exclude skills from the performance evaluation based on a belief that performance is defined by what you accomplish and how you act, not what you know. Performance may be influenced by the skills you have, but actual performance depends entirely on how you apply your skills to achieve job goals. However, there are some positions where it may make sense to explicitly include skills as an element of the performance definition. These are jobs where employees must demonstrate skill proficiency to be qualified for certain functions—for example, insurance sales jobs where people must pass licensing certifications to sell specific products, or health care jobs where employees are legally required to demonstrate certain knowledge and skill qualifications. Companies might also use skills as part of the performance evaluation if they are trying to encourage employees to build their capabilities for future roles and job demands. When skills are used to measure performance evaluation, they tend to be weighted much less than goals and competencies (e.g., basing 10 percent to 25 percent of an employee's overall evaluation on skills proficiency).

THE ROLE OF COMPETENCIES IN PERFORMANCE MANAGEMENT

Competencies define behaviors that employees are expected to display in a job or company. Assessing performance based on competencies provides detailed information about a person's effectiveness in his or her job. Because the best predictor of future behavior is past behavior, measuring competencies also provides insight into what employees are likely to do in the future in either the same job or a new role. Competencies also help create more effective dialogue between managers and employees in these ways:

- Clarifying the behaviors that define what it means to be a high performer

- Illustrating the values of the company in observable behavioral terms

- Giving employees specific feedback on behaviors they need to "start doing" or "stop doing" to be more productive

- Defining the different behavioral requirements between an employee's current role and other jobs he or she may be interested in pursuing

Competencies are particularly valuable for coaching employees. Managers tend to describe employee performance in terms of goals they have achieved or using broad adjectives or adverbs about their attributes. For example, managers will talk about employees being "top performers," "the A players," "problem cases," or "people who don't have what it takes." These terms may mean something to the manager, but they are highly subjective and provide little useful information to guide employee development and performance. Competencies help managers become better coaches by giving them descriptive behavioral language to support performance management discussions. This enables managers to provide employees with specific guidance around what behaviors they can "do more of" or "do less of" to increase their effectiveness.

To illustrate the value of competencies in the context of coaching, consider this exchange between a manager and his employee before and after the introduction of competencies into the conversation:

Manager: You aren't hitting your goals

Employee (to himself): Thanks for telling me something I already knew.

Employee (to manager): Any suggestions on how I can be more successful?

Manager: You need to work smarter, not harder.

Employee (to himself): So I'm a failure because I haven't hit my goals, and I'm an idiot because I don't work smarter, whatever that is.

Employee (to manager): Is there anything I can do differently to be more successful?

Manager [now using competencies]: I suggest you get some training on planning and organizing your territory so you can spend more time building relationships with customers.

Employee (to himself): Finally, some feedback that makes sense and doesn't just make me feel bad. Now I know how I should change my behavior to be more successful.

This example is not that far off from conversations managers and employees have every year during performance reviews. The tone and results of these conversations can be quickly and vastly improved by incorporating competencies into the discussion.

Building Competency Models The first step in defining performance is deciding on the emphasis to place on goals, competencies, and skills for different roles in your organization. The next step is to determine what specific goals, competencies, and skills are relevant for each job. Because competencies play a particularly critical role in performance management, we will spend some time discussing competency modeling techniques. (For information on how to define job goals and job skills see the discussion in chapters 4 and 5 on how to get the right people [skills] and focus them on the right things [goals].)

A competency model is a predefined set of competencies that describe behaviors that drive performance for a specific job, group of jobs, or organization. Competency models focus on critical behaviors that make or break performance. Competency models should not list every behavior employees must display to be effective. They should highlight behaviors that distinguish high performers from average or low performers. As one HR manager told me, "Competency models highlight the differences between employees that make a difference."

Here are some questions to address:

• *What does a well-defined competency look like?* Figure 6.2 provides an example of a well-defined competency. The title of the competency in figure 6.2 is "Supporting Change." Supporting change could mean a lot of different things to different people. What makes the competency in the figure useful is not its title but the behavioral anchors that define effective and ineffective performance. Based on the competency in figure 6.2, employees who are effective at supporting change do things like "enthusiastically participate in new change initiatives and programs" and "abandon outdated or obsolete practices." These behavioral descriptions help managers and employees reach agreement on what "effective" looks like with regard to this competency. Employees who are good at supporting change consistently display the positive behaviors and rarely display the negative behaviors listed in the figure. Figure 6.2 is just an example of one way this competency might be defined. Other companies might define "supporting change" using different behaviors, or they might use an entirely different competency. What is important is ensuring that competencies are defined using observable, job-relevant behaviors. These behaviors are things that people could be asked to "stop" or "start" doing.

Appendix A contains a library of competencies that can be used to build competency models. This library is based on research studying behaviors that influence job performance across a wide range of jobs. Competency libraries provide an efficient way to build performance definitions. Rather than developing new competencies, companies can select content from competency libraries to quickly configure competency models that make sense for their particular jobs. No single job requires all of the competencies listed in appendix A. However, the library is likely to contain the competencies that make or break performance in most jobs and organizations.

Clearly defined behavioral competencies provide several advantages for performance management. First, they communicate what people are expected to do (or not do) in their jobs. Second, they provide a set of criteria to assess performance, which helps create more consistent performance evaluations across managers. Third, competency definitions contain content that managers can use to provide constructive behavioral feedback to support employee coaching. To achieve these benefits, competency descriptions must include observable behaviors and should avoid subjective adjectives or adverbs whose interpretation might vary across people.

Figure 6.2
What a Well-Defined Competency Looks Like

Supporting Change
Enthusiastically participates in new change initiatives and programs; focuses on reasons that changes will work and how they will be beneficial

Negative Behavioral Anchors	Positive Behavioral Anchors
• Views changes as ineffective or unnecessary	• Embraces and encourages new ideas and initiatives
• Demonstrates resistance toward change; clings to existing methods and practices	• Looks for positive aspects of changes; focuses on reasons that changes will work and how they will be beneficial
• Focuses on reasons that changes will not work	• Enthusiastically participates in new change initiativies and programs
• Views change from perspective of how they will "take things away" or otherwise be unfair	• Abandons outdated or obsolete practices; willing to try new things

• *How many competencies should be in a competency model?* It is ideal to limit competency models to between five and ten competencies. Models with more than ten competencies are difficult and cumbersome to use. It takes managers too long to evaluate performance using so many competencies. Conversely, models containing fewer than five competencies are likely to overlook key dimensions of job performance or may contain competencies that are so broadly defined they lack clear meaning.

• *How many competency models does my company need?* Some companies use the same competency model for every job in the organization. Others build different models for specific jobs and functions. Using job-specific models makes it possible to more accurately describe performance for different roles. Using a smaller set of generalized competency models makes it possible to compare the performance of employees across different jobs. It is also easier to build and manage a few general models as opposed to creating and maintaining multiple job-specific models.

Figure 6.3 shows an approach for balancing the trade-off between job-specific versus generalized competency models. This approach breaks competencies into three categories:

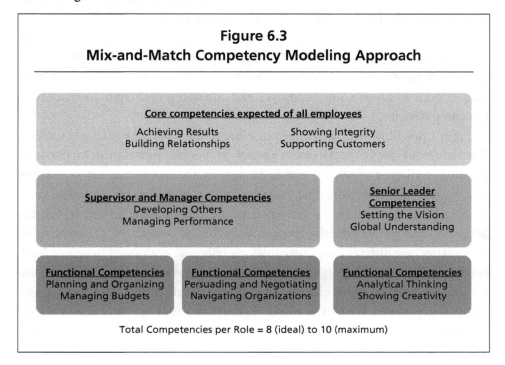

Figure 6.3
Mix-and-Match Competency Modeling Approach

Core competencies expected of all employees
Achieving Results   Showing Integrity
Building Relationships   Supporting Customers

Supervisor and Manager Competencies
Developing Others
Managing Performance

Senior Leader Competencies
Setting the Vision
Global Understanding

Functional Competencies
Planning and Organizing
Managing Budgets

Functional Competencies
Persuading and Negotiating
Navigating Organizations

Functional Competencies
Analytical Thinking
Showing Creativity

Total Competencies per Role = 8 (ideal) to 10 (maximum)

- *Core competencies* expected of all employees regardless of their position. These are competencies that drive success across the organization and reflect core company values.
- *Level-specific competencies* that influence performance in jobs with different levels of responsibility (e.g., individual contributor, manager, senior director, executive).
- *Functional competencies* that influence performance for jobs in certain areas of the company (e.g., finance, sales, human resources).

Some companies evaluate all employees on the same set of core competencies and do not create level-specific or functional competencies. Other companies create different models for different job levels or job functions. For example, many companies have a competency model for individual contributors, a model for managers, and another model for executives.

Another approach is to mix and match competencies across job categories. The competency model for a specific job might include three to five core competencies, two or three level-specific competencies, and one or two functional competencies. The mixing and matching approach allows companies to keep the total number of competencies to a manageable number. It also captures similarities across different types of jobs while providing flexibility to ensure performance definitions capture critical level or functional specific competencies. If you choose to use this mix-and-match approach, be sure to do it in a way so no employee ends up being evaluated on more than ten competencies.

Figure 6.4 illustrates a competency modeling approach that shows how the nature of job expectations changes as people move into higher-level positions. All employees are evaluated against the same core set of competencies, but the behaviors that define effective performance for each competency shift depending on the job level. In the example in figure 6.4, the behaviors that define effective performance for the competency "Encouraging Innovation" are different for individual contributors compared to senior leaders. Individual contributors are expected to accept change, while senior leaders are expected to drive change. This approach lets a company use a single competency model across the whole organization that captures different performance expectations based on job level. It also helps employees understand

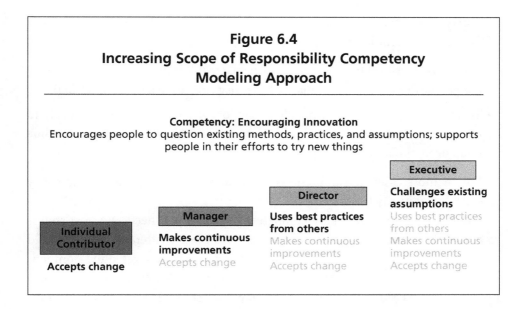

Figure 6.4
Increasing Scope of Responsibility Competency
Modeling Approach

Competency: Encouraging Innovation
Encourages people to question existing methods, practices, and assumptions; supports people in their efforts to try new things

Executive
Challenges existing assumptions
Uses best practices from others
Makes continuous improvements
Accepts change

Director
Uses best practices from others
Makes continuous improvements
Accepts change

Manager
Makes continuous improvements
Accepts change

Individual Contributor
Accepts change

how job expectations change as people move into positions with higher levels of responsibility.

The approaches in figures 6.3 and 6.4 are both effective for developing competency models. Which one is preferable depends on the nature of your organization and the goals you are seeking to achieve through performance management. If your primary goal is to accurately evaluate performance of people in their current roles, the more job-specific approach in figure 6.4 may be more useful. If you want to encourage career advancement, the multilevel approach in figure 6.5 may be more effective.

Companies can also build job-specific competency models that are relevant to only one type of job—for example, creating a unique competency model for "field repair technician" and a totally different model for "product sales representative." Job-specific competency models can provide highly detailed descriptions of behaviors that influence performance in specific roles. This makes them very effective for accurately evaluating current job performance and providing detailed coaching feedback. The problem with job-specific competency models is they take a lot of time to create, do not support comparing employees across jobs since each job has different competencies, and can be difficult to maintain.

It may make sense to build job-specific competency models when one or both of the following conditions exist:

- The job is so critical to business performance that it is important to make finely grained distinctions in performance levels (e.g., nurses in a hospital setting).
- There are large numbers of people in the job, and most of them are likely to remain in this same role during their tenure with the company (e.g., frontline retail or manufacturing jobs).

But in most cases, the limitations associated with job-specific competency models do not justify the benefits.

Once you decide how many competency models you need, the next step is to create the actual models. Entire books have been written on how to build competency models.[4] Competency modeling projects can get quite complex, often lasting several months. But companies have also built effective competency models through a single one-day workshop. These workshops take subject matter experts through a structured process to select the appropriate competencies from competency libraries such as the one in appendix A. What competency modeling approach to use depends on factors such as the size of your organization, the goals of your performance management process, and the limits of your budget. Whatever approach you use, make sure the final competency models provide clear, relevant, and meaningful behavioral descriptions of what "effective" and "ineffective" performance looks like for jobs in your company (see the discussion: "The Devil Is Often in the Details in Building Competency Models").

THE DEVIL IS OFTEN IN THE DETAILS IN BUILDING COMPETENCY MODELS

Competency models are critical for performance management because they provide clear, behaviorally based descriptions clarifying the difference among effective, average, and ineffective job performance. These models communicate the behaviors that employees are expected to display and provide managers with a standardized vocabulary for discussing, evaluating, and coaching employee performance. Because the best predictor of future behavior is past behavior, competency models also give organizations a useful benchmark to assess employee potential to take on future job roles and assignments.

Creating competency models has become fairly easy due to the development of standardized competency libraries. Rather than developing new competency descriptions, companies simply pick and choose from competency libraries to build competency models that highlight key behaviors that are important to success in a certain job or set of jobs. Many companies go one step further by modifying the standardized content from preexisting libraries to create tailored competency models that include language reflecting the unique culture and nature of their organization.

Considerable advantages can be gained from using competency libraries to build competency models. However, problems can also arise from this approach. Following are four common problems associated with building competency models and guidance on how to manage them:

- *Missing the mark*. This happens when competency models fail to capture key behaviors important to performance. It can be the result of not having the right subject matter experts involved in building the model or when companies focus too much on defining what effective performance looks like but do not pay adequate attention to the behaviors that limit or derail success. I saw an example of this when developing a competency model for a sales job. Much attention was paid to the behaviors that made high performers successful. Then a veteran manager noted that one of the main sources of performance problems was a failure to complete administrative tasks to support sales forecasts and process contracts. As he said, "It doesn't matter how good they are at building relationships if they don't file the contract before the end of the quarter." His comments emphasized that poor performance is not just the opposite of effective performance. In fact, sometimes poor performance is a result of overusing performance strengths (e.g., the person who is too assertive in his or her efforts to drive results). The best way to avoid missing the mark is to have the right mix of subject matter experts in the room and make sure they look at both effective and ineffective performers when identifying competencies.

- *The kitchen sink.* This happens when companies are unwilling to prioritize what competencies are the most critical for performance. Rather than identifying a few well-defined competencies, they create vague or extremely heterogeneous competencies that contain so many different types of behaviors that no employee could possibly be good at all of them. A single competency may even contain behaviors that contradict each other. I have seen models with competencies like, "Getting things done: focuses on the big things but also manages the details and little things." This sort of competency does not give managers clear, easy-to-use language for accurately describing performance. It is likely to create inconsistent performance evaluations since employees can be rated high or low on these sorts of competencies depending on what behaviors a manager chooses to emphasize.

- *The generic model.* This occurs when companies use off-the-shelf competency libraries and do not modify the content to fit the company's unique culture. The language used in generic models may have little resemblance to the words managers and employees actually use when discussing performance. I saw an example of this when working with a Norwegian company that adopted a competency model based on a library created by a US consulting firm. One of the competencies was called "Learning on the Fly." When reading this title, a manager responded, "What does this mean? It's so stereotypically American." The key to avoiding generic models is to change competency titles and definitions so they use the language common in your company. Often changing just a few words will have a significant impact on people's acceptance of the model.

- *Emotional but meaningless.* Many leaders give competencies emotionally laden titles and definitions that sound inspiring but lack behavioral detail. While the language may be inspiring, it provides little value for accurately evaluating performance. In one company, subject matter experts determined that one of the competencies needed for a job was, "Responding quickly to customer issues." The CEO said this sounded too boring and changed it to, "Passionately pursuing customer excellence." When this model was rolled out, managers and employees joked about starting romantic liaisons with customers to show them more passion. A little inspirational language is fine when developing competencies, but it has to be backed with definitions outlining clearly observable, job-relevant behaviors.

When building competency models, think about how the competencies will be used. Managers will sit down with their employees and use these competencies for serious and often difficult conversations about performance, pay, and career growth. The managers may have personally recruited, hired, and worked with these people for years. Some of these people will be close friends. Others may not particularly like each other but still need to effectively work together. In all cases, managers will want to appear confident and credible when talking with employees about their performance, pay, and future career prospects. Now look at your competency model. Does it contain words you can imagine a manager using when explaining why employees are not getting a raise or are being let go due to an organizational change? Does it describe observable behaviors that differentiate poor, average, and great performance?

The reality test I use for competencies is to imagine a manager looking a long-term employee in the eye and saying, "I am not giving you a raise this year because you don't [insert the actual words from the competency model]." If your competency model does not contain the right terms to support this sort of serious conversation or contains cute or emotional terms that would sound silly used in this context, then change the model. A good competency model provides words that clearly describe the difference between effective and ineffective performance—take care to make sure these words are the right ones.

6.4.3   How Will You Structure Your Performance Management Cycle? When Will You Evaluate Performance?

Performance management is best thought of as three interrelated cycles, which are illustrated in figure 6.5. The innermost cycle is about managing business operations through ongoing goal management. The next cycle is about managing employee effectiveness through performance measurement. It focuses

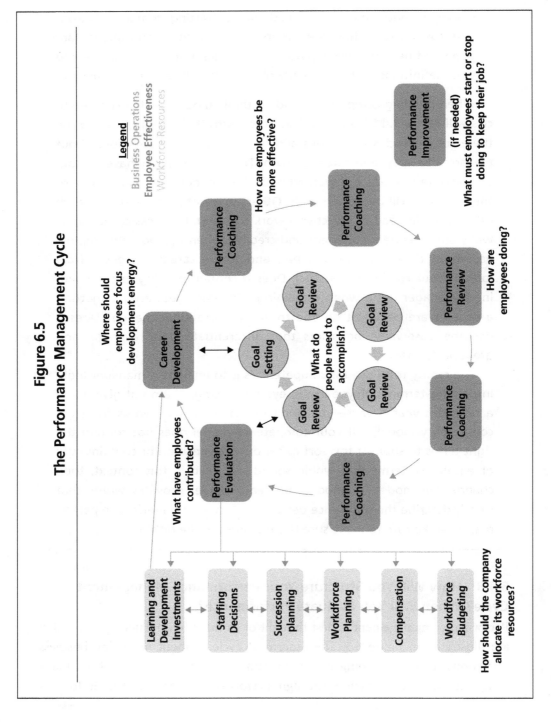

Figure 6.5
The Performance Management Cycle

on assessing employees' behavior and providing coaching feedback to increase effectiveness in their current role. The outermost cycle is about managing workforce resources through talent decisions. It focuses on evaluating overall employee contributions and using this to guide decisions related to compensation, job transfers and promotions, and developmental resources.

Managing Business Operations   The performance cycle starts with the manager defining what business goals need to be accomplished by their group. The manager then works with employees to agree on the specific goals they will achieve to support the group's overall goals. The most frequent performance management activity is tracking and updating goals so employees have a clear sense of whether they are accomplishing what the company expects them to achieve. This is usually done through daily, weekly, or monthly operating meetings. The business operations cycle uses goal management to keep employees aligned on activities that are critical to the company's business objectives.

Managing Employee Effectiveness   The second cycle of performance management involves assessing employee performance and providing coaching advice and feedback. It is about increasing employee awareness of what behaviors to start, stop, or continue doing to be more effective in their jobs. Informal performance coaching should take place throughout the year as part of regular work discussions. Companies should also periodically conduct more formal, systematic assessments of employees' contributions to the organization. This is usually done on an annual basis, although for many jobs, it makes sense to do it more frequently.

It is important to schedule performance assessments at specific times during the year for four reasons:

- *Measurement accuracy.* Performance management is used to measure the contributions employees are making to the organization. The foundation of accurate measurement is consistency. Part of consistency is standardizing time frames used to measure employee performance. Performance appraisals can be influenced by environmental factors such as the company's current performance and the manager's work schedule. Even the weather could potentially influence how managers evaluate employees. Standardizing performance appraisals so employees are evaluated in the same time frame increases the accuracy of performance measurement.

- *Linking to business cycles*. Virtually all companies manage financial resources and strategic objectives against an annual calendar. It is important to synchronize talent decisions with this calendar. There should be a clear link between the steps used to set business strategies and plan budgets and the steps contained in the performance management cycle.

- *Manager accountability*. Performance management is largely about assessing employee contributions and providing employees with feedback to increase their effectiveness. In a perfect world, all managers could be counted on to voluntarily meet with their employees to provide detailed, constructive performance feedback. We do not live in such a perfect world! Creating formal steps that require managers to assess employee performance and provide employee feedback is critical to ensuring that managers are doing the job of managing.

- *Legal compliance*. Many companies are legally required to formally document employee performance to justify decisions related to pay and employment. Formal, standardized performance evaluations are often a fundamental component for meeting these legal requirements.

A common question when developing performance management methods is whether to include formal midcycle reviews (e.g., by requiring managers to conduct a midyear performance assessment in addition to an end-of-year performance evaluation). The disadvantage of adding these reviews is they increase administrative burden. The advantage is they ensure managers are giving employees some feedback throughout the year and thus decrease the risk that surprises will occur during the end-of-year evaluation. Because midyear reviews are more about communication than evaluation, they may not include any formal rating. Managers and employees are simply asked to write comments about performance strengths and development areas. One company even reduced the midyear review to a single question: "Has your manager met with you in the past thirty days to provide you with meaningful coaching feedback about your performance?" Reponses to this question were used to remind managers of the importance of providing ongoing coaching throughout the year.

Most companies include optional steps in this cycle to address serious performance problems. Called things like "performance improvement plans," these are specialized performance reviews that address employee behaviors that could lead to formal corrective action up to and including termination of employment.

These plans ensure that employees are aware of the difference between development opportunities and serious performance issues. They can be important for complying with laws and regulations that govern compensation and staffing decisions used to address counterproductive employee behavior.

Managing Workforce Resources The third cycle of performance management considers the overall value that employees are providing to the organization. It focuses on determining where to invest scarce resource such as pay, promotions, and limited development opportunities. This cycle requires comparing employees against one another to determine which employees are the most valuable in their current roles, which ones may be ready for more responsibility, and which ones need to improve their performance or be managed out of their current position. This cycle is ideally timed to a company's financial cycle and linked to the creation and allocation of workforce budgets.

Linking Business Operations, Employee Effectiveness, and Workforce Management Thinking through how the steps in figure 6.5 link together is central to building an integrated strategic HR approach that ties together the 4R processes of right people (staffing), right things (goal management), right way (performance management), and right development (succession, learning, and career development). This is critical to aligning business operations, employee effectiveness, and workforce management. Business strategies should guide the development of employee goals; employee goals should be incorporated into performance evaluations; performance evaluations should influence compensation and staffing decisions; and succession management and career development conversations should incorporate all of these elements to integrate information about what employees have done in the past, what the company needs employees to do in the future, and what employees want to achieve in their careers.

A big part of performance management design is deciding on the frequency and formal structure of the steps in figure 6.5 and how they tie to each other. There are, of course, significant differences in how companies approach these steps. For example, some companies do not include formal steps for goal setting or midyear performance reviews. There is also considerable variation in the frequency and complexity of the cycles for different types of jobs. Jobs that compensate people based on weekly, monthly, or quarterly goals require increasing the frequency of certain steps. In some jobs, pay decisions are determined by contracts, tenure, or other variables unrelated to actual employee performance. These jobs may benefit from having formal performance reviews to support coaching and staffing decisions, but it does not make sense to tie performance reviews for these jobs to compensation.

Companies do not need to build out every step in figure 6.5 when implementing a performance management process. It is usually more effective and manageable to phase in different steps over several years. Start by determining which steps provide the greatest value with the least effort. Then focus energy around designing and deploying those steps so they are effective. Remember that you will probably want to build the other steps at some point. Think about how all the steps will ultimately come together, even if it takes three to five years to get the entire process up and running.

Additional Guidelines for Structuring the Performance Management Cycle The following are additional design guidelines to keep in mind when prioritizing what performance management steps to build and how they will fit together.

Goal Feedback Should Be More Frequent Than Performance Feedback Goal feedback is about progress toward achieving business outcomes. Performance feedback is about employee behavior. Managers and employees should be constantly talking about goals and what they can do to accomplish them. Much of this discussion will be about strategies, resources, market challenges, and other business issues that are not controlled by employees. These conversations about goal progress should be happening regularly. Coaching conversations about employee behavior should occur far less frequently unless there is an ongoing issue that the manager and employee are trying to address.

Performance Coaching Should Occur throughout the Year It is often said that there should be no surprises in an annual performance review. Employees should not wait for a formal performance evaluation to learn about their performance strengths and concerns. The design and communication of performance management cycles should emphasize the importance of managers' meeting informally with employees throughout the year to provide recognition, share feedback, and discuss what employees can do to increase their effectiveness. This does not have to happen every day, but it should happen more than once a quarter for most jobs.

Avoid Tying Performance Reviews to Employment Anniversary Dates Some companies conduct employee performance reviews based on when employees were hired, typically on the first-year anniversary of being hired and every year on that date thereafter. People like anniversary dates because they spread performance reviews over the course of the year so managers do not have to evaluate large numbers of employees at the same time. But there are three reasons that anniversary dates are often a bad idea:

1. Evaluating employees at different times of the year introduces inconsistency and potential measurement error into the process.

2. Conducting performance reviews based on anniversary date makes it hard to synchronize talent management activities with business operations.

3. It can be an administrative challenge to keep track of when different people need to have their reviews completed. This becomes even more challenging when people shift jobs internally and no longer have a clear employment start date.

To avoid these problems, companies often limit the use of anniversary date reviews to conduct probationary performance appraisals for new employees. Once employees have been in the company past a certain time, they are shifted to a common performance appraisal calendar. Shifting away from anniversary dates will create more pressure on managers to complete multiple performance reviews in a short amount of time. This concern can be addressed by designing efficient performance appraisal forms, providing managers with tools and resources to write performance reviews easily, and giving managers several weeks in which to complete the reviews.

Separate Performance Reviews into Descriptive Assessment and Normative Evaluation Encourage managers to start the performance appraisal by describing the employee's accomplishments, strengths, weaknesses, and developmental needs. Then move to a separate step of evaluating the employee's overall performance compared to others in the company. Separating the action of describing performance from the action of evaluating performance will lead to more effective reviews.

Keep Compensation and Staffing Decisions Distinct from Performance Evaluation One of the uses of performance evaluations is to guide compensation and staffing decisions. But there are several reasons to keep these actions separate. First, performance reviews provide a lot of value outside staffing and compensation decisions. This includes providing employees with coaching feedback and supporting employee career development. Second, a number of factors influence staffing and compensation decisions that are unrelated to employee performance (e.g., overall business performance, salary freezes). Third, if you tie performance management too closely to compensation, people will start to think of it solely as an exercise to justify compensation decisions. Never design a performance management process that might lead a manager to say something like, "Why should I complete my employees' performance reviews if there is a salary freeze?"

Keep Performance Appraisal Feedback Separate from Communication of Compensation Decisions If performance appraisal feedback includes information about compensation decisions, employees may focus only on their pay without processing what the review is saying about their behavior. Communicate performance reviews in a manner that encourages employees to understand what the reviews say about their performance strengths and development areas independent of how it affects their compensation. I typically recommend that companies conduct performance feedback discussions at least a week apart from communication of any compensation decisions, although this is not always possible.

6.4.4   How Will You Evaluate Performance?

Determining how to evaluate performance requires looking at three things. First, how do you define performance? What do you need to measure to determine if someone is effectively performing their job? Second, what is the reason for evaluating performance? Is it to provide coaching, determine compensation, assess career potential, or some mixture of these and other things? Third, how much time and effort do you want to put into the appraisal process? In general, the more time and effort put into the evaluation process the more accurate it will be. But how much accuracy is necessary? Let's look at these in more detail:

• *How is performance defined?* If performance is defined in terms of objective, clearly measurable goals, then performance evaluation is largely just a matter of accurate goal measurement. For example, some jobs are evaluated entirely based on the amount of revenue generated through sales. The only thing required to evaluate performance in these jobs is keeping track of sales numbers associated with each employee. If, however, performance is defined using behavioral competencies or goals that cannot be measured in a purely objective fashion, then more thought is required to create an effective evaluation method. Most jobs fall into this category. There are also jobs where managers may not have the expertise needed to evaluate the technical performance of employees. For example, many health care administrators do not have the training required to evaluate the performance of the doctors or nurses they manage. In situations where job performance is less well defined or more difficult to measure, the most common approach used to evaluate performance is through a standardized performance rating process.

• *What is the reason for evaluating performance?* Performance evaluations can be used for multiple purposes, including providing coaching and feedback, determining how to allocate pay and other scarce resources, or providing a consistent, fair, and legally defensible basis for making personnel decisions. If the sole purpose of performance evaluations is to support coaching and feedback, then you may choose to limit the evaluation to highly descriptive, qualitative measures. If performance evaluations will be used to guide decisions related to pay, staffing, or allocation of development resources, you will need some method to categorize employees based on different performance levels. The only way to do this is to rate employees, although this does not necessarily mean using numeric rating labels. I discuss ratings in greater detail later in this chapter.

• *How much time and resources will you invest in evaluating performance?* Performance evaluation methods can be as simple as asking managers to place their employees into general categories of "good versus bad" or as complex as lengthy calibration sessions where managers work together to systematically categorize employees using highly detailed performance benchmarks. Typically the longer and more involved the method is, the more accurate the evaluation is, although there is certainly a point of diminishing returns. An important question when designing performance evaluations is, "How important is it to measure and categorize employees accurately?" The answer will influence how much time is spent on the evaluation. Evaluation methods that take a few hours per employee are typically fine for most jobs. For critical roles such as senior executive, it may make sense to use more extensive methods that could take several days to complete. And for relatively unskilled jobs such as frontline retail sales clerks, the evaluation methods may take as little as ten minutes per employee.

Like most other aspects of talent management, there is no one best way to evaluate performance. What makes sense for some roles may not be effective for others. However, most methods use some version of rating scales, multirater input, and performance calibration. For that reason, we discuss each of these in a bit more detail.

Designing Rating Scales Most performance management processes include a step where managers categorize employees to indicate their overall level of performance using a standardized scale. This does not necessarily mean assigning a numerical rating such as 1, 2, 3, 4, or 5. It may mean labeling employees based on their contribution to the organization using such descriptors as "valued contributor," "exceeds expectations," or "not achieving goals." What is important is that employees are placed into categories where certain groups are considered to be performing at a higher level than other groups.

Rating employees is necessary to guide decisions around allocation of scarce resources such as pay, promotions, and training opportunities. Unless you treat all employees exactly the same regardless of performance, or assign rewards solely based on things like tenure and union job code, then you need some method to group employees based on performance levels. This cannot be done without some form of rating. The reality is that all companies rate employees, but not all companies make ratings in a consistent, well-defined, and transparent fashion.

Companies vary considerably in the emphasis they place on identifying and communicating employee ratings. Some companies make the rating a central focus of the performance management process by directly tying it to pay increases and promotion eligibility. In these cases, the performance management process is largely a series of steps leading up to the assignment and communication of ratings. Other companies do not share performance ratings with employees: they give employees qualitative feedback on their performance but are never told what ratings they received, although they can often infer their ratings based on whether they get pay increases, receive promotions, or keep their jobs.

Hiding performance ratings from employees is counter to using performance management to create a culture where everyone knows exactly where they stand in terms of their performance effectiveness. But considerable care needs to be taken when sharing performance ratings, or they can significantly damage employee motivation and morale. I discuss this more when examining the kinds of training managers must receive to use performance management methods effectively.

Assuming your company is going to make formal performance ratings, the next question is what sort of rating to use. This is one of the few areas of talent management where there are some well-tested and highly specific best practices.

Use a Five-Point or Seven-Point Rating Scale   Research shows that five-point rating scales typically result in the most accurate evaluations.[5] Seven-point scales may be slightly better if you provide managers with a lot of training on how to assign ratings. The advantage of five- or seven-point rating scales is they have a midpoint and allow for enough differentiation to be effective without overly complicating the rating process. It probably does not matter if a rating of 1 is good or if a rating of 5 is good, just as long as the meaning of the ratings is clearly communicated.

Here is how one company instructed its managers on using a five-point scale:

> You will probably rate most of your employees as 2s, 3s, or 4s. These ratings represent solid performers at slightly different levels of effectiveness. Use the 1 and 5 as exclamation points to indicate a clear need for action with regard to an employee's performance. You want to have clear implications for employees rated as 1s or 5s. Employees rated a 1 need to quickly improve or be managed out of their current role. In other words, performance is such a problem the company needs to act now to address it. Conversely, employees rated a 5 are so good the company should take near-term action to provide them with significant rewards or career opportunities.

You might wonder, *Why not use three-point scales, even-numbered scales, or scales with nine or more ratings?* The problem with three-point scales is they tend to function as two-point scales in application. Managers are unlikely to give someone the lowest possible rating (a 1) unless they are ready to either fire the employee or accept his or her resignation, so they end up grouping everyone into the 2 and 3 categories, which leaves little room for performance differentiation. The problem with even-numbered scales is that many employees truly are average. It frustrates managers when they are forced to rate average employees as being above or below expectations. The problem with scales with nine or more rating points is they create inconsistency without increasing measurement precision. Most managers cannot effectively differentiate more than seven levels of performance, and so nothing is gained by giving them more rating points.

Furthermore, since some managers tend to use higher ratings than others, rating scales with more than about seven points decrease rating consistency across managers without increasing rating accuracy.

Provide Descriptive Labels to Guide How Ratings Are Assigned   The accuracy and value of performance ratings increase when companies define rating scales using descriptive labels instead of numbers.[6] Table 6.3 provides examples of descriptive labels that have been used with five-point scales. There are two reasons that descriptive labels are better than numerical ones. First, they define the difference between rating categories. For example, it is easier for a manager to distinguish between a "solid performer" and someone who is "exceeding

Table 6.3
Examples of Descriptive Rating Labels

Rating	Example 1	Example 2	Example 3
1	Significant concerns; results must change or serious disciplinary action will follow	Unsatisfactory performance. Performance must improve significantly within a reasonable period of time if the individual is to remain in this position.	Not meeting expectations. Employee is not performing to the requirements of the job.
2	Not meeting expectations; has some performance areas that need to be improved	Needs some improvement. Performance is noticeably less than expected.	Needs improvement. Usually performs to and meets job requirements; however, the need for further development and improvement is clearly recognized.

Rating	Example 1	Example 2	Example 3
3	Solid performer; valued contributor who effectively performs core duties of the role	Meets expectations. Performance clearly and fully meets all the requirements of the position in terms of quality and quantity of work.	Meets expectations. Minor deviations may occur, but the overall level of performance meets or slightly exceeds all position requirements.
4	Exceeding expectations; high performer who contributes above and beyond core role	Exceeds expectations. Performance is sustained and uniformly high with thorough and on-time results.	Exceeds expectations. Performance frequently exceeds job requirements. Accomplishments are regularly above expected levels.
5	Role model; exceptional performer who is having a major impact on organizational success; sets the bar for performance in his or her role	Exceptional performer. Performance levels and accomplishments far exceed normal expectations.	Outstanding. This category is reserved for employees who truly stand out and clearly and consistently demonstrate exceptional accomplishments in terms of quality and quantity of work that is easily recognized as truly exceptional by others.

expectations" than it is to distinguish between a 3 and a 4. Second, descriptive labels make it easier to communicate the results of performance evaluations to employees. It is more meaningful to tell an employee that she is a "solid performer" than to tell her that she is a "3."

Base Ratings on Well-Defined Performance Criteria Managers should be given specific guidelines on how to evaluate performance based on an employee's goals and competencies. They should not make ratings based solely on their personal opinions of what constitutes effective performance. It is usually most effective to have managers start by rating employees against specific job competencies and goals and then make an overall performance rating based on these individual ratings. To maximize the accuracy of performance ratings, require managers to explain their ratings using behaviors and metrics linked to job-relevant competency models and goal plans.

Avoid Overly Complicated Performance Weights It is a good idea to have managers rate their employees on specific goals and competencies, and then evaluate their overall performance based on these initial ratings. This approach helps ensure managers base their overall performance evaluations on appropriate performance criteria. Some companies go a step further and assign mathematical weights to different competencies or goals that reflect their relative importance to the overall job. These weights are then used to automatically calculate an overall performance rating.

There are pros and cons to using mathematical weighting. Weights are good because they indicate that certain goals or competencies are more important to the job than others. For example, attendance and customer service are both parts of being a parking lot attendant, but performance may depend more on good attendance than good customer service, so it may make sense to weight attendance ratings more heavily.

Weights are bad because they can complicate the performance evaluation process. Weights create another level of complexity that people have to think through, and this added complexity may not be worth the value that weights provide. It is also often difficult to set weights. People struggle to place specific numbers on the relative importance of different goals and competencies. This is particularly true for competencies. You also need to define the criteria for setting weights. For example, should goal weights be based on "relative importance" or "relative difficulty"? Most companies base weights on relative importance, but this needs to be clarified and communicated. Finally and perhaps most important, the way weights are typically used does not accurately reflect how people actually evaluate performance.

Most performance systems that use weights have simple additive formulas where ratings are multiplied by the relevant weight and then just averaged or added together. But people don't actually evaluate performance using simple additive formulas. They judge overall performance based on whether people fall above or below certain thresholds on individual goals and competencies. This is called noncompensatory scoring, and it is hard to effectively replicate using weights (see the discussion: "Why Automatically Calculating Overall Performance Ratings Is a Bad Idea").

WHY AUTOMATICALLY CALCULATING OVERALL PERFORMANCE RATINGS IS A BAD IDEA

Some performance management processes ask managers to rate employees on individual competencies and goals and then automatically average or add these individual ratings to create an overall performance rating. Although this approach sounds reasonable, it is generally not a good idea. First, it can result in creating an overly engineered rating process that suggests a level of mathematic precision that doesn't truly exist. Second, it does not reflect how people actually evaluate overall performance.

Manager evaluations of overall employee performance tend to follow what is called a noncompensatory decision-making approach. Managers typically do not rate each competency or goal and simply add them together to come up with an overall rating. What managers do is decide whether employees have achieved certain thresholds of performance for different competencies and goals and then use these thresholds to guide their overall evaluation. The use of thresholds allows managers to make exceptions when rating employees who are really good or bad at certain parts of their job. If performance on a specific competency or goal is exceptionally good or bad, then managers may weight that competency as being more important regardless of how the employee has performed in other areas. For example, an employee who fails to meet certain minimum levels of performance related to "achieving results" might be considered to have poor overall performance no matter how good he or she is at other competencies, such as "getting along with others" or "following rules and processes."

Averaging or adding performance ratings to calculate an overall performance score does not reflect the noncompensatory way managers actually evaluate performance. Consider the following illustration. Imagine performance of a retail job was based on five competencies: attendance, customer service, problem solving, attention to detail, and supporting coworkers. The company rated employee performance using the following five-point scale: 1: unacceptable; 2: needs improvement; 3: meets expectations; 4: exceeds expectations; 5: outstanding.

Suppose an employee was exceptional when she was at work but constantly showed up late for her scheduled shifts. This employee might receive the following individual competency ratings:

Attendance	1—unacceptable
Customer service	5—outstanding
Problem solving	5—outstanding
Attention to detail	5—outstanding
Supporting coworkers	5—outstanding
Total	21

The mathematically calculated overall performance rating based on averaging these five ratings is 4.20 (21 divided by 5). An overall rating of 4.2 suggests the employee's performance "exceeds expectations." But until the employee gets attendance above some minimum level, her manager is unlikely to view her as a high performer no matter how good she is at the four other competencies. In fact, the manager might rate the employee's overall performance as 1 (unacceptable) based on attendance alone in order to justify removing the employee from the position.

You might ask, "Why not use HR technology to create automatic scoring algorithms that use noncompensatory methods?" This is possible, but there are three reasons not to take this approach. First, creating noncompensatory scoring algorithms can be relatively complicated, and many HR technology systems cannot easily support these types of calculations. Second, it implies that performance evaluations have a level of mathematical precision that is beyond the true accuracy of most manager performance ratings. Third, and most important, it removes the manager from having full ownership over the final overall rating. Performance management processes should not give managers the chance to say things like, "The system automatically calculated the overall rating, and it is different from what I would have given if I was allowed to do it myself." It is important that managers own the overall evaluation they assign to employees and be able to effectively explain why they gave this rating. The easiest way to do this is to have managers assign ratings themselves and require that they justify those ratings based on well-defined competencies and goals.

There is value in having managers rate individual goals and competencies independently before making an overall performance evaluation. Such individual ratings focus managers on the criteria that define effective performance. But rather than averaging or adding these ratings together into an overall rating, it is better to ask managers to make the overall rating independently. The overall rating should reflect the ratings made on individual competencies and goals but should not be a simple linear addition of these ratings. Instead, it should take into account the importance of meeting or exceeding certain performance thresholds for different competencies and goals. And most important, managers should be able to easily and clearly explain to employees how they arrived at their overall performance rating. This approach creates stronger manager ownership for the overall rating, is simpler to understand, and reflects how people actually make overall performance evaluations.

Taking these pros and cons into account leads to the following recommendation for the use of weights:

- Carefully consider whether the value gained by using weights in the performance appraisal process justifies the work it will take to use them effectively.

- It is usually better to use weights for individual goals than for individual competencies. This is because it is easier to evaluate relative importance and define weights for goals compared to competencies.

- It is reasonable to use weights to balance the overall importance of goals versus competencies because this is fairly easy to understand—for example 70 percent assigned to goals and 30 percent assigned to competencies.

Weights can provide a general guide to help managers make their final overall performance evaluation. But the final evaluation should not be mathematically determined because such formulas do not account for the noncompensatory nature of performance. Managers should be given leeway to set their final evaluation based on their interpretation of the employee's overall performance. This evaluation should be reflective of the individual competency and goal ratings and their associated weights, but it should not be automatically determined by them.

Designing the Performance Evaluation Process The foundation for effective performance management is accurate performance measurement, which is critical for providing employee feedback, supporting coaching and development, and guiding staffing and pay decisions. Accurate performance measurement depends on clearly defining the criteria that determine performance and consistent, systematic collection of performance data based on these criteria.

How you collect performance data depends on the types of data you are collecting and who you are collecting it from. There are three steps to performance data collection:

1. Define what sort of data you are collecting.

2. Define what sources you will use to obtain the data. The primary sources are usually employees and their managers, but you may also want information from peers and customers, as well as objective data such as financial metrics or assessment test results.

3. Decide how to collect information from these sources.

Figure 6.6 illustrates the three types of performance data that are used to evaluate employee performance:

- *Competency data* are usually based on ratings provided by employees and their manager. These data can also be collected from coworkers and customers. The use of social technology tools in the workplace is also leading to the use of crowdsourced competency data (see the discussion: "Using Social Technology and Crowdsourcing Applications to Evaluate Employee Performance"). It is also possible to evaluate competencies using job simulations or psychometric assessments, but these methods are better suited for staffing and are rarely used for performance management.

- *Goal data* usually come from employee and manager evaluations of whether goals were accomplished. Goals for some jobs can also be measured using objective metrics such as customer satisfaction surveys, productivity metrics, or sales revenue.

- *Skills data* are included as part of the performance management process for some jobs. These data are usually based on certification tests, by having managers or subject matter experts rate the employees on skills proficiency, or by having employees provide evidence that they have performed certain tasks or gained certain experiences.

USING SOCIAL TECHNOLOGY AND CROWDSOURCING APPLICATIONS TO EVALUATE EMPLOYEE PERFORMANCE

Social technology applications similar to Facebook or Twitter are now common in the workplace, and people have suggested that data from these systems can be used to replace formal performance reviews. Instead of managers rating employees on different competencies, might it be better for employees to be evaluated directly based on comments, popularity rankings, and posts made on these sites? It makes sense to explore how social technology can improve on more traditional performance rating processes. But it does not make sense to assume social technology can or should replace current performance evaluation methods.

Social technology provides tremendous value for supporting ongoing coaching and communication around performance. But when it comes to making formal evaluations of someone's value to the organization, these tools have a lot of problems:

- *Poor measurement.* Social technology metrics often reflect how often a person comments on different sites and the reactions others show to those comments. One could argue that social technology is more about impression management, popularity, and knowing who to ask for feedback than rigorous, consistent measurement. There is also a distinct absence of well-defined performance criteria in most social technology systems (e.g., well-defined goals or competencies).

- *Lousy analytics.* Social technology tends to rely heavily on qualitative statements as opposed to quantitative ratings. This is a strength from a coaching and feedback perspective but a problem from the perspective of calibration, measurement consistency, and workforce analytics.

- *May not work in competitive environments.* People competing for limited resources might distrust or actively try to game social technology. For example, employees may intentionally make online comments or posts simply to increase their crowdsourcing scores.

- *Potential to create disruption in the company.* Constructive feedback requires sharing negative comments from time to time. But posting of negative comments on social sites is likely to create more problems than it solves. Providing effective critical feedback is a sensitive topic. Many cultures are averse to making critical comments about someone else's performance. There is a reason that it is not possible to "dislike" something on Facebook. One cringes to think what might happen if someone posts a comment on a company's social performance technology system saying, "His work is bad," or, "He is an idiot."

- *Legal concerns.* Ask your corporate legal counsel what they think about using social technology systems as a primary source of data for evaluating employee performance. I suspect they might describe it as a plaintiff's gold mine of inappropriate comments.

People once said the Internet will be the end of brick-and-mortar retail stores. That didn't happen, although it certainly has changed how people shop. The same is true for social technology and traditional performance reviews. Social technology is unlikely to completely alter the future of performance management. It will create some changes to how performance management data are collected, but at the end of the day, it is just another tool, even if it is a unique and valuable one.

It is important to think about what types of data you need to conduct performance evaluations. The nature of the data you use will have a significant impact on how you design the evaluation process.

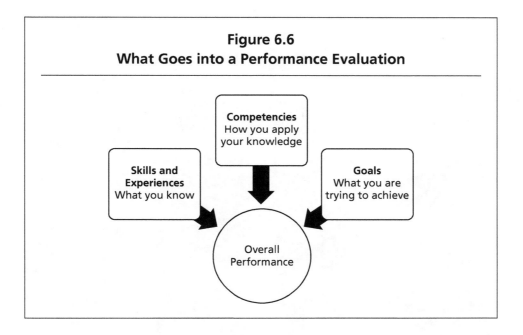

Figure 6.6
What Goes into a Performance Evaluation

Competencies
How you apply
your knowledge

**Skills and
Experiences**
What you know

Goals
What you are
trying to achieve

Overall
Performance

Performance Evaluation Process Steps   After determining what data will be used in the performance review, the next step is determining how these data will be collected and analyzed to create performance ratings. Figure 6.7 provides an overview of steps commonly used to evaluate employee performance. The steps in dark gray are necessary for implementing consistent performance evaluations. The steps in medium gray are commonly found in many performance management processes but are not always necessary. The steps in light gray work well for some companies and jobs, but these are less widely used because of the resources they require or their limited relevance to certain types of positions.

Here is what a performance evaluation process would look like for a company that did the fewest possible number of steps and what it would look like for a company that used every step in figure 6.7.

For the minimal process, the manager drafts and submits a review of the employee, including an overall performance evaluation based on the manager's opinion of the employee's performance (combining steps D, F, and J into a single step). The manager meets with the employee to review his or her performance evaluation and communicate pay or staffing decisions that were based on the evaluation (combining steps E, K, and L into a single step). This minimal

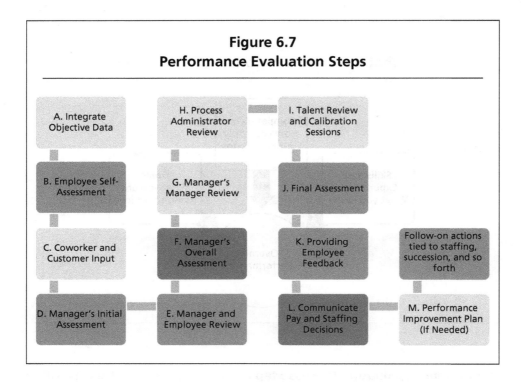

Figure 6.7
Performance Evaluation Steps

A. Integrate Objective Data

H. Process Administrator Review

I. Talent Review and Calibration Sessions

B. Employee Self-Assessment

G. Manager's Manager Review

J. Final Assessment

C. Coworker and Customer Input

F. Manager's Overall Assessment

K. Providing Employee Feedback

Follow-on actions tied to staffing, succession, and so forth

D. Manager's Initial Assessment

E. Manager and Employee Review

L. Communicate Pay and Staffing Decisions

M. Performance Improvement Plan (If Needed)

process might take two weeks or less to complete and require fewer than three person-hours per employee. It could take as little as thirty minutes if a very simple rating form is used and managers are not expected to spend time coaching employees.

In the comprehensive process, information is imported from sales and financial data systems to create a profile of the employee's performance based on objective business metrics (step A). The employee creates an initial assessment of his or her performance based on these metrics combined with other information about his or her performance collected over the year (step B). Several of the employee's coworkers send information to the employee's manager expressing their opinions of the employee's strengths and developmental areas. This may include getting input from the employee's own direct reports if the employee is also a manager (step C). The manager reviews the employee's business metrics, the employee's self-assessment, comments from the employee's coworkers, and the manager's own record of the employee's performance to draft an initial evaluation of the employee's performance (step D).

The manager and the employee meet to discuss the manager's initial performance assessment and make modifications to address areas of misalignment (step E). The manager drafts and submits his or her overall assessment for further review and approval (step F). The manager's manager reviews the assessment and makes relevant changes based on his or her perspective on the employee's accomplishments (step G). Representatives from the HR department review the assessment to ensure it is appropriately written and contains all required information (step H).

The manager discusses the assessment with other managers during a calibration session and if necessary changes the evaluation based on input from their peers (step I). The manager makes a last round of changes to the assessment based on input from previous steps and finalizes the review (step J). The manager meets with the employee to discuss the final assessment and discuss ways to increase his or her performance and achieve his or her career goals (step K). The manager shares information with the employee about decisions regarding pay or job position that were based on the results of the performance evaluation (step L). If the employee's performance is well below expectations, the manager may put the employee on a performance improvement plan (step M).

This comprehensive process would probably take about three to four months from start to finish and require around ten to fifteen person-hours to complete for each employee.

The minimal process might work for some very basic positions, but is too simplistic to be effective for most jobs. In contrast, the comprehensive process is way too long and involved for most organizations. The best process usually lies somewhere between these two extremes. The challenge is finding which sequence of steps is appropriate for your setting. With that in mind, we review the steps in more detail and discuss their strengths and potential concerns.

A. Integrate Objective Data   This involves bringing together data from different sources that will be used in the performance review. These sources might include financial results, sales numbers, customer satisfaction survey scores, productivity metrics, workforce metrics (e.g., staff turnover, engagement levels), or any other data assumed to reflect an employee's performance contributions. This step is common for jobs tied to objective metrics such as sales or production positions. It is less common for support and professional jobs where it is difficult to tie performance directly to objective metrics. It is important to think through what data to include because pulling together this information can be a labor-intensive effort. Also important is taking care in using objective data just because they are easily obtainable. This can result in treating data as important merely because of availability. Finally, these data should be presented in a way that will be easy for employees and managers to interpret.

B. Employee Self-Assessment   In this step employees evaluate their own performance against job-relevant competencies, goals, and skills. Employee self-assessment has several advantages. First, employees have a vested interest in presenting their performance strengths. They are likely to put a fair bit of effort into presenting information that describes their accomplishments. Having employees conduct a self-assessment also reduces the workload placed on managers because employees gather and document many of their accomplishments so managers do not have to do it. Having employees review their performance also encourages them to critically compare themselves against job-relevant performance criteria. This increases employee self-awareness regarding performance strengths and weaknesses. The only significant downside to employee self-assessment is the tendency for underperforming employees to view themselves as being more competent than they actually are.[7] This can create difficulty for managers who are faced with the task of giving employees a candid dose of reality about their true level of effectiveness.

C. Coworker and Customer Input   This step involves asking people who work with the employee to provide input into the performance assessment. This step can be initiated by employees or managers. Companies often ask employees to provide a list of coworkers to their manager, which the manager approves or changes based on who will provide the most useful and accurate input. Companies also use this step to gather input from direct reports when assessing the performance of managers (see the discussion: "Evaluating Manager Performance: When 120 Is Worth More Than 360").

There are a few things to remember when gathering coworker and customer input. First, it is usually wise to limit input to fewer than five people, or this step can become very time intensive and the amount of information collected can become difficult to process. Second, avoid asking coworkers to rate the performance of their peers. It is better to ask for descriptive comments by using such prompts as, "What are two things this employee does well?" and, "What are two things this employee could change to improve her job effectiveness?" Third, be sensitive to the number of times people are being asked to provide input. Coworkers who work with a large number of employees could easily be asked to provide comments on ten or more reviews, which can be a significant time demand and can have a negative impact on the quality of information provided.

EVALUATING MANAGER PERFORMANCE: WHEN 120 IS WORTH MORE THAN 360

A major aspect of managerial performance is the ability to motivate, develop, and guide direct reports. Yet surprisingly few companies formally collect information from direct reports when evaluating manager performance. Fortunately, this is starting to change, largely because technology is making it much easier to get input from direct reports in an efficient and confidential manner.

Companies are using a modified version of the 360 survey process to do this. The traditional 360 survey collects ratings on an employee's performance from his or her supervisor, peers, and direct reports. The modified version collects ratings only from a manager's direct reports but not his or her supervisor or peers. This type of survey is sometimes called a "120" because it surveys only people who have one of three possible perspectives, which makes the process more focused and manageable. These surveys tend to be very short and look at only competencies related to managing and developing others. Some companies send the results to the manager's manager, who then compiles them for the formal assessment, while others send the results to both the manager and the manager's manager. This tends to vary based on employee concerns about providing critical feedback directly to their managers.

These 120 surveys provide managers with a more complete sense of their performance. It also allows companies to address the longstanding problem of managers who "kiss up and kick down," that is, managers who excel at looking good to their superiors but are abusive and intimidating toward those working for them. By providing greater transparency into how managers truly treat their employees, companies can reward managers who achieve results through building the strengths of their teams, develop managers who may achieve results but do it at the expense of those working for them, and remove managers who should never have been allowed to manage people in the first place.

Most companies I have worked with that use 120 surveys have been satisfied with their results. However, there is a risk that these surveys might create a bias for managers to avoid doing things that might lead their employees to give them low ratings such as confronting poor performance or challenging employees to set difficult goals. Like all other strategic HR methods, there are pluses and minuses to the use of 120 surveys. What is important is to be aware of these risks so they can be recognized and managed.

D. Manager's Initial Assessment   During the initial assessment, the manager provides his or her first evaluation of the employee. This step can be done in parallel with the employee self-assessment, as a response to the employee self-assessment, or by itself if the company is not including an employee self-assessment step. It is important to indicate that this assessment may be revised during subsequent steps. Most companies have managers provide an initial overall performance rating with the understanding that the rating is not final. Other companies ask managers to provide only descriptive information and ratings on employees' individual goals and competencies in this step and wait until the talent review session to collect an overall performance rating (step I).

E. Manager and Employee Review   The manager and employee meet to review the performance evaluation and discuss its accuracy and completeness. This step can occur at many places in the overall process. For very simple processes, it may occur shortly after the manager's initial assessment and may represent the end of the process. Companies may use this step to ensure the manager has thoroughly assessed the employee's performance before discussing it during manager, administrator, or calibration reviews (steps G, H, and I).

F. Manager's Overall Assessment   The manager revises the review based on information from previous steps and submits an overall assessment of the employee. At this point, the manager and employee are assumed to accept the review as final unless additional changes are made during reviews by the managers' manager, the process administrator, or during calibration meetings.

G. Manager's Manager Review The manager's manager reviews the assessment to ensure it meets quality expectations and aligns with his or her perceptions of the employee's performance. This step has several advantages. It helps ensure that evaluations reflect a consistent set of performance standards, reduces the risk of having managers evaluate their employees more harshly or leniently than their peers, and creates an opportunity to coach the manager on conducting performance reviews. It also gives the manager's manager greater knowledge of employees in the organization, which can promote talent mobility and inform workforce strategies.

The main disadvantage of this step is that it is time-consuming. A manager's manager may be responsible for looking at scores of performance reviews if they have several managers reporting to them. The manager's manager may also struggle to provide useful feedback on the assessment if he or she has only limited exposure to the employee being evaluated. Finally, this step assumes the manager's manager is skilled at performance reviews, which is not always the case.

H. Process Administrator Review The assessment is reviewed by a process administrator with expertise in performance management, typically someone from the HR organization. This step creates more consistency in performance reviews across the organization since the process administrator typically looks at reviews across multiple departments and functions. Having the review conducted by someone with expertise in performance appraisals can also increase the quality of performance reviews and decrease legal risks associated with inappropriate evaluation comments. This step can also help identify managers who need performance management training. The main disadvantage is that this step is time intensive, requires dedicated resources to conduct the reviews, and increases the overall bureaucracy of the performance management process.

I. Talent Review and Calibration Sessions These sessions bring together groups of managers to compare and discuss the performance levels of their direct reports. Talent review sessions create more consistent performance evaluations, help managers share ideas for conducting performance reviews and developing employees, and increase awareness of employee capabilities across the company, which enables better utilization and mobility of internal talent. The disadvantage is that they are time-consuming. They must also be effectively structured and facilitated to ensure the sessions remain productive, focused, and non-confrontational.

J. Final Assessment The manager now integrates information from all the previous steps and develops and submits his or her final assessment of the employee's performance. It is critical that managers be clearly responsible for the content and consequences of reviews they submit. Do not design a process that allows managers to say, "This isn't what I would have said, but I was required by the performance management process." It is appropriate to ask managers to explain why they have given employees certain performance ratings. But managers should not be forced to submit a review they do not agree with unless there is an openly acknowledged difference of opinion between the manager and his or her supervisor about the employee's performance. Forcing managers to make ratings they do not agree with will cause them to question the entire performance management process and resist using it to improve employee productivity.

K. Providing Employee Feedback The manager meets with the employee to discuss the final review. Ideally this step is spent discussing how to use the information contained in the review to help the employee increase his or her future performance and achieve his or her career goals. But performance management processes do not always require extensive development coaching to be effective. In some cases, simply making employees aware of their performance levels is enough. We discuss this in more detail in the section on providing employee feedback.

L. Communicating Pay and Staffing Decisions Normally the manager will tell employees about any pay and staffing decisions that come out of the performance management process. Communicating these decisions is ideally integrated with the performance appraisal process but is preferably done separately from communicating the results of the appraisal itself. Compensation and staffing decisions are not technically part of the performance review process, although they should be influenced by performance appraisals. The purpose of performance reviews is to measure the performance contributions of employees. This is not the same thing as deciding how much people should be paid or who should be promoted. Many factors influence pay and promotion decisions other than performance. We discuss this more in the section on using performance management data to guide talent decisions.

M. Performance Improvement Plan (If Needed) If an employee is performing below a certain level, then companies may place him or her on a formal performance improvement plan. Performance improvement plans are intended to do what they say they do: improve performance. These plans may also be necessary to ensure compliance with relevant legal guidelines in case the company has to terminate a person's employment contract.

The performance appraisal process is the most visible part of performance management. When deciding which performance appraisals steps to include, carefully consider the overall objectives you want to achieve from performance management. If your main goal is to increase employee productivity, then you are likely to include a lot more steps than if your goal is just to ensure legal compliance. The number and nature of the steps will also be influenced by the resources available for performance management, including the level of support shown by business leaders toward the process. As a general rule, it is better to do a few steps really well than risk doing a lot of steps poorly. It is usually the most effective to start with a simple process and steadily build on it over time rather than trying to go directly to a highly detailed, multistep process.

6.4.5 How Will You Calibrate Performance Evaluations?

Calibration is used to make sure evaluations of employee performance are based on a common and accurate set of standards. Calibration drives differentiation between employee performance ratings, creates consistency across managers in how they evaluate performance, and helps ensure that employees are rated based on their actual behavior and accomplishments and not just the subjective opinions and attitudes of their managers. Calibration methods are frequently used for making decisions about which employees should be given rewards or opportunities that will not be made available to the entire workforce—for example, deciding who will receive limited organizational resources such as promotions, compensation, or development opportunities. It also addresses one of the most common problems in performance management: the tendency to rate all employees as being at the same general level of performance (see the discussion: "Why Managers Struggle to Differentiate between High and Low Performers and How to Help").

WHY MANAGERS STRUGGLE TO DIFFERENTIATE BETWEEN HIGH AND LOW PERFORMERS AND HOW TO HELP

People often complain that performance management processes do not adequately identify high- and low-performing employees. This might seem odd since virtually every performance management process encourages managers to make this differentiation. What makes it so difficult for managers to rate certain employees as being more effective than others?

Answering this question starts with understanding how managers approach performance management. Managers think about several things when they are starting the performance management process.

- *Is it easy?* This is not just about the time is required to complete performance management tasks. It is about whether the tasks associated with performance management are simple or difficult. Performance management tasks such as delivering critical feedback are not easy for many people. Making performance management easy requires building simple and intuitive tools and processes. It also requires training managers on how to set goals, evaluate performance, and provide feedback. Otherwise managers may avoid the tasks altogether.

- *Will it increase workforce productivity?* To maximize productivity, it is necessary to provide employees with feedback that illustrates what they can do differently to increase their effectiveness. If this feedback does not contain the right information or is not delivered in the right way, it may decrease productivity and increase the turnover of valued employees. One of the challenges managers ask before giving critical feedback is, "Will this lead to more or less effective performance?" How they answer this question will depend on whether they know how to hold effective coaching conversations.

- *Does it have a positive impact on the work environment?* Giving someone critical feedback can be motivating when that person is fully engaged in fulfilling his or her performance potential. But it can also be stressful due to the expectation that people must improve to be successful. Managers may avoid critically evaluating people's performance for fear of the stress and potential interpersonal conflict it can create.

- *Will managers be rewarded for confronting poor performance?* All companies say they want managers to hold employees accountable for meeting performance expectations, but many companies do not back this up with action. Managers who call attention to underperforming employees are sometimes told to live with the poor performer because it is politically or legally difficult to manage that person out of the organization. Rather than supporting managers for addressing performance issues, these managers are treated as troublemakers. At other times, managers are punished for not having teams entirely composed of "high performers."

Any manager who truly strives for high performance will at some point encounter employees who are not meeting expectations. The true test of effective managers is not whether they have performance issues on their teams, but how they address these issues when they occur. It is important to examine how the company reacts when managers call out employees who are not meeting expectations. Are managers supported or punished for acknowledging and addressing performance issues?

From a manager perspective, the main goal of performance management is not to accurately document employees' past performance but to positively influence their future performance. Using performance management to critically evaluate employees and place them into different performance categories does not necessarily have a positive impact on the lives of managers. Why would managers risk evaluating employees if it might lead to decreased productivity and a stressful work environment? If a manager is not confident in his or her ability to use performance management to increase workforce productivity, he or she may logically take the path of least resistance and simply rate everyone as "above average." This may not increase performance, but it may not significantly decrease it either, at least in the short term.

The best way to get managers to differentiate between low- and high-performing employees is to give them clear performance criteria, train them on using these criteria to accurately evaluate employees, show them how to provide critical performance feedback in a way that will motivate employees to change for the better, and support and reward managers who are willing to distinguish between low- and high-performing employees. Managers will not truly embrace using performance management to differentiate between employees until they are confident that such critical evaluations will help them more than it will hurt them.

The three most common uses of calibration are for performance management, compensation, and succession:

- *Performance calibration.* Managers are required to explain or justify why they gave certain employees higher performance ratings than others. This ensures they have a consistent definition of performance and effectively differentiate between high-performing employees and less valuable contributors. It decreases the influence of managers' subjective opinions and attitudes on employee performance ratings. Performance calibration can have a significant impact on how employees are rated. For example, I once encountered a manager who said, "I never give employees the highest rating because I always want them to have something to strive for." During a calibration session, it was pointed out that if this manager never gave employees a rating of 5, then the highest rating employees could hope to obtain is a 4. Furthermore, the manager's unwillingness to acknowledge high performance hurt motivation rather than helping it.

- *Compensation calibration.* Managers are required to allocate financial rewards such as pay increases or bonuses in a way that meaningfully differentiates the rewards given to high performers from those given to others in the organization. This is primarily used to maximize the motivational value of compensation for high performers, avoid the risk of overpaying underperformers, and build a pay-for-performance culture. Research has found that even slight differences in pay significantly influence motivation, provided people know that these differences are tied to performance.[8] For example, the difference between a 2 percent and 3 percent salary increase may not seem like a lot in terms of absolute value, but it can mean a lot in terms of showing recognition for superior performance. And the difference between a 2 percent increase and no increase at all sends a very strong message to underperformers.

- *Succession calibration.* Managers or other organizational leaders compare and contrast the potential of employees to assume roles with increasing leadership or job responsibility. This is primarily used to ensure the company has a realistic sense of its internal talent pool or bench strength, develop common definitions of potential for different roles, and promote development and sharing of internal talent across the organization. (Methods for assessing potential are addressed in chapter 7.)

These three types of calibration work best when they are integrated with each other, and they all start with effective performance management calibration. A well-run performance management calibration process can eliminate the need for compensation calibration and significantly reduce the effort required to conduct succession calibration.

Implementing Calibration Methods Calibration is not always easy to implement, but it doesn't need to be overly complicated. Large companies have successfully deployed calibration methods across thousands of employees in a matter of months. As with most other talent management methods, there is no one best way to use calibration. Methods that make sense for one organization may be impractical or ineffective in another. Carefully thinking through the following calibration methods will provide a solid foundation for deploying calibration within your company.

Clearly Defined Performance Definitions Clear definitions support calibration by providing a common standard to evaluate employees. The most effective performance definitions use goals and competencies to describe specific achievements and behaviors associated with different levels of performance. If calibration is being used to compare employees who are working in different jobs, then it is valuable to identify core competencies that influence performance across all these jobs. Core competencies are particularly useful for comparing the performance of employees who have vastly different sets of skills and experiences.

Rating Distribution Guidelines Guidelines indicate the approximate numbers of employees who are expected to fall into different performance categories.

Companies tend to expect overall employee performance ratings to approximate a normal distribution for most jobs. Here is an example of a rating distribution guideline for a five-point performance scale:

Percentage of Employees Expected to Be Placed in Different Performance Categories

5—Top performer: 10 percent

4—Strong performer: 35 percent

3—Solid performer: 45 percent

2—Needs improvement: 7 percent

1—Poor performer: 3 percent

Rating distribution guidelines encourage managers to evaluate their employees more critically. They can create "performance pressure" by flattening the curve so more employees are rated as high or low performers (e.g., requiring that 20 percent of employees fall in each of the five categories shown in the example). Forced ranking is the most extreme form of this because it asks managers to place every employee in a different performance category from most effective to least effective (see the discussion: "The Truth about Forced Ranking and Forced Distributions").

THE TRUTH ABOUT FORCED RANKING AND FORCED DISTRIBUTIONS

Forced distributions are calibration methods that require managers to place a certain percentage of employees in different performance categories ranging from most to least effective. Forced ranking is the most extreme form of forced distribution because it requires managers to list each employee in order of performance from most valuable to least valuable.

Forced distribution methods received a lot of publicity in the 1990s due to their use at GE under CEO Jack Welch. Subsequent research has shown that these methods increase workforce productivity in certain limited settings but can have a negative impact on productivity in others.[a]

Forced ranking and forced distributions can increase workforce productivity when a company has a high percentage of underperforming employees. But their value quickly wears off as the company begins to weed out poor performers. At this point, forced distribution methods begin to damage workforce quality and employee morale. These methods also do not work well if managers compare only the direct reports on their teams, as opposed to making comparisons across much larger groups of employees such as entire departments. Forced ranking and forced distributions can punish managers who have been "slow to hire and quick to fire" in terms of building a team entirely consisting of high performers, which, while rare, is possible. It can also create unnecessary and unhealthy conflict. For example, when an engineering company implemented strict forced ranking, some of its most talented engineers became upset when they were rated number 2 instead of number 1 on their teams. In reality, there was little difference between the performance of the number 1 and number 2 engineers. But the number 2 engineer resented the implication that he was not the equal of his peer.

Few companies do strictly forced ranking or strongly forced distributions. Even GE stopped doing it years ago. It is usually far more effective to use calibration talent review sessions. In these sessions, managers must explain their performance ratings to their peers or supervisors and reach mutual agreement on the final ratings. A manager may initially give everyone on his or her team high ratings, but must justify why the team deserves these ratings or adjust the ratings downward. Calibration sessions help address the problem of some managers rating more leniently or severely than others. The calibration process also helps managers to develop a common definition of what high performance looks like. Finally, it provides managers with insight into talent in other parts of the organization, which can facilitate talent movement across the company.

[a]Scullen, S. E., Bergey, P. K., & Aiman-Smith, L. (2005). Forced distribution rating systems and the improvement of workforce potential. *Personnel Psychology, 58*, 1–32.

Rating distribution guidelines are a useful tool for calibration, but they create risks if they are not appropriately managed or do not match the true nature of the performance distributions found in a company. They are particularly problematic if managers are required to strictly adhere to the guidelines (e.g., requiring that managers always place a percentage of employees in the highest and lowest performance categories even if managers do not believe this placement represents a true portrayal of their team's performance). Rating distribution guidelines also work best when comparing groups of at least thirty or more employees since smaller groups of employees are less likely to conform to expected distributions.

Rating Reviews Reviews involve having someone review a manager's performance evaluations for accuracy and appropriateness. The most common rater review is the second-level-manager review. In this method, employees are rated by their manager, and then the manager's manager reviews the ratings for accuracy and differentiation. Rating reviews are sometimes conducted by members of the HR department instead of the second-level manager. Rating reviews are time-consuming, but they help ensure that employee ratings are reasonably accurate based on broader company expectations. They can also be used to monitor the overall quality of performance assessments.

Talent Review Sessions These sessions bring together groups of managers, senior leaders, and talent management specialists to compare and discuss the performance of employees drawn from multiple teams, departments, or organizations. There are many ways to structure and conduct talent review sessions. The common feature is that people from different parts of the company discuss and contrast the performance of employees who may not directly report to them.

Talent review sessions are the most powerful form of calibration because in a single meeting, you can clarify common performance definitions, reinforce rating guidelines, and conduct rating reviews. They also allow managers to coach each other on how to manage different kinds of employees and promote transparency and sharing of talent across the organization. The downside is that these sessions require significant resources to be done well and can create major problems within the workforce if they are done poorly.

Each of these calibration methods can be implemented independently. But they are most effective when implemented as part of a single performance appraisal process.

What calibration methods to use will depend on the results the organization wants and the resources it has available. However using some form of calibration is highly recommended because of the multiple positive outcomes these methods provide—for example:

- *Shared definitions of performance.* One of the fundamental aspects of a high-performance work environment is a clear and well-understood definition of what success and failure look like. Common performance definitions and talent review sessions support the creation and use of rigorous performance standards. These force managers and employees to candidly and honestly compare their actions against the expectations of the organization.

- *More accurate performance data.* Calibration methods have a significant impact on the accuracy of performance appraisals by creating clear guidelines for performance evaluations and encouraging discussion and debate around the validity of managers' ratings.

- *Increased equity and fairness.* Calibration increases the transparency of performance ratings and decreases the potential for managers to unfairly rate certain employees leniently or harshly. Employees know their performance evaluation has been critically reviewed by people other than just their manager. This can reduce concerns of being rated poorly "just because my manager doesn't like me."

- *Improving the quality of the workforce.* Ongoing performance calibration helps ensure that underperformers are identified and not continually overlooked and tolerated year after year. This does not mean calibration should be used to constantly winnow the workforce every year by removing the bottom x percent. In fact, there are significant problems with this type of use of calibration. But it does mean taking action to address problems caused by underperforming employees.

- *More effective compensation allocation.* Calibration enables companies to more closely link pay decisions to employees' performance contributions. This increases the motivational value of compensation. Pay increases have a much stronger impact on motivation and retention when employees see a clear relationship between performance levels and pay. The motivational value of paying for performance is significant even when the relative difference in pay given to high versus low performers is fairly small.[9] There are also cost savings associated with reducing the amount of pay provided to low-performing employees.

- *Better insight into workforce capabilities.* Because calibration increases the accuracy of performance appraisal data, it makes performance management data more useful for evaluating workforce strengths and weaknesses. The conversations that occur during calibration reviews also promote understanding across the company around relationships between business needs and current workforce capabilities.

- *Greater coaching and sharing of talent.* Talent reviews give managers a forum to discuss performance issues with their peers. This creates an opportunity for sharing ideas on how to accelerate employee development and address employee performance issues.

Which of these outcomes are most pronounced depends on how the calibration process is designed. But taken as whole, there are relatively few strategic HR actions that have a greater impact on workforce productivity than the use of effective and well-designed calibration.

6.4.6 How Are Data from Performance Evaluations Used? What Is the Relationship among Performance Evaluations, Pay, Promotions, Development, and Workforce Management?

One of the ways performance management drives business execution is through enabling more accurate decisions related to investing company resources to increase workforce productivity. Most of these decisions have to do with pay, staffing, development, and workforce management. It is important to think how these decisions are currently made in the organization and how performance management data will be used to improve their effectiveness. Here are a few high-level issues to consider when tying performance management to compensation, staffing, and development decisions.

Compensation Decisions   Creating a stronger pay-for-performance culture is a common goal for implementing performance management methods. Pay for performance is a more complex concept than it might initially seem, but the basic notion of paying high performers more than low performers is generally a good strategy for increasing workforce productivity (see the discussion: "Do We Really Want Pay for Performance?"). Here are some considerations for building pay-for-performance processes:

DO WE REALLY WANT PAY FOR PERFORMANCE?

A pay-for-performance culture is one in which people receive monetary rewards based on the contributions they provide to the company: the more you contribute, the more you are paid. The assumption is that people will contribute more value if they are financially incented based on their contributions. Adopting a pay-for-performance mind-set is generally a good idea, but the idea can also oversimplify what business leaders truly want and what actually motivates employees. To illustrate this, consider the following four pay-for-performance cultures in order of best to worst to somewhere in-between:

- The best scenario: Performance without pay. From a strictly financial perspective, business leaders don't necessarily want to pay for performance. What they ideally want is performance without having to pay. But most employees are not willing to accept this proposition. We rightfully expect to be paid for what we contribute. Nevertheless, it is possible to inspire people to achieve high levels of performance without focusing on pay. Volunteer organizations do this all the time. There are a lot of things that motivate people. The motivational value of pay varies depending on the type of job and employee, and business leaders who use pay as the sole tool for motivating employees risk adopting a very expensive and marginally effective leadership approach.

- The worst scenario: Pay for poor performance. The worst-case scenario for a business occurs when employees are rewarded for doing things that undermine company performance. This occurs more often than companies would like to admit, particularly in companies whose managers have to comply with restrictive personnel policies, rules, and regulations. Rewarding poor performance encourages counterproductive behavior and destroys the motivation of high performers. High performers dislike it when they do not receive recognition or rewards for their contributions. But they hate it when they see rewards going to poorer-performing colleagues.

- A lousy scenario: Performance only for pay. One of the problems with creating a direct link between pay and performance is that some people will never feel they are getting paid enough. No matter how much pay these people receive for doing something, over time they always want more. Payouts can quickly switch from being a reward to being an expectation. Today's financial bonus is tomorrow's entitlement. Once this happens, pay ceases to be a motivator and becomes a source of dissatisfaction.[a]

- The pragmatic scenario: Performance influences but does not completely determine pay. There should be a positive relationship between how much people are paid and how much they contribute to the company, but the relationship between pay and performance does not need to be perfect to be effective. Many things influence pay levels beyond individual performance (e.g., overall company financials). Conversely, pay is only one of many factors that influence performance.

Companies should create a link between performance and pay, but they should not overemphasize pay as the only reason that employees should seek to perform at higher levels. Establishing links between pay and performance does tend to increase productivity. But it is not just the promise of pay that drives the productivity. When you link pay to performance, employees and managers get much more serious around defining what they mean by "performance." And clearly defining performance expectations drives all kinds of benefits for increasing workforce productivity, regardless of pay levels.

[a]This can also be an issue when companies adopt gamification approaches to employee recognition. Gamification involves creating systems so employees receive points or badges for doing certain things considered to be desirable by the company, customers, or peers. These points can be redeemed for cash awards or financially valuable prizes. Gamification can be an effective way to encourage positive behaviors, particularly since companies tend to do a poor job recognizing employees in general. But it can also lead to employees trying to game the system where they strive solely to get points or rewards without considering whether they are truly helping the organization overall.

- *How will performance management data be used to guide compensation decisions?* Simply providing managers with a table that compares performance ratings with compensation recommendations can substantially improve the relationship between pay and performance. Just making managers aware that there is little associated between performance ratings and pay decisions can lead them to take action to create a stronger pay-for-performance relationship for people on their team. Many companies also give managers specific restrictions or recommendations for pay increases based on performance levels. For example, employees who receive the highest performance rating may be eligible for 4 to 8 percent pay increases, while employees who receive middle-level ratings may be eligible for only 3 to 5 percent increases. It is better to give managers pay ranges as opposed to dictating a specific pay number (e.g., "All employees who receive the highest rating will get 6 percent"). Providing ranges gives managers some leeway to adjust pay up or down based on other factors, such as an employee's turnover risk or current pay levels, while still retaining the general relationship between pay and performance. In addition, if companies create an automatic relationship between specific ratings and specific pay increases, then managers will start manipulating performance ratings merely so they can pay employees a certain amount.

- *What is the relationship between different types of pay increases and different aspects of performance?* The three most common types of pay increases roughly correspond to the three categories of criteria used to evaluate performance (see figure 6.8):

  - *Base salary increases* raise pay by a fixed amount. This typically occurs when someone moves from a lower-paying job to a higher-paying job. Base salary increases tend to reflect skill acquisition. Employees who acquire new skills are qualified to take on greater job responsibilities and thus qualify for higher base salaries. Base salary adjustments can also be used to prevent turnover of employees who possess skills that have become highly sought after in the labor market.

  - *Merit increases* raise pay based on a percentage of current salary. These are the most common types of annual pay increases. Merit increases tend to reflect competency ratings because competency performance tends to be stable over multiple years. As people's competency performance increases, they become more valuable employees overall.

  - *Variable pay bonuses* provide a one-time financial award as a fixed amount or as a percentage of current salary. These are usually tied to achievement of specific goals. Variable pay bonuses are typically used to reward employees for something they accomplished during the previous year or pay period but may not do again in the future.

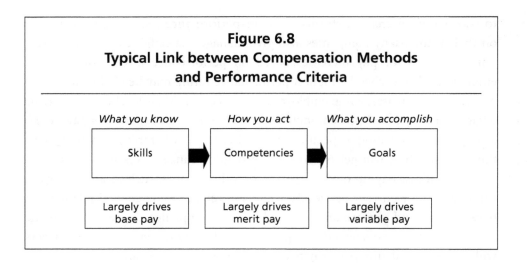

Figure 6.8
Typical Link between Compensation Methods and Performance Criteria

What you know → *How you act* → *What you accomplish*

Skills → Competencies → Goals

Largely drives base pay | Largely drives merit pay | Largely drives variable pay

Companies do not always create strict links between the different types of pay and these three aspects of performance. But this framework can help explain general compensation strategies. Base pay is a function of what skills employees possess and therefore what jobs and tasks they are qualified to perform. Merit pay is a function of performance related to stable, underlying job performance competencies that increase a person's overall value in their current role. Variable pay is a reward for an employee's most recent goal accomplishments.

• *What factors have an impact on pay outside of performance, and are people aware of them?* Performance is an important factor when making compensation decisions, but it is not the only one. Other factors important to pay decisions include an employee's current salary relative to others in similar positions, turnover risk, and overall criticality to the business. The financial performance of the company also has a major impact on pay decisions. It is useful to provide managers with guidelines on how to account for these other factors when making these decisions. Employees should also have some sense of these factors so they better understand how decisions are made about compensation. Performance management data are important pieces of the puzzle in setting compensation, but not the only piece.

Staffing Decisions It might seem obvious to use performance management data to guide internal staffing and promotion decisions. Yet many companies do not systematically include performance reviews in the staffing selection process.

This is often because companies do not feel they have accurate performance management data. But regardless of the state of your performance management data, it is important to consider performance management ratings when filling internal positions. Excluding performance ratings from the staffing process sends a message to employees and managers that the performance management process is not important. The following are a few additional considerations when creating links between performance management data and staffing:

- *Establish guidelines or minimum performance levels for internal transfers or promotions.* Communicate minimum performance requirements that employees must meet to be considered for other positions in the company. For example, you might require that employees have performance ratings of "meets expectations or above" in order to be qualified for internal transfers. Employees should not be able to deal with poor performance reviews by escaping to another role elsewhere in the organization. Similarly, managers should not be allowed to pass poor performers to other parts of the company without some discussion of their performance issues. The practice of "dumping poor performers onto other departments" is particularly common in companies that do not support managers who confront underperformance.

- *Balance the what and how of performance when making staffing decisions.* I have discussed performance being a function of "what you accomplish" (achieving goals) and "how you accomplish it" (demonstrating competencies). There is a tendency to promote people based on goal accomplishment while overlooking performance issues related to competencies. This sends the message that results are all that matter, and how you achieve those results is of little importance. This sort of staffing approach can create a business culture where ethics and values become unimportant as long as employees hit their numbers.

- *Clarify that performance is one of many things that influence staffing decisions.* The decision to promote or transfer an employee should depend in part on how effectively he or she is performing. But it also depends on the employee's overall commitment to the organization, whether this person possesses underlying skills and attributes to perform different roles beyond what he or she is currently doing, and whether the company has the talent needed to backfill the employee's current position if he or she is moved to another job. Employees should understand that even if they may be the best performer in their current job, this does not necessarily mean they are the best candidate for other roles.

• *How you measure employee performance to guide staffing decisions may be different from how you measure performance in current roles.* When companies use performance assessments to guide staffing decisions, they should emphasize those parts of job performance that are similar to the new role. This may represent only a small part of a person's current role. For example, when you are evaluating the performance of someone in an individual contributor role for a potential promotion into a management role, you should emphasize those aspects of his or her current job that have to do with guiding and influencing others (e.g., building relationships), while downplaying parts of their role that reflect individual contributor tasks that you might not want managers to do themselves (e.g., solving technical problems). Because performance assessments done for staffing put more emphasis on some parts of the job than others, it is not uncommon to find that the best candidate for a new job may not be the employee who had the highest overall performance rating in their current role. This is important to explain if a high-performing employee did not get a promotion they were expecting.

• *Do not wait until a formal performance review to address counterproductive performance.* We usually think about staffing in terms of promotions and job transfers. But staffing also includes removing people from jobs in which they are underperforming. Staffing actions to manage out underperformers should be initiated as soon as a manager determines that an employee's performance does not meet the needs of the role. This includes putting employees on a performance improvement plan so they have an opportunity to correct performance issues. If it is determined that an employee needs to be removed from a role, this action should take place immediately and independent of the formal performance review cycle. You do not want to tolerate a clearly underperforming employee longer than you have to. You also do not want the performance review cycle to become associated with an annual weeding out of poor performers.

Development Decisions The primary way performance management supports employee development is by providing constructive, actionable feedback that employees can use to increase their effectiveness and career success. Delivering performance feedback is an essential step in the overall performance management cycle. This step depends heavily on the skills of an employee's manager, which I discuss in the next section covering performance management training. There are other ways performance management can support development beyond just providing feedback. Performance management results can be used to guide creation of career development plans, determine employee training needs, or allow employees to qualify for development programs designed for high-potential employees. Following are a few suggestions to consider when integrating performance management with development activities:

• *Stand-alone development planning forms usually provide little value.* Many performance management processes include a step where employees are asked to complete a development planning form based on their performance review. These plans are used to document developmental goals and actions the employee hopes to take in response to the performance feedback he or she received. Conceptually this makes a lot of sense. We want employees to use information from the performance evaluation to increase their effectiveness. But these sorts of development forms often go unfilled because there is no compelling reason for employees to use them. The key to creating effective development planning forms is to make sure one or more of the following conditions exists:

- The development plan provides the employee with links to training catalogues and other resources to support his or her development goals.

- The content of the development plans is actively reviewed by the employee's manager or training experts within the organization who can provide the employee with suggestions regarding his or her development strategies.

- The employee's development plan is used to make decisions that are important to the employee's career growth. An example is basing assessment of future potential in part on the progress an employee is making toward fulfilling the development objectives listed on his or her development plan.

The main point is to create some compelling reason to use the form. There has to be a clear benefit for employees if they are going to take time to record their development goals and accomplishments on development plans.

• *Treat development resources as a strategic investment.* Many organizations view training and development resources as something that all employees should have access to. At a general level, this is true since all employees are capable of improving their performance to some degree. However, many development opportunities can be considered to be both a reward for the employee and an investment for the organization. It makes sense to focus development resources such as training on employees whose performance suggests they will most effectively use these resources. Make sure employees realize that receiving certain development resources is in recognition of their performance contributions and potential.

• *Put more focus on developing high performers than fixing low performers.* There is a tendency to view development as something done to address poor performance. But investing in the development of high performers often generates far more benefits than trying to fix issues limiting the effectiveness of low performers. Furthermore, if training is mainly used to address performance problems, then being given a training assignment will be viewed as a sign of incompetence. I saw an example of this in one organization where a manager told me that "being sent to training was a sign that you are at risk of getting fired." Avoid this problem by stressing the use of development activities designed to make good performers better.

• *If you are serious about development, track it.* Most companies say they expect employees to develop their capabilities, but not all companies track employee progress against development goals. If you want to send the message that development matters, require employees and managers to build development plans based on performance reviews, track employee performance against these plans, and hold employees and their managers accountable for progress.

• *Development is the employee's responsibility; enabling development is the manager's responsibility.* The only way employees will develop is if they are truly committed to their developmental goals. From this perspective, development is an employee responsibility. At the same time, it also depends on the work environment that their manager creates. The decisions and actions of managers significantly support or constrain the ability of employees to develop. As a result, both employees and managers should be held accountable for the development progress of employees.

Workforce Management Decisions Performance management data allow companies to shift workforce planning and analytics from an exercise focused on workforce quantity to one that includes workforce quality. For example, rather than just tracking average employee turnover, companies can focus specifically on the turnover of high-performing employees. Or analytics can be used to identify the recruiting sources that lead to hiring the best employees as opposed to just looking at which sources provide the most candidates. The following are a few tips to consider when integrating performance management data into workforce planning and analytics activities:

- *Performance management data are more interesting when compared to data from other processes.* Most companies treat business metrics as though all employees performed at the same level, even though one of the biggest variables affecting business outcomes is variance in employee performance.[10] Performance management data can be used to investigate relationships between business metrics such as profit, customer satisfaction or product quality, and characteristics of the employees responsible for these metrics. Consider the value of having insight into the following kinds of questions:
  - What performance competencies are associated with higher sales numbers?
  - What manager competencies are associated with retention of high-performing employees?
  - What impact does a training program have on the performance levels of employees?
  - What impact do high-performing employees have on customer satisfaction levels compared to average or low-performing employees?

- *The more you use performance management data, the better the data will become.* Many companies do not use performance management data to guide workforce management decisions because these data have historically been of poor quality. But the reverse is true as well: the reason a lot of performance management data are of poor quality is that no one uses these data. The more that performance management data are used to make business decisions, the more effort managers will invest to ensure the data are accurate and useful. The best way to create this virtuous cycle is to start looking at performance management data in leadership meetings. If managers complain that "it's not accurate," your reply might be, "It came from managers, so managers are the ones who can improve its quality."

- *Approach performance management data with the same mind-set used for budget forecasts.* Performance management data are often criticized as being based on subjective opinions that lack accuracy. The same can be said for budget forecasting data. A significant part of budget forecasts is based on managers' subjective estimates of what resources will be needed in the future. These estimates may be based on some actual records of past business performance and resource consumption, but they also include a healthy dose of speculation about the future. Like budget forecasts, performance management data are based largely on managers' subjective evaluations of employees' competencies, backed up with some actual records of goal metrics and behavioral examples. If these data are systematically collected and thoroughly reviewed, they can provide accurate information for forecasting future business outcomes. When someone complains about the subjectivity of performance management data, it may help to remind the person that the same thing is true for budget forecasts, yet we regularly use those data to guide effective business decisions.

6.4.7   What Training and Incentives Do Managers and Employees Need to Effectively Use Performance Management Processes?

Implementing more rigorous performance management processes invariably requires managers and employees to do things they have not done before or have not done very effectively. Performance management can also require HR personnel to support tasks they have not previously performed (see the discussion: "Why Some HR People Fear Rigorous Performance Management"). Many performance management processes fail because managers and employees are unable or unwilling to use them as intended.

WHY SOME HR PEOPLE FEAR RIGOROUS PERFORMANCE MANAGEMENT

You might assume that HR professionals will be strident advocates for effective performance management. But the reality is that some HR professionals find performance management personally challenging and anxiety provoking.

Many HR professionals developed careers conducting administrative duties such as processing payroll and answering questions about benefits. A common stereotype of HR professionals describes them as "people who like people." While this is certainly not always true, there are some HR professionals who would rather be viewed as a confidant, coach, and friend than as the person who ensures talent is assessed using consistent, rigorous, and accurate methods. They have never been at the center of major business discussions and may be uncomfortable driving managers to critically evaluate and address performance issues. As a result, barriers to effective performance management can come from within a company's own HR department. These are some of the reasons that HR professionals may resist rigorous performance management methods:

- *Unwilling to challenge managers.* Effective performance management requires challenging managers to give honest, candid, and accurate evaluations of their employees. Some HR professionals do not know how to push back on managers effectively or do not want to risk managers' disliking them or otherwise reacting negatively to their challenges.

- *Uncomfortable facilitating crucial business conversations.* Performance management conversations focusing on performance calibration and compensation can generate intense discussion among managers regarding the value of different employees and their relative impact on the business. HR professionals should actively encourage and facilitate these discussions, working to keep them on track and productive. Yet HR professionals may lack the skills needed to manage these sorts of intense debates. In addition, they may have concerns about how they will be treated if they challenge managers to justify their talent decisions. For example, one global organization had a stated goal to increase gender and ethnic diversity at senior levels of the company. The head of HR called out staffing practices among senior executives that were perpetuating the status quo. One practice was hiring executives from the CEO's personal network who all shared his demographic characteristic (e.g., white males who played golf). The HR leader quickly learned that pursuing leadership diversity was okay as long as it did not require the CEO to change his behavior!

- *Lack confidence dealing with difficult performance issues.* If performance management processes are working well, at some point they will uncover performance concerns in employees who are considered key to business operations. These are people who possess crucial skills and talents yet behave in a manner that limits the overall effectiveness of the company or group (sometimes they are referred to as prima donnas). Managers often tolerate performance issues in these people for fear they might leave if anyone gave them honest feedback. It is one thing to call out performance problems of employees whose loss is not going to create major issues for the business. It is another to note flaws in people who are viewed as critical talent. Evaluating these people in a manner that motivates them to change rather than quit requires considerable talent management skills. Some HR professionals do not feel up to this task.

- *Don't want to explain unpopular decisions.* Effective performance management results in employees being treated differently based on their relative contributions to the organization. This means that someone has to explain to average and low performers why they are not considered to be high performers and encourage them to accept the decision as fair and equitable. Managers are primarily responsible for this discussion, but it is common for disgruntled employees to also take their concerns to HR. HR managers may not want to be put in a position where they have to hold these conversations and be seen as the bearer of bad news.

The self-identity and self-confidence of a company's HR professionals is an important factor in deploying and supporting a rigorous performance management process. For performance management to work, HR must own the role of experts in creating high-performance work environments. Other support functions such as finance and IT tend to be far more comfortable than HR in this sort of expert role. It is the rare finance organization that lets line managers decide whether they want to comply with budgeting guidelines and requirements. Similarly, IT departments are quite comfortable telling managers what technology systems their teams are required to use based on company policy. HR needs to be similarly comfortable owning the role of talent management experts. This doesn't mean being arrogant and inflexible. It does mean being confident enough to challenge managers who think performance management processes and guidelines are something they can ignore.

It is also important to provide HR professionals with the tools, knowledge, and resources to handle the challenges that arise when implementing performance management processes. It takes specialized skills to facilitate calibration sessions, constructively challenge manager opinions, and deliver critical feedback to valuable employees. HR professionals need to be trained on these skills and given access to resources that support them. Finally, HR leadership must set clear expectations for members of the HR department toward supporting and facilitating performance management practices. HR professionals must be evaluated based on how well the departments they support carry out performance management. Little tolerance can be shown toward HR professionals who actively or passively resist the adoption of more rigorous performance management methods.

Implementing stronger performance management also requires getting line leaders to appreciate and respect the specialized skills and knowledge associated with strategic HR in general. This can be a challenge as many people like to think they are experts in people. This makes HR different from support functions like IT or finance. People will readily admit they do not understand the technical aspects of IT and finance. But managers often claim to be good at judging and influencing the performance of others, despite countless examples of management incompetence that clearly demonstrate that many managers do not understand the best ways to increase employee performance.

Table 6.4 summarizes changes that managers and employees must accept if performance management is going to work as intended. The table lists benefits each change provides if done well, reasons that managers and employees may resist the change, and enablers that will drive acceptance of the change.

Table 6.4
Changes Affecting Manager and Employee Adoption of Performance Management

Key Changes[a]	Benefits	Concerns	Change Enablers
Managers must:			
Communicate specific goals and performance expectations to employees	Increased role clarity allows employees to more effectively self-manage performance	Time required to set goals and communicate expectations	Training on how to set goals
			Tools to support setting goals and communicating expectations
Provide regular feedback during the year so there are no surprises in the performance review	Increase employee performance and engagement through ongoing coaching	Taking time to give feedback. Knowing how to give effective feedback	Tools to support and remind managers to give feedback.
			Training on delivering feedback
Systematically assess employees based on specific competencies and goals	Accurate, fair, and job-relevant performance evaluations	Having to comply with a structured process	Tools that increase efficiency of reviews
		Time needed to do reviews	Short, meaningful performance criteria
Critically compare employees and avoid rating everyone the same	Development of a high-performance work environment	Having to explain to employees why some are rated higher than others	Clear criteria to justify ratings
	Consistent performance standards across the company	Admitting they have low performers	Training on how to deliver potentially critical feedback
		Having to conform to a shared performance standard	Support for dealing with low performers
Explain and justify performance ratings to peers and HR	Resolve issues decreasing workforce productivity	Time and potential stress associated with giving what may be seen as critical feedback	Accountability for complying with the process
Provide accurate behavioral and goal-based performance feedback to employees	Retain and better use high-performing talent	Time and disruption to business operations resulting from having to address underperformance	Accountability for meeting with employees.
	Increase return on investment associated with workforce costs and expenses		Clear criteria to justify ratings and training and support for providing feedback
Identify and address low-performing employees			Support and resources to minimize issues related to addressing underperforming employees
Recognize high-performing employees		Having to justify staffing and pay decisions based on clear criteria	Resources to recognize high performers
			Rewarding managers for providing talent to the company
Use performance data to guide compensation, staffing, and development decisions			Accountability for making talent decisions in a consistent and transparent manner

Employees must:[a]			
Accept and commit to specific performance expectations	Knowing exactly what is expected of them	Loss of autonomy; dislike being told what to do	Involve employees in process of defining expectations; participative goal setting
Accept and act on ongoing feedback from managers	Receive guidance on how they can be more successful	Dislike being told "what they are doing wrong"	Emphasize development as a key part of job performance
Be reviewed against a rigorous, consistent set of standards	Fairer and more consistent performance process	Threat of being evaluated to standards they may not meet	Ensure managers know how to provide constructive feedback
Accept that they may not be rated as highly as others	Understanding gaps between current performance and ideal performance	Feeling that they are not valued or their career at the company has derailed	Provide transparency into how the performance management process works, who is involved, and how decisions are made
See actions taken to address underperforming coworkers	Not having to tolerate and work with underperforming coworkers	Concerns about the welfare of coworkers who may be friends	Reinforce that average employees are valued; stress that performance levels can and do change over time
Receive feedback that they are an underperformer	Get help and direction to improve their performance	Fear of negative consequences resulting from performance issues (pay, dismissal)	Provide transparency on how performance issues are identified and addressed; emphasize use of fair and consistent methods
Be recognized as a high performer	Knowing their contributions are appreciated; tangible benefits (e.g., pay, promotions)	Uncertainty of whether they will be able to maintain this level	Provide transparency on how performance issues are identified and addressed; emphasize use of fair and consistent methods
Receive critical, detailed feedback on their performance, including strengths and weaknesses	Clear awareness of current effectiveness and how to improve, valuable information for career development	Concern about having performance weaknesses documented and used against them	Stress benefits of being a high performer and how to maintain this level
		Fear of being "labeled"	Emphasize confidentiality of performance data
			Clarify how data are used
			Note performance is expected to change over time

[a]Some changes apply only to certain types of performance management processes or are relevant only for specific employees based on their level of performance.

Managers' Use of Performance Management   The main reason for managers to adopt performance management is to increase the productivity of their employees. This requires having a well-designed performance management process and using it correctly. Many managers have had unrewarding experiences with performance management because the previous processes they used were not well designed or they did not know how to use them. Expect these managers to voice one or more of the following objections when you ask them to adopt more rigorous performance management methods:

- *"It takes too much time."* Most managers are constantly pressed for time and frequently view performance management as a bureaucratic exercise that takes them away from operational business issues. There are several ways to overcome this objection. First, make sure the performance management process has a direct impact on decisions managers care about. If performance management data do not influence allocation of pay, staffing, or other organizational resources, then managers have a valid complaint that it's a pointless administrative exercise. Second, have managers rate employees on well-defined, concise, and clearly job-relevant performance criteria. Third, design the process to provide maximum impact with minimal work. If you don't know how a rating or item of information is going to be used, don't ask managers to provide it. Never ask for information just because it seems that it might be useful. Fourth, remind managers how much time and resources are spent dealing with problems that arise as a result of poor performance management. Evaluating performance and providing feedback may seem time-consuming, but it is far less costly than tolerating poor performance.

- *"It creates friction between me and my employees."* One reason managers avoid performance management is they do not want to talk with employees about sensitive and potentially volatile performance issues. Most managers won't say this openly, but many think it. There are two ways to address this issue. First, make sure managers are setting clear performance expectations. Discussing performance issues is basically a three-step process: (1) agreeing on what the employee did or did not do, (2) ensuring the employee understands the impact of his or her actions and why he or she needs to change, and (3) working with the employee on strategies to act on the feedback.

The first step is the most important and most sensitive. It is much easier to discuss performance problems with employees if the issues are clearly visible to both the employee and the manager. Well-defined performance criteria are critical to making this run smoothly. As one colleague told me, "The best time to educate managers on how to set goals and performance expectations is right after they finish last year's performance review sessions. That's when they are most aware of the value of setting clearly defined expectations because they are wishing they'd taken the time to do it twelve months ago!" The second action is to give managers training on how to provide feedback (see the discussion: "The COACH Method for Increasing Employee Performance" for an example of what this training might include). If managers say they already know how to deliver feedback, don't necessarily believe them. Almost all successful deployments of performance management include considerable manager training on how to deliver constructive feedback.

THE COACH METHOD FOR INCREASING EMPLOYEE PERFORMANCE

Effective managers know that success does not depend on what they do; it depends on what their team members do. Being a good manager is like being a good soccer coach. Coaching is not about what you do on the sidelines; it is about how your actions influence what the players do on the field. The challenge of management is figuring out what you can do on the sidelines that will effectively influence the behavior of your players on the field. If you want to become a truly great leader, think less about "what I can do to increase my performance" and think more about "what I can do to increase the performance of the people I manage."

Increasing the productivity of a team requires changing other people's behavior. The only way to increase direct reports' performance is to get them to act differently in the future from how they have acted in the past. Getting people to change their behavior is not easy. In fact, many highly capable, hard-working professionals choose not to take management positions because they do not want to be accountable for the behavior of others.

The following five basic managerial actions help inspire and guide employees to increase their performance through changing their behavior. These five steps are referred to using the acronym COACH (Credibility, Objectives, Awareness, Consequences, Help).

Establish Credibility

Most people do not respond well to being told that they need to change. Before you can create a productive dialogue with employees about changing behavior, they must believe that you are someone they should trust and listen to. Until you establish a basic level of credibility with employees, they are unlikely to listen to your advice. The fastest way to build credibility is to ask employees what they want to achieve from their job and then take actions that demonstrate that you are serious about helping them achieve their goals. Employees don't change to support your goals; they change to support their goals. If you want to be a credible source of feedback for your employees, start by making sure you understand what it is they want to achieve by working for you.

Set *Objectives*

Performance is about getting things done. This requires making sure employees understand what they are supposed to be doing. Setting objectives is not about telling people what they are supposed to do. It is about working with them to reach agreement on how to align their career goals and interests with the objectives and needs of the company. Actively tracking objectives with employees is often the biggest opportunity managers have for improving performance. Try this exercise with your employees. Ask them to write down the five to ten most important things they need to accomplish to be successful in their roles. At the same time, independently write down the five to ten things you believe they must accomplish. Compare these two lists and make sure they align.

Increase Awareness

Increasing awareness is about providing employees with insights that help them accomplish their objectives. Helping them understand what they are doing well and what they need to change to maximize their productivity is a key skill of an effective manager. It is also one of the most difficult managerial skills to develop. Several basic techniques help ensure feedback is viewed as a gift and not a punishment. One is to tie feedback to goals: let people know how their behaviors are helping or hurting their ability to achieve their objectives. You do not want them to change just to change; you want them to change so they will be more successful. Another technique is to give feedback based on clearly observable behaviors. Be very specific in suggesting what sort of actions employees can "start doing," "stop doing," or "continue doing" to be more successful.

Create Consequences

Setting clear objectives and increasing employees' awareness of how to achieve these objectives often provides enough information to increase employee performance. But some employees need additional incentives to change their behaviors. Managers are responsible for ensuring that employees understand what they need to do to be successful and making sure employees know what will happen if they do or do not do these things. More often than not, managers are the ones who must deliver these consequences, both good and bad. Be extremely transparent about how you are evaluating employee performance and what consequences are tied to those evaluations. People can usually accept that they will not get everything they want as long as rewards are allocated based on a consistent and clearly communicated set of criteria and they are confident that in the future they can do better than they may have done in the past.

Providing *Help*

Employees are responsible for their own performance. But it is the manager's responsibility to create an environment that supports employee success. Do little things every day that foster learning, development, and productivity among your direct reports. Performance management is not a quarterly or annual event. It is an ongoing activity. Look for things you can incorporate into your day-to-day routine to ensure you are creating a high-performing work environment for your team.

• *"It will hurt the productivity of my team."* This is a result of managers not understanding the importance and value of performance management activities. Empirical research shows that effective performance management is a critical component of high-performance organizations. When managers say, "Our performance management process doesn't work," the appropriate response is not to get rid of performance management altogether. Engage with managers to understand the source of their concerns, and then address them through communication, training, and process redesign.

- *"It doesn't matter if I don't do it."* Check to see if this is true. Does your company track metrics that provide insight into whether managers are fulfilling their performance management responsibilities? Are they held accountable for following the process? Are managers who excel at performance management rewarded and recognized? Do senior leaders role-model effective use of performance management? If the answer to one of these questions is no, then revisit your business leaders' commitment to performance management. The HR department can support and facilitate the performance management process, but it cannot hold managers accountable for using the process. This is the responsibility of business leaders.

Managers have the most difficult tasks in the performance management process: they have to sit down with employees, tell them what they are doing wrong, and explain the impact this has on their pay and career goals. They need to do this in way that makes employees feel confident about their ability to improve, not despondent about their future in the company. This is not a simple administrative exercise, so do not treat it as one. Manager adoption of performance management depends on managers understanding what they are being asked to do and being clear on why it is important, providing training so they know how to do it, and measuring and holding them accountable for actually doing it.

Employees' Use of Performance Management Effective performance management has many benefits for employees. It ensures they are fairly evaluated and appropriately rewarded for their contributions. It provides critical information to guide career development. It gives greater role clarity around the importance and purpose of their jobs. And it addresses frustrations caused by incompetent or unmotivated coworkers.

Like managers, many employees have experienced previous performance management processes that were poorly designed and applied. These employees may approach performance management activities with a mixture of skepticism and anxiety. Most employee concerns will center around two basic themes.

The first theme is questioning the fairness and accuracy of the performance management system. Employees may be concerned whether the process will accurately evaluate their contributions and take fair and appropriate actions based on their performance. Research on employee perceptions of justice shows that employees evaluate fairness of performance management processes based on three criteria:[11]

- *Distributive justice*, which focuses on the outcomes of performance management decisions ("What did I get in terms of recognition or rewards?")

- *Procedural justice*, which focuses on the processes used to make these decisions ("How did they decide what I deserve?")

- *Interpersonal justice*, which focuses on how decisions are communicated ("Did they inform me of the decision in a respectful, sensitive, and appropriate manner?")

Procedural justice has the most influence on perceptions of fairness in an employment setting. Most employees can accept that they will not always get what they hoped for as long as the processes used to make decisions are clearly communicated and fairly and consistently applied. Interpersonal justice can also be critical if the outcome of a decision is particularly negative for an employee (e.g., being told you will not get a raise or will lose your job due to poor performance).

The justice research indicates that it is extremely important to communicate to employees exactly how the performance management process works. Be transparent about how the company makes decisions about employment outcomes such as pay and promotions. Employees should know what information is considered when making performance decisions, who is involved in reviewing the information and making the decisions, and what guidelines those people follow during this process.[12] It is also important that managers be trained on how to appropriately deliver bad news to employees who may not be getting the performance outcomes they had hoped for.

The second theme is concerns about the impact of performance management on the employee's future career objectives. Employees may express concern that negative performance reviews could have a permanent impact on their future career opportunities within the organization. On one hand, this is true. If someone has performance problems, then the company can and should take this into account when making decisions about pay, promotions, or development opportunities. On the other hand, even the most effective employees have opportunities for performance improvement. Employees should not fear that having negative comments in their performance review will forever limit their career opportunities within the organization unless the goal is to have these employees leave the company.

Two messages should be stressed when giving negative performance feedback to employees. First, all employees, no matter how effective, have areas where they could improve. One purpose of performance management is to give them feedback that will help them be more successful, no matter how successful they already are. Second, just because something is a performance concern now does not mean it will be a concern in the future. The purpose of giving employees feedback is to help them address issues that are limiting their success.[13] If companies did not believe employees could improve their performance, there would be little reason to tell them the results of their performance reviews. The key to effectively delivering these two messages lies with the manager. This is another reason that manager training is so critical to the successful deployment of performance management processes.

6.5 INCREASING PERFORMANCE MANAGEMENT PROCESS MATURITY

Figure 6.9 illustrates five general levels of performance management maturity. The lowest level of performance management maturity is making sure employee performance is evaluated using consistent, standardized methods (e.g., the traditional annual performance review). The basis of performance management lies in accurately measuring if employees are doing things in the right way, and a requirement for accurate measurement is consistency. Thus, conducting regular performance reviews is important.

Level 2 emphasizes creating clear performance definitions, competency models, and goal criteria to guide performance evaluations. Level 3 focuses on using performance data so they have impacts on decisions related to employee pay, development, and staffing. Level 4 emphasizes the use of calibration processes that build consensus across managers regarding performance expectations and employee evaluations. At level 5, business leaders leverage performance management data to gain insight into the workforce itself—for example, determining what competencies are most relevant to success in different roles, assessing

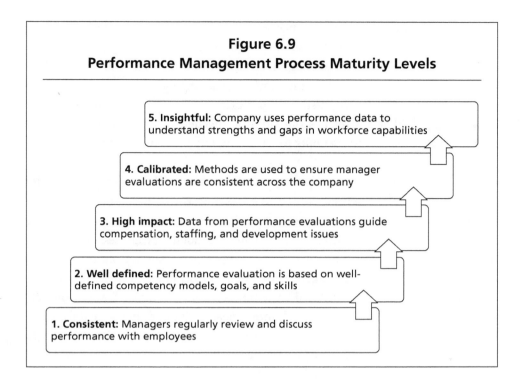

Figure 6.9
Performance Management Process Maturity Levels

5. Insightful: Company uses performance data to understand strengths and gaps in workforce capabilities

4. Calibrated: Methods are used to ensure manager evaluations are consistent across the company

3. High impact: Data from performance evaluations guide compensation, staffing, and development issues

2. Well defined: Performance evaluation is based on well-defined competency models, goals, and skills

1. Consistent: Managers regularly review and discuss performance with employees

overall strengths and weaknesses of the workforce, and identifying actions to increase overall workforce productivity.

Higher levels of performance management maturity create stronger results, but it is not necessary to always strive for the highest level possible. Each level provides more value than those below it, but moving up each level also requires more resources and change management. What level is best depends on the objectives associated with performance management in your company. If all you want is to ensure compliance with legal guidelines, then level 1 may be adequate. If the goal is to increase coaching and dialogue, levels 2 and 3 may suffice. And if you want to create a true high-performance culture, you will want to strive for level 4 or higher.

There are two ways to increase performance management maturity in organizations. The most obvious is to start at the bottom and work up. Start by introducing annual performance reviews using basic competency models and goal plans. Expand on this by adding more job-specific competencies and creating stronger links between performance evaluations, pay, and promotions. Move up further by adding calibration sessions and reviewing talent reports at senior-level meetings to track development and retention of high performers. The advantage of this approach is that it allows managers to gradually learn the skills needed to support more sophisticated performance management methods. The disadvantage is that it stretches out the time needed to reach higher maturity levels that provide greater benefits for the company in terms of increased work-force productivity.

It is also possible to start by focusing on higher levels of process maturity and use this to drive the organization to adopt lower-level processes. One of the fastest ways to do this is to implement an integrated calibration process using well-defined competency models, goal plans, and talent review sessions (level 4 on the maturity curve). When a company implements calibration, three things will happen. First, when managers know their performance ratings are going to be reviewed and discussed in a talent review session with other leaders, the ratings process suddenly becomes much more meaningful and they take it far more seriously (level 3). Second, because they know they'll have to justify the ratings, they also show more interest in using well-defined performance criteria (level 2). Finally, since they know they'll have to share their ratings, they are driven to get their performance evaluations completed on time and in the proper format (level 1). Calibration can pull an organization up through levels 1, 2, 3, and 4 on the performance process maturity curve in less than a year. It does require considerable manager training and change management, but it is an achievable objective if an organization approaches it with clarity and focus.

6.6 CONCLUSION

Performance management is probably the most widely used and most widely criticized strategic HR process. This chapter explained why performance management is crucial for maximizing workforce productivity and why it is often difficult to do well. It provided guidelines for creating effective performance management processes and called out problems that occur when performance management methods are poorly designed or improperly deployed.

All companies treat certain employees differently from others based on their performance. In other words, all companies practice performance management. But relatively few do it extremely well. Companies that make a concerted effort to clearly communicate performance expectations, fairly and accurately assess employees against these expectations, and use this information to guide employee development, compensation, and staffing decisions have a significant and lasting advantage over companies that manage people using poorly defined, highly subjective, and poorly communicated techniques.

Companies that believe in the value of performance management believe that employees should know what is expected of them and should be fairly and consistently evaluated and rewarded based on those expectations. These companies value transparency and meritocracy. They dislike talent decisions based largely on personal opinion and unfounded claims about employee value. It basically comes down to this question: Do you believe employees should understand how their performance is defined, evaluated and rewarded? If the answer is yes, then you believe in the value of performance management.

NOTES

1. Toppo, L., & Prusty, T. (2012). From performance appraisal to performance management. *Journal of Business and Management, 3*, 1–6.

2. Aguinis, H. (2007). *Performance management.* Upper Saddle River, NJ: Pearson Prentice Hall.

3. Borman, W. C., White, L. A., & Dorsey, D. W. (1995). Effects of ratee task performance and interpersonal factors on supervisor and peer performance ratings. *Journal of Applied Psychology, 80*, 168–177.

4. Brannick, M. T., Levine, E. L., & Morgeson, F. P. (2007). *Job and work analysis: Methods, research, and applications for human resource management.* Thousand Oaks, CA: Sage. Cooper, K. (2000). *Effective competency modeling and reporting: A step-by-step guide for improving individual and organizational performance.* New York: AMACOM. Gael, S. *Job analysis: A guide to assessing work activities.* San Francisco: Jossey-Bass. Lucia, A. D., & Lepsinger, R. (1999). *The art and science of competency models: Pinpointing critical success factors in organizations.* Hoboken, NJ: Wiley.

5. Eichinger, R. W., Lombardo, M. M., & Ulrich, D. (2006). *100 things you need to know: Best people practices for managers and HR.* Minneapolis: Lominger.

6. Jacobs, R., Kafry, D., & Zedeck, S. (1980). Expectations of behaviorally anchored rating scales. *Personnel Psychology, 33,* 595–640. Kingstrom, P. O., & Bass, A. R. (1981). A critical analysis of studies comparing behaviorally anchored rating scales (BARS) and other rating formats. *Personnel Psychology, 34,* 263–289. Latham, G. P., & Wexley, K. N. (1977). Behavioral observation sales for performance appraisal purposes. *Personnel Psychology, 30,* 255–268.

7. Kruger, J., & Dunning, D. (1999). Unskilled and unaware of it: How difficulties in recognizing one's own incompetence lead to inflated self-assessments. *Journal of Personality and Social Psychology, 77*(6), 1121–1134.

8. Lawler, E. E. (1987). Pay for performance: A motivational analysis. In H. R. Nalbantian (Ed.), *Incentives, cooperation, and risk sharing: Economic and psychological perspectives on employment contracts* (pp. 69–86). Lanham, MD: Rowman & Littlefield. Rynes, S. L., Gerhart, B., & Parks, L. (2005). Personnel psychology: Performance evaluation and pay for performance. *Annual Review of Psychology, 56,* 571–600.

9. Kreps, D. M. (1997). Intrinsic motivation and extrinsic incentives. *American Economic Review, 87,* 359–364. Rynes, S. L., Gerhart, B., & Minette, K. A. (2004). The importance of pay in employee motivation: Discrepancies between what people say and what they do. *Human Resource Management, 43,* 381–394.

10. Fleming, J. H., & Asplund, J. (2007). *Human sigma: Managing the employee-customer encounter.* New York: Gallup Press.

11. Greenberg, J. (1986). Determinants of perceived fairness of performance evaluations. *Journal of Applied Psychology, 71,* 340–342. Korsgaard, M. A., & Roberson, L. (1995). Procedural justice in performance evaluation: The role of instrumental and non-instrumental voice in performance appraisal discussions. *Journal of Management, 21,* 657–669. Erdogan, B., Kraimer, M. L., & Liden, R. C. (2001). Procedural justice as a two-dimensional construct: An examination in the performance appraisal context. *Journal of Applied Behavioral Science, 37,* 205–222. Taylor, M. S., Tracy, K. B., Renard, M. K., & Carroll, S. J. (1995). Due process in performance appraisal: A quasi-experiment in procedural justice. *Administrative Science Quarterly, 40,* 495–523.

12. This does not mean reporting who said what during calibration reviews. Sharing such personal information is likely to be seen as a violation of confidentiality and could cause serious damage to work relationships.

13. It is worth making a brief note about strength-based performance management methods. These methods argue that employees should be told to leverage their strengths and not waste time trying to address weaknesses. This approach is partially true. Employees are likely to succeed through making more effective use of their current strengths. But this success will be limited if they fail to appropriately manage their weaknesses. This does not mean turning weaknesses into strengths. It does mean finding a way to keep weaknesses from derailing their careers.

Creating the Right Development Experiences

Executing business strategies requires having the right people doing the right things in the right way. Maintaining business execution over time requires developing employees to meet changing business demands. This chapter discusses concepts associated with employee development. Emphasis is placed on integrating development methods to maximize business impact and addressing process design and organizational issues that often limit the effectiveness of development methods.

The term *development* refers to processes designed to build the capabilities of employees and leaders within the organization. It is a result of giving people experiences that enable them to acquire new skills, knowledge, and insights. It also involves providing tools that help people maximize the learning obtained from these experiences, as well as putting people in roles that expose them to novel tasks and environments, establishing relationships that support learning and development, and providing training and development resources to acquire job-relevant knowledge, skills, and capabilities. Development is also about transfer of training to help people use skills acquired in one setting to address business challenges encountered in a different setting.

Development is arguably the most complicated area of strategic HR. First, there are many ways to influence learning. Designing effective development

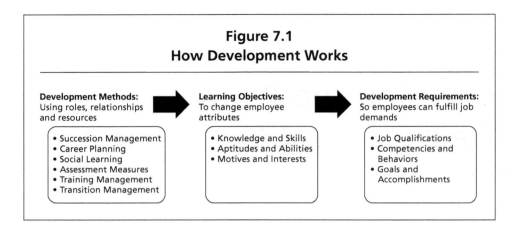

Figure 7.1
How Development Works

Development Methods:
Using roles, relationships and resources

- Succession Management
- Career Planning
- Social Learning
- Assessment Measures
- Training Management
- Transition Management

Learning Objectives:
To change employee attributes

- Knowledge and Skills
- Aptitudes and Abilities
- Motives and Interests

Development Requirements:
So employees can fulfill job demands

- Job Qualifications
- Competencies and Behaviors
- Goals and Accomplishments

programs requires coordinating multiple talent activities toward a common goal. Second, development requires changing who employees are in terms of their skills, knowledge, and self-insights. Most strategic HR processes use communication and motivation to influence employee behavior. In contrast, most development methods are used to change the employee attributes that underlie different job behaviors (see figure 7.1). Changing people's underlying capabilities by giving them new experiences, awareness, and knowledge tends to be far more difficult than changing their behaviors through giving them direction, rewards, and feedback. It can be likened to the difference between asking someone to read a document versus actually teaching this person how to read.

This chapter discusses several methods of development and emphasizes the importance of integrating them into a single development program. Section 7.1 describes the four basic components of a development process. Section 7.2 provides an overview of six major development methods. Section 7.3 discusses the value of building integrated development programs and suggests ways to do this. One of the reasons many development programs struggle is that they focus too much on individual development methods by themselves and not enough on using multiple methods in a coordinated fashion (see the discussion: "The 360 Survey Fad: A Lesson in Misguided Development"). Section 7.4 reviews seven critical questions for designing and implementing integrated development programs. Section 7.5 describes five levels of development process maturity and discusses methods for achieving each level.

THE 360 SURVEY FAD: A LESSON IN MISGUIDED DEVELOPMENT

Companies often implement development methods like training, 360 surveys, or succession management without fully defining how these methods will affect business needs or integrate with other strategic HR processes. What often happens in these situations is that a good development method fails because it is not targeting learning objectives that really matter for the company's strategy. The 360 survey fad that began in the late 1990s is an excellent example of this happening on a widespread basis.

These surveys are assessment measures that ask an employee's manager, peers, and direct reports to provide ratings on the employee's strengths and weaknesses. These surveys are used to provide employees with in-depth feedback to guide self-development. They were considered something of a major innovation when they were developed, and many HR departments and their consulting partners touted them as a key tool for developing employee performance. In a relatively short amount of time, 360 surveys were being used across a wide range of companies.

Problems started to emerge as more and more companies rushed to take advantage of these surveys. Although they can be an effective development method in some situations, they do not work equally well all the time. And several studies were published showing that they can actually decrease performance if they are deployed in the wrong setting or using the wrong process.[a] This awakened people to the fact that 360 surveys were not the developmental silver bullet that many had hoped they would be.

The lesson to be learned from the 360 survey fad is that no development method is effective all the time. These surveys can be very effective in some settings but not in others.

It is costly and potentially detrimental to implement development methods that are not well aligned with the company's business needs. Development strategies should never start with the question, "How can we use this development method?" They should start with this question instead: "What are our business needs, and what learning objectives do we need to achieve to address them?" Only after this is answered should companies begin to consider what development methods to use.

[a]Toegel, G., & Conger, J. A. (2003). 360 degree assessment: Time for reinvention. *Academy of Management Learning and Education, 2,* 297–311.

7.1 THE BASIC COMPONENTS OF A DEVELOPMENT PROCESS

The discussion in this chapter is built around understanding four basic components of development and how they interrelate: talent requirements, learning objectives, development methods, and development programs.

- *Talent requirements:* The term *talent requirements* is used to describe things employees in the workforce must be able to do in the future that they may not be able to do now. Most business strategies require employees to do things in the future that they have not done in the past such as performing current tasks more effectively and building qualifications to take on new roles and responsibilities. The purpose of development is ultimately to address talent requirements. Talent requirements can be tied to specific operational needs like "train sales employees so they can demo the new mobile product application," or they can reflect more general workforce capabilities like "maintain a steady supply of internal talent available to staff all of our global leadership positions."

- *Learning objectives:* Learning objectives describe the attributes employees must develop to meet talent requirements. They define specific types of knowledge, skills, aptitudes, abilities, motives, and interests that influence employee performance now and in the future. Development is used to help employees achieve learning objectives that support the company's talent requirements. Like talent requirements, learning objectives can be specific or more general—for example, "ensure employees know how to install the mobile product application onto their smart phones" or "educate leaders on methods for managing a virtual workforce." Learning objectives define what capabilities employees need to develop. Talent requirements define why they need these capabilities.

- *Development methods.* Development methods are used to achieve learning objectives. There are six primary categories of development methods: succession management, career planning, training resources, social learning, assessment measures, and transition management (see table 7.1). All development methods use a combination of three basic techniques to build employee capabilities: giving people roles that expose them to learning experiences, creating relationships that help employees learn from others, and providing resources that support the learning of new skills, knowledge acquisition, and self-insights.

Table 7.1
Common Development Methods

Method	Purpose and Characteristics	Primary Talent Requirements Addressed
Succession management	To identify and develop talent to fill key positions in an organization. Includes nine box talent reviews, job rotation programs, high-potential identification, and leadership development programs.*	Helps ensure a steady supply of high-performing talent in critical roles Engage, retain, and use high-potential employees
Career planning	To help employees build their capabilities and achieve their career goals. Includes career development plans, career paths, and career interest inventories.	Engage, retain, and develop employees who are seeking to build a career
Training resources	To provide employees with specific knowledge, training, and skills needed to perform their current roles or prepare for future roles. Includes online and classroom training.	Provides employees with access to knowledge needed to perform current roles or move into future roles
Social learning	To provide employees with guidance on how to advance their careers and build relationships to increase engagement and knowledge sharing. Includes formal and informal career coaches, mentors, and online learning communities.	Provides employees with knowledge and relationships that help them advance their career Emphasis on learning through relationships, which increases employee retention

(Continued)

Method	Purpose and Characteristics	Primary Talent Requirements Addressed
Assessment measures	To provide employees with insight into performance strengths and development opportunities. Includes 360 surveys and psychometric measures of work style, personality, and motives.	Increases employees' self-awareness and understanding of strengths and limitations Focuses development energy on things that matter the most
Transition management	To help employees adapt and rapidly reach full productivity in new positions. Focuses on technical training as well as methods to socialize people into new companies or groups.	Helps employees to reach full productivity in new roles while decreasing the risk of turnover in new staff

*Nine box talent reviews are a method commonly used in succession management to evaluate employees based on their performance and potential. A nine box is a three-by-three grid where one axis is used to categorize employees according to three levels of performance and the other axis is used to categorize employees based on three levels of potential.

- *Development programs.* A development program is a process for leveraging one or more development methods in combination with other talent management activities to achieve learning objectives that address a specific set of talent requirements. Companies typically implement development methods in combination with other activities to form integrated development programs.

An example illustrates how these four components come together to create an integrated development process. When a utility company realized that over 25 percent of its skilled power line workers were eligible for retirement, it identified a "talent requirement" to hire and develop internal talent to fill these roles within the next five years. To fill these roles, employees had to achieve the learning objectives of mastering technical skills needed to work the lines, as well as gain experience working on the line in specific types of challenging environments (e.g., during storms or large-scale power outages). The company designed a development program that integrated four development methods: succession management to identify high-potential employees and determine who could move into specific roles over the next three to five years, career planning to help high-potential employees map out the actions and experiences they needed to be qualified for more specialized jobs working on the line, training resources to teach specialized technical skills to high-potential employees so they could perform critical job tasks, and social learning to build mentoring relationships between high-potential employees and highly experienced employees currently working on the line.

Before you can create an effective development program, you need to clearly define the talent requirements the program will address, determine the learning objectives the program must support to meet those requirements, and identify what development methods make the most sense given the program's learning objectives. Too often companies start with looking at development methods first and then try to show how these methods address talent requirements. This is akin to picking a solution first and then trying to find a problem that matches it. Remember that many business leaders don't care a lot about development methods, but all business leaders care about addressing talent requirements that have a direct impact on business performance. Start where their interest lies.

7.2 THE SIX PRIMARY DEVELOPMENT METHODS

Table 7.1 summarizes the six methods commonly used to support employee development: succession management, career planning, training resources, social learning, assessment measures, and transition management. The names used for these categories highlight what is unique about each method in terms of its focus and design.[1]

Succession management methods are used to ensure a steady supply of qualified talent for critical job roles. Historically succession management focused on figuring out who would replace top executives. Organizations now use succession management for roles across the company, including key individual contributor positions. Succession management in some companies extends all the way to frontline employees. Many tools have been created specifically to support succession management (e.g., nine box talent reviews), but much of succession management is actually about coordinating other talent processes such as workforce planning, staffing, and career planning to forecast, identify, develop, and place talent in critical positions.

Career planning methods help employees define strategies to achieve their career goals. Career planning focuses on acquiring skills and building competencies to take on new roles and responsibilities and improve effectiveness in current roles. Career planning can be thought of as the flip side of succession management. Succession management takes a top-down organization-based approach to ensure a supply of talent for future business demands. In contrast, career planning uses a bottom-up employee-based approach to build individual skills to meet requirements for future jobs or job assignments.

Training resources are structured classes, workshops, webinars, books, and other resources used to provide employees with specific knowledge, skills, and insights. Training resources are often deployed using learning management systems (LMS), which are technology platforms that coordinate, deliver, and manage costs associated with providing training resources to a company's workforce. Training resources can be delivered in person, online, or through books or other materials. They are typically used to help employees more effectively perform their current jobs and achieve their future career goals. Training resources are also used to comply with regulations that ensure employees are qualified to perform specific tasks or understand key job policies. Training resources tend to fall into two categories: formally developed activities created and delivered by professional instructional designers and educators, and informally developed activities built and delivered by employees themselves (e.g., employee-created training videos).

Social learning methods create personal relationships that support employee development. These methods emphasize development through social interaction. Social learning methods tend to fall into two categories: methods focused on creating one-to-one development, such as mentoring and coaching relationships, and methods focused on creating learning communities such as online groups where employees with common development goals can share questions, ideas, and suggestions.

Assessment measures are structured tools used to evaluate employee attributes and increase awareness of performance strengths, developmental opportunities, and underlying work tendencies and motives. They tend to fall into three categories:

- 360 surveys, where an employee's coworkers respond to structured questions about the employee's behavior and developmental needs

- Personality questionnaires, simulation exercises, and other structured tools that measure underlying work style, decision-making abilities, and career interests

- Tests where employees must answer questions or perform tasks that demonstrate proficiency with regard to specific knowledge and skills

Transition management methods focus on helping employees assimilate to new jobs and work environments. The methods tend to fall into two categories: onboarding programs that help newly hired employees adjust to their roles within the organization and role transition programs to support internal job transfers within a company, such as moving from an individual contributor to a managerial position. Most transition management methods focus on providing administrative information that people need to perform their jobs (e.g., instructions on how to fill out expense reports), training on job-relevant skills (e.g., product training for new salespeople), and socialization activities designed to help people adjust to the company and culture (e.g., establishing "new hire buddies" who help new employees adjust to the organization).

Companies often treat these methods as individual activities rather than different parts of a single development program. Similarly, many HR professionals will specialize in one or two of these methods without recognizing how the methods they support can and should integrate with other methods. The result is that companies often fail to realize the value that comes from approaching all six methods as parts of a single integrated process for developing workforce capabilities.

7.3 APPROACHING DEVELOPMENT PROGRAMS FROM AN INTEGRATED PERSPECTIVE

Creating an integrated development program requires aligning different development methods so they support one another in a coherent fashion. For example, succession management methods often use assessment measures to identify leadership potential, training resources to develop leadership skills, and social learning to establish high-potential mentorships and learning communities. It makes sense to think of succession management, assessment measures, training resources, and social learning as all being components of a single development program. Yet companies do not always think of development this way.

One of the reasons for poorly integrated development programs is a tendency for companies to treat the six methods listed in table 7.1 as separate programs managed by separate groups. For example, training resources, succession management, and career planning are often administered by different groups within a company. The problem becomes worse when each group uses its own set of tools and technology without planning how to share data and information with the others. Different development groups may even compete against one another for resources rather than collaborating to build integrated development programs. It sometimes feels as if the only things integrating different development methods in these companies are the employees who have to use them.

One can argue that companies need separate departments for these methods since each one requires attending to a variety of unique details and logistics. This may be true, but these methods are still fundamentally tied together by a common focus on building employee capabilities. They work best when they are coordinated with each other. The best way to create integrated development programs is to treat all development methods as aspects of the same overall function. People charged with designing and supporting different development methods should be encouraged to work together, leverage common technologies and models, and create direct links between each other's processes.

It is also common for the six development methods described in table 7.1 to be deployed as separate activities rather than presenting them as integrated programs. Organizations frequently emphasize going live with individual development methods in as a short a time as possible rather than taking time to coordinate multiple development methods into a single program. Implementing development methods in isolation can be easier than deploying an integrated development program. Although there is value in getting development methods up and running quickly, failure to tie development methods together can result in a poor use of resources. Even worse, it can lead to abandoning development methods because they cannot be sustained as isolated activities. The history of human resources is littered with defunct development methods that were launched with great fanfare, only to be dropped because they were never effectively linked into the broader talent management strategy.

Understanding common threads and interdependencies across development methods allows companies to leverage development resources for multiple purposes and avoid duplication of effort. Creating integrated development programs also allows managers and employees to experience development as a coherent sequence of steps rather than a disjointed series of events. It also decreases the risk of creating development methods that conflict with one another, such as encouraging employees to pursue career plans that do not align with the company's succession management needs.

Adopting the following perspectives helps to ensure that development programs are designed with integration in mind:

- All development methods should leverage other development methods.

- All development is based on roles, relationships, and resources, and the most effective development programs use methods cutting across these three areas.

- Development is most effective when it is integrated into ongoing business operations.

7.3.1 All Development Methods Should Leverage Other Development Methods

Figure 7.2 illustrates some ways the six primary development methods interrelate. Every development method provides information or tools that can be used to support each of the other five methods. For example, succession management influences the kinds of career planning that should be encouraged among employees. Employees' career plans affect the types of training resources and social learning the company will want to support. A company's training resources and social learning methods will influence how it designs and uses assessment measures. No development method should be approached in isolation. How you design and use one method should influence and be influenced by how you use the other methods.

In addition, do not assume that one type of development method is inherently more valuable or important than another. The method that is most important depends on the circumstance. A company may allocate more money to support training resources than to support succession management, but that does not mean training is always more critical to business success than succession. The value of development methods depends on the talent requirements facing the organization.

Figure 7.2
Relationships between Developmental Methods

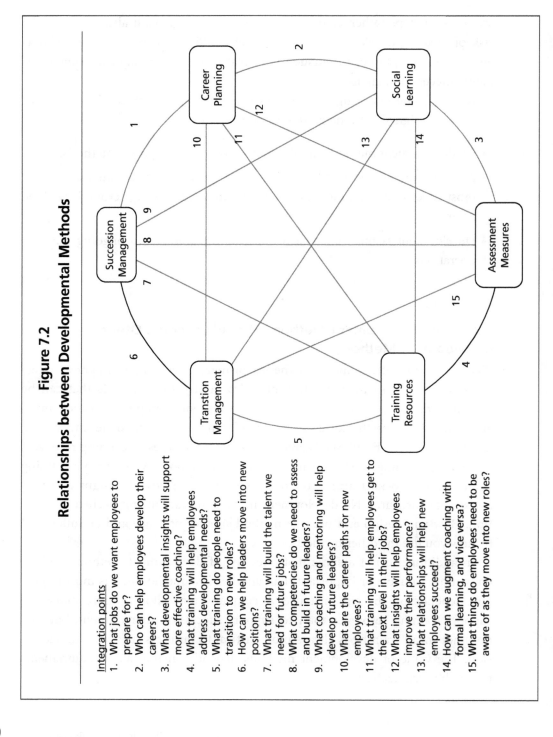

Integration points
1. What jobs do we want employees to prepare for?
2. Who can help employees develop their careers?
3. What developmental insights will support more effective coaching?
4. What training will help employees address developmental needs?
5. What training do people need to transition to new roles?
6. How can we help leaders move into new positions?
7. What training will build the talent we need for future jobs?
8. What competencies do we need to assess and build in future leaders?
9. What coaching and mentoring will help develop future leaders?
10. What are the career paths for new employees?
11. What training will help employees get to the next level in their jobs?
12. What insights will help employees improve their performance?
13. What relationships will help new employees succeed?
14. How can we augment coaching with formal learning, and vice versa?
15. What things do employees need to be aware of as they move into new roles?

7.3.2 All Development Methods Use Roles, Relationships, and Resources to Achieve Learning Objectives

There are three ways companies can help employees achieve learning objectives:

- *Roles:* Give employees job tasks or goals that allow them to acquire new capabilities by learning from experience.
- *Relationships:* Build relationships between employees and people that support development, such as coaches, mentors, observers, or supportive colleagues.
- *Resources:* Provide employees access to training, assessment measures, and other resources that enable them to acquire new skills, knowledge, and developmental insights.

Roles involve giving employees jobs and work assignments that expose them to certain environments, tasks, people, tools, or technology—in other words, asking people to do things they have not done before that enable them to learn from experience. This is arguably the most powerful form of employee development.[2] If you want someone to develop a competency, then give that person a job assignment that requires him or her to build this competency to succeed. This doesn't necessarily mean throwing people in the deep end and seeing if they can swim, although such an extreme approach to development can be effective in some situations. It does mean recognizing that the strongest development comes from hands-on experience.

Relationships help employees establish connections with people who can support their development by providing constructive feedback, offering guidance and instruction, and giving moral support and encouragement. Development relationships can be with anyone in a position to teach employees new skills, help them learn from job experiences, or succeed when they face developmental challenges. Development relationships may come in the form of formal mentoring programs, work interactions between an employee and his or her manager or coworkers, and online collaborative learning communities where employees share knowledge and developmental support with other people with similar career challenges or aspirations.

Resources are tangible tools that help employees acquire new skills, knowledge, and developmental insights. Training is the most common development resource, whether it is in the form of classroom instruction, online courses, or written materials. Another widely used set of resources is represented by 360 surveys and development assessments. Companies are also increasingly providing development resources in the form of social learning videos and online instructional tools created by coworkers to share job-relevant knowledge and information.

Table 7.2 shows how the six major development methods use roles, relationships, and resources. Succession management and career planning are largely about determining what job assignments will best support a person's ongoing development. Training resources provide employees with courses, books, and other materials that help them acquire knowledge and skills to perform their current jobs and develop capabilities for future roles. Assessment measures are a specialized type of development resource. Social learning methods are all about relationships. Transition management methods use a combination of roles, relationships, and resources to help people move into new positions.

Table 7.2
Mapping Roles, Relationships, and Resources to Six Common Development Methods*

	Roles: Giving People Job Assignments That Enable Learning from Experience	Relationships: Helping People Learn from Others	Resources: Providing Tools and Information to Increase Knowledge and Self-Insight
Succession management	✓✓✓	✓	✓✓
Career planning	✓✓	✓✓	✓✓
Training resources			✓✓✓
Social learning	✓	✓✓✓	✓
Assessment measures		✓	✓✓✓
Transition management	✓	✓✓	✓✓

*The check marks indicate the emphasis different development methods place on the use of roles, relationships, and resources, for example, social learning methods rely heavily on establishing mentoring and coaching relationships that support employee development and typically rely less on the use of structured tools to support learning.

Development methods that emphasize roles usually have the biggest impact on employee development. This is because employees tend to learn the most from on-the-job experience. But role-based development methods like succession management and career planning work best when they incorporate relationship-based and resource-based development methods such as training, assessment measures, and social learning. Integrating role-based, resource-based, and relationship-based development methods maximizes people's ability to learn from job experience. For example, if you want to develop an employee's managerial skills, the best results are likely to come from giving that person a task that requires him or her to manage others (e.g., leading a team project). But if you want to maximize the learning value of this assignment, also provide him or her with training resources on how to manage others and help them establish relationships with experienced managers who can coach them in their new role.

When creating a development program, try to draw broadly across different types of development methods. Think about development in terms of the roles, relationships, and resources that will provide the most developmental value given your talent requirements. Figure this out first, and then determine how to combine succession management, career planning, training resources, social learning, assessment measures, and transition management to address key learning objectives. Do not limit yourself to one method just because it happens to be readily available. For example, many companies overly rely on resource-based development methods like training because they are relatively easy to obtain—even though role-based and relationship-based methods are often much more effective. Challenge the organization to leverage the methods that make the most sense given its particular talent requirements.

7.3.3 Development Is Most Effective When It Is Built Directly into Business Operations

Every business leader will say that development is important. Yet managers commonly complain about having to attend a development program or engage in a development exercise instead of being allowed to focus on running the business. Similarly, employees often approach development activities as something they do instead of actual work. This is a result of people failing to see the connection between development programs and talent requirements (see the discussion: "Why Development Has No Inherent Business Value and What to Do about It"). The way to address this challenge is to ensure that development activities are integrated into work itself rather than being treated as stand-alone activities.

Employee development has no inherent business value. Development becomes valuable only when it leads to addressing talent requirements that are important to business operations. Furthermore, most development activities are two or more steps removed from actual business results. Consider the example of training. The immediate result of employee training is increased employee knowledge and skills. But this training does not have an impact on business results until employees use their newly acquired knowledge and skills to solve business challenges. The business value of training depends on whether employees have opportunities and motivation to apply the knowledge gained through training to address business objectives.

Because most development methods do not directly affect business results, it is important to demonstrate how development methods will support learning objectives that are critical to talent requirements. Business leaders should never wonder, "How does this development method help me achieve my department's business objectives?" The link should be obvious. If leaders do not see clearly how development methods and talent requirements help business operations, they will resist using or funding these methods.

Linking development methods to talent requirements in order to affect business outcomes may seem like an obvious action, yet many development departments struggle to do this effectively. This may be due in part to a tendency of HR professionals to assume that "development is its own reward." However, many business leaders do not actually care strongly about employee development; they care only about the business results it creates. HR people tend to talk about how development methods make employees smarter (more skilled, more self-aware) without realizing that business leaders don't want smart employees. They want effective employees. There are certainly jobs where employees have to be smart in order to be effective, but being smart is not the same as being effective.

Development methods are often sold to business leaders based on what they will enable employees to do. But a better approach may be to talk about what will happen to the company if it does not provide development to its employees. Leaders should understand how the organization will be affected if a development program is discontinued. What will people fail to do in the future unless they are developed? How will business results be affected if the company chooses not to develop people? If you cannot answer these questions clearly, then do not be surprised when your development program is suddenly discontinued.

Development should not be something managers and employees do in addition to their regular jobs. It should be part of their regular jobs. Development processes should be closely integrated with processes used to support ongoing business operations.[3] Development activities should have an immediate and clear link to people's business objectives or personal career goals. Following are a few examples of what this looks like in practice:

- A consulting company wanted to increase the number of employees who were qualified to support a new technology. To build these skills, it gave people job assignments that required using this technology. Then the company gave people training on the technology just before the assignments started.

- A manufacturing company wanted to build leaders with greater levels of cross-functional experience. It asked leaders to set learning objectives on their career plans that were related to cross-functional experience. Progress toward these objectives was used as a measure of readiness for promotion into higher-level leadership positions.

- A food processing company needed more cross-cultural leaders to support its growth plans, so it changed its monthly operations meetings to include a discussion of how near-term operational assignments could be used to give high-potential leadership candidates cross-cultural experience.

All of these examples focused on issues directly related to business objectives. The companies had to meet these objectives, and they did it in a way that also supported employee development.

Employees are ideally developed through their day-to-day work, not in addition to it. Blurring the distinction between work and development makes it easier for employees to see how development is helping them achieve their career goals. Making development part of ongoing work creates a direct link between development activities and business results. In my experience, some of the best development experiences are things people never thought of as actually being developmental experiences. They just thought it was part of their job.

7.3.4 Integrated Development as a Way of Thinking

To ensure the creation of effective, well-integrated, long-lasting development programs, it is important to get people who manage different development methods to interact with one another. Avoid organizational structures and technology systems that create silos between succession management, career planning, training resources, assessment measures, social learning methods, and transition management methods. Think how different developmental methods can be used in combination to address talent requirements.

Also solicit the opinions of line managers and employees regarding the business value of development methods. Clarify the link between development programs and ongoing business operations. Show how development methods have a direct impact on employees' ability to achieve their job objectives and career goals and improve managers' ability to improve the productivity of their teams. Overall, remind everyone that the ultimate goal is not to implement development methods or build employee capabilities. It is to address the company's talent requirements.

7.4 CRITICAL DEVELOPMENT DESIGN QUESTIONS

There are seven key design questions related to building and deploying integrated development programs:

1. What talent requirements are you addressing?

2. What positions or people do you need to develop?

3. What employee attributes do you need to develop to achieve your learning objectives?

4. How will you build and maintain development methods?

5. How will you administer and support development programs?

6. How will you measure the impact of development programs?

7. How will you create an environment that supports use of development methods?

These questions are applicable to the design of any development program regardless of the methods used. The answers to them depend on your company's particular talent requirements, the nature of its workforce, and existing talent management processes. Failure to address any of these questions adequately can result in a suboptimal developmental program.

7.4.1 What Talent Requirements Are You Addressing?

Many development programs take several years to become fully effective, for two reasons. First, the effectiveness of these programs is limited by the rate at which people can learn and apply new knowledge, skills, and capabilities. You can teach employees basic facts and procedures in as little as ten minutes, but creating global leaders or specialized technical experts takes years. Second, considerable operational logistics go into building high-impact development programs. You can get simple methods running in under three months. It takes quite a bit more time to build the infrastructure and organizational change to support development programs integrating multiple development methods such as workforce planning, succession management, performance management, career planning, training resources, social learning, and staffing.

Before building a major development program it is important to ask, "Why do this at all?" The following are talent requirements that can be addressed through development programs (see table 7.3):

- *Staffing critical roles.* In every company, certain jobs disproportionately affect overall company performance. These include senior leadership roles such as the CEO, but also key technical and operational roles. Examples of critical roles include merchandise buyers in retail organizations, software architects in technology companies, and nurse managers in hospitals. Failure to identify and develop talent for these roles can have devastating consequences on overall company performance. Extended senior leadership vacancies create confusion and may generate organizational politics and infighting in an effort to fill the power vacuum. Extended vacancies in critical operational positions can have a significant impact on profitability, quality, and service. In many cases, the best and most cost-efficient way to ensure you have the people you need when you need them is through proactive development of internal talent.

- *Sustaining and increasing performance.* Even your best employees will become poor performers over time if they are not given resources to develop and maintain

Table 7.3
Talent Requirements Addressed by Development Processes

Talent Requirements	Questions for Assessing Talent Requirements
Staffing critical roles	What are the critical roles in the organization? What is the financial impact of filling these roles with average compared to high-performing employees?
	What is the time required to fill a vacancy in each critical role? What is the cost per hire to fill these roles?
	How many internal succession candidates are identified for each critical role in your company? How many of these candidates are ready now?
Sustaining and increasing performance	What methods are used to measure employee performance? How do we ensure performance is at acceptable levels?
	Are performance levels in the organization increasing or decreasing?
	What development methods are used to ensure that employees keep their knowledge and skills current?
Accelerating performance	How are new people transitioned into the organization?
	How long does it take them to reach full productivity?
	What methods are in place to support employees' transition into new roles?
Managing turnover	What are the projections for turnover across critical roles? How many people must be hired to support these roles in the future?
	What is the current retention risk of employees in critical roles? How does the company assess employee engagement in these roles?
	What methods are used to transfer knowledge across and ensure smooth hand-offs from one employee to another during job transitions?
Preventing avoidable turnover	Who are the high-potential employees in the organization? How are they being developed?
	What actions are being taken to build a sense of commitment and engagement among these employees?

Talent Requirements	Questions for Assessing Talent Requirements
Avoiding skilled talent shortages	What skills and capabilities will be critical for future organizational performance?
	What are the projected gaps between the skills found in the current workforce and the skills the business will need three, five, and ten years into the future?
Workforce diversity	Does the diversity of employees in key roles in the organization match the diversity profile of the company as a whole? Does it align with the diversity profile for customers?
	How does the company encourage career development among underrepresented employee populations?
Regulatory compliance	How does the company monitor whether employees have the training and knowledge required to perform critical job tasks?
	What methods are used to ensure your company is complying with relevant training requirements and policy guidelines?

their skills. Sustaining and increasing performance levels requires giving employees methods to hone their skills and keep their knowledge current with changing business demands, technology innovations, and market conditions.

- *Accelerating performance.* Each time an employee moves into a new role, there is a drop in workforce productivity as that employee adjusts to the new job demands. Development methods that support onboarding of new employees and internal role transitions significantly decrease the time required for employees to achieve full performance.

- *Managing turnover.* All employees are going to leave at some point. Development methods cannot eliminate turnover, but they can lessen the impact that turnover has on company performance. If managed effectively, turnover can even be used as an opportunity to increase organizational capabilities by moving high-potential talent into key roles. This works only if a company has development processes that anticipate and manage turnover events.

- *Preventing avoidable turnover.* High-performing employees are inherent retention risks. The attributes that make them high performers, such as a strong record of accomplishment, also make them attractive to other companies. These employees also tend to focus on the next opportunity to advance their careers—inside or outside the company. The best way to keep high-potential talent is to implement development methods that let them know that the career opportunities in your company are better than those they might find elsewhere.

- *Avoiding skilled talent shortages.* Much has been written about shortages of skilled labor across the globe. Companies that fail to acknowledge and address this shortage may soon find that they no longer have the skilled talent needed to perform even basic operational tasks. Development plays a key role in addressing future skill shortages before they occur.

- *Workforce diversity.* Many organizations struggle to build demographically diverse workforces in certain technical, customer-facing, or leadership roles. Demographically diverse workforces can have a significant impact on business issues related to customer service, attraction of talent, and regulatory compliance.[4] Actively developing talent from targeted demographic groups is pivotal to building and maintaining a diverse workforce. Coaching and mentoring methods are particularly effective for addressing this challenge.

- *Regulatory compliance.* Many jobs have legal policies or other rules that require employees to have certain training and knowledge to perform different functions. Well-managed development programs are critical to ensuring employees are fully qualified to fill these jobs.

Any of these talent requirements can have a significant impact on business performance. But it is unrealistic and unwise to try to address all of these needs at the same time. Not only would this cost a lot; it could result in overwhelming the organization with change. It is important to work with line-of-business leaders to determine which of these talent requirements are most relevant to your company's business strategies and why they matter. Then take a targeted approach toward addressing those requirements first. Having a strong understanding of the company's talent requirements will have a positive influence on how you design and deploy development programs. It ensures that you invest resources where they matter the most and will help get managers and employees to adopt development methods (see the discussion: "Making a Case for Development").

MAKING A CASE FOR DEVELOPMENT

To gain support for development business leaders must understand relationships between talent requirements and business performance. Managers do not always think a lot about development, and when they do, it may not be in a positive light. For example, many business leaders do not think about preventing turnover and building talent to staff critical roles until after a valued employee quits. And when this happens, they often focus on applying a short-term fix by hiring someone externally without actually resolving the problem through investing in long-term employee development. In some cases, managers may even question the value of developing employees who may subsequently leave the organization.

Strong development organizations excel at recognizing and publicizing the gains that have been made as a result of development—for example, highlighting dollars saved by hiring from within instead of relying on external staffing, monitoring and reporting the percentage of employees who have received critical training for their roles, and calling attention to the impact that employee development has on engagement, retention, workforce diversity, and productivity. Development is often a matter of investing a little bit now or paying a lot later. Leaders must be reminded of this from time to time. When managers say things like, "Why should we spend all this money on training if employees can quit and work for someone else?" ask them, "What happens if we don't train employees to do their jobs and they stay?"

7.4.2 What Positions or People Do You Need to Develop?

Development is an investment. Like any other investment, you want to put it where it will provide the greatest return. Not all jobs or employees need the same amount of development resources. But it is not always obvious where to focus development resources. For example, where should a company invest development resources to avoid talent shortages in leadership positions? Does it require developing all leadership positions or just certain roles? Should the development be designed for all employees in these roles or just those who have the most leadership potential? Determining where to focus development resources is critical when a company is seeking to address broad talent requirements like "preventing avoidable turnover," "managing turnover," or "avoiding talent shortages in key roles." The following five approaches can be used to determine where to invest development efforts:

- *Based on job levels.* This approach assigns development resources based on people's level in the organization. For example, some succession management methods target senior-level positions starting with the CEO and extending two levels below him or her. Similarly, many companies define training programs specifically for employees moving to first-level manager roles.

- *Based on job roles.* This approach focuses development resources on specific roles in the company that are crucial to the current and future performance of the organization. Job roles can be used to determine which employees are eligible for development methods such as training, mentoring, developmental assessments, or participation in succession management. These roles tend to fall into three categories (two of these categories were previously discussed in chapter 4 in the context of staffing):

  - *Pivotal* positions are roles where small differences in performance have a significant impact on company profitability. This includes strategic leadership roles but may also include key operational roles such as plant managers in manufacturing companies or technical experts in software and biomedical research companies. It may also include roles that include very large numbers of people such that small changes in performance have big impacts on profitability (e.g., frontline jobs in a retail organization).

  - *Critical* positions are roles that are necessary to maintaining key company operations and where there is a significant shortage of talent—for example, nurses in health care companies or maintenance specialists in utility companies.

  - *Development* positions are roles that are viewed as feeder positions for providing employees with the skills and experiences needed to move into critical or pivotal roles. For example, many retail companies view assistant store manager positions as critical development roles for creating future store managers.

- *Based on functions.* Many companies create development programs for functions related to a common business area or area of expertise. Function-based development programs can be particularly effective for companies that have relatively stable organizational structures where it makes sense to build out five- to ten-year career plans. One example is succession management programs found in some large companies that move employees through a series of finance jobs to prepare them for senior financial leadership positions. Another example can be found in many retail organizations that have programs to help employees progress through field operations functions starting with shift supervisor and moving up to assistant manager, store manager, district manager, and regional vice president.

• *Based on employee types.* Companies may build development programs that are designed specifically for employees meeting certain criteria. For example, many companies create succession management programs designed for employees who have been formally identified as high potentials. Companies also create performance improvement training programs for employees who are underperforming in their current roles. Development programs can also increase workforce diversity by creating mentorships for employees belonging to certain demographic groups. When using employee types, it is important to develop clear and consistent methods to determine employee eligibility; otherwise some employees may feel unfairly denied access to development resources.

• *Based on employee populations.* Some development processes involve every employee in a certain department or organization. These processes are usually implemented to address a mixture of the following talent requirements:

- Managing turnover by encouraging employees to engage in knowledge sharing so others can assume their responsibilities when they leave their current position
- Retaining employees by providing and engaging them around possible career paths they can pursue within the company
- Avoiding talent shortages by leveraging the employee population as a source of possible candidates for internal positions
- Ensuring all employees have completed required training programs

Whether it makes sense to allocate development investments based on levels, roles, functions, types, or populations will depend on the talent requirements being addressed and the resources available to invest in development programs. Succession management programs using costly executive coaching and leadership assessment centers probably have to be limited to a few high-potential employees in select roles. In contrast, social learning programs based on web-based learning communities and chat boards can be effectively and economically scaled across entire employee populations.

Deciding where to invest development resources is basically a three-step process:

1. Define your talent requirements. What problem are you seeking to solve through the use of development?

2. Determine what positions need to be included in the development program.

3. Determine whether it is necessary to apply development to every employee in these positions, or if development should be targeted on a subset of employees meeting certain criteria.

Build development programs with a clear understanding of who the end users will ultimately be. Do not invest development resources in certain groups just because they asked for it or because it "seems like the right thing to do." Determine where development resources will provide the greatest positive return on investment for the company, and give those areas priority.

7.4.3 What Employee Attributes Do You Need to Develop in Order to Achieve Your Learning Objectives?

The primary purpose of development is to give employees capabilities to perform new job tasks or more effectively perform existing job tasks—in other words, developing attributes that allow employees to do things in the future they have not or could not have done in the past. This means giving employees new skills, knowledge, experiences, and insights that make them more effective members of the workforce. It requires getting people to make personal changes that will influence their job performance.

Getting people to change can be very difficult. The first principle for changing people is ensuring they understand why the change is beneficial to them. If they do not clearly understand what's in it for them, they are unlikely to do it. And even then, they may struggle to make the change. This is why it is critical to tie development programs to personal career ambitions. The second principle for changing people is to be very specific about what you are trying to change. This means clearly and precisely answering the question, "What attributes do we need to develop in employees for this development program to be successful?"

Employee attributes can be divided into three basic categories: experience, aptitudes, and motives. Understanding these categories and how they relate to your learning objectives is important for determining what development methods to use. It also provides insight into the time and effort that will be required to achieve their learning objectives:

- *Experience* (what people have done): Knowledge, skills, and qualifications that are acquired and demonstrated through previous job assignments, training programs, and certification exercises.
- *Aptitudes* (what people can do): Traits primarily associated with personality, temperament, and cognitive ability. Aptitudes comprise a major portion of what is commonly referred to as potential (see the discussion: "Assessing and Developing Potential").
- *Motives* (what people want to do): Interests, career goals, and personal constraints that influence whether someone will pursue, accept, and remain committed toward certain jobs and work environments. Motivation is a function of what people want to do (e.g., make money, develop skills, increase influence) and what they are willing to sacrifice to achieve these goals (e.g., willingness to move, willingness to work long hours).

Understanding what types of attributes you are trying to develop is critical for determining what development methods to use. If the purpose of a development program is to ensure employees have learned basic job policies or regulations, then all that may be needed is a simple online course. If the purpose is to build expertise in solving problems that require a mix of experience, personality, and ability traits, then the program will have to use a much broader range of development methods such as on-the-job learning and developmental interactions with peers and mentors. Examples include job rotation programs that multinational companies use to develop global leaders and the extensive apprenticeship programs used to develop master electricians and carpenters.

Development programs can be used to influence employee motivation and engagement toward career opportunities and can be effective for increasing

A common goal of many development programs is helping employees "achieve their full potential." This usually means developing attributes that allow people to take on new roles and responsibility. So what are the attributes that influence people's capability to assume future roles?

Whether someone has the capability to perform a future job or task depends on two things: what the person knows how to do and how he or she responds to work environments and job challenges. What people know how to do is primarily a function of what they have done in the past (e.g., training programs they have completed, jobs they have held). In contrast, how people respond to work environments and job challenges is heavily influenced by underlying personality and ability traits. For example, just because someone has the technical training to be a software engineer does not mean he or she will perform this job effectively under stressful or competitive situations. Similarly, an individual salesperson may possess the sales knowledge needed to lead a sales team, but this does not mean he or she has the right disposition needed to manage others effectively.

A common mistake companies make when assessing and developing potential is to overemphasize the importance of experience, knowledge, and skills and underemphasize the impact that personality and ability traits have on future performance. Measuring and changing knowledge and skills is far easier than measuring and changing underlying personality and ability traits. When people perform poorly, it is more often due to problems with how they act than what they know. Or to put it another way, companies typically hire people based on their experience and fire them based on their personality.

The key to assessing and developing potential is to look at both experience and aptitude. This requires defining and measuring the aptitudes that influence potential. Measures of aptitudes can range from simple manager ratings to complex psychometric tools that evaluate underlying personality and ability traits associated with success in different kinds of job roles. Most measures of potential tend to focus on three broad areas:

- *Cognitive traits* reflecting the ability to deal with the kinds of information and problems that people will encounter as they move into positions with increasing responsibility

- *Social traits* that influence the ability to build and manage different types of relationships

- *Change management* traits reflecting the ability to manage the stresses and ambiguity associated with different positions

If your development goal is to build employee potential to assume future roles, then it is a good idea to pay attention to these three areas. Also be aware that many of the personality and ability traits that influence potential are relatively hard to change.

Finally, note that aptitudes associated with potential are different from motives that influence career direction. Even if someone can effectively perform a role, that does not necessarily mean he or she will want to move into that role. Developing motivation tends to be even more difficult than developing aptitude. If you explain the benefits of a job to someone and this person is not interested in it, then the better approach is usually to avoid asking him or her to do it rather than trying to develop his or her interest.

---

long-term employee retention. The following are some ways to influence employee career choices:

- Using assessment measures that help employees understand what they want to achieve from work and help them align their personal motives to opportunities within the company

- Social learning methods that establish coaching and mentoring relationships that help employees define their personal career goals and find ways to match these with company job opportunities

- Career planning and succession management methods that provide employees with a sense of possible future jobs they could pursue within the company and a general plan on how to pursue them

- Transition management methods that help new employees build social networks so they feel a sense of belonging and commitment toward the organization

- Social learning methods that help employees create a sense of community with their peers at work

Like all other development methods, these tend to be most effective when implemented in a coordinated fashion with each other and with other strategic HR processes such as staffing and performance management.

Table 7.4 indicates the development methods that tend to be the most effective for changing different types of employee attributes. Providing employees with experience related to specific knowledge and skills can often be done with resource-focused development methods (i.e., training resources and assessment measures). Building aptitudes associated with leadership potential and specialized expertise tends to rely more heavily on role- and relationship-focused methods such as succession management, career planning, and social learning. Influencing motivation also tends to be more affected by role- and relationship-based development methods than ones focused on resources.

While table 7.4 provides a general sense of relationships between attributes and development methods, the best methods for developing specific attributes will depend far more on the attribute itself than the general category it belongs to. For example, knowing how to run a meeting and knowing how to speak a foreign language are both elements of knowledge and skill that depend on experience. But the development methods used to teach a language are quite different from those used to teach people how to run a meeting.

Creating an effective development strategy starts by first answering, "What talent requirements are we addressing?" and then, "What jobs employees do we need to develop to address these needs?" This is followed by another question: "What employee attributes do we need to change to achieve our development learning objectives?" The answer to this question will determine the types of development methods to incorporate into the development program.

Development programs are usually most effective if they leverage a combination of development methods. For example, if you want to build a skilled workforce or train future leaders, you will want to look at a mixture of methods incorporating elements of succession management, career development, onboarding, training, social learning, and assessments. There are exceptions, such as training programs that target specific regulatory requirements. But stand-alone development methods tend to have less impact than integrated development programs that use multiple methods.[5]

Table 7.4
Development Methods That Are Most Effective for Influencing Different Types of Attributes

Attributes to Change	Using Roles	Using Relationships	Using Resources
Experience/have done (knowledge, skills, qualifications)	Succession management and career planning methods that give people tasks and job assignments that enable them to acquire and use the skills and knowledge you wish to develop	Social learning methods where people work alongside others who possess the skills and knowledge you want people to acquire	Training materials that address specific skills and knowledge you wish to develop Transition management methods that provide access to training and knowledge resources needed in new roles
Aptitudes/can do (abilities, work style, temperament)	Succession management and career planning methods that give people assignments or positions that require them to display job behaviors and acquire experiences associated with demonstrating potential	Social learning methods such as coaching that improve people's self-awareness and ability to identify and leverage their strengths and manage weaknesses that could affect their long-term potential Transition management methods that help people establish supportive relationships with colleagues	Assessment measures that give people insight into their natural strengths and weaknesses Training materials that help people effectively manage their behaviors to maximize their capabilities
Motives/want to do (interests, career goals)	Succession management and career planning methods that give people a sense of long-term career paths and ensure their current job assignments are moving them in a direction that aligns with their personal career goals	Social learning methods that help people find links between their personal career interests and career development opportunities within the company Onboarding programs that help employees establish social connections with the others in the company	Assessment measures that help people identify their career interests

7.4.4 How Will You Build and Maintain Development Methods?

It would take several books to thoroughly discuss all the development methods that can go into an integrated development program. Entire industries have been created to support development methods like succession management and training resources. But here are a few general guidelines to keep in mind when defining and assembling development programs:

- *Avoid doing it all yourself.* The development industry is one of the largest segments of the human resource market. Chances are someone has already built tools, technology, and other resources needed to support the development methods you need. Actively scan the marketplace and take advantage of others' work. It is usually much faster, easier, and more cost-effective than building it yourself.

- *Avoid unnecessary learning.* Development requires people to change, which tends to be difficult. When assembling content, focus on development methods that directly address the employee attributes tied to your learning objectives. View any development methods that do not directly target your core objectives as distractions, not opportunities.

- *A little tailoring goes a long way.* When adopting off-the-shelf development methods, look for ways to make minor modifications so the content aligns with the language and concepts in your organization. For example, if a training program talks about "objectives" and your company talks about "goals," change the language in the training program so employees don't have to make this translation in their head. What may seem like trivial modifications can significantly improve the adoption and use of development methods (see the discussion: "Aligning New Ideas to Familiar Concepts: Why Words Matter").

ALIGNING NEW IDEAS TO FAMILIAR CONCEPTS: WHY WORDS MATTER

The goal of many development programs is to change how employees approach work situations—for example, getting employees to recognize how their behaviors influence the actions of others or getting them to adopt more effective methods to solve work problems. The challenge these types of programs face is they require people to do more than just act differently; they must learn to think differently. You cannot simply show them what to do; you have to change the mental methods they use to understand, interpret, and act toward situations.

One of the more effective techniques to influence how people think is to point out similarities between new ideas and familiar concepts. This is why analogies are such a powerful tool for communication. They enable people to understand a novel concept using frameworks they already understand. This is also why it is important to minimize the use of new or unfamiliar words and models when deploying development programs. The more you tie the concepts you are teaching to things people already understand, the more easily they will understand and adopt these new concepts.

I saw a great example of this during a program used to teach specialty coffee shop managers how to select job candidates. The challenge was getting managers to adopt a structured interview process to systematically evaluate candidates. Rather than trying to explain psychological concepts related to measuring and matching applicant traits to job demands, the company used an analogy between interviewing candidates and tasting coffee. They talked about the fact that there isn't just one best type of coffee and the importance of matching different types of coffee based on the meal or time of day. They then pointed out that the same concepts apply to hiring. Whether a candidate will be a good fit depends on the job he or she is being hired for. They extended the analogy to the importance of evaluating coffee using a consistent, structured tasting process and noted that this same concept applied to interviewing candidates using the same set of questions asked in the same way.

This analogy to interviewing and coffee would probably confuse hiring managers in other companies. But it made absolute sense to these managers because of their experience with coffee tasting. What's more, the managers did not have to learn a bunch of new interviewing terms and models that were originally included in the off-the-shelf version of the training. Instead they became more effective interviewers by using terms and concepts that were already familiar to them. The lesson to be learned from this is to avoid introducing new words and models when you can achieve your development objectives using words and concepts that are already familiar to people in the company.

- *Plan scheduled maintenance and upgrades.* No matter how much work goes into the creation of a development program, it is going to contain limitations and eventually will become outdated. Define a time line for reviewing, updating, and refreshing development methods. Schedule sufficient time between upgrades for the methods to become familiar to end users, but do not wait so long that people become frustrated by their limitations. How often upgrades should occur will depend on the type of method and how it is used, but for most development methods, a three-year upgrade cycle often works well.

- *Explore user-generated learning resources.* A distinction can be made between user-generated "organic" development content and more formally designed "structured" content built by training and development experts.

  - Organic content includes things like web posts and short videos created by employees to share ideas and knowledge (see the discussion: "User-Generated Learning: Where the Future Meets the Past"). It has the advantage of usually being fairly current because it emerges in real time from employees working on the front lines. Organic content development methods are particularly useful when the types of content needed are rapidly changing due to constant shifts in technology, markets, or business structures. But it tends to pose risks associated with poor quality and lack of integration with other development content.

  - Structured content such as formal training programs and manuals tends to have better quality control but costs more to create and can quickly become outdated as the business changes. Structured content development methods are well suited for situations where employees have to learn specific things that are unlikely to change over time or when employees are working in relatively stable jobs or organizational structures.

USER-GENERATED LEARNING CONTENT: WHERE THE FUTURE MEETS THE PAST

More and more companies are discovering that development programs that rely solely on classroom training and structured courses are not effective or efficient enough to meet their growing demands for skilled labor. As a result, companies are looking at alternative methods for developing employees. One of the more promising innovations is the ability to use social technology to leverage user-generated learning content. What is interesting about this trend is that in many ways it represents a shift back to the future when it comes to learning. To explain this, let's take a look at the rise of formal classroom training.

Going to class is not the natural way for people to learn. Humans did not develop classrooms until fairly late in our evolution. For centuries, we managed to learn without structured courses. So how did we do it? The answer is that we learned from experience and observation. People acquired skills by working alongside others who knew more than they did, that is, by being apprentices. The problem with the apprenticeship approach was that it did not scale well: there weren't enough apprenticeship opportunities available to produce the number of skilled employees needed. In addition, not all experts make good mentors and coaches. Classroom training was created in part to respond to shortages of mentors and apprenticeships.

Social learning technology is starting to change this. YouTube is probably the best widespread example of how technology is allowing skilled mentors to share their expertise with people around the world. Want to learn to play guitar like rock musician Brian Setzer? There's a video where you can virtually "sit down" with him for an hour while he shows you various tips and tricks. Want to learn how to cook like Emeril? Check out videos where he'll walk you through what he does to create unique flavors. Social learning technologies are addressing the historic challenge of scaling expertise through mentorships.

Companies are also using social communication technology to enable greater collaboration and knowledge sharing among employees. Chat sites, blogs, and community web pages allow employees to learn much more from each other than was possible when learning was limited to the person you happened to be working with that day. Colleagues working different shifts or in different locations can readily share ideas, pose questions, provide recognition, and offer constructive coaching to one another. The result is that many workplaces provide much richer sources of learning than did those that existed just a few years ago.

Social learning technology provides an alternative way to teach and enable new skills that is cheaper, easier to access, and in many ways complementary to more traditional training programs. I am not suggesting this technology will totally replace formal educational programs. But the upsides of this technology are considerable. Instead of people having to go to training to acquire new skills, they can increasingly leverage the expertise embedded within their broader working community.

Assembling and maintaining development methods to support a large-scale integrated development program is a major undertaking. Paying attention to the concepts presented here and thinking through how different methods will integrate into a larger development program will have major benefits later. Remember that the value of most development methods is not determined by your ability to deploy them in the short term but by whether the method is still considered useful several years into the future.

7.4.5   How Will You Administer and Support Development Methods?

After defining the goals of your development program, identifying which people to develop, defining what they need to develop, and deciding what methods will be used to develop them, the next step is to ensure these development methods are effectively administered within the organization. Unless you are a very small company, technology is going to be a central component for administering and supporting development methods here. The logistics associated with implementing most development methods to more than one hundred or so employees can become overwhelming without the right technological tools.

It is beyond the scope of this book to detail all the features you might consider when choosing technology to support development methods. What you will want depends on the development methods you are deploying, the people you are deploying it to, and the impact you want to have. For example, the technology features needed to deploy customer service training to frontline hotel employees across the globe are much different from the features needed to deploy succession management for executives in a regionally based financial services organization. Technology systems used to support career planning for managers in an engineering company may be set up differently from those used to support career planning for nurses in a hospital. Given the variety of ways you are likely to use development technology, it is best to look for systems that provide a range of options and features that can be configured to support different needs. This allows you to support all your development programs through the same core technology platform.

It is also important to choose technology that allows you to integrate and share data across development methods and with other talent management processes. Table 7.5 lists integration features to consider when evaluating development technology. These feature fall into three areas:

- *Integrating development methods with each other.* It should be possible to access content and data associated with one development method through other development methods. For example, succession management technology should give you the ability to access elements of employees' career plans. Employees should be able to access training resources from within their career plans. Social learning and assessment measures should be accessible from within the platform used to manage traditional training. Ideally, it

---

Table 7.5
Integration Features to Consider When Evaluating
Development Technology

Features that enable integrating development methods with each other such as

- Links between career plans and succession management that support examining what succession candidates are doing to develop themselves and adding activities to high-potential candidates' development plans as a result of succession conversations
- Links between career development and training resources so employees can sign up and access training directly from their career plans
- Features that allow blending traditional training programs and curricula with social learning communities and user-generated training content
- Accessing training and social learning resources directly from the tools used to support transition management and onboarding programs
- Incorporating development assessments and 360 surveys into career plans and succession management processes

(Continued)

Features that enable integrating development with other talent management processes such as

- Creating links among performance management, succession management, and career plans
- Creating links among staffing processes, succession management, and onboarding programs
- Linking compensation methods to career plans and training resources to enable rewarding employees for skills development
- Linking goal management programs to career plans and succession management to support the use of job assignments to build employee capabilities
- Linking goal management to social learning communities to promote knowledge sharing tied to job activities
- Creating links between succession management and workforce planning processes

Features integrating development method with administrative data such as

- Creating links between career plans, onboarding, and succession management to human resource information systems data on job codes and employee data to enable links between job types and different development activities
- Creating links between assessment measures and organizational charts and employee job codes to enable more effective selection of raters for 360 surveys
- Linking career plans and succession management to organizational charts and job codes enabling more effective creation of career paths and identification of succession candidates
- Linking training programs to data on job types in order to manage training requirements for different jobs
- Creating links between development programs and data on employee turnover, promotions, and productivity in order to more effectively evaluate the impact of training programs on workforce productivity
- Creating links between development programs and data from financial, productivity, and sales systems to evaluate the impact of development methods on workforce productivity

should be possible to link every development method to every other development method directly or indirectly.

- *Integrating development methods with other talent processes.* Most development programs are used to increase employees' current job performance or build their potential and qualifications to move into new roles. To support these goals, technology should support linking development programs to the processes used for staffing, workforce planning, performance management, goal management, and compensation.

- *Integrating development methods with administrative data.* There are several reasons to link development technology to administrative systems used to track employees job titles, reporting structures, salary, tenure, and work history. First, the nature of development activities like succession, onboarding, and training is often based on where employees are placed in the company (e.g., requiring employees in certain jobs to complete specific training programs). Second, knowing where employees are located in the company and having data on their managers, coworkers, and direct reports can be extremely useful for supporting development methods such as succession management, social learning, and 360 surveys. Third, being able to link employee participation in development activities with outcomes associated with turnover, promotion, and productivity is critical to evaluating the impact of development methods.

It is important to define development program needs first and then evaluate technology against those needs. But keep an open mind when looking at the capabilities and constraints of technology systems. It is unlikely that any technology system will perfectly support every feature you might ideally want. And you may find that many technology systems provide features you might benefit from but might not have considered. Selection of technology always comes with some level of trade-off between what is wanted, what is needed, and what is possible. This is particularly true when looking at technology used to support systems as complex as integrated talent development. Do not compromise on critical features, but remember that there may be more than one way to support your requirements.

7.4.6   How Will You Measure the Impact of Development Programs?

Development methods typically do not have a direct impact on short-term business results (see the discussion: "Why Development Is Like Routine Maintenance"). Development programs build the capabilities of employees, but these capabilities do not improve business performance until employees apply them to address talent requirements. In other words, just because someone has acquired new knowledge and skills does not mean he or she is using them on the job. This difference between developing knowledge and applying knowledge is often referred to as the transfer-of-training problem.

WHY DEVELOPMENT IS LIKE ROUTINE MAINTENANCE

Funding for development programs is often the first thing to get cut when companies are looking to reduce costs. This is particularly true if business leaders do not see a clear link between the capabilities employees acquire through development and the results they achieve on the job. Companies can and often do achieve results without spending much money on development, at least for a little while. What these companies do not realize is the degree to which lack of development is limiting the performance they could achieve if they had a more fully engaged and capable staff. Nor do they recognize the risk that a lack of development creates for maintaining long-term performance.

An analogy can be made between development and routine engine maintenance. Most engines can run for a while without regular tune-ups to improve timing, ensure adequate oil, and check seals for a good fit. The performance of engines will start to decline as timing drifts and oil gets dirty, but because this decrease is gradual, drivers may not notice that the engine has become less efficient and powerful than it once was. In contrast, people are immediately aware of the costs and short-term lost productivity associated with taking the engine off-line and hiring a mechanic to tune it up. Often the only time people recognize the value of routine maintenance is after something goes catastrophically wrong due to a failure to fix a problem that could have been easily addressed had it been recognized earlier (e.g., having an engine seize up because it ran out of oil).

The reasons people ignore routine maintenance on engines are similar to the reasons that many companies fail to invest in employee development. People don't recognize the value of development programs because this value plays out in subtle improvements in productivity over time, as opposed to giving a company a highly visible short-term boost in profits. Companies often do not appreciate the value of performance levels they will achieve or talent shortages they will avoid as a result of investments in development they are making right now. This is why it is so critical to ensure that business leaders understand how development programs affect business results and long-term productivity. As one person told me, "Failing to invest in employee development is like failing to change the oil in your car: you may not regret it right away, but eventually it hurts you in a way you will regret for a long time."

One way to ensure the transfer of training and demonstrate the value of development programs is to track the impact of development methods. Table 7.6 lists several metrics that can be used to evaluate development methods. The metrics are separated into three categories: usage, impact, and outcomes.[6]

Usage metrics provide insight into whether people are using development methods at all. They track things such as how many employees have attended training classes, completed career plans, identified succession candidates, accessed onboarding resources, or used assessments. Usage metrics for development methods like career planning, social learning, and succession should not just track whether employees use the method, but also how frequently they use it—for example, how often people update goals in career plans, contribute new content to online learning communities, or meet with career coaches or mentors. Tracking usage is important because if people are not using development methods, then obviously the methods will not have any impact. Usage also provides insight into whether methods are perceived as valuable or easy to access.

Impact metrics provide insight into whether development methods are improving the capabilities of the employees using them. For example, these metrics can be used to determine whether a succession management program results in greater numbers of high-potential candidates or whether a training program enables more employees to pass a knowledge certification test.

The simplest impact measures assess whether employees felt the development method was valuable. The problem with this type of metric is that just because employees liked participating in a program does not mean it actually improved their capabilities. Conversely, effective development interventions are

Table 7.6
Examples of Development Metrics

Development Method	Usage Metrics	Impact Metrics	Development Outcomes
Succession management	Percent of employees with completed talent profiles	Percent of roles with ready-now candidates identified	Employee engagement and commitment survey scores
	Percent of updated talent reviews/nine boxes	Number of ready-now candidates identified for key roles	Percent of positions filled with internal promotions or transfer
	Percent of employees identified as high potentials	Changes in employee performance and potential ratings over time	Time to fill for key roles
			Retention rate of high-performing employees
Career planning	Percent of employees with career plans	Progress against development objectives	Demographic diversity in key roles
			Increased revenue per employee
	Percent of employees using development resources available through career planning (e.g., training programs)	Percent of employees with well-defined career paths	Development of workforce pipeline to support future talent requirements
		Percent of managers using career development plans to evaluate employee potential	Decreased time to competence in new roles
Training curriculums	Number of people completing courses	Percent of people passing certification tests tied to training	Employee, manager, and executive ratings of career development process
		Trainee ratings on course quality	Increased retention
			Increased internal promotion rates

Social learning	Percent of employees participating in social learning forums Number of people volunteering to participate in mentor programs or social learning groups Number of mentor-mentee relationships established Number of user-generated training videos or posts created	Employee evaluations of quality and utility of social learning programs Number of employees accessing social learning sites or user-generated training content Percent of employee recommending mentoring programs for others	Increased internal job transfers Decreased turnover Time to reach full productivity in new roles Percent of employees who are in compliance with certification requirements
Onboarding and other transitions	Trainee ratings of onboarding course value Percent of new employees using onboarding development resources	Employee ratings of the overall onboarding or job transition process	
Assessments including 360 surveys	Number of employees receiving developmental feedback such as 360s Number of employees completing assessments	Percent of employees recommending assessments, 360s for coworkers Relative changes or improvements in employees assessment, 360 scores over time	

not necessarily enjoyable. Consider the use of 360 surveys to give people constructive but critical feedback on their performance. Learning painful truths about one's developmental needs can be valuable, but it is rarely pleasant. The best impact measures assess the degree to which development programs improve employee capabilities without asking employees to simply report their perceptions—for example, formally testing employee skills after a training course or collecting manager and coworker evaluations of how employee performance has changed as a result of a coaching or succession management program.

Impact measures can also provide evidence to support the cost of a development program. Simply showing that a development program is improving the skills of employees may provide justification to continue the program. On the other hand, impact measures do not necessarily indicate that a development program is improving business performance. This is because of the transfer-of-training problem. Even if employees have developed new capabilities, this does not mean they are using them to address business challenges. Companies that rely solely on impact measures to assess the value of development programs may find these programs in jeopardy if the company needs to cut costs. The only way to ensure that development programs are fully effective and appreciated is to create links between the use of development methods and outcome metrics.

Outcome metrics illustrate the true business value of development processes. They do this by linking development methods to data reflecting workforce productivity, efficiency, sustainability, scalability, and governance. The ultimate value of development programs is their ability to improve things like revenue generated per full-time employee, cost per hire, retention of high-performing employees, time required to onboard new employees, time to fill critical positions, and percentage of employees certified to perform key job tasks.

Some outcome metrics are closely related to certain types of development methods (e.g., succession management, time to fill critical positions). But most outcome metrics depend on multiple development methods as well as factors that have nothing to do with development. For example, turnover can be influenced by onboarding, mentoring, and succession management. But turnover is also influenced by compensation and changes in the external labor market. This can make it difficult to establish direct links between development methods and specific outcomes. Nevertheless, tracking outcome metrics is critical if you want to build a strong case for the business value of development.

The relationship between development methods and outcome metrics does not need to be sophisticated to be effective. The following are examples of simple but effective use of outcome metrics to demonstrate the value of development methods: showing that new salespeople who completed an onboarding program achieved quota several months faster on average than salespeople who did not participate in or finish the program, demonstrating that employee retention significantly increased after a new career development program was put in place, and showing an increase in internal promotion rates that occurred after implementation of a succession management process. None of these examples required a lot of sophisticated workforce analytics. They simply pointed out changes that occurred in the workforce that could reasonably be attributed to the use of different development programs.

The success of most development methods does not depend on the opinions of human resources or even the employees participating in the program. It depends on the opinions of the line-of-business managers who must decide whether the time and money they and their employees spend on a development program generate enough business value to justify the cost. One way to determine what development metrics to track is to simply ask line-of-business leaders, "What data would demonstrate whether this development method was adding real value to business operations?" It is a good idea to also provide the leaders with a list of possible metrics, or they may recommend metrics that are difficult or impossible measure.

7.4.7 How Will You Create an Environment That Supports Use of Development Methods?

The final issue to explore when building a development strategy is whether people are adequately rewarded and supported for using development methods. On the positive side, development is in many ways its own reward: most people like to learn new things, assuming these things are relevant to their jobs and appropriately matched to their skills and capabilities. Few doubt the importance of development as a key element for long-term success. On the negative side, most organizations contain a range of direct and hidden barriers to development. Even the best development methods will fail if people in the organization are unwilling to adopt them.

Potential barriers to development range from tangible policies to more subtle cultural traits. Most of these barriers can be placed into four general categories:

- *Does the company reward actions associated* with development? Most development methods require making sacrifices to short-term productivity to build capabilities to accomplish higher levels of long-term performance. Yet many companies reward short-term productivity far more than long-term performance improvement (see the discussion: "Some Companies Punish People for Development: Is Yours One of Them?"). What criteria does your company use to evaluate employee and manager performance? Do these criteria include metrics and ratings that encourage people to invest time and energy into developing themselves and others? Or are the metrics focused solely on past performance with little reward for doing things that build the long-term capabilities of the company?

SOME COMPANIES PUNISH PEOPLE FOR DEVELOPMENT: IS YOURS ONE OF THEM?

You can tell a lot about how much a company values development by looking at the criteria used to guide compensation and promotion decisions. Are managers and employees rewarded for investing time in building long-term talent? Or is it all about last quarter's business results? Here are some examples of ways companies punish employees, managers, and human resource leaders for investing time toward development.

Punishing Employees

The best way for employees to develop is by taking on goals that require performing new job roles, adapting to new work environments, and learning new capabilities. These goals are typically harder to complete than familiar ones because they require learning new things. Many companies do not distinguish between developmentally challenging goals and familiar goals when evaluating employee performance. All that matters is whether employees meet their targets. As a general rule, if an employee hits 100 percent of his or her goals year after year, these goals are not challenging. Yet employees who achieve familiar goals with little development value may appear to have stronger performance than employees who set unfamiliar and far more challenging goals.

Punishing Managers

From a short-term operational standpoint, investing in employee development is a lousy managerial strategy. Why should a manager risk short-term targets by giving stretch job assignments to employees who have not done them before? Why take time away from daily operations to invest in employee learning? And why encourage employees to pursue career opportunities or promotions elsewhere in the company? How does giving away talent help the manager? The degree to which a company supports developmentally minded managers can be assessed by evaluating whether managers who promote people past them are rewarded or punished. Are these managers celebrated as talent creators or looked down on as people who have hit a career plateau and are now being passed by? Similarly, are managers rewarded for hiring and developing less-experienced and less-costly candidates? Is there any incentive for managers to save on salary costs by developing talent instead of buying it? Are there metrics related to talent development and retention on the scorecards used to evaluate managers?

I once asked a business leader how his company rewarded managers who developed and promoted people out of their teams. His answer was, "We don't; we punish them by not backfilling their positions." Given this, it is little wonder that a lot of managers express skepticism toward the relative value of development programs.

Punishing HR

The saying that what gets measured gets managed is as true in HR as anywhere else. Many of the things that are easy to measure in HR do not support investment in development programs. For example, it is far easier to track the cost of training than to track the value created by training. As a result, more emphasis may be placed on using inexpensive development methods instead of effective ones.

HR metrics can also create conflict within the HR organization itself. An example of this occurred in a company I was working with where the director of leadership development was rewarded based on the percentage of positions filled by internal candidates while the director of recruiting was rewarded based on number of external hires. This placed the recruiting organization in direct competition with the development organization. Rather than cooperating to see if it made more sense to treat specific positions as opportunities to develop internal talent versus opportunities to bring fresh talent into the company, it was just a race to see who could fill them first.

No company intentionally creates rules and cultural norms to discourage development. These things result from a failure to think through the implications of organizational policies and leadership decisions. Compare these examples to the methods your company uses to recognize and reward performance. Are you truly supporting people who invest in developing themselves and others, or do you merely give lip-service to the value of development without actually rewarding it?

- *Does the company provide adequate time and resources to support development efforts?* Development takes time. This is particularly true if employees are working to build significantly new skill sets. Think about the first time you learned to perform a highly novel task, whether it was driving a car or managing a large-scale project. Learning something requires far more energy and attention than it takes after you have been doing it awhile. Managers must be patient and supportive of employees who are challenging themselves to develop. This means giving employees both moral support and additional time until they acquire some level of mastery. It may also mean temporarily decreasing productivity expectations for them so they can focus more energy on development activities.

- *Does the company culture encourage people to take on development challenges?* Development is about self-improvement. The best development occurs in environments where people are comfortable openly discussing strengths and weaknesses and actively enlist help from others to get advice on how they can improve. Employees should trust that their managers and coworkers will encourage their growth, help them learn from mistakes, and not punish or mock them for taking on novel tasks that may be difficult for them at first. Not all companies have this sort of supportive culture. If your company is not a place where people feel comfortable and encouraged taking risks in order to build their skills, then employees are likely to resist attempts to get them to step outside their comfort zone.

- *Does the company support internal career growth and advancement?* The main reason employees pursue development is to achieve their career goals.

Supporting the talent requirements of the organization is secondary to this primary goal. Yet many organizations have norms and policies that discourage employees from pursuing career advancement within the company. For example, managers may explicitly or implicitly punish direct reports who apply for jobs elsewhere in the company. Rather than supporting these employees' career interests, managers treat them as though they were being disloyal. Some companies also create norms and rules to restrict internal talent movement, ignoring the fact that high-potential employees will seek jobs in other companies if they feel it will more quickly advance their careers (see the discussion: "Talent Poaching: A Concept That Shouldn't Exist").

TALENT POACHING: A CONCEPT THAT SHOULDN'T EXIST

A common complaint made about development programs is the concern that it will create employee turnover. As employees develop new capabilities, they will be dissatisfied staying in their current roles and will begin seeking opportunities elsewhere. People argue that "if we develop our employees, other people will hire them away." Or as some managers put it, "Why should I develop people just so others can poach them from me?"

Concerns about talent poaching are misguided and extremely detrimental to long-term organizational health. First, what company wants to employ people whom no one else is interested in hiring? Do you want your organization to be the place that hires people no one else wants? Second, not developing people for fear they will be hired away is like refusing to maintain your house for fear that it will look more attractive to thieves. Although there is risk of developing people, only to have them leave, it is far worse to not develop them and have them stay. Third, retaining employees by discouraging career advancement is a great way to build teams of employees who lack ambition and energy.

A manager who complains of losing an employee because he or she was poached by someone else is blaming the wrong person. The problem is not with the employee or the poacher; it is with the manager who failed to create a more desirable career path for the employee. If a valued employee unexpectedly leaves to pursue opportunities elsewhere, the fault for the turnover lies on the manager for failing to recognize the employee's career ambitions and the organization for failing to give the employee access to career opportunities that match their long-term interests. The only loyalty companies should ask for and expect from employees is loyalty toward a work environment that provides them with opportunities to fulfill their career goals.

The concept of talent poaching should be stricken from any organization that is committed to development. It may make sense to have guidelines on internal transfers in order to avoid excessive turnover in specific roles. But it never makes sense to punish employees for exploring alternative career options within the company. Nor should managers be discouraged from talking with employees in other groups about internal positions that will help advance their careers. Remember that the question is not whether employees with strong performance and potential are going to seek new job opportunities; the question is whether they will look for these opportunities within their current company.

Many companies also set up compensation plans that do not reward employee loyalty and internal career development. Employees who are promoted internally often receive smaller salary increases than they would have gotten had they quit the organization entirely and applied for the job as an external candidate. Years ago a manager advised me to "change companies every three to five years as it's the only way to get a really meaningful pay increase." Take an honest look at how you establish compensation for internal transfers and make sure that statement could not be applied to your organization.

Some of the organizational issues that limit the adoption and value of development methods can be quickly addressed and changed (e.g., eliminating overly restrictive policies for internal transfers, changing compensation strategies to reward managers who invest in employee development). Others are more subtle and may take years to change (e.g., creating a culture that encourages taking risks to support development). To ensure the success of your development programs, have a discussion with company leaders about barriers in the organization that could hinder development efforts. Be realistic about what sorts of changes leadership will or will not support; then adjust your development objectives accordingly.

If leaders in the company are not willing to reward managers for promoting talent out of their departments, then it is probably a waste of time to implement succession management methods that encourage managers to share talent with others. If employees are not given time to engage in self-development activities and training, then there is little sense in providing these sorts of resources to them. When employees are encouraged to develop capabilities but are not given job assignments where they can use them, the company is wasting its investment in development, and employees are likely to become frustrated at having learned something they don't have an opportunity to use. It is often better to do nothing than to deploy development methods that are not supported by managers or senior leadership or that do not help employees advance their careers within the organization. A likely outcome is that you will increase employees' sense of frustration over the lack of support for their personal career development in the organization.

7.5 INCREASING DEVELOPMENT PROCESS MATURITY

Development is arguably the most complex area of talent management for at least three reasons. First, development encompasses six different methods, each with its own unique set of tools, techniques, and design features. Setting up these methods can be a significant undertaking. This becomes even more complicated when attention is placed on integrating the methods with one other. Second, development programs can be used to improve a range of employee capabilities, each requiring different types of development approaches. The nature of development changes depending on whether the focus is on building technical skills, leadership potential, career motivation, teamwork, or other attributes. Third, development processes must be able to change based on the learning objectives of employees. The more extensive a development program becomes, the more flexible it needs to be to support career growth across a diverse range of employees. Development programs must support basic training for new employees and career growth for highly experienced leaders and professionals. Achieving high levels of development process maturity is not about creating a single system that does one thing really well; it is about creating a flexible system that can be used to support a range of developmental needs that shift over time.

It is important to approach development as an ongoing series of projects and activities. Companies can implement individual development methods that quickly add value in a matter of months. For example, implementing a new 360 survey assessment or training program takes very little time. But it typically takes years to build a fully comprehensive development program (for an example, see appendix B). Companies with highly mature development processes constantly modify them to leverage new development methods and adapt to shifting business requirements. Do not think of the development process as a house you design once, build once, and then maintain. Think of it as a garden that you build and nurture over time, constantly finding ways to improve and modify it as it grows.

Figure 7.3 illustrates five basic levels of development process maturity. Understanding these levels provides a framework for structuring a long-term development strategy. Level 1 is focused on individual development planning to improve employees' performance in their current roles. This is about making sure employees have discussed development needs with their managers, have some form of development plan, and have access to development resources such as job-relevant training materials.

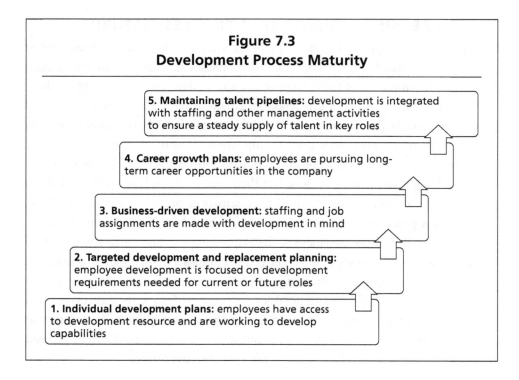

Figure 7.3
Development Process Maturity

5. **Maintaining talent pipelines:** development is integrated with staffing and other management activities to ensure a steady supply of talent in key roles

4. **Career growth plans:** employees are pursuing long-term career opportunities in the company

3. **Business-driven development:** staffing and job assignments are made with development in mind

2. **Targeted development and replacement planning:** employee development is focused on development requirements needed for current or future roles

1. **Individual development plans:** employees have access to development resource and are working to develop capabilities

Level 2 emphasizes targeted development to build employee capabilities for taking on new tasks or preparing for future job roles. Within the context of succession management, this level is often thought of as "replacement planning" to develop internal people who can replace more experienced employees if they leave or move into different roles. This level also includes focused training programs to help employees qualify for expanded responsibilities within their current jobs.

Level 3 emphasizes business-driven development where managers staff jobs, assign goals, and structure work groups in a way that stretches employees to develop new skills and capabilities. This level requires integrating career planning and social learning with staffing and goal management so employees build new capabilities as a result of the work they are doing and whom they are working with. Level 4 shifts the time horizon to the future by providing employees with guidance on identifying and achieving long-term career objectives within the organization. Mentoring, career planning, and succession management are highly important to achieving this level.

Level 5 is about integrating employee development with workforce planning and staffing to maintain a steady supply of high-performing talent in key jobs across the company. At this point, development becomes entirely intertwined with workforce staffing (see discussion: "Staffing and Development: Two Sides of the Same Coin").

STAFFING AND DEVELOPMENT: TWO SIDES OF THE SAME COIN

Companies can increase workforce productivity in four basic ways: put the right people in the right jobs, focus people on the right things, ensure people are performing their jobs in the right way, and give people assignments and tools that ensure they are getting the right development. All of these processes are interrelated, but two are particularly intertwined: right people and right development.

Having the right people requires having staffing processes that attract, identify, and select employees whose attributes match the demands of the jobs they are hired to perform. Providing the right development is about creating processes that build employee attributes to meet current and future job demands. A company's ability to staff future jobs using internal talent depends on its ability to develop the attributes of current employees. Conversely, the best way to develop employees is to put them in positions that allow them to learn through on-the-job experience. And one of the main motives for employees to develop their attributes is to create future job opportunities for themselves.

At the highest levels of talent process maturity, staffing and development become completely intertwined. Staffing focuses on creating talent pipelines that ensure access to adequate numbers of qualified candidates needed to fill ongoing job demands. Development focuses on keeping talent flowing through these pipelines by creating internal talent pools of employees who have the attributes needed to perform critical job roles. Staffing leaders are in regular communication with development leaders to align long-term workforce needs with near-term development activities so the company builds talent before it needs it. When a critical position opens, staffing and development leaders discuss whether it makes sense to fill it externally or use it to build the career of current high-potential employees. In addition, the development opportunities provided by the company become integral to the sourcing strategies it uses to attract talent into the organization.

Companies cannot do staffing at a high level of effectiveness without focusing on development, and vice versa. These processes are two sides of the same coin.

There are two general approaches to increasing development process maturity: starting with employee career goals and working upward, or starting with organizational talent needs and working down. The bottom-up approach focuses on providing tools and resources to help employees build their careers. Supporting employee career development is the primary focus in this approach. Process maturity is built through steadily adding tools and resources to help employees define career goals and pursue career paths to achieve these goals. The top-down approach focuses on building a steady supply of high-performing talent for critical roles in the company. Building talent pipelines is the primary goal in this approach. Process maturity is achieved by identifying what sort of talent the company needs and then building staffing and development programs to ensure the company has access to this talent.

The advantage of the bottom-up approach is that it can generate some very quick wins. The organization determines what sort of development resources will help employees achieve their career objectives and then finds ways to provide these resources. Career planning, training resources, social learning, and assessment measures typically play a major role in the early phases of this approach. These methods are tied directly to the career goals of employees so employees are likely to appreciate their value.

There are a few major limitations of the bottom-up approach. Employees' career goals do not always align with their company's talent requirements. The development methods that employees use may not necessarily be building the workforce capabilities the company truly needs. It is also common for development process maturity to get stuck at level 1 or 2 of the maturity curve. Development methods like training and assessments that work well for individual development and targeted development cannot by themselves get companies to higher levels of process maturity. Achieving these higher levels requires implementing methods like succession management, which requires companies to change how they assign job tasks or make staffing decisions. These higher levels also require coordinating development with staffing and goal management. This coordination can be difficult for companies that are used to treating development as an activity primarily focused on supporting employee career goals. It requires a shift in mind-set within HR and within the line of business. HR leaders have to coordinate development processes with those used for staffing, performance management, and goal management. Business leaders have to start thinking about job assignments and promotions as tools for long-term development in addition to viewing them from the perspective of short-term business operations.

The top-down approach starts with a focus on succession management and talent pipelines. Starting from a higher level has several benefits. Because it is focused on the talent needs of the organization rather than the career goals of employees, it will inherently be aligned with the company's talent requirements. It also forces the company to build development methods that support high levels of process maturity. Building talent pools requires getting line leadership to approach staffing and job assignments with a developmental mind-set. Once this higher-level mind-set has been accepted and adopted, it is much easier to build out the resources needed to support lower levels of development process maturity. For example, if managers know they will be rewarded for developing and promoting talent out of their teams, they are going to be much more supportive of efforts focused on individual and targeted employee development.

The main challenge with the top-down approach is that it requires considerable cross-functional integration and leadership commitment. Rather than focusing on the development needs of individual employees, the focus is on addressing longer-term talent needs identified by line leadership. Business leaders have to agree on where the company is going strategically and what sort of talent will be needed to execute this strategy. The top-down approach also emphasizes the use of cross-functional development methods like succession management that require close integration with other talent management areas, including development, staffing, workforce planning, and performance management. In sum, the downside of taking a top-down approach is that it requires a lot of coordination to define and launch the process. The benefit is that once it is launched, it is likely to have a much stronger business impact over the long term.

Most development programs are built through a mixture of top-down and bottom-up approaches. To be successful, development programs must support both the talent needs of the company and the career objectives of employees. True development success is achieved when an organization effectively aligns what the company needs employees to do, what employees are able to do, and what employees want to do.

7.6 CONCLUSION

Development can be one of the most rewarding areas of talent management. It provides a means to ensure you have the talent needed to achieve your company's business goals and is critical to maintaining employee skills and knowledge to meet the changing nature of business. When done exceptionally well, development can even be used to acquire and keep high-performing employees from joining competitors. It achieves all of this through helping employees achieve their potential while supporting the talent requirements of the organization. In this sense, development truly embodies the concept of a win-win partnership between employees and companies.

Development can also be one of the most frustrating areas of strategic HR. It is frustrating because many development programs fail to have a meaningful impact on employee development or business performance. This failure is usually the result of implementing development methods as stand-alone initiatives without adequately linking them to talent requirements and other strategic HR programs. Many failed development programs are classic examples of good concepts implemented in the wrong place at the wrong time in the wrong way.

This chapter discussed how to approach the design and deployment of development methods in an integrated fashion that will effectively address talent requirements tied directly to business needs. The chapter addressed fundamental concepts and design philosophies that underlie high-impact development programs. Attending to the questions reviewed in this chapter will help ensure that the development methods you build and deploy will be grounded in a robust, well-integrated, and effective overall development program.

NOTES

1. There is a tendency to give development methods more expansive names than the ones used here. This is done to encourage people to think of development more broadly—for example, referring to training resources as "learning management" to emphasize that training is not just about attending courses. I have intentionally chosen to use more narrowly defined names to clarify what it is that makes each of these methods unique from one another.

2. McCall, M. W. (2004). Leadership development through experience. *Academy of Management Executive, 18*, 127–130.

3. The only time it might make sense to run a development program in isolation is when it is being used purely for regulatory purposes (e.g., when employees must complete a training course mandated by law).

4. Stockdale, M. S., & Crosby, F. J. (2004). *The psychology and management of workplace diversity*. Malden, MA: Blackwell.

5. Burke, M. J., Sarpy, S. A., Smith-Crowe, K., Chan-Serafin, S., Salvador, R. O., & Islam, G. (2006). Relative effectiveness of worker safety and health training methods. *American Journal of Public Health, 96*, 315–324. Blume, B. D., Ford, J. K., Baldwin, T. T., & Huang, J. L. (2010). Transfer of training: A meta-analytic review. *Journal of Management, 36*, 1065–1105.

6. These three categories of metrics are similar in many ways to Kirkpatrick's levels of training criteria, which are widely used in the HR field. See Alliger, G. M., & Janak, E. A. (1989). Kirkpatrick's level of training criteria: Thirty years later. *Personnel Psychology, 42*, 331–342. The difference is that Kirkpatrick's framework does not include usage metrics since it assumes people have already completed training. But in practice, one of the main reasons development methods fail to work is that managers and employees never even use them.

Creating an Integrated HR Strategy

This chapter is about defining the changes you want to create through strategic HR and how to use strategic HR processes to create them. The previous four chapters described critical features to consider when designing each of the 4R strategic HR processes. This chapter discusses how to incorporate these four processes into an integrated HR strategy. The reason this chapter appears toward the end of the book is that it is easier to develop a strategy if you are familiar with the tactical methods, tools, and techniques that will be used to execute it. In application, the topics in this chapter might be addressed before addressing many of the topics discussed earlier in the book. Before building out specific processes for recruiting, goal management, performance management, and development it is useful to have an picture of what you want to achieve with strategic HR overall. This includes prioritizing whether certain processes should be developed and deployed before others. In sum, it is valuable to know what you want to accomplish with your overall HR strategy before you begin designing specific strategic HR processes.

The following issues are central to determining how to use strategic HR methods:

- *Identifying the change you want to create.* Strategic HR methods deliver business value by changing how the organization manages its people. Change requires effort and resources. Changing too much too fast can create stress, resistance, and confusion. HR strategies should identify the changes that are needed to support the company's business execution needs. They should also map out how to implement these changes over time in a way that balances the need for business improvement against the risk of overwhelming the company with excessive change.

- *Defining what the change will look like.* After identifying the general nature of the changes you are seeking to create, the next step is to define exactly what these changes will mean for employees, managers, senior business leaders, and HR professionals. This is done by describing the visible events that will result from the change—the sorts of conversations, information, and decisions that will be created as a result of implementing new strategic HR processes.

- *Defining how you will create the change.* Decide at a high level how strategic HR processes can be used to create the necessary changes. This includes identifying the metrics to evaluate if the changes are successful.

- *Operationalizing the change.* This is where you dive into the details of designing, deploying, and using the 4R strategic HR processes of right people, right things, right way, and right development to create the change. It also includes determining the technology you will use to enable these processes.

This chapter is divided into four sections reflecting these themes. Section 8.1 provides tools for assessing your organization's current level of strategic HR process maturity and using the assessment to define what sort of change you want to create. Section 8.2 provides examples of visible events that can be used to define and guide strategic HR efforts. Section 8.3 reviews steps to define how you will create these visible events. It also addresses metrics that can be used to guide and focus integrated strategic HR initiatives. Section 8.4 revisits how to use the 4R strategic HR processes to create change in your company and highlights concepts related to HR technology and data that will help increase the overall impact of integrated strategic HR processes.

8.1 IDENTIFYING THE CHANGE YOU WANT TO CREATE

Creating effective HR strategies requires both defining what you need to change and clarifying what you do not intend to change. Chapter 3 discussed the importance of viewing talent management maturity as a pyramid whose sides reflect the 4R strategic HR processes of right people, right things, right way, and right development. When developing an HR strategy, use this model to define what level of change you need to create to meet your business objectives. This includes recognizing that your company does not necessarily need to be at the highest levels of process maturity to address its business execution needs.

Table 8.1 provides descriptions of the different maturity levels for each of the 4R strategic HR processes. This table can help clarify what changes you wish to create through your strategic HR initiatives. To do this, work through the following steps:

1. *Define the business needs.* What are the most critical commitments the company must fulfill to meet the expectations of its shareholders? When answering this question, think about what time frame makes the most sense for your company. In larger companies, you may want to look at commitments spanning five years or more. For smaller companies, the focus may be on the next one to three years.

2. *Identify workforce impacts.* How do you need to change the workforce to meet these commitments? Will you need to add talent to the workforce that you do not currently have? What will people need to do in the future that they are not doing now?

3. *Prioritize business execution drivers.* Which of the six business execution drivers introduced in chapter 3 are the most important based on these commitments and changes? What business execution drivers are most critical to achieving the company's strategic objectives? Are the changes focused on increasing alignment, productivity, efficiency, sustainability, scalability, or governance?

4. *Determine how you will need to change your strategic HR processes to support these drivers.* Review the different maturity levels in table 8.1 and identify which ones are most critical to supporting the business drivers, workforce changes, and strategic commitments identified in steps 1 through 3. Use this analysis to clarify the general nature of the changes you need to make to your strategic HR processes.

Table 8.1
Talent Process Maturity Grid for Determining the Actions Most Critical to Supporting Your Company's Business Execution Needs

	Right People	Right Way	Right Things	Right Development
Level 5 (highest level of maturity)	*Maintaining Talent Pipelines:* Integrating external staffing and internal development processes to create a steady flow of talent into and across the company	*Influencing Strategy:* Analyzing data on employee performance to gain insights into overall strengths and weaknesses of the workforce	*Operational Use of Goals:* Providing leaders with clear insight into the types of goals employees at all levels are pursuing and progress made toward achieving them.	*Building Talent Pipelines:* Integrating the processes used to create jobs, hire and promote people, and develop employees based on a single strategy focused on building workforce capabilities to meet future talent requirements
Level 4	*Forecasting Talent Needs:* Forecasting future talent needs to ensure we have the talent to support our business growth and performance over the long term	*Calibrating Performance:* Making sure managers across the company evaluate employee performance using a common, consistent set of standards and expectations	*Coordinating Effort:* Creating collaboration and cooperation between people who share similar or interdependent goals	*Encouraging Career Growth:* Supporting and investing in high-potential employees to encourage them to build long-term careers within the organization

	Staffing	Performance Management	Goal Setting	Development
Level 3	*Building Talent Pools:* Increasing the number of qualified candidates available to meet our current job requirements	*Basing Decisions on Performance:* Creating alignment between people's performance and the company's pay and promotion decisions	*Creating Meaningful Goals:* Giving employees business goals and job assignments that are meaningful and relevant to their personal career objectives	*Business-Driven Development:* Giving people jobs and work assignments that challenge them to develop new skills and capabilities
Level 2	*Selecting High Performers:* Accurately evaluating candidates to ensure we are hiring the best employee and avoiding hiring mistakes	*Establishing Well-Defined Expectations:* Identifying and clearly communicating well-defined performance expectations for different job roles	*Aligning Goals:* Making sure employees understand the link between the goals they are working on and the overall strategic objectives of the company	*Targeted Development:* Identifying gaps between people's current capabilities and the capabilities they need to take on future job assignments
Level 1 (lowest level of maturity)	*Filling Positions:* Efficiently processing new employees and onboarding them into the organization	*Consistently Evaluating Performance:* Ensuring the performance of employees is reviewed on a regular basis using a standardized and agreed-on process	*Setting Tangible Goals:* Ensuring employees have clear goals and know exactly what they are expected to achieve	*Individual Development:* Providing training and development resources that help people perform their current jobs

It is important to have representation from all areas of strategic HR when addressing these questions. This includes leaders who manage staffing, performance management, compensation, training, and leadership succession and development. Higher levels of HR process maturity require greater levels of HR process integration. Even if the processes overseen by these leaders are not highly integrated now, they will ultimately have to come together to achieve higher levels of HR process maturity.

Also recognize that what you need to change is driven in part by what you are currently doing. For example, imagine a company is launching a new product line and wants to increase alignment around this strategy by increasing the maturity of processes used to focus employees on the right things. If the company currently has no goal-setting process, then simply achieving level 1, "setting tangible goals," may represent a major step forward. In contrast, if the company has a well-established goal-setting process, then the focus might be on achieving higher levels of process maturity such as "coordinating effort" or "operational use of goals."

It is also important to recognize that achieving higher levels of process maturity may not be possible until you establish processes to support lower levels. For example, if a company wants to achieve "maintaining talent pipelines," the highest level of "right people," then it has to first create processes to support filling positions, selecting high performers, and building talent pools. Overlooking lower levels of maturity can create significant problems. For example, I worked with a technology company that needed to increase productivity to more quickly respond to market changes. To achieve this goal, it implemented a rigorous calibration process to identify top performers and address low performers (level 4 of maturity for the process "Right Way"). But they never clearly defined the criteria used to evaluate performance (level 2 of maturity). As a result, the calibration sessions often turned into bitter arguments between managers over whose employees were best, without any consensus around what "best" actually meant.

Defining what level of process maturity you are seeking to achieve allows you to define the sorts of strategic HR processes you need to put in place and how they need to be designed. It also gives you a sense of what level of effort will be required to achieve the necessary changes. It is usually not too difficult to move an organization up one level of process maturity in less than two years. But moving up multiple levels of maturity can take three years or more (see the discussion: "Why Most Strategic HR Initiatives Take Three Years to Reach Full Effectiveness").

WHY MOST STRATEGIC HR INITIATIVES TAKE THREE YEARS TO REACH FULL EFFECTIVENESS

A common question associated with deployment of HR initiatives is how long it will take to get the processes up and running. The answer depends on the process, but in most cases, a good answer is, "It will take less than a year to get under way, but it will take three years to become fully effective."

There are two reasons "three years" is the magic number when it comes to achieving strategic HR process effectiveness. First, the purpose of these processes is to change how managers and employees act and think about things like setting goals, making staffing decisions, or developing potential. This requires overcoming past habits and instilling new patterns of behavior. Such changes will not occur all at once. They must be ingrained through educating, demonstrating, and reinforcing actions over time. Second, many HR processes occur annually. The first year a new process is rolled out, people have to go up a learning curve simply to use it. The second year, they start to get comfortable with it. It is often not until the third year that they truly begin to master it. One could argue that managers and employees are not familiar enough with HR processes until this third year to provide educated evaluations of process effectiveness. In essence, you need to have some mastery of a process before you can truly say whether it works well.

Because many strategic HR processes have a three-year time line, be direct with business leaders about the level of sustained commitment needed for these processes to fully deliver value. Business leaders should agree to support the process for three years before making significant changes to it. Making major changes to HR processes more often than every three years can create confusion and uncertainty in the company. This doesn't mean a process has to stay exactly the same through all three years. But companies should refrain from making radical changes in years 1 and 2 unless the process is clearly not working. In sum, you need to give the process time to work before you can accurately say whether it is working.

8.2 DEFINING WHAT THE CHANGE WILL LOOK LIKE

It is important to define the changes that an integrated HR strategy will create when the strategy has been successfully deployed. In other words, what will people be doing in the future that they are not doing today? This is especially important if the goal is to create transformational change (see the discussion: "Distinguishing between Process Automation and Business Transformation"). Clearly defining what the change will look like ensures that process design decisions emphasize the right features and methods to support it.

DISTINGUISHING BETWEEN PROCESS AUTOMATION AND BUSINESS TRANSFORMATION

Companies often talk about using strategic HR methods to create business transformation. But what does it mean to "transform" a business through HR? And how is this different from other ways HR processes might affect the business?

Strategic HR processes, particularly those supported by HR technology, provide two types of value. One source of value is through automating and simplifying HR methods. This is about making it easier for managers and employees to complete activities they are already doing—for example, putting existing paper processes online or standardizing the methods used across the company to conduct performance reviews. Automation and simplification add value through increasing efficiency.

The second source of value comes through transforming how a company manages its workforce. This is about improving workforce productivity through creating better conversations, decisions, and actions related to staffing, goal management, performance management, and development. There are three basic kinds of transformation:

- *Tactical*—changing the things that employees and managers actually do. This is the most concrete aspect of transformation. It includes completing performance rating forms and filling out development plans. Tactical transformation is associated with aspects of a process that you can easily measure (e.g., have employees recorded their job goals in an HR technology system).

- *Interpersonal*—changing how employees and managers interact with each other. This includes coaching sessions by managers with employees; meetings of employees with managers and coworkers to establish goals that align with business strategies; and conversations between new and existing employees to build relationships and facilitate job transitions.
- *Conceptual*—changing how employees and managers make decisions. This is the most significant form of transformation because it requires changing how people think. This includes having managers incorporate data on employee performance into compensation decisions, ensuring all managers use the same criteria when evaluating employee performance and potential, and providing senior leaders with data that influence their perceptions of the company's workforce strengths and weaknesses.

Achieving tactical transformation tells you a lot about process compliance but does not necessarily indicate whether people are using the process effectively. Achieving interpersonal and conceptual transformation is the primary goal of most transformational strategic HR initiatives.

Table 8.2 highlights differences between process automation and business transformation. Automation provides fewer benefits but is much easier to implement. The risk of automation is that it may have a negative impact on a company if the processes being automated are ineffective to begin with. Automating a lousy process can be described as "doing bad things quickly." Transformation is more difficult to achieve but provides more significant performance improvements. Because transformation requires significant effort on the part of managers and employees, there is also less risk of implementing processes that do not add value as people will simply refuse to do them.

Strategic HR initiatives should clarify whether the end goal is process automation or business transformation. Both types of change can provide value, and it is possible to create HR processes that provide both. There is also risk of creating processes that achieve automation but do not accomplish the extra, more difficult step of achieving true transformation. In order to manage this risk, it is important to clearly define the kinds of transformational change you are seeking to achieve and then establish processes and measures that effectively support and assess this change.

Table 8.2
Process Automation versus Business Transformation

Process Automation	Business Transformation
Makes existing methods more efficient	Fundamentally changes how you do things
Accelerates good and bad performance	Creates new experiences while eliminating others
Can lead to doing bad things quickly	Enables doing things you could not do before
Does not require a mental mind shift	Qualitative changes in performance or experience
Easily duplicated by others	Difficult to copy
Easier to implement	Harder to implement

It is also far easier to get people to adopt new HR processes if they understand exactly what they are expected to do differently and why. A common myth is that people fear change. In reality, people do not fear change. They do dislike uncertainty and may fear changes they do not fully understand. The more clearly you can paint a picture of what the organization will look like after a new HR process has been implemented, the easier it is to get people in the organization to accept it. Do not just define the outcomes you will create through more effective strategic HR processes; describe the actual things people will have to do in order to create these outcomes.

Table 8.3 provides examples of visible events associated with the use of strategic HR processes. The events in the table correspond to the process maturity levels described table 8.1. These visible events illustrate changes a company can create through implementation of strategic HR methods. The events range from things associated with low levels of HR process maturity such as, "When asked, employees will be able to list the five to eight most important goals they are seeking to accomplish this year and explain how they link to the goals of the CEO," to things associated with high levels of maturity such as, "Senior leaders will be given quarterly reports highlighting where the company is at risk of experiencing critical staffing shortages one, three, and five years into the future." The common characteristic underlying the events in table 8.3 is that they are tangible

Table 8.3
Examples of Transformation Events Associated with HR Processes

	Right People	Right Way	Right Things	Right Development
Level 5 (highest level of maturity)	*Maintaining Talent Pipelines:* Senior leaders will be given quarterly reports showing the rate of internal transfers, external turnover, and new hires associated with specific roles and departments in their organization.	*Influencing Strategy:* Senior leaders will receive quarterly reports indicating trends in revenue per full-time-equivalent employee for their departments and their relationship to employee skills, competency ratings, and development activities.	*Operational Use of Goals:* Leaders and managers will update or refine their goals at least once a quarter to reflect changing business demands.	*Building Talent Pipelines:* Leaders will meet once a quarter to discuss staffing needs and determine how these can be used to accelerate development of high-potential talent.
Level 4	*Forecasting Talent Needs:* Senior leaders will be given quarterly reports highlighting where the company is at risk of experiencing critical staffing shortages one, three, and five years into the future.	*Calibrating Performance:* Managers will meet twice a year to agree on which employees are among the top 20 percent most influential contributors to the company.	*Coordinating Effort:* All employees and leaders will have goals that are public and visible to other employees.	*Encouraging Career Growth:* Mentorship relationships will be established for at least 50 percent of employees identified as key talent.

(Continued)

	Right People	Right Way	Right Things	Right Development
Level 3	*Building Talent Pools:* Recruiters will receive automatically generated reports indicating the number of applicants hired from different recruiting sources.	*Basing Decisions on Performance:* The merit increases of top-performing employees will be at least two times larger than the increase given to average-performing employees.	*Creating Meaningful Goals:* Every employee will be able to identify at least one goal he or she is working on that is significantly building that person's capabilities and requiring him or her to learn new things.	*Business-Driven Development:* Managers will be evaluated based on internal transfer versus external turnover and rewarded for retaining and providing talent to the organization.
Level 2	*Selecting High Performers:* All candidates will be interviewed by at least three people using structured interview guides built around key job competencies.	*Establishing Well-Defined Expectations:* Employees will receive behavioral feedback on their performance based on key competencies at least twice a year.	*Aligning Goals:* Managers will meet at least once a quarter with employees to review their goals to ensure they align with business priorities.	*Targeted Development:* All training investments will be clearly linked to specific business needs and job-relevant competencies.
Level 1: (lowest level of maturity)	*Filling Positions:* Managers will automatically generate job requisition and job postings by selecting from existing job description libraries.	*Consistently Evaluating Performance:* Performance of employees will be reviewed at least once a year using consistent evaluation process.	*Setting Tangible Goals:* When asked, employees will be able to list the five to eight goals they want to accomplish this year and explain how they link to the goals of the CEO.	*Individual Development:* Every employee will have at least one but no more than three specific development objectives listed in his or her development plans.

things that can be seen in a company. The tangible nature of these events helps leaders, managers, and employees fully understand how the organization is going to change and why. It also helps guide the design of strategic HR processes by clarifying exactly what the processes have to create or support.

The events in table 8.3 are a small sample of the kinds of visible events you might create through the use of strategic HR processes. Use this sample as a starting point to define the specific changes you need to create in your organization to support your company's business goals. Some of these events define specific success metrics (e.g., "Every employee will have at least one development objective in his or her development plan"), while others are more qualitative or conversational in nature (e.g., "Managers will meet twice a year to agree on which employees are among the top 20 percent most influential contributors"). Use the events in table 8.3 to engage with HR and line-of-business stakeholders in your company to define what changes make sense for your company given its business needs. Again, consider this question: When the new HR processes are implemented, what will people in the organization be doing that they are not doing now?

8.3 DEFINING HOW YOU WILL CREATE AND MEASURE THE CHANGE

Once you have defined the visible events you are seeking to create, link these events back to the HR processes that will be used to create them and the business goals they are addressing. This further clarifies exactly what you are trying to accomplish and why. It also provides a useful check to make sure you have not drifted away from the original business objectives. Remember that you have now taken several steps since the original step of defining the company's business goals and linking them to business execution drivers.

Defining how you will create the change with these higher-level goals in mind involves working through the following questions:

- *What visible events are you going to create?* Describe the actual events—for example, "Managers will meet once a quarter with employees to review their goals and sure they align with business priorities."

- *What is the organization trying to accomplish with this event?* Tie the event back to the business execution drivers that it addresses—for example, "This will increase alignment in the organization to support our business plans."

- *Why is this important?* This is where you justify why this change is worth the effort by linking the change to specific business objectives—for example, "Our company's business plan requires increasing revenue in new markets. To do this, we need to ensure employees' goals effectively support products and regions they have not supported in the past."

- *How is the organization going to make this happen?* Explain the HR processes that are going to be used to facilitate and support this change—for example, "We will deploy a goal management process along with manager training on goal-cascading methods to ensure every employee has goals clearly aligned to the new business plan. We will use HR technology to support the goal-cascading process and track whether managers are meeting with their teams to set goals."

- *How will you measure success?* Identify metrics you can use to determine whether the change is being successfully implemented—for example, "Goal plans for 90 percent of employees will be updated at least once a quarter. Senior leaders will be provided with quarterly reports showing the number and types of goals that have been set to support the new business plan along with progress against these goals."

This last question is particularly important to ensuring the success of the initiative. Clearly defining measures of success not only allows you to determine if the HR strategy is ultimately successful, but also helps you to avoid drifting off course when working through the myriad of questions that you have to address during process design.

Table 8.4 lists some of the metrics that can be used to measure the success of different strategic HR processes. These metrics are broken into three categories: workforce data, process usage data, and employee attitude data.

Workforce data provide descriptive information about workforce operations and characteristics. These data, which provide insight into workforce quality, efficiency, and cost, can be used to track the number of people in different roles, employee productivity rates, turnover in different jobs, and the length of staffing vacancies for various positions, for example.

Process use data is used to track adoption and use of strategic HR processes. Examples include the percentage of people with completed performance appraisals, the frequency with which goal plans are updated, and the number of succession candidates identified for key roles. These data provide insight into how employees are using strategic HR methods.

Table 8.4

Metrics of Strategic HR Process Impact

	Right People	Right Things	Right Way	Right Development
Workforce Data	Number of people hired	Number of employ-ees assigned to work on different strategic initiatives	Increase in workforce productivity metrics	Time to fill for key roles
	Time-to-hire		Greater variance in performance ratings	Number of cross-functional moves
	Time-to-fill	Percentage of leaders using goal reports to make talent decisions	Percentage of leaders using performance management to make talent decisions	Percentage of posi-tions filled with internal promotions
	Cost per employee hired			
	Applicant quality			
	Applicant-to-hire ratio			Percentage of key positions unfilled
	Offer-to-acceptance ratio		Decrease in fairness complaints, litigation	High-potential turnover
	Productive performance			
	Counterproductive performance		Correlation between performance ratings and salary increase or bonus	Employee demographics for key roles
	Tenure			
	Training performance/time to competence			Changes in employee performance and potential ratings over time
	Turnover costs			
	Employee demographics, equal employment oppor-tunity statistics			Average tenure in current position
	Internal promotions and transfers			
	Time and attendance			

(Continued)

	Right People	Right Things	Right Way	Right Development
Process Use	Applicant volume Applicant source Applicant demographics Assessment scores Interview scores	Percentage of employees with completed goal plans Percentage of employees who regularly update goal progress Time communicating goals Time developing goal plans Percentage of goals completed Percentage of employees with effective goals (based on auditing goal quality) Percentage of employees with aligned goals	Percentage of employees with performance reviews Percentage of managers regularly updating performance management files Percentage of executives who regularly access performance reports Time spent completing performance reviews Percentage of managers providing effective performance feedback (based on review quality) Greater variance in performance ratings	Percentage of employees with completed profiles Percentage of employees with current career development plans or using training resources Percentage of key positions with identified candidate slates Percentage of "ready=now" candidates for key roles
Employee Attitude	Applicant reactions Hiring manager Attitudes Employee attitudes Turnover reasons	Employee, manager, and executive ratings of goal management process Employee engagement and alignment ratings	Employee and leader ratings of performance management process Employee engagement and fairness ratings	Employee engagement Employee, manager, and executive ratings of career development process Employee engagement and commitment survey scores

Employee attitude data measure broad attitudes like employee engagement and job satisfaction, as well as attitudes related to specifics, such as the value of a training course or the efficiency of a staffing process. These data provide insight into the beliefs and perceptions that managers and employees have toward the organization in general, as well as toward specific strategic HR methods.

Although there is value in tracking all the data in table 8.4, it is usually most effective to pick three or four metrics that get at the nature of the change you are seeking to create and use these to focus your change efforts on what matters most. Workforce and employee attitude data tend to provide the most insight into the value and effectiveness of strategic HR process. But it is important to also include some process usage metrics to ensure the process is being adopted. If a process is not adopted, then obviously it is not going to be effective. And methods used to fix problems associated with a lack of process adoption are quite different from those used to fix problems associated with lack of process effectiveness.

8.4 OPERATIONALIZING THE CHANGE

After you have defined the change you are seeking to create, clarified how it will have a positive impact on the company's business objectives, and identified metrics to evaluate project success, it is time to begin designing, building, and deploying strategic HR processes that enable and support the change. Chapters 4 through 7 discussed the major issues to consider when designing these processes. The following are few additional things to keep in mind when you begin the process design phase:

- *Establish a cross-functional steering team.* Companies often create different teams to focus on redesigning specific HR processes such as staffing, performance management, or development. Having small, focused teams is important to efficiently working through the design questions that arise with each of these processes. But these different HR processes must also integrate with each other. To ensure effective integration of HR processes, it is useful to create a cross-functional steering team consisting of representatives from different areas of HR (e.g., staffing, development, compensation). This team is tasked with periodically looking across all the strategic HR processes to make sure they are aligned around common models and are able to share data effectively with one other.

- *Use the right technology to support process integration and process design.* It is virtually impossible to implement large-scale strategic HR processes without some use of technology. The technology does not always need to be leading-edge software, but it must provide features that support the kinds of HR processes needed to support your business execution goals. It is important for this technology to support integration across different HR processes.

- *Do not allow yourself to be overly constrained by relying on technology systems that were not designed with integrated, strategic HR in mind.* This can be a particularly significant issue for organizations that have historically treated HR as an administrative function. Many of these companies use HR technology systems that were primarily built to support financial operations. These systems may be called "HR technology," but they lack the rich set of features and functions needed to support strategic HR methods. Strategic HR is a specialized area, and it requires the use of specialized, highly configurable technology. If you are a small company, you may be better off modifying some general form of technology like Excel rather than trying to get an administratively focused HR system to perform strategic HR tasks. If you are a large company, you may need to seriously challenge your IT department to provide you with the tools you need to perform your job effectively.

- *Achieve perfection through application.* Some companies spend months on process design before they move to process deployment. These efforts to create the perfect process never work. No matter how much time is spent using whiteboards to think through process design, you never really know how well a process will work until you try it. It is usually better to launch a good process quickly than to spend months trying to design a great process that takes years to go live. Realize that no matter what you implement, you are going to want to make changes. Make sure the technology you are using is flexible enough to allow modifications after the process has been launched.

- *Pace the change.* Introduce change into the organization at a pace that will challenge but not overwhelm managers, employees, and HR. It can be useful to categorize the different changes you are creating based on business value and ease of adoption. Changes that are both easy to implement and provide considerable value should be given priority. Consider spreading out deployment for changes that provide high value but are also more difficult to implement. See if there is a way to introduce changes at a more gradual pace so you do not overwhelm the organization. But do not lose sight of the ultimate reasons for driving the implementation of new strategic HR methods. If a change is critical to supporting the company's business execution needs, do not shy away from making it happen. The most difficult changes are often the most beneficial and long lasting.

- *Strive to move from a push to a pull.* When you start changing your strategic HR methods, be prepared to encounter considerable resistance. This is particularly true if your organization has historically treated HR as an administrative function. People will initially wonder why the company is changing its HR processes and are likely to view these changes with skepticism. But as managers and employees begin to see the value of using more effective HR methods for staffing, talent management, and development, they will start to ask what else HR can do to help them be more successful.

The beauty of strategic HR is that increasing process maturity in one area creates tension to increase maturity in other areas. For example, if a company starts measuring and rewarding employees based on clearly defined competencies, then employees will start asking for resources to develop these competencies. As employees start developing competencies, they will become more valuable as a source for internal hires. This will create interest in tools to support long-term career development and succession planning, which will lead to more interest in workforce planning, and so on. The more you improve one area of strategic HR, the greater the desire in the company to improve other areas (see the discussion: "Developing Our Own: How One Company Created a Virtuous Cycle of Strategic HR").

DEVELOPING OUR OWN: HOW ONE COMPANY CREATED A VIRTUOUS CYCLE OF STRATEGIC HR

The interconnected nature of strategic HR processes can be both a challenge and benefit. It is a challenge because the ability to increase maturity in one area of strategic HR is constrained by maturity levels in other areas. For example, a company's staffing department will struggle to create strong talent pipelines if the company lacks effective methods for developing internal talent. Similarly, a performance management process will never become highly effective if the data from this process are not used to guide decisions related to compensation, promotion, and development.

The interconnected nature of strategic HR is a benefit because increasing maturity in one area of strategic HR creates pressure to improve other areas. For example, when a company starts using performance management data to make internal staffing decisions, it creates pressure to create methods that ensure performance management data are accurate and complete. When employees know that performance management results affect their career opportunities, they will start asking for development resources that allow them to take action on the results of their performance assessments. The result is a virtuous cycle where improvements in one area of strategic HR encourage and support improvements in others areas.

Over my career I have seen virtuous cycles of strategic HR play out in many companies. One of the most interesting is a retail company that early in its growth chose to adopt a policy of filling operational leadership positions only through promoting internal talent. The president of this company believed that the best way to maintain a strong culture and build employee engagement was to build leaders internally rather than hire from outside. This policy created a domino effect in terms of its impact on strategic HR.

The promote-from-within policy forced the company to develop effective processes for identifying and selecting internal leaders from frontline staff. The company could not afford to promote employees who could not perform these leadership roles, so it established a variety of methods to develop and measure leadership potential through on-the-job assignments. The company also had to hire frontline staff with the capabilities to become future leaders. This led to creating more rigorous selection methods. As the company's promotion-from-within policy became more widely known, it started to attract a higher caliber of talent for frontline jobs than would normally apply. People were not just applying to fill a job; they were applying so they could start a career with the company. As the company began hiring frontline staff with stronger capabilities, it was able to raise the bar on what was required to be promoted into leadership roles. This in turn led to creating even more rigorous methods to develop and assess potential.

This company's decision to promote from within created pressure to build stronger development programs, which led to the need to create better hiring methods to ensure employees could succeed in these programs. As the quality of the workforce increased, the expectations of the company toward employees also increased. The result is a workforce that in many ways is getting stronger and stronger over time.

To be clear, I am not saying that companies should adopt strict promote-from-within policies. Such policies are neither feasible nor beneficial for many organizations. There are also downsides to overrelying on internal promotions in terms of innovation and diversity of thinking. But for this company, a strong promote-from-within policy worked extremely well. Much of the reason it worked was not due to the promotions themselves, but due to the pressure the promotions put on developing better strategic HR methods for staffing, performance management, and employee development. The key lesson from this example is that strongly focusing on improving one area of strategic HR often creates pressure to improve other areas.

8.5 CONCLUSION

This chapter walked through concepts related to designing and implementing strategic HR initiatives. This starts with defining the business reasons of why it makes sense to change how your company currently hires, manages, and develops people. Do not change HR processes just because it seems like a good idea; change them because they are critical to supporting key business execution drivers.

The next step is to define what changes are required to meet your business execution needs and articulate the visible events and metrics that will result from these changes. In particular, what will managers and employees do in the future that they may not be doing now? Finally, use these envisioned changes to guide the redesign of your strategic HR processes. This includes thinking through the role technology will play in enabling and supporting these processes.

The challenge to developing and implementing an integrated HR strategy is that it requires approaching HR at a holistic, interconnected level. Staffing, performance management, goal management, and development cannot be thought of in isolation from each other. But the benefits of this integrated approach are multiple. Integrated HR strategies drive more effective and lasting results by leveraging multiple levers to drive positive workforce change. They create a more coherent experience for the managers and employees who ultimately have to adopt and use HR methods. And they create a virtuous cycle where improvements in one area of HR create pressure to make improvements in the other areas.

Strategic HR Process Deployment and Adoption

The value of strategic HR is not a result of HR departments identifying processes needed to drive business execution but from getting managers, employees, and senior leaders to adopt these processes to drive stronger business execution. It is not enough to build great processes. These processes must be effectively used to be successful.

This chapter discusses four actions that underlie successful deployment and adoption of strategic HR methods:

1. *Establishing HR leadership credibility.* Do people in the company trust the HR organization enough to take their advice? Are the HR team members viewed as experts in business execution, or does the company view HR as an administrative support function?

2. *Defining the change and change requirements.* Have you clearly defined what it is you want people to do differently in the future from what they have been doing in the past? Have you determined what critical barriers and enablers are going to affect this change?

3. *Providing tools and training to support the change.* Are you giving people the technology, methods, and knowledge they need to make the change? Are they able to do what you want them to do?

4. *Enlisting line leadership to drive the change.* Do line leaders actively support the deployment of HR processes? If not, these processes are likely to be branded as "stuff HR is asking us to do." Such processes almost always fail.

This chapter discusses each of these four deployment actions in more detail. All of these actions assume that the strategic HR process you are deploying is well designed. Chapters 2 through 8 addressed elements of good process design, so we will assume this criterion has been met.

9.1 ESTABLISHING HR LEADERSHIP CREDIBILITY

To drive business execution, strategic HR processes must change how senior leaders, managers, and employees think about staffing, job assignments, performance, and development. People will not follow the advice of HR if they do not perceive HR as credible experts in these areas—and not all HR organizations have this sort of credibility. Rather than being seen as people who can help line-of-business managers and employees be more effective, HR is often viewed as a necessary but nonstrategic services function built around matters like payroll processing and legal compliance with employment laws. Changing this perception requires HR to do the following things:

• *Understand the business problems that leaders and line managers face.* Take time to learn about the strategic objectives leaders and managers are being held accountable for and the challenges they are facing in meeting these objectives. Then show how HR processes can support their needs. Revisit the discussion of business execution drivers in chapter 3 for guidance on how to do this. As a general rule, always begin discussions about HR processes by reviewing the business goals these methods will address.

• *Start conversations with leaders by talking about the operational challenges that are on their minds.* Imagine being in front of a group of business leaders and saying, "We have a solution that will help the company address this business need." What business needs will get leaders, to lean forward in their seats wondering, "How can you help us with that?" Link HR processes to these business needs, and keep reminding leaders that this is why HR matters.

• *Keep in mind that most non-HR people do not care about HR processes.* They care only about the things these processes have an impact on. For example, managers care a lot about whether their employees achieve their business goals. But this does not mean they have an inherent interest in goal management processes. This is why it is critical that managers see a clear connection between strategic HR processes and the objectives that are important to their personal career success. Furthermore, unless managers ask for more detail, do not tell them any more about HR processes than is absolutely necessary for them to use them successfully. Most managers do not have time or interest to learn the theories behind HR processes. They just need to be confident that they will improve their success and understand how to use them effectively.

- *Show employees how HR can help them achieve their career goals.* Employees will not embrace HR methods because they are valuable to the company. They will embrace them if they believe the methods will help them achieve their career objectives. You may be able to get basic compliance by saying HR methods are mandatory conditions of employment. But if you want employees to truly engage in HR processes, they must see a link between these processes and personal career advancement. This comes from linking HR processes to pay, promotions, and development opportunities. This can also be achieved by showing how HR processes make employees better at their job.

- *Be simple, clear, and easy to understand.* Much of the value of HR processes comes from helping the organization effectively communicate and make decisions about people. This starts with creating a common, well-understood vocabulary that people can use to talk about job requirements, employee attributes, goals, performance, and development. When possible, adapt the language of HR to match the language of the business. Never introduce a new word to the company if an old word will do. Do not introduce new terms unless they describe something that is critical to using certain HR techniques. When you introduce terms, make sure they are clearly defined, and then always adhere to this definition. For example, it may be important to introduce concepts like skills, competencies, and goals to managers so they understand the levers that drive performance. But be sure these terms are used in a consistent fashion across all HR processes. Over time, the language of HR should become embedded in everyday communication and be indistinguishable from the language of the business.

- *Focus on fundamentals, and avoid trends.* The field of HR is often criticized for its tendency to embrace trends. HR departments have a history of rolling out new concepts and models, only to abandon them a year later in favor of something else, frequently before these processes have had any real impact. Employees and managers ignore new HR initiatives as they are confident they will soon be abandoned for another "flavor of the month."

- *Be alert to HR's reputation for following fads.* In general, approach HR deployments as being a three-year undertaking and avoid making major changes to HR processes more often than once every other year. A good mantra for strategic HR might be, "simple, fundamental methods rigorously and consistently applied over time." Remember that the fundamentals of strategic HR come down to four basic things: getting the right people in the right jobs, focusing them on the right things, ensuring they are doing things the right way, and providing them with the right development. Master these fundamentals, and let competitors waste their time chasing after the current "next big thing in HR."

- *Take leadership risks*. Strategic HR adds value by creating change. HR leaders must be willing to advocate and take accountability for the changes they are seeking to create. This requires engaging business leaders in discussions around the best way to manage people

- *HR leaders must be confident in their expertise*. Most HR leaders would not presume to tell finance leaders how the company should manage its bank accounts or tell marketing leaders how the company should segment its customer base. Conversely, HR leaders must earn the respect of their peers by giving confident and effective guidance to other areas of the company on how to attract, hire, manage, develop, and retain the talent needed to drive business execution.

Convincing non-HR business leaders of the value of HR methods typically does not come from theoretical explanations of the value of HR techniques— for example, trying to explain to managers why intrinsic motivation is so important to driving employee engagement and why engagement is so important for performance. Nor does it come from pure monetary arguments (see the discussion: "Problems with Using Return on Investment to Justify HR"). It comes from clearly articulating to business leaders how HR can provide them with a better way to manage their workforce. This involves tying HR methods to the company's business execution needs, and then clearly and succinctly explaining how these methods can be adopted in a manner that will significantly increase the organization's business execution capability.

PROBLEMS WITH USING RETURN ON INVESTMENT TO JUSTIFY HR

A book on talent management included the following statement about the return on investment (ROI) of talent management methods:

Researchers have begun to try to determine the return on investment of various HR initiatives [and] determined that . . . performance management is three times more powerful than better selection interviewing and decision making, and training and developing current employees is two times more powerful than just hiring better employees in the first place.[a]

This quote suggests that scientific research can provide an accurate empirical estimate of the relative ROI associated with different strategic HR processes. But what the authors also report is that staffing, performance management, and training and development applications "are extremely difficult things to compare." The study they reference used meta-analysis, a statistical technique that relies on a range of assumptions that can hide variance in ROI found across different organizations using the same talent management interventions.[b] So while the relative value reported for performance management, training, and staffing may be accurate in general, the actual value that individual companies may realize varies substantially.

This research highlights the notoriously ambiguous and ill-defined nature of ROI estimates applied to strategic HR processes. It is possible to demonstrate clear empirical relationships between HR methods and employee behaviors, and employee behaviors and business outcomes at the level of individual employees. But it is difficult to create mathematical models that accurately estimate the level of direct impact that HR processes have on financial outcomes at the company level. The reasons are complex, but suffice it to say that most HR ROI studies are based on statistically complex assumptions about the relationship of process design, workforce characteristics, and business results. As a result, ROI estimates tend to be relatively poor tools for convincing non-HR leaders of the value of HR processes. In fact, ROI models can undermine HR credibility because financially minded business leaders frequently find them to be empirically unsound.

The purpose here is not to criticize research focused on calculating the ROI of talent management interventions. Such research is valuable for understanding the utility of different strategic HR interventions and calling attention to business gains associated with investing in programs to increase workforce productivity. But caution needs to be taken when interpreting ROI estimates that require estimating the financial value of human performance. Strategic HR is ultimately about predicting or changing the behavior of people, and people are complex creatures. Interventions that greatly increase the productivity of one person might hurt the productivity of someone else. Programs that work in one company culture can fail in another. In addition, companies are notoriously bad at measuring the productivity of individual employees, and any study that attempts to report changes in employee performance is inherently at risk of reporting statistics based on faulty data.[c]

There is value in empirically examining the ROI of different strategic HR methods, but care needs to be taken when interpreting the results of these studies. Just because a program had a significant impact in another company does not necessarily mean it will have the same impact in your organization. But if empirical research suggests that certain interventions have had little or no positive impact in previous companies, then you should probably seriously question their value before trying them in your company. ROI studies are useful for showing the general financial benefits associated with the use of strategic HR methods, but they tend to be questionable for showing exactly how much money you will gain or save as a result of their implementation.

[a]Eichinger, R. W., Lombardo, M. M., & Ulrich, D. (2006). *100 things you need to know: Best people practices for managers and HR*. Minneapolis: Lominger, pp. 208–209.

[b]Spencer, L. (2001). The economic value of emotional intelligence competencies and EIC-based HR programs. In C. Cherniss & D. Goleman (Eds.), *The emotionally intelligent workplace: How to select for, measure, and improve emotional intelligence in individuals, groups, and organizations* (pp. 45–82). San Francisco: Jossey-Bass.

[c]Austin, J. T., & Villanova, P. (1992). The criterion problem: 1917–1992. *Journal of Applied Psychology*, *77*(6), 836–874.

9.2 DEFINING THE CHANGE AND CHANGE REQUIREMENTS

That "people fear change" is a common misconception. To the contrary, most people actively seek change: they travel to new countries, take up new hobbies, and pursue new career opportunities. It is the human ability to adapt to changing environments that allowed us to genetically outcompete larger and stronger animals. In fact, people do not fear change—but many fear the uncertainty

Figure 9.1
HR Process Stakeholders

Stakeholders Employees Managers Senior Leaders Human Resource Professionals Information Technology Professionals	Changes: What must they do in the future that they might not be doing now?
	Benefits: How will this change help them acheive their goals?
	Challenges: Why will they resist this change?
	Enablers: What resources and incentives do they need to accept this change?

caused by changes they do not understand. And all people dislike putting effort into changes that they do not see as beneficial.

The best approach to change management is to be extremely clear about what you are changing, why you are changing it, how it will benefit the people affected by the change, and what support you are providing that will help people make the change. Figure 9.1 provides questions that help clarify the nature of changes created by implementing new HR processes. Prior to implementing a new HR process, think about how the change will affect the following groups of people:

- *Employees*. What impact will this process have on frontline employees and individual contributors? How will it affect their perceptions toward their jobs, careers, managers, and the organization in general? Is this change something they will find easy to accept or hard to do?

- *Managers*. How will this process help managers achieve their career goals and business needs? What knowledge and skills will they need to carry out the changes required of them? Do they view this change as something that will make their lives easier or harder?

- *Senior leaders.* Senior leaders may not be directly affected by many HR processes, but they must support these processes by encouraging and holding managers and employees accountable for using them. In cases where senior leaders are expected to actively use an HR process, they must act as visible role models on process adoption and use (e.g., setting clear goals, making staffing decisions based on clearly defined criteria). Senior leaders may also be expected to use data from HR processes to guide business decisions. This requires providing data to them in a usable format, making sure they know how to effectively interpret these data, and giving them some means to act on insights they gain from their analysis.

- *HR professionals.* HR professionals are typically expected to be the first line of support for employees and managers using HR processes. The job experience of many HR professionals is based more on carrying out administrative HR tasks than supporting strategic HR processes. The skills needed to answer questions about benefits programs are much different from those needed to facilitate a talent review session. Are HR professionals able to make the transition to support strategic HR processes? Do they want to? Do they have the skills to consult and advise managers, employees, and senior leaders on how to conduct strategic HR activities and interpret strategic HR data?

- *Information technology (IT) professionals.* Deploying, scaling and maintaining most strategic HR processes requires the use of technology. What role will IT professionals play in deploying and supporting this technology? Do they understand how the technology works? Do they have the time and resources needed to support it?

For each of these groups, systematically walk through the following questions:

- How will the change affect them? What will they be asked to do differently in the future that they were not doing in the past?
- How will the change benefit this stakeholder group?
- What things might they resist or find confusing or challenging?
- What will be key to getting them to accept these changes?

Also think about what other groups play a role in the success of the deployment. For example, will the new processes affect customers, suppliers, or contractors? If so, what actions will be needed to ensure the support of these groups?

Systematically working through these questions will provide a comprehensive picture of what you are changing, what factors will enable this change, and what challenges you need to address or overcome for the change to be successful. Once you have answered these questions, it is likely to be fairly obvious what types of communication, change management, and training will be needed to make the change successful.

Finally, remember that change management does not end when the process is deployed. It takes several years for people to fully master many HR processes. There will also be a constant stream of new employees, managers, senior leaders, and HR professionals who must be trained on how to use the process. Change management starts with process deployment, but it does not end there. As one HR leader told me, "We shouldn't talk about 'going live' with a new HR process; we should talk about 'going to live' with the process."

9.3 PROVIDING TOOLS AND TRAINING TO SUPPORT THE CHANGE

Chapters 4, 5, 6, and 7 discussed what is involved in getting members of the organization to adopt and effectively use processes associated with getting the right people in the right jobs, ensuring they are focusing on the right things, doing things the right way, and getting the right development. In addition to the information discussed in these previous chapters, it is important to consider two additional topics related to supporting HR process change. First, does the technology used to support the process effectively facilitate the changes you want to create? Second, have you positioned and branded the change in a manner so that it comes across as compelling and valuable, or does it feel like just another administrative exercise?

9.3.1 How Technology Enables Change

Throughout this book, I have mentioned that many strategic HR processes cannot be effectively deployed and maintained without the use of technology. Technology does not create change, but it does make change possible that would be impossible or unsustainable without it. But this will happen only if the technology meets certain criteria. It is important to consider four things when evaluating HR technology from a change management perspective: functionality, usability, accessibility, and transparency.

Functionality Does the technology support the process steps you are seeking to create? When examining functionality, do not just focus on whether a system supports different types of process steps, forms, and database requirements. Think about how it affects conversations and decisions. Will it influence how employees and managers think about jobs and careers? Does it support conversations between employees and managers around performance, development, and job assignments? Can it be used to guide and facilitate meetings to discuss talent strengths and needs across the organization? Does the system provide reports and dashboards that will help managers and leaders incorporate HR data into how they make decisions about the company?

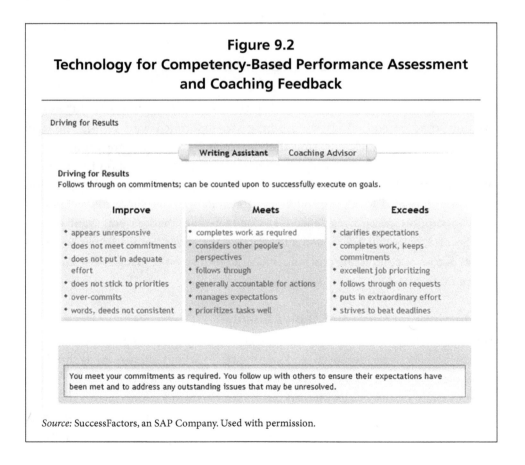

Figure 9.2
Technology for Competency-Based Performance Assessment and Coaching Feedback

Driving for Results

Writing Assistant   Coaching Advisor

Driving for Results
Follows through on commitments; can be counted upon to successfully execute on goals.

Improve	Meets	Exceeds
• appears unresponsive	• completes work as required	• clarifies expectations
• does not meet commitments	• considers other people's perspectives	• completes work, keeps commitments
• does not put in adequate effort	• follows through	• excellent job prioritizing
• does not stick to priorities	• generally accountable for actions	• follows through on requests
• over-commits	• manages expectations	• puts in extraordinary effort
• words, deeds not consistent	• prioritizes tasks well	• strives to beat deadlines

You meet your commitments as required. You follow up with others to ensure their expectations have been met and to address any outstanding issues that may be unresolved.

Source: SuccessFactors, an SAP Company. Used with permission.

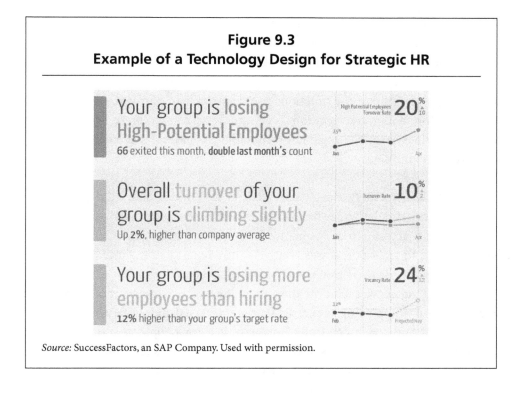

Figure 9.3
Example of a Technology Design for Strategic HR

Your group is losing
High-Potential Employees
66 exited this month, **double last month's** count

High Potential Employees Turnover Rate **20**%

Overall turnover of your
group is climbing slightly
Up **2%**, higher than company average

Turnover Rate **10**%

Your group is losing more
employees than hiring
12% higher than your group's target rate

Vacancy Rate **24**%

Source: SuccessFactors, an SAP Company. Used with permission.

Figures 9.2 and 9.3 contain examples of HR technology designed to influence how managers and leaders think about their workforce. The first example is a tool that helps managers assess employee performance and provide coaching feedback. It gives managers observable behavioral examples that define effective and ineffective performance. This influences how managers evaluate employees by giving them specific criteria to differentiate between effective and ineffective performance. It also provides managers with suggestions on how to provide developmental feedback to employees. The availability of these coaching suggestions increases the likelihood that managers will actively engage employees in conversations around how to improve their performance.

The second example displays data on workforce trends in a manner designed to capture the attention of business leaders. Presenting the data as observations rather than simple numbers encourages leaders to reflect on what these data mean and whether they warrant further action. The interface is specifically designed to grab the attention of leaders and pull them in to explore workforce data in more detail.

When you consider technology, remember that the goal of strategic HR is not about completing forms and carrying out process steps. It is about changing how employees, managers, and leaders think about, talk about, and act on workforce issues that are important to business execution. The value of strategic HR technology is less about the functions people are able to perform within the system and more about conversations, decisions, and actions these functions create outside the system. Strategic HR technology should not just enable actions; it should shape thinking.

Usability   Many HR processes are used on an annual, quarterly, or monthly basis. This is particularly true for processes related to matters like compensation, staffing, and succession management. Employees and managers might access the systems used for these processes relatively infrequently, so the user interface for these systems needs to be intuitive. People will become frustrated if they have to go up a learning curve each time they log in. Ease of use is even more important for technology-supporting processes that are accessed more often, such as goal management and coaching. Think how easy it is for people to use commercial software applications such as search engines, shopping sites, and other online tools. HR technology should ideally be on par with those systems when it comes to intuitive, efficient user interfaces.

Usability does not mean building the easiest or simplest strategic HR processes possible. The user experience must guide the user to perform process steps appropriately. The goal is not to complete the process quickly but to complete it as quickly as possible without sacrificing accuracy and quality. To illustrate this concept, look at the user interface in figure 9.4, which shows a tool for collecting performance management ratings. This interface is likely to appeal to managers because it allows them to efficiently evaluate everyone on their team at one time. It also allows them to easily access information on team members and performance criteria by clicking on the names of the employees and the names of the competencies. At the same time, the visual layout of this system addresses one of the most common performance rating mistakes that managers make: giving all employees the same or similar ratings. If managers start to rate everyone the same, they receive immediate visual feedback that makes them aware that they may be making this error. This is a great example of blending efficient and effective HR technology user interface design.

Performance Evaluation Competencies

Save | Cancel | Print Preview

	Marcus Hoff	Richard Maxx	Sid Morton	Wilma Sown	Vic Stokes
Communication	4	3	2	5	4
Customer Focus	4	4	2	3	5
Hiring	3	3	1	4	2
Teamwork	5	2	2	4	4
Summary	4.00	3.00	1.75	4.00	3.75

Source: SuccessFactors, an SAP Company. Used with permission.

Accessibility   One reason HR processes often fail to have the impact they should is they are often supported with technology that is difficult to access. For example, many companies' performance management processes are supported using systems that can be accessed only if employees are working on a company computer, have provided security passwords to get past the company's firewall, and have logged in and entered another password to get into the HR system itself. Compare this to the steps required to access company e-mail.

If you want people to access HR systems on a regular basis, strive to make it as easy to access as it is to access e-mail. This means using technology that works on smart phones and tablets and does not require lengthy log-in procedures. (For additional thoughts on the use of mobile strategic HR technology, see the discussion: "Virtual Workforces + Mobile HR Technology = Better Workforce Management.")

VIRTUAL WORKFORCES + MOBILE HR TECHNOLOGY = BETTER WORKFORCE MANAGEMENT

Over the past twenty years, workforces have become increasingly global, virtual, and mobile. The era of expecting that a company's employees will all work from the same physical location is over. In many companies, employees are required to report in to work at a specific location only if their job literally requires them to be physically present (e.g., to use certain types of machinery or provide personal service to customers or patients). Technology has played a central role in making the shift to virtual workforces possible. Thanks to communications technology available through the Internet and smart phones, employees can now effectively work together without actually being together.

The shift to virtual workplaces was made possible by technology but was largely driven by two other things. First, employees did not want to have to move to a new city or lose time commuting to an office if they did not have to. Many people value the autonomy and flexibility that comes from working in a virtual office.[a] Second, companies did not want to spend money on expensive office real estate or pay fees to relocate employees and their families from one area to another. But a third somewhat unexpected benefit has also emerged from the move to virtual workforces: it is creating better workforce management.

Managing virtual employees requires companies and managers to invest in the use of more effective management methods. Managing virtual employees forces managers to be purposeful about setting clear goals, checking in with employees to ensure they are making progress on objectives, and scheduling times to talk to employees about longer-term career development. You cannot simply show up in the office and look over at an employee to see if that person is doing his or her job. In a physical office, managers often just left these things to chance, assuming that they'd cover these topics in the course of naturally occurring conversations. But in a virtual organization, you cannot wait to run into someone in the hallway. You have to be much more proactive when it comes to setting up conversations and communicating expectations. In my experience, virtual managers often tend to become better managers overall. These managers also challenge their HR organizations to provide more effective strategic HR systems to manage goals, provide feedback, and support the career growth of virtual employees.

Companies have had to invest in better HR technology to support virtual employees. As one client told me, "When it comes to our virtual employees, what the company looks like is mainly about the experiences they have with our company web pages and online tools. It is not about what the office looks like." Virtual companies need to use strategic HR processes and technology that engage employees and make them feel appreciated. Sending a virtual employee to a cumbersome, nonintuitive HR technology system is like sending an on-premise employee into a dirty office closet to fill out forms. As more and more companies come to this realization, we are starting to see the creation of more effective HR technology systems.

The shift to increasingly global, virtual, and mobile organizations was largely a result of innovations in communications technology combined with employees' desire for autonomy and companies' desire to save on real estate costs. But this shift is resulting in better management, better HR technology, and more productive workforces overall.

[a]Gajendran, R. S., & Harrison, D. A. (2007). The good, the bad, and the unknown about telecommuting: Meta-analysis of psychological mediators and individual consequences. *Journal of Applied Psychology*, *92*, 1524–1541.

Transparency Technology allows managers and employees to easily perform strategic HR activities like setting and updating goals, providing performance recognition and coaching, and using data to make informed decisions about people and their careers. Technology also allows companies to track whether managers and employees are taking these actions. For example, are managers working with employees to establish goals, and are they regularly reviewing and updating these goals throughout the year? Are managers meeting with employees on a regular basis to discuss career development, and are employees making progress on their career objectives? These can all be tracked using HR technology provided the systems are designed to gather and present this data in an easy-to-use fashion. Providing process transparency creates visibility, and visibility drives process adoption.

Companies have a tendency to overemphasize cost and ease of deployment when they evaluate HR technology. This is particularly true when the evaluation process is driven by IT professionals instead of strategic HR leaders. IT professionals are not trained to recognize the difference between effective and ineffective strategic processes. They often underestimate how much of an impact functionality and user interface design have on the value of a strategic HR technology system. The purpose of strategic HR processes is to create conversations, provide information, and support decisions that lead to more effective use of the workforce in driving business execution. For this to happen, the technology used to support strategic HR processes must be highly engaging and accessible to end users. Compatibility with existing IT platforms and ease of deployment are important factors for assessing system cost, but functionality, usability, accessibility, and transparency have a far greater impact on actual system value. This is why it is so important for HR organizations to clearly define the functionality they need from HR technology systems. Just because an application says it has "performance management" or "staffing" functions does not mean it can support effective performance and staffing processes.

9.3.2 Branding HR Processes

HR processes tend to be viewed by managers and employees as relatively uninteresting administrative activities. One way to shift this mind-set is to market how HR processes will support the goals of managers and employees. This is referred to as "branding the HR process." For example, employees tend to view the term *performance management* from a negative mind-set, dwelling on the aspects that focus on identifying and addressing underperformance. They may not give enough credit to the role that performance management plays in supporting recognition and career development of high-performing employees. Rather than referring to a process as being "about performance management," a company might refer to it as a "recognition and career development program" to encourage employees to see the process in a more positive light.

The best brands call attention to how HR processes help employees and managers achieve their career objectives and create a tie between the HR process and the mission, culture, or external brand of the company. For example, a mobile telephone company promoted its performance and development processes using the tagline, "It's about the conversation." This emphasized that the process was focused on getting managers and employees to talk about performance and development. But it also resonated with the company's identity as an organization that built and sold tools that help people communicate.

When building a brand, start by examining how the process will address the goals of employees and managers. Why should they be excited about this process? What's in it for them? Next, develop a short phrase that captures these benefits and highlights the brand promise. Ideally this phrase will resonate with other aspects of the company culture or market reputation. For example, a large health care organization called its strategic HR program "Compass" because it helped employees navigate the organization and identify appropriate career paths. A global hotel organization called its succession and development program "Profile" because employees had complained that no one in the company outside of their local hotel knew them or their career potential and goals. The Profile brand emphasized that the process is a way for the company to get to know all of its employees at a detailed level.

After you develop a brand, review it by asking and answering these questions:

- Is it truthful? Can you back it up with real examples and practices? Can you show how the strategic HR process is fulfilling the promise made by the brand?

- Is it compelling and appropriate? How will it be perceived by different stakeholder groups, divisions, and cultures? Is it interpreted by people in a positive and appropriate manner? Does it speak to things employees care about?

- Is it unique? It is distinct from how other companies portray themselves? Does it "feel" like the company?

- Is it comprehensive? Can it be used to support a range of strategic HR programs? It is ideal if all strategic HR processes can fit under the same brand. Trying to maintain multiple brands for different processes is time-consuming and confusing for employees, managers, and senior leaders.

Brands can help get employees and managers to view HR processes as tools for creating positive change. But if the brand does not reflect process reality, it can create cynicism about the sincerity of the company and HR initiatives in general. In sum, use brands, but use them wisely.

9.4 ENLISTING LINE LEADERSHIP TO DRIVE THE CHANGE

All change management programs emphasize the importance of having executive support. When it comes to strategic HR processes, it is important to be particularly clear about what you mean by "executive support." Specifically, what do executives actually have to do to demonstrate that they are supportive of an HR process?

Figure 9.5 illustrates three types of executive support that can be used to support deployment of strategic HR processes, listed in order of least effective to most effective.

- *Endorsing.* Executives promote the process through presentations, written messages, and other means of communication. This is the easiest and least effective form of support.

- *Enforcing.* Executives hold people accountable for following the process. HR can provide leaders with data indicating compliance levels, but direction to drive compliance must come from line leadership to be effective. It is extremely important that process enforcement come from line leadership, not HR. Efforts by HR to drive compliance tend to have little impact, can lead managers to resent HR as the "process police," and often result in employees complying with the minimum requirements without putting in the effort needed to actually benefit from the process.

- *Exhibiting.* Executives act as role models by personally completing process steps in a visible manner. Technology can be particularly valuable for role modeling as it often makes it possible for employees and managers to literally see what their leaders have done (e.g., looking at their leaders' goal plans or

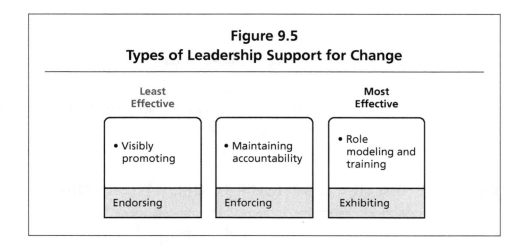

Figure 9.5
Types of Leadership Support for Change

Least Effective		Most Effective
• Visibly promoting	• Maintaining accountability	• Role modeling and training
Endorsing	Enforcing	Exhibiting

checking to see how many of their leaders have completed coaching sessions with their direct reports). Exhibiting can also involve having line leaders take an active role in training managers and employees on how to use the process. Exhibiting is by far and away the most effective type of leadership support.

To illustrate the differences among endorsing, enforcing, and exhibiting, consider the following examples associated with deploying a goal management process:

- *Endorsing:* The CEO's office sends an e-mail to all employees asking them to complete their goal plans in the system.

- *Enforcing:* The HR office reports which employees have not entered their goals, and the CEO's office sends them a message reminding them to enter their goals into the system or they will be held accountable.

- *Exhibiting:* The CEO creates and shares her goal plan with all employees and asks them to work with their managers to create similar goals for their jobs.

Think how you would react to these three examples as an employee. In the first example, your CEO asks you and all the other employees to create a goal plan even though it's not clear if she has completed one. In second example, your CEO tells you to create your goal plan or face some sort of negative consequence although she has not necessarily created a goal plan herself. In the third example, your CEO publishes her goal plan to the company and asks you and all of the other employees to create a similar goal plan. It is fairly obvious which of these is the most positively motivating.

Truly enlisting line leader support requires agreeing on specific things that leaders will do to demonstrate their support for the process. If possible, find ways they can personally role-model using the process. It is amazing how much easier it is to get employees to comply with process actions if they know that their leaders have already completed these actions themselves. And if you discover that leaders are not willing to do what is necessary to demonstrate true commitment and support for the process, then it may be time to reconsider whether you should deploy the process at all.

9.5 CONCLUSION

The history of HR is littered with well-designed processes that failed during deployment. This chapter reviewed major issues that affect whether organizations adopt strategic HR processes to drive business execution or resist the use of these methods by treating them as relatively unimportant administrative activities. Successful deployments start by establishing HR leadership credibility. The next step is to understand how the changes that HR is proposing will affect different stakeholders senior leaders, managers, employees, HR, and IT. This needs to be followed through by supporting strategic HR processes with effective change management communication and well-designed, easy-to-use technology. Finally, and most important, leaders within the organization must actively support the change through personally endorsing, enforcing, and exhibiting effective use of strategic HR processes.

Remember that the single biggest boost to HR process deployment and adoption is the process itself. If the process is well designed, easy to use, and clearly tied to business execution needs, then senior leaders, managers, and employees are likely to push for its adoption. You won't have to ask them to adopt it because they will already be asking you when they can start using it. While most HR process requires some level of branding and change management it is remarkable how quickly people embrace processes once they realize that they will help them achieve their personal career objectives.

Improving the World through Strategic HR

The past fifty years have seen companies make major advances in the methods used to manage business operations such as financial accounting and investment, information management, maintaining supply chains, managing manufacturing processes, and marketing products. But relatively few organizations apply the same rigor to processes used to maximize the value of their workforce. Due to the rapidly changing nature of work and the growing labor market skills shortages, we have now reached a point when human resource management can and must be given the same leadership attention and strategic focus that has been shown to other areas of business.

Here are a few of the reasons that companies need to aggressively pursue the use of strategic HR methods to drive business execution:

- *It has an impact on the bottom line.* The largest source of performance variance in most companies is due to differences in the performance of people. Research has shown that high-performing employees generate far more revenue than average or poorly performing employees do. Furthermore, hiring and tolerating low-performing employees directly saps a company of financial resources, hurts workforce morale, and damages its brand reputation in the general market. The most effective way to build and increase long-term profitability in most organizations is to increase the performance of its employees.

- *We know how to do it.* The profession of human resources has known how to maximize employee productivity for decades. This is mainly about consistently doing a few fundamental things really well. It starts with putting the right people in the right jobs through the strategic use of staffing methods. The next step is focusing people on the right things through the operational use of goal management and ensuring people are doing things the right way through effective use of performance management. Finally, for long-term success, ensure that people are given job assignments and access to training resources that provide them with the right development for what you want them to do in the future.

- *We have the technology to do it.* Until recently, one of the major barriers to the effective application of strategic HR methods was the inability to scale these methods across multiple employees, managers, and departments. Innovations in strategic HR technology have largely eliminated this barrier. The technology is available to drive significant improvements in workforce productivity. Companies just have to use it correctly.

- *It reduces human trauma.* The quality of a person's work has a major impact on his or her happiness, health, and general well-being. How employees are managed not only impacts the lives of employees, but also it affects their families, their customers, and their communities. We often joke about bad management, but the reality is that bad management hurts people. Given that we know how to manage people in a productive and respectful manner, there is no reason for companies or societies to tolerate ineffective, incompetent, or otherwise inappropriate management practices.

This book provides insight into and advice on using strategic HR process to create positive business outcomes. How you use the information in this book will vary depending on your company's unique business needs, company culture, and employee population. But every company can benefit from applying the concepts I have discussed. As one of my mentors told me early in my career,

> Strategic HR is relevant to every company because it is relevant to every manager. There is no manager in the world who isn't struggling with some sort of people-related issue. When you ask leaders to describe the top three business challenges they are facing, invariably at least one, and usually all three, are people related. Every manager has concerns about whether they have the right people to do the work and whether the people they have are doing their work in the right way.

10.1 NEXT STEPS

HR professionals have the knowledge and tools to significantly improve the performance of companies and the happiness of the people in those companies. It is just a matter of using our knowledge and tools in a manner that makes a difference. We know what needs to be done, and we know how to do it. Now it is up to us to make it happen.

Part of this is avoiding the tendency in HR to get caught up in trends or to become overly enamored with the processes, theories, and techniques we use to increase employee productivity. Managers and employees care a lot about the things that HR methods affect, but many of them do not care much about HR methods themselves. An analogy can be made to how most people feel about IT systems: we don't really care what IT database platforms or servers our company uses, but we do care about being able to access our e-mail accounts. The same can be said for how most managers feel toward staffing, management, and development methods: they don't care what these processes are called or why they work; they just want to get the right people in the right jobs doing the right things the right way.

I titled this book *Commonsense Talent Management* in reaction to the tendency of some HR professionals to overcomplicate the field of strategic HR. HR authors and consultants often talk about the newest innovations in talent management when in reality the most effective strategic HR methods are the simplest and most obvious: hiring people based on well-defined job descriptions, for example, and setting clear goals for employees and giving them actionable feedback on how to improve their performance. These aren't sophisticated or novel concepts, yet most companies struggle to do them consistently and effectively.

Strategic HR basically comes down to two things. First is determining how the workforce needs to change to support the company's business strategies. This is about prioritizing business execution drivers. Does company success depend more on increasing workforce alignment, productivity, efficiency, sustainability, scalability, or governance? Second is determining how the company can use HR methods to create the change. Remember that there are basically only four things you can do to change the workforce: (1) put the right people in the right jobs by staffing based on clearly defined job requirements, (2) focus people's attention and motivation on the right things through effective goal setting, (3) ensure people are doing things the right way by measuring their performance and giving them feedback they can learn from either directly through coaching or indirectly through staffing and pay decisions, and (4) provide people with job experiences and resources that give them the right development to do the things you want them to do in the future. Strategic HR processes can get complicated when you get into the details. But don't lose sight of the fact that ultimately it is just about getting the right people doing the right things in the right way while getting the right development. The easier it is to explain strategic HR, the easier it is to get business leaders to appreciate the value of strategic HR methods and use these methods.

There isn't one best way to do strategic HR. What models and process designs work best will change depending on the nature of the organization and the issues it is facing. No matter what processes you put in place, you will make minor modifications over time. But avoid making major changes too often because such changes can be quite disruptive. An analogy I use for HR process design is sailing a small boat with three or four sails. When you are sailing this type of boat, you constantly make minor modifications to the tension and position of the sails based on changes in the wind and water. How you change one sail will affect the performance of a different sail, so the process of modification never really stops completely. And every so often when there is a significant change in the weather, you will need to make a major adjustment by putting up a different type of sail entirely. The same thing can be applied to how you use the 4R strategic HR processes. There are slight modifications you can make to these processes every year to make them a bit more effective. And every so often, you may need to significantly rework one or more of the processes based on a significant change in your company's business strategy or business execution drivers.

10.2 PARTING THOUGHTS

I have worked in the field of strategic HR for over twenty years. During this time, I have seen some pretty horrific HR practices. Many of these were perpetrated by managers who were doing things that might have made sense to them but not to anyone else. In most of these cases, the problem was that these managers did not understand the factors that drive employee behavior and performance. In many others, HR practitioners were hopelessly overcomplicating what are basically fairly simple processes. In both cases, the problems could have been easily avoided if people had just thought through things a bit more carefully. Helping companies avoid these problems is one of the reasons I wrote this book.

The other reason I wrote this book is to help and inspire companies to achieve ever greater levels of workforce productivity. While I have seen my fair share of HR horror stories, I've also seen a great number of HR successes. I've seen what happens when HR is done well: improving the quality of HR practices has a direct impact on the health and well-being of employees, managers, customers, their families, and society in general. HR is about people, and people matter.

Good luck in your journey to make the world a better place through better use of strategic HR processes!

ACKNOWLEDGMENTS

This book is a result of my having had the good fortune to spend time with a lot of really smart, kind, and at times incredibly patient people. Many ideas in the book were refined through work done with current and former colleagues at SuccessFactors/SAP, including Jessica Kane, Mark Bissell, David Verhaag, Laurie Donahoo, Will Doolittle, Philip Haine, Tony Ashton, Dmitry Krakovsky, Lisa Hartley, Adrienne Whitten, Erik Berggren, Anastasia Ellerby, Karie Willyerd, Peter Howes, Sally Hackett, Newt Swain, Mary Poppen, Conrad Voorsanger, Alex Shevelenko, Jay Larson, Sylvia Lehnen, Andrew Clark, Kelsey Herb, and countless others that I should list by name but won't purely due to limited space and an imperfect memory (I hope you will forgive me). I also thank Lars Dalgaard for building a company whose mission, culture, and products so strongly align with my personal and professional beliefs regarding meritocracy and workforce productivity.

This book was mostly written during my tenure at SuccessFactors but is based on over twenty years of experience spent in the field of strategic human resources. The stories in the book are a result of my having had the pleasure of working with hundreds of companies of all sizes and industries from around the world. The genesis of several of the models and concepts in this book can be traced back to events that occurred in graduate school and before. The names of the people I should thank are too numerous to list, but I at least give a general thanks to my former colleagues at the Pacific National Laboratory, The Ohio State University, PDI, SHL, Starbucks, Unicru, and Kronos. Pete Olsen, Brian Stern, and Joe Murphy are whom I am referring to in chapter 10 when I quote my earlier mentors. They may not realize how much great advice they gave me when I left graduate school and came to work with them, but I remember it and use it constantly.

Three people reviewed this book in draft form and made suggestions that greatly improved its quality. My father, Earl (Buz) Hunt, provided detailed advice on how to present many of the ideas in the book more effectively. My father's knowledge, insight, and candid and constructive feedback have been tremendous resources for me as an author, psychologist, and person in general. Gabby Burlacu called out areas in the book where my personal opinions were at risk of going beyond what the scientific research actually supports. She also provided many citations contained in the book and made suggestions on areas where I needed to provide a bit more explanation. Brigid O'Donnell read the book from the perspective of someone relatively early in her HR career and let me know where I had made the mistake of substituting jargon for meaning.

My family and friends served as an enduring source of inspiration, support, tolerance, and entertainment throughout the process of creating this book. My sons, Robbie and Antonio, provided a welcome source of distraction whenever I needed to talk about something that had nothing to do with HR. My wife, Cynthia, kept me healthy, well fed, and happy even when I was at my most stressed. In addition to my immediate family, I am blessed to have amazing parents, siblings, nieces, nephews, aunts, uncles, cousins, and friends who collectively supported me with ideas, encouragement, and camaraderie. Their intellectual brilliance, interpersonal charm, and amazing accomplishments inspire me every day.

APPENDIX A
A COMPREHENSIVE LIBRARY
OF BEHAVIORAL COMPETENCIES

This competency library is based on research on the structure of job performance. Table A.1 groups the competencies into categories reflecting broad dimensions of job performance. The actual competencies are presented in alphabetical order. In the interest of space, the competency definitions are limited to a few positive behavioral examples and do not include behavioral examples illustrating ineffective performance. It may be helpful to develop such additional "negative" anchors before using these competencies to support staffing or talent management decisions. Sample interview questions are also provided for each competency. A short guide to conducting structured interviews is provided at the end of the appendix.

DEFINITIONS OF COMPETENCIES AND RELATED QUESTIONS

- *Accepting direction:* Accepts and follows directions from others; respects authority; complies with requests; does what is asked.

  Describe a time when you were given incomplete or conflicting instructions from a supervisor. What was your reaction? What steps did you take to make sure you were clear on your instructions?

Source: SuccessFactors, an SAP Company, used with permission.

Table A.1
Categories of Competencies Reflecting Job Performance

Change Management Competencies

- Adapting to change
- Working with ambiguity
- Using feedback
- Supporting change
- Displaying confidence and composure
- Managing stress
- Maintaining work-life balance

Analytical Competencies

- Maintaining objectivity
- Working with financial information
- Making accurate judgments and decisions
- Learning quickly
- Solving complex problems
- Thinking broadly
- Acquiring information
- Critical thinking
- Testing and troubleshooting

Innovation Competencies

- Displaying creativity
- Evaluating and implementing ideas
- Driving continuous improvement
- Acting as a champion for change

Project Management Competencies

- Navigating organizations
- Managing resources
- Delivering high-quality work
- Managing time
- Coordinating project activities
- Developing plans
- Prioritizing and organizing work
- Managing from a distance

Achievement-Oriented Competencies

- Serving customers
- Entrepreneurial thinking
- Driving for results
- Thinking globally
- Leveraging opportunities
- Demonstrating tenacity and perseverance
- Championing customer needs
- Managing risk
- Supporting organizational goals

Interpersonal Competencies

- Attentive listening
- Establishing relationships
- Communicating effectively
- Making a strong impression
- Presenting and public speaking
- Managing meetings
- Negotiating agreements
- Making convincing arguments

Directing and Motivating Competencies

- Setting a strategic vision
- Showing community and social responsibility
- Managing performance
- Delegating responsibility
- Acting decisively
- Demonstrating initiative
- Assembling talent
- Developing talent
- Inspiring and motivating others
- Acting strategically
- Demonstrating beliefs and principles
- Accepting responsibility

- Driving projects to completion
- Controlling costs
- Setting objectives

Social Competencies

- Supporting coworkers
- Demonstrating appreciation
- Building and supporting teams
- Working with diverse populations
- Showing caring and understanding
- Interacting with people at different levels
- Managing political situations
- Creating and maintaining networks
- Sharing information
- Teaching
- Resolving conflict
- Adapting to others

Personal Competencies

- Assessing and understanding people
- Performing physical or mechanical tasks
- Displaying technical expertise
- Working safely
- Using math
- Reading effectively
- Pursuing self-development
- Demonstrating self-insight and awareness
- Using computers and technology
- Composing and writing text

Fundamental Work Competencies

- Following policies and procedures
- Accepting direction
- Acting with integrity
- Meeting basic work expectations

Tell me about a time you disagreed with a supervisor. What was the nature of the disagreement? How did you handle it? What was the outcome?

- *Accepting responsibility:* Takes accountability for delivering on commitments; owns mistakes and uses them as opportunities for learning and development; openly discusses his or her actions and their consequences, both good and bad.

Describe a time when you felt you let someone down by not meeting a commitment you had made to him or her. What was the situation? What had you promised? What barriers prevented you from keeping it? What did you do when you realized you might not meet the commitment? How did the other person react?

Tell me about a time you realized you would not be able to meet a deadline at work. How did you come to realize this? What steps did you take when you realized you would not meet the deadline? What, if anything, do you wish you had done differently?

- *Acquiring information:* Consults the appropriate resources to obtain information. Asks the right questions and knows who to go to for information.

  Tell me about a problem or question you faced at work where you initially didn't know the right answer. What did you do to find out the answer? What things do you do in general to make sure you are able to get the right answers to work-related problems and questions?

  Describe a time when you had to track down some particularly hard-to-find information in order to accomplish a task or business objective. Why was this information important? How did you go about finding it?

- *Acting as a champion for change:* Challenges the status quo; encourages people to question existing methods, practices, and assumptions; supports people in their efforts to try new things.

  Tell me about a change or proposal you made that had a widespread influence within your organization. Why were you able to have such a large influence?

  Tell me about a time when someone else in your organization suggested a change that you did not fully agree with. How did you react to the suggestions? What actions did you propose instead? What was the outcome?

- *Acting decisively:* Moves quickly to make decisions and commit to a clear course of action; comfortable making decisions based on partial information; willing to take risks in order to maintain momentum; shows a strong bias toward action.

  Prioritizing tasks and projects can be challenging. Tell me about a time you think you could have done a better job identifying the key priorities that you should have focused on. What was the situation? What happened? What could you have done differently to achieve a more favorable outcome?

  Tell me about a time you had to make a decision very quickly. What was the situation? What led you to your decision? How do you think your decision would have been different if you had had more time?

- *Acting strategically:* Identifies key issues and relationships relevant to achieving long-range goals or vision; commits to course of action to accomplish goals after developing alternatives based on logical assumptions, facts, available resources, constraints, and organizational values. Develops priorities with the right balance of short- and long-term wins.

Tell me about a time when you sacrificed a short-term goal in order to stay focused on a longer-term objective. What prevented you from achieving both the short- and long-term goals? Why did you decide to give the long-term goal priority?

Tell me about a time when you were responsible for implementing a strategy that took your organization in a new direction. What was the strategy? What did you do to get people aligned around the strategy?

- *Acting with integrity:* Follows through on commitments; lets others know his or her true intentions; admits mistakes.

Tell me about a time you made a significant mistake or error at work. What caused the problem? How did you find out about it? What actions did you take when you realized you had made a mistake?

Tell me about a time when someone else accused you of failing to meet a commitment or otherwise failing to do things appropriately. What was the situation? Why did this person blame you for the problem? What was your reaction? Was the problem ever resolved? If so, how?

- *Adapting to change:* Accepts and adapts to change in a professionally appropriate and thoughtful manner. Knows when and how to stand down graciously and accept a well-thought-out decision. Embraces change.

Describe a time that you dealt with a sudden, major change at work. What was the situation? How did you handle the change?

Tell me about a time when you changed your approach or objectives to accommodate the needs and interests of others. Why did you decide to change your approach? How did you become aware of the need to change direction?

- *Adapting to others:* Changes interpersonal style and approach based on circumstance or audience; works hard with all kinds of people and work groups; does not judge others.

Describe the time when you most needed to cooperate and coordinate your work with someone else to get things done right. What was the need? What conflicts or difficulties came up, and how did you handle them? What worked well, and what didn't?

Tell me about a project you led that required gaining collaboration across a variety of areas of the organization. Why was collaboration so critical to the project? How did you figure out who needed to be involved? What strategies did you use when approaching people about the project? What was the outcome?

- *Assembling talent:* Actively works to recruit, hire, and retain high performers; constantly looking for talent to add to the organization; creates a challenging and rewarding work environment; has a reputation as a great person to work with.

    What sort of things do you consider when hiring someone? Give me an example that illustrates how you used your basic beliefs and approach toward a staffing decision. How were your actions or decisions different from what others might have done?

    Tell me about a situation in which you were able to attract a talented person to join your team. What did you do to recruit this person and get him or her on board?

- *Assessing and understanding people:* Gets the right sense about people; understands many different types of personalities and motivations; good at pinpointing talents or incompetence.

    Tell me about a time when you tried to understand somebody else's point of view—a time when you tried to "get inside someone else's head" in order to understand their motives and thinking. Why did you want to learn so much about this person? What methods did you use to explore his or her motives and thoughts? How did you use this information? What was the outcome?

    Tell me about a time when you were counting on someone to perform in a certain way and he or she did not. What was the situation? Why do you think your judgment about this person was off target?

- *Attentive listening:* Uses active listening techniques to avoid distractions and show interest in what the speaker has to say; is open to other viewpoints and clarifies points of contention; demonstrates patience while listening to others and does not interrupt.

    Provide an example of a work conversation or meeting where you had to show effective listening skills. What did you do to promote communication and information sharing during the meeting? How did your approach differ from what others might have done?

Describe the hardest time you've had understanding someone in a work-related interaction. What did you do to better understand this person? How much did you understand at the end?

- *Building and supporting teams:* Is an honest and dependable team player who contributes to group collaboration and consensual decision making and shows empathy and respect for others. Builds and maintains good working relationships.

  Describe the most successful work team you have worked on. What made this team so successful? What did you personally do that contributed to the team's success?

  Describe a time when you were on a team that seemed to be stalled and not functioning very effectively. What kinds of things did you do to jump-start the team and get everyone back on track and working together again?

- *Championing customer needs:* Provides timely and professional service to both internal and external customers; is responsive to customer needs and requests; is always courteous to the customer and considers the needs of the customer when making decisions.

  Tell me about a time at work that you had to show sensitivity toward a customer's concerns and feelings. What did you do to demonstrate your concern?

  Tell me about a time when you acted as an advocate for a customer who was experiencing significant difficulties but was not receiving any support. Why did you offer to help this person? What did you do to alleviate some of the issues facing them? What happened?

- *Communicating effectively:* Shares information. Listens and involves others. Clearly conveys ideas in a manner that engages others and helps them understand and retain the message.

  How do you keep your team members informed and generally on the same page? What methods do you use to communicate decisions and information to coworkers? Give me an example that illustrates some of these methods.

  Tell me about how you have set up systems and processes to facilitate information exchange and knowledge sharing within your organization. How do you get other people to share information?

- *Composing and writing text:* Writes documents that are easy to read and understand; uses correct spelling, grammar, and sentence structure; able to create effective written documentation in a short amount of time.

  Tell me about some of the things you do to ensure that the work-related documents you write are easy to understand and effectively communicate the appropriate information. Give me an example of a time when this led to making improvements to something you had written.

  Of all the documents you have written over the past year, which one do you consider to be the best written in terms of clarity and comprehensibility? What are some of the things you did that make this document so easy to read? What prompted you to take these actions? Do you do these things with everything you write? Why or why not?

- *Controlling costs:* Manages resources to achieve maximum value with minimum cost. Accurately estimates, invests, and monitors resources and budgets to optimize returns and control waste. Makes good use of company assets.

  Tell me about a time when you realized an activity or project was going to require more money than you had originally planned for. What was the situation? What did you do about it? Why were you unable to accurately forecast the budget? How often has this happened in your work?

  What kinds of things do you do to ensure that you stay within spending limits for projects and assignments? Give me an example of a time you were able to successfully and accurately plan for the costs of a project.

- *Coordinating project activities:* Is knowledgeable in project management; plans for and assigns tasks and resources appropriately.

  Tell me about a time you had to manage a project that required coordinating efforts from several different people. How did you keep everyone focused and moving in the right direction? What did you do to avoid potential conflicts or duplicate efforts?

  Tell me about a time when you had to carefully coordinate a variety of schedules to ensure a task was carried out successfully. What tools did you use to keep track of all of the schedules? How did you make sure you avoided creating schedule conflicts?

- *Creating and maintaining networks:* Makes strong impressions; forms lasting relationships; has a positive and kind demeanor.

Tell me about a time when you had to rely on your personal relationships to get something done at work. What was the situation? Why were your personal relationships so critical to accomplishing the objective? How did you use your relationships to get the job done?

How do you maintain your business relationships? Give me an example of a time when you let a relationship fade and you needed to rebuild it. What did you do? Why was this important? How does the relationship stand today?

- *Critical thinking:* Able to assess a problem or situation using effective logic. Uses important information to make logical assessments.

Tell me about a time when you were able to make sense of an extremely complex or challenging problem or situation. How did you approach the issue? What led you to the insights and observations that allowed you to fully understand the problem?

Tell me about a time when you had to build a case for an argument you were making. How did you approach this task?

- *Delegating responsibility:* Enables others to act, allocating appropriate decision making authority or responsibility to others to maximize organizational and individual effectiveness. Understands the increased influence and results of delegating work. Sets direction and expectations and delegates appropriately, demonstrating confidence in team to deliver. Removes obstacles.

Give me an example that illustrates how you typically assign tasks and responsibilities to others. What methods do you use to delegate tasks? What issues and factors do you pay particular attention to when assigning tasks?

Describe a time when you delegated a task or set of tasks to someone, and this person was unable to effectively complete the assignment. What was the situation? Why was he or she unable to perform the tasks you assigned? How, if at all, do you think you could have approached the situation differently to ensure a higher chance of success?

- *Delivering high-quality work:* Makes sure responsibilities central to the role meet all requirements and expectations. Finishes tasks promptly and critically reviews work to ensure quality and accuracy. Considers impact of work on others and takes any necessary steps to mitigate. Seeks additional work after finishing tasks.

How do you evaluate the quality of your work? What do you do to make sure you are doing things the right way? Provide an example that illustrates how you have used this approach on past assignments or tasks to ensure you are delivering high-quality work.

All work involves balancing accuracy and speed. Provide an example of how you have managed this trade-off in your work. What did you do that was different from how others might have approached the task? How do you typically decide when something is good enough to pass on to someone else?

- *Demonstrating appreciation:* Shows others appreciation when hard work or a need for help is demonstrated. Seeks opportunities to thank others for their hard work.

   What do you do to provide coworkers with recognition for doing a good job? How do you let people know they are doing a good job? Tell me about a time when you gave a coworker recognition for a job well done. What was the outcome?

   Tell me about a time when you were working on or leading a team that achieved a major goal or objective. What actions did you take to celebrate this achievement?

- *Demonstrating beliefs and principles:* Openly confronts actions or decisions that do not align with his or her core beliefs, values, and principles; let's people know where he or she stands on issues and why; willing to agree to disagree when appropriate.

   Tell me about a time when one of your coworkers was doing something that you felt was inappropriate or in conflict with the values and ethics of your organization. How did you handle the situation?

   Describe a time when you felt pressured to bend the rules in order to accomplish a critical task. What was the situation? How did you react?

- *Demonstrating initiative:* Takes action on his or her own without being prompted; handles problems independently; able to resolve issues without relying on extensive help from others; does more than is expected or asked.

   Tell me about a time when you acted on something before anyone else did; where you were the first one to do something decisive to address a problem or opportunity. What prompted you to take action? Why do you think you were the first one to act? What was the outcome?

Tell me about a time when you encountered an unexpected problem at work and took the initiative to solve the problem yourself. Why did you decide to take that approach? What was the outcome?

- *Demonstrating self-insight and awareness:* Has a good sense of personal strengths and developmental areas; knows what he or she is good at; gives people a realistic sense of his or her capabilities and talents; seeks out roles that complement his or her capabilities.

  Describe your two greatest strengths and two most significant development needs. What led you to identify these as strengths or weaknesses? What information is your self-evaluation based on? How has your knowledge of your strengths and weaknesses affected your performance?

  Describe some of the more significant things you have learned about yourself through you work experience. What do you know about yourself now that you did not know several years ago? How did you become aware of these things? How has this affected your behavior?

- *Demonstrating tenacity and perseverance:* Demonstrates high levels of enthusiasm and energy; takes charge of projects and does not give up until alternatives are exhausted; pushes self and others when needed.

  Describe a time when you experienced a major setback at work—a time when things did not go as you had hoped. What went wrong? How did you respond? What was the ultimate outcome?

  Tell me about a time when you had difficulty with a particular assignment or project. What was the nature of the difficulty? How did you handle it? What, if anything, do you wish you had done differently?

- *Developing plans:* Proactively develops plans that meet the organization's goals; engages in short-term as well as long-term planning, including contingency plans and ways to maintain focus on key objectives; considers wise use of resources in setting plans.

  Tell me about a time when you had to translate a broad organizational strategy or direction into a specific, actionable plan. How did you make sure your actions were aligned with the broader strategy? How did you communicate the plan to others?

  Tell me about a time when you were directly responsibility for determining assignments, schedules, and time lines for a project you were managing. How did you go about developing the project plan? How did the project turn out?

- *Developing talent:* Values the difference that each employee makes and connects that role to organizational and team success. Provides direction and guidance in team and collaborative settings. Provides timely guidance and feedback to help others strengthen specific knowledge and develop skill areas to accomplish tasks or solve problems.

  Tell me about some of the experiences you have had developing high-potential talent in your organization. How do you determine a person's potential? Do you treat high-potential people differently from other employees? What sort of results have you achieved in terms of working with high-potential individuals?

  What do you do to encourage people to take responsibility for their development? Provide some examples of things you have done to create a more developmentally focused work environment and workforce. Which of these things appeared to be the most effective?

- *Displaying confidence and composure:* Is aware of the situation and is confident in abilities. Maintains composure during stressful times.

  Describe a time when you were faced with multiple conflicting demands at work and very tight deadlines. How did you deal with the stress caused by this situation? What actions did you take to make things easier for you?

  Describe one of the most stressful times you have had with a customer. What was the situation? What did you do? Were you able to satisfy the customer?

- *Displaying creativity:* Uses creativity appropriately to drive progress and encourages others to do the same; makes innovation a priority among team members; encourages reasonable risk taking.

  People often say, "If it ain't broke, don't fix it." Tell me about a time when you challenged this assumption and experimented with changing an existing method or process at work because you felt it could be more effective. What made you think that this could be done more effectively? What changes or ideas did you suggest? How did you come up with these ideas?

  Tell me about a time when your standard approach to something didn't work. What did you do?

- *Displaying technical expertise:* Keeps his or her technical skills current; effectively applies specialized knowledge and skills to perform work tasks; understands and masters the technical skills, knowledge, and tasks associated with his or her job; shares technical expertise with others.

  > Tell me about a time when you experienced difficulty implementing a technology that was designed to simplify or improve your job. What was the situation? Why did you have problems getting up and running on the new technology? Is there anything that you could have done differently to have made it work better for you?

  > Describe a time when a new technology dramatically improved your job. What was the technology? How did you incorporate it into your work routine? Why do you think it was so successful?

- *Driving continuous improvement:* Uses formal and informal tools and techniques to achieve operational excellence. Maintains a constant focus on efforts to improve performance, quality, and efficiency of work processes.

  > Tell me about some of the tools and methods you have used to monitor and improve the performance of a business process or method. How can you tell if something is performing well or poorly? Give me an example of when you used these methods to identify and resolve a performance problem.

  > Tell me about a time when you found a significant quality problem in your work or the work of another person. What did you do?

- *Driving for results:* Follows through on commitments; can be counted on to successfully execute on goals.

  > Tell me about a project you were working on that was not going as well as you would have liked. What was the situation? What did you do to get things moving forward again? How did it turn out?

  > Tell me about a time when you were faced with an overwhelmingly difficult or otherwise challenging project or assignment. What made the project so demanding? How did the project affect your general level of effort and motivation? How did the project turn out?

- *Driving projects to completion:* Develops project plans that clearly define relevant goals, resources, actions, time lines, and stakeholders. Monitors and communicate project status, tracks resources, and drives projects to completion.

What sort of things do you do to ensure projects and tasks stay on track? Give me an example of a time when you got a project back on track.

Tell me about a project you were involved in that was failing to achieve its objectives. What sort of problems was the project experiencing? How did you become aware of these problems? How did you handle the situation? What was the outcome of your efforts? What might you have done to cause things to go differently?

- *Entrepreneurial thinking:* Recognizes opportunities for business growth; understands the company's strategy for growth.

  Tell me about a time when you developed a new source of revenue or business that had been overlooked or ignored by previous members of your company. What led you to take advantage of this source of business? What approach did you use to develop this new business? How successful were your efforts?

  We all encounter times when business is down. Tell me about a time when business was going badly for you or your department, business unit or organization. What did you do to improve the situation?

- *Establishing relationships:* Able to relate to all kinds of people regardless of background; finds topics and common interests that he or she can use to build rapport with others.

  Tell me about a time you had to quickly build a sense of rapport and connection with someone you had never met before. Why was it important to establish a connection with this person? What did you do to develop rapport with him or her? What was the outcome?

  Tell me about a time when you reached out to build a relationship with someone who initially did not know you at all (for example, cold-calling a specific customer or business contact). Why did you want to get know this person? How did you reach out to him or her? What resistance or obstacles did you face in terms of getting to know this person? How did you overcome these challenges? What was the outcome?

- *Evaluating and implementing ideas:* Uses creativity appropriately to drive progress and encourages others to do the same; makes innovation a priority among team members; encourages reasonable risk taking.

Often people come up with great ideas that are just not practical. Describe a time when you had to take a visionary idea and get it into a workable state. What was the idea? What did you have to do to make it more manageable and user friendly? What happened?

Describe a time at work when you were able to take an idea and turn it into reality. What was your idea? What steps did you take to turn it into something actionable? What was the outcome?

- *Following policies and procedures:* Follows relevant policies and procedures; encourages others to follow work rules and calls attention to violations.

    Tell me about a time when you had to follow a new procedure for completing a familiar task. What was the situation? Why did the process change? How did you incorporate the new method into your work?

    Describe a time when you became aware of a coworker or peer who was violating company policy in some way. What did you say or do to try to rectify the situation? What was the outcome?

- *Inspiring and motivating others:* Emphasizes the importance of people's contributions; lets people know why their work is important and how it will benefit themselves and others; ties work activities to people's personal career goals and life interests.

    What things do you do to get the best out of the individuals and teams you are managing? Tell me about a time you were able to get a team or individual to deliver results that exceeded other people's expectations. What did you do to inspire and motivate the team or person?

    What things have you done to foster commitment and motivation within your work group? How do you get people excited about objectives? Describe a time when you put these techniques to use. What challenges did you experience, and how did you handle them?

- *Interacting with people at different levels:* Comfortable interacting with people at all levels of the organization; gauges audiences effectively; talks to everyone as equals.

    Describe the different types of relationships you built in your current or last job. Who did you build relationships with, and why? What methods did you use to build these relationships? How would you characterize your relationships with these people today?

Sometimes it can be difficult to work across organizational levels. Tell me about a situation in which you had difficulty working with someone who was at a much different level (higher or lower) in the organization than you were. What challenges did you face? How did you overcome these obstacles? What was the result?

- *Learning quickly:* Able to learn things the first time. Self-learner who is curious about adding to his or her knowledge base and seeking different perspectives. Approaches learning in multiple ways.

  In any job, there are things we seem to pick up quickly and other things that take us more time to learn. In your most recent job, tell me about something you learned quickly and something that took you more time to master.

  How did you learn everything you needed to know when you started in your most recent position? How did you get up to speed on everything? What difficulties did you encounter? How did you overcome them?

- *Leveraging opportunities:* Scans the environment for opportunities to develop the business or accelerate performance; encourages people to execute on opportunities to drive the business forward.

  Tell me about a time when you foresaw or predicted an opportunity that others had missed. What enabled you to predict it? How did you prepare for it? What was the outcome?

  Describe several unique opportunities that you have been able to identify and leverage over the years. How did you uncover these opportunities? What methods do you typically use to scan the environment for business opportunities?

- *Maintaining objectivity:* Acknowledges one has existing assumptions and beliefs that might influence his or her views. Effectively controls potential biases and negative assumptions. Capable of seeing things objectively.

  Describe an example of how you once reached a good decision by carefully reviewing the available options. How did you get the facts? How did you come up with options? What criteria did you use to evaluate the options? How much did you study the issue? How hard was it to make a choice?

Describe a time when you weighed the pros and cons of an issue and decided not to take any action. How did you arrive at your decision? Were you happy with your decision? What might have happened if you had made the decision to take action?

- *Maintaining work-life balance:* Finds the appropriate balance between work and nonwork demands; effectively manages work pressures.

  What strategies have you used to encourage a healthy work-life balance within your organization? Describe some of the ways you help other people manage their workloads. How do you keep people from pushing themselves too hard and burning out?

  Tell me about a time when a demand or expectation you had at work was in direct conflict with a commitment or expectation you had outside of work—a time when your life inside and outside work were in conflict with one another. What led to this conflict? How did you respond to the situation? What was the outcome?

- *Making a strong impression:* Has a good understanding of the audience; effectively communicates message; leaves a positive lasting impression.

  Tell me about a time when it was critical that you made a strong first impression on someone. Why was it so important to make a good first impression? What did you do to make sure you made a positive impression? What was the outcome?

  Describe a time when you did not get off on the right foot when meeting with someone—a time when you had difficulty building a strong rapport with someone. What was the reason you had difficulty? How did this affect your behavior with this person? What sort of relationship did you end up having with this person?

- *Making accurate judgments and decisions:* Makes confident, timely, fact-based decisions drawing on a broad range of resources. Acts on decisions with a sense of calculated risk taking. Ensures others understand the decision before moving forward.

  Tell me about the most difficult decision you have had to make at work. Why was it difficult? How did you decide what to do? What was the outcome?

  Tell me about a decision you made at work that did not turn out as planned. What went wrong? What, if anything, should you have done differently?

- *Making convincing arguments:* Makes compelling arguments; able to persuade others; presents information in a logical manner.

    Tell me about a time when you had to ask someone else for help or assistance that you felt he or she might not want to provide. How did you phrase your request? What did you do to increase the chance that this person would comply with your request? What was the outcome?

    Describe a time when you had to convince someone else to change his or her opinion or support something he or she had initially doubted. Why was it important to influence this person? What method did you use to win him or her person over? What was the result?

- *Managing from a distance:* Gets results from people and groups at multiple locations; works well managing virtual teams.

    Tell me about a time when you had to manage an individual or group of individuals e located in a wide variety of different geographical locations. How did you coordinate communication and effort across the individuals in this group? What methods did you use to track performance and make sure everyone was on the same page?

    What methods do you employ to make up for the lack of face-to-face contact with remote associates? How have these methods been effective? Give me an example.

- *Managing meetings:* Uses meeting time effectively; involves participants in discussion; plans ahead; achieves positive outcomes.

    Tell me about a time you had to manage a project that required coordinating efforts from several people. How did you keep everyone focused and moving in the right direction? What did you do to avoid potential conflicts or duplicate efforts?

    Tell me about a time when you had to carefully coordinate a variety of different schedules to ensure a task was carried out successfully. What tools did you use to keep track of all the schedules? How did you make sure you avoided creating any schedule conflicts?

- *Managing performance:* Has an authentic interpersonal style that engages others and encourages high performance. Uses personal influence to encourage and support.

Tell me about a time you had to address performance issues with a direct report or coworker. What prompted you to take action? How did you deal with the issues? What was the result?

Describe how you have established performance standards for a team member. What processes did you use to ensure he or she understood your expectations?

- *Managing political situations:* Is able to diffuse conflict; encourages negotiation and workplace diplomacy; is a good communicator who uses group decision making in order to encourage positive group dynamic.

    Describe a time when you had a disagreement with someone at work. What was the nature of the disagreement? How did you handle it? What was the outcome?

    Tell me about a time when you had to deal with a highly political situation at work. What were the politics behind the situation? How did you become aware of its political aspects? What actions did you take to deal with these political issues?

- *Managing resources:* Manages resources to achieve maximum value with minimum cost. Accurately estimates, invests, and monitors resources and budgets to optimize returns and control waste. Makes good use of company assets.

    Tell me about a project you had to manage that required getting a lot of resources or time, or both, from other people. How did you figure out what resources were needed and ensure you had access to them? What was the project outcome? Was it successful?

    Describe a time when you had to get a lot done with very few resources. What was the cause of the resource shortage? How were you unable to get additional resources? How did you ensure that resources were being used efficiently and effectively? What was the outcome?

- *Managing risk:* Effectively balances risks and opportunities; thinks through potential positive and negative outcomes; looks for ways to mitigate risks.

    Tell me about a time when you had to make a risky decision. What made this decision a risk? How did you determine what actions to take? What did you do to minimize or control the potential risk? What was the outcome?

Describe a time when you took a risk that you later wished you hadn't taken. What was the situation? What happened? Do you regret taking the risk?

- *Managing stress:* Manages stress in an effective manner. Stress does not cripple performance.

  Tell me about the most pressure you have been under in the last year from any aspect of your life—school, work, something else. Tell me in particular what you did in the situation. What caused the stressful situation? What did you do to solve the problems? What was your reaction when the pressure was the greatest? How long were you affected by this stress?

  What strategies do you use to reduce pressure and stress? Are there things you do to keep things from becoming too stressful or tense on the job? Give me an example of how you have used these strategies in previous jobs.

- *Managing time:* Accurately estimates time required to complete actions and activities; adheres to schedules and timetables; sensitive to the use of other people's time.

  Tell me about a time when you effectively organized a lot of activities that all had to get done in a short amount of time. How did you balance the time required for each of the activities? How did you determine priorities? What planning or organizing aids or materials did you use?

  What strategies have you used to coordinate meetings with a variety of busy people? Tell me about a project you were involved in that required balancing the schedules of several people. How did you manage the process of coordinating schedules and keeping meetings on track?

- *Meeting basic work expectations:* Complies with basic job requirements and tasks; arrives at work on time as scheduled; informs others when encountering problems that may limit his or her ability to meet expectations.

  Tell me about a time when you were unable to work your assigned shift. What happened? What actions did you take when you realized you weren't going to be able to work?

  Tell me about a time when you had to leave work unexpectedly. What was the situation? How did you handle it in terms of notifying colleagues and superiors?

- *Navigating organizations:* Has an understanding of how an organization is structured. Shows effective navigation strategies when seeking information.

What do you do when someone else is keeping you from accomplishing your objectives? Give me an example of a time when you had to overcome obstacles caused by someone else at work. What was the outcome? How did this event affect the relationship between you and this person?

What sort of things have you done during your career to increase your understanding of the politics and informal networks within an organization? How do you determine who the key decision makers are in an organization? Describe a time when you were able to complete a task more effectively because of your understanding of these networks.

- *Negotiating agreements:* Effectively leverages negotiating strategies and tactics to reach mutually agreeable solutions; focuses on win-win solutions; outlines requirements, contingencies, and timetables that help drive discussions toward completion.

  We have all encountered conflicts with others—times when we don't see eye-to-eye with another person or group. Tell me about a time you experienced this sort of conflict. What was the outcome?

  Tell me about a time when you had to negotiate expectations with someone. What did you do to try to reach a mutually agreeable solution?

- *Performing manual tasks:* Comfortably understands how financial information is collected and used to guide and evaluate business decisions. Effective at creating ways to share financial information so others can understand it.

  Tell me about a time when you had to do something that required a high-level of hand-eye coordination. What made this task hard? How effective were you at the task? What things caused you the most difficulty?

  Tell me about a time when you had to use a particularly complex piece of machinery in your work. How did you learn how to use the machine? What parts of it were easy for you? What parts of it were difficult for you?

- *Presenting and public speaking:* Presents ideas in a manner that is clear, concise, and easy to understand. Succinctly and effectively communicates information in writing and through presentations.

  Tell me about a time when you were asked to represent your organization in a public setting—for example, a community event or interview. How did you prepare? How did it go?

What are some things you do during presentations to keep the audience's attention and interest? Describe some times when you have used these techniques during presentations. What prompted you to use a particular technique? How did the audience respond?

- *Prioritizing and organizing work:* Allocates time and attention based on what is most important to achieve key goals and objectives. Effectively organizes and balances tasks and priorities to keep multiple projects on track.

  How do you prioritize tasks during your workday? Provide an example of a time when you had to make a tough decision related to prioritizing tasks. What led you to give one of the tasks higher priority over the others?

  Describe a time when you or your work team faced two conflicting tasks at work. What was the nature of the conflict? How did you decide which to focus on first? How, if at all, did you incorporate the opinions and viewpoints of other people into that decision?

- *Pursuing self-development:* Demonstrates ambition and desire to move forward in his or her career; engages others in discussions about career development; seeks feedback on ways to increase his or her performance; takes advantage of opportunities to build new skills and capabilities.

  How do you make sure that what you learn in training is applied to your job? Give me an example of a time when you realized a significant improvement in the way you do things at work from development you received. What was the benefit for the organization?

  It is sometimes difficult to fit in development when your work schedule is already full. What efforts have you made to pursue development opportunities, even when you were busy at work? Tell me about a time when you thought it was important to engage in a development activity even though you didn't have a lot of time.

- *Reading effectively:* Accurately interprets written information associated with his or her job; able to follow logic and arguments contained in written materials; able to process large amounts of written information in a relatively short amount of time.

  Describe the most complex written documentation you have had to read as part of your work. What made this document so complex? How long did it take you to read through it? How did you make sure that you were interpreting it correctly?

Tell me about a time when you had to summarize the key points of a complex written document for another person. How did you know what was important? How did you present the information to this person? What was the result?

- *Resolving conflict:* Handles confrontation in a professional and constructive manner; avoids conflict when possible but does not shy away from addressing issues when necessary; is a skilled mediator when needed.

  People often have to work with customers or coworkers who seem unreasonable or expect too much. Tell me about a time you had to deal with such a person. What actions did you take?

  Tell me about a time when you found yourself engaged in an argument or heated discussion with a colleague. What led to this discussion? How did you resolve it?

- *Serving customers:* Has sufficient knowledge of products and services and helps customers enthusiastically; communicates well with customers and follows up as necessary; is always professional and represents the organization positively.

  Give me an example of when you went above and beyond the call of duty for a customer. What did you do? What prompted you to take this action? What was the outcome?

  What things have you done in the past to ensure you are providing good customer service? How have you measured customer satisfaction with your service? How do you stay in touch with customers in your organization? What methods do you use to monitor customer interests, needs, and concerns?

- *Setting a strategic vision:* Creates and communicates a compelling vision that motivates others; conveys the purpose and importance of the corporate vision and mission; links department, team, and individual initiatives to those of the organization.

  Describe a time when you had to translate a broad, long-term goal or strategy into a more short-term, action-oriented plan. How did you create a connection between high-level strategic objectives and more tactical short-term actions? How did you ensure ongoing alignment between the longer-term strategy and day-to-day actions? What were some of the challenges you faced in terms of sticking to the strategy?

Tell me about time you were able to get a group or team to rally around a longer-term goal or vision. How did you communicate the long-term goal? What did you do to build excitement and enthusiasm? How did you leverage people's motivation toward the long-term goal to create shorter-term actions and results? What were the main challenges to keeping people motivated and focused on working toward the goal?

- *Setting objectives:* Sets meaningful, challenging performance objectives with clear measures of success.

  Tell me about a time when you had to set goals and a long-term direction for a group. How did you communicate these goals? What did you do to make sure people understood the goals?

  Tell me about a time when you had to translate a broad organizational strategy or direction into a specific, actionable plan. How did you make sure your actions were aligned with the broader strategy? How did you communicate the plan to others?

- *Sharing information:* Shares useful information with the team. Provides insight and offers knowledge and experience.

  Tell me about a time when you provided information to someone that his or she did not ask for but that you felt he or she should know. Why did you think this person needed the information? How did you communicate the information to him or her? What was his or her reaction?

  Tell me about how you have set up systems and processes to facilitate information exchange and knowledge sharing within your organization. How do you get other people to share information?

- *Showing caring and understanding:* Shows empathy toward challenges, concerns, and problems of others; takes a tolerant and patient approach with people who are struggling with difficult challenges; helps to put people at ease and make them feel more comfortable.

  Give me an example of a time when you treated a coworker with fairness and respect, even though he or she had not treated you in a similar fashion. Why did you do this? What was the outcome?

Tell me about a time when you were very frustrated with someone at work. What was the situation? What did the person do that made you feel that way? What did you do about it? What was the outcome?

- *Showing community and social responsibility:* Supports social and community events; discusses how the organization fits into the larger community.

    Describe a time when you became aware of a community issue that was very important to a coworker or customer. How did this issue affect how you worked with him or her?

    Tell me about a time you sought to create a more sustainable process in your organization, either economically or environmentally. What were some of the issues with the process you wanted to change? How did you communicate the need for a change to your work team? What was the outcome?

- *Solving complex problems:* Effective at thinking through complex problems and information; uses traditional and innovative approaches to identify effective solutions. Seeks to accept and build off the ideas of others for solutions others may not have considered.

    What was the most complex work-related problem you have had to solve? How did you work through the problem? What was the outcome?

    Tell me about a time that you solved a complex work-related problem and needed to communicate your solution to others. How did you present your thinking? What, if anything, do you wish you had done differently?

- *Supporting change:* Supports change and innovation. Is comfortable with a changing environment and is adaptive to such an environment.

    Most of us have been part of organizational changes that we did not fully agree with. Tell me about your experience dealing with an organizational strategy, initiative, or decision that you did not fully agree with. What was the situation? How did you voice your concerns? What was the outcome?

    Tell me about a time when you were asked to communicate a change in company polices or strategy that you did not personally agree with. How did you present this strategy or plan to others on your work group?

- *Supporting coworkers:* Contributes to team performance by providing encouragement and support. Helps others overcome obstacles and successfully accomplish goals.

Tell me about a time where you went out of your way to help someone else at work. What did you do that was different from what others might have done in the same situation? How did this benefit you?

Tell me about a time when you changed your approach or objectives to accommodate the needs and interests of others. Why did you decide to change your approach? How did you become aware of the need to change direction?

- *Supporting organizational goals:* Actively supports organizational goals and values; aligns actions around organizational goals; gives priority to organizational needs and concerns when making decisions.

  Provide an example of a time when you did something that reflected well on the company you were working for—something that helped to improve the company's general image. What led you to take this action? What was the outcome?

  Tell me about a time when you sacrificed your personal goals for your team or the company. What was the situation? Why did you set aside your goals in favor of the company's needs?

- *Teaching:* Explains things in a simple and educational way. Works patiently with others so they learn new tasks and concepts.

  Tell me about a time when you had to show someone how to perform a certain task or procedure. What prompted you to teach this person? What methods did you use to teach? What were the main challenges you faced? How successful was the person at mastering the task?

  Tell me about some of the techniques you use when teaching or instructing others. How did you develop these techniques? Provide some examples that illustrate how you have used these teaching techniques on the job.

- *Testing and troubleshooting:* Effectively tests and detects problems using a variety of methods and approaches. Suggests appropriate solutions and anticipates problems and helps prevent them.

  Tell me about a time when you were given responsibility for maintaining the performance of a complex system, process, or operation. What instructions were you given regarding how to maintain the system? What approach did you take to ensure things ran smoothly? Did you encounter any problems? What were they?

Describe a time when you had to diagnose a system, process, or operation in order to improve its performance. What approach did you take to assess the performance of the system? How did you decide to take this approach? What did you learn about the system? What did you do to improve its performance? What was the outcome?

- *Thinking broadly:* Able to approach problems from different perspectives; considers far-reaching implications of actions.

  Describe a time when you were able to trace problems in your company to aspects of the broader work environment. How was the environment affecting performance? What approach did you take to solve the problem?

  Tell me about a time you had to solve a particularly complex problem with an overall process or system in your company. What factors did you look at when diagnosing the problem? What things did you consider when developing a potential solution? What was the eventual outcome?

- *Thinking globally:* Is knowledgeable of the global climate in the industry; is aware of global trends in technology and understands the global market; deals effectively with global partners and is aware of multicultural issues.

  Tell me about a time when you were asked to work on a project with people from different nationalities. What was the nature of the project you were working on? How was your work approach affected or changed as a result of having to work with people from other cultures?

  Tell me about a time when your knowledge of global economics or markets led you to change or modify your strategic approach to something at work. What were the global factors or issues that affected your approach? How did you become aware of these issues? What changes did you make to your strategic approach? What was the outcome?

- *Using computers and technology:* Maintains expertise in technical and professional knowledge and skills critical to performing the role. Adept at using technology, machines, or tools fundamental to the job.

  How have you incorporated the use of technology in your current or previous job? Did you have to learn new technologies for your work? What parts of this process were easy for you, and where did you face some challenges?

  Describe a time when a technology you regularly used for work became outdated or replaced in your company. How did you handle this change?

What steps did you take to ensure you knew how to properly use the new system?

- *Using math:* Capable of using and explaining mathematical computations; creates accurate predictions.

  Tell me about a time you had to make sense of or otherwise solve a problem that required analyzing a large amount of data. What was the problem? What approach did you take toward working through the data? What conclusions did you reach?

  Describe a time when you had to use numbers or data to back up a claim. How did you approach this? How did you incorporate the numbers into your presentation? What steps did you take to make sure that everyone understood the nature of the data and how it fit into the larger picture?

- *Using feedback:* Committed to personal and professional growth and development through feedback from others. Provides appropriate and reinforcing feedback to others.

  Tell me about a time when someone criticized your ideas or work. How did you respond to these comments? What was the outcome? What sort of relationship do you have with this person now?

  Tell me about a time when you received feedback that was not what you had expected. What was the situation? How did that discussion go?

- *Working safely:* Respects and follows safety policies and regulations; scans the environment for things that may pose a safety risk; encourages others to use safe and healthy work practices.

  Tell me about a time at work when you noticed something that was potentially dangerous or unsafe. How did it come to your attention? What actions did you take?

  Tell me about a time when you had to deal with a safety or security issue at work. What happened? How did you react? What was the outcome?

- *Working with ambiguity:* Handles uncertain situations professionally and reasonably; recognizes that ambiguity is inevitable in some processes and accepts that some risks must be taken to make progress.

  Tell me about a time when you were given conflicting directions or instructions. How did you respond to these directions? What actions did you take to get resolution?

Describe a time when you were asked to work on a project where the goals or process steps where not clearly defined. How did you figure out what to do? What was the outcome?

- *Working with diverse populations:* Works well with people of diverse backgrounds and is able to effectively leverage individual difference. Encourages diversity and mutual respect among team members and demonstrates compassion and sensitivity.

Tell me about a time when you consciously changed your work behavior out of respect or recognition toward someone else's culture or cultural background. What did you do differently? What was the cultural difference you were concerned with? How were your actions received?

How have you encouraged associates to incorporate cultural awareness into their day-to-day work activities? Give me an example.

- *Working with financial information:* Comfortably understands how financial information is collected and used to guide and evaluate business decisions. Effective at creating ways to share financial information so others can understand it.

Tell me about a time you had to make sense of or otherwise solve a problem that required analyzing a large amount of data. What was the problem? What approach did you take toward working through the data? What conclusions did you reach?

Tell me about a time when you used numbers and mathematics to help back up your views. Why did you decide to use numbers to make your point? What was the basis for your argument? How did you explain the argument to others? What was the result?

GUIDE FOR CONDUCTING A STRUCTURED INTERVIEW

To maximize the accuracy of hiring decisions, it is important that each person in the interview process focus on a predetermined set of job competencies and questions.

Please use the following guidelines to conduct the interview.

Preparing for the Interview

❏ Review résumé. Note career accomplishments or events to explore during the interview; note topics you might use to build candidate rapport.

❏ Review job description. List key challenges associated with the position; discuss position with other stakeholders who have a strong interest in the hiring decision.

❏ Review interview guide. Review questions before meeting with the candidate.

❏ Prepare meeting space. Arrange to interview the candidate in a professional work space; if meeting in a shared space, arrive early to make seating arrangements and advise others of the need to avoid interruptions.

Building Rapport with the Candidate

❏ Treat candidates as customers. Candidates will be evaluating our company as a prospective employer during the interview. Exceed their expectations.

❏ Be on time. Do not make the candidate wait for you.

❏ Show hospitality. Warmly welcome the candidate. Start the conversation by discussing a neutral subject; weather, travel, the city you are in, and general comments about the industry are all safe topics.

❏ Explain the process

❏ You will be asking questions primarily about their past work experience.

❏ All candidates are asked the same questions to ensure a consistent review of their skills.

❏ You will need to move at a steady pace to cover all the questions.

❏ There will be time for the candidate to ask you questions at the end of the interview.

Asking Interview Questions

❏ Ask, listen, probe, listen, and move on. Read the first part of the initial question as written in the interview guide; follow up with probes until the candidate has given a thorough response; try to spend three to five minutes on each question.

❏ Use the SARI model: Situation candidate was facing that led him or her to take action, Actions he or she took, Results or outcomes of his or her actions, and Interesting features about the situation /or the candidate's actions, or both.

❏ Get the information you need. Be courteous but persistent in getting information to evaluate the candidate effectively.

❏ Keep it legal. Do not say, ask, or write anything that you would not want to have repeated in court (see below).

Closing the Interview

❏ Answer the candidate's questions. Respond to questions only where you are certain of the answer; commit to getting information about questions you cannot answer.

❏ Do not make promises. Avoid statements that could be interpreted or alleged to create an unwarranted expectation in the candidate's mind of an employment contract; remember that you have not made your hiring decision yet.

❏ Give the candidate a clear time line. Let the candidate know when and who he or she can expect to hear back.

❏ Thank the candidate for his or her participation in the interview. Walk the candidate out or to the next meeting.

Legal Dos and Don'ts

❏ Focus on job-relevant topics. The easiest way to do this is to restrict your questions to those in the interview guide.

❏ Respect the candidate's privacy rights; do not probe into topics that are not directly job relevant.

❏ Don't ask questions that the law may prohibit. These may include questions about sex; race; color; creed; national origin; religion; age; marital status; pregnancy; physical, mental, or sensory disability; sexual orientation; gender identity; and any other basis protected by federal, state, or local law. For specific legal advice, consult the company attorney.

❏ Ask all candidates the same questions.

Rating Candidates

❏ Rate each candidate as soon as possible. Avoid interviewing other candidates before your ratings are completed.

At the end of the interview, provide the following information to the person assigned to manage the candidate:

- Rating for each topic you addressed during the interview (1 to 5, where 5 is outstanding)

- Overall candidate evaluation (1 to 5, where 5 is very strongly recommend)

- Any unique observations, recommendations, or other thoughts you have regarding the candidate

Succession management is one of the most powerful and most complicated development methods available to companies. At least seven components need to be built out to create a fully robust succession management process:

- *Succession framework:* Creating a well-defined calendar of events and actions associated with succession such as nominating high-potential candidates, conducting talent reviews, and assigning development actions to identified successors for different roles. At the simplest level, this may be an annual talent review. At advanced levels, it becomes a dynamic process for integrating talent management into ongoing business operations and strategic planning activities.

- *Critical roles:* Determining which jobs will be included in the formal succession process and defining the succession methods needed for different kinds of jobs. The simplest methods rely solely on using the organizational chart or manager opinions to decide what jobs are critical. At advanced levels, this is done through leadership opinion combined with a complex analysis of workforce and labor market data to prioritize critical roles across the company.

- *Candidate identification:* Defining the criteria and decision-making process for identifying and nominating employees to include in the succession talent pool. At the basic level, this often consists of manager nominations and employee self-identification. At advanced levels, companies may use statistically validated measures of potential combined with multipart assessment centers.

- *Talent reviews:* Building a framework and resources to support talent review meetings where leaders convene to discuss succession needs and talent resources. At the most basic levels, this usually involves using a method to systematically compare candidates based on performance, potential, and readiness. At advanced levels, these meetings use interactive technology to support dynamic conversations that integrate discussions of business strategy and operations with targeted dialogue around key talent necessary to support business needs.

- *Development programs:* Creating career development and training programs to help employees realize their full potential and assume positions with greater responsibility. The most basic levels may involve just setting specific development objectives for high-potential employees based on the results of talent reviews. At advanced levels, companies may incorporate extensive development programs spanning multiple years that incorporate job rotations, 360 survey reviews, mentoring, and a range of other training and development courses and resources. An important strategic choice related to development programs is whether to intentionally build differentiated engagement programs that actively target high-potential employees as a distinct population within the organization. These programs may assess for potential early in an employee's career, even on entry into the organization, and then actively guide career development to engage and retain high potentials over years or even decades. Differentiating high-value talent and addressing their unique needs and risks can span from just communicating to them that they are valued to providing special compensation and deep development investments that can include supporting their interests outside the organization such as accommodating living preferences or supporting volunteer activities.

- *Staffing and pay decisions:* Defining how succession management processes will be used to guide staffing decisions and investment of development and pay resources. At the basic level, this means encouraging managers to make workforce management decisions that take into account succession management discussions and data. Advanced levels may include formally rewarding managers based on their ability to attract, retain, and develop talent. It may also incorporate the use of advanced analytics to determine optimal pay and promotion strategies based on comparing past measures of performance and potential against current job success and retention.

- *Succession resources:* Assembling the staffing resources and HR technology needed to support large-scale succession management methods. The simplest succession management process can often be supported by one person provided this person has access to sufficient succession technology so is not overwhelmed by administrative tasks. Advanced succession programs require the use of technology that integrates succession with other talent management activities, most notably staffing, development, and workforce planning. World-class succession management also requires developing a center of excellence for succession, staffed by people who focus full time on monitoring and guiding the flow of talent through critical job roles across the organization.

Table B.1 lists what each of these components looks like at basic and advanced levels.

All seven components described in table B.1 are critical to support an effective succession management process. But not all components need to be fully developed for succession management to work. It is usually far better to build each component incrementally over time rather than investing massive resources up front in an effort to create a flawless succession management process in year 1. For example, if your primary succession goal is to identify candidates for key positions, then focus on "critical roles" and "candidate identification" in year 1, but don't worry as much about other components such as "development programs" or "staffing and pay decisions." If you need to drive talent retention, start with a clear emphasis on "candidate identification," "development programs," and "staffing and pay decisions," but do not put as much effort into "critical roles." Or if the initial goal is creating a common definition of performance, you might emphasize "talent reviews" in year 1 and not invest a lot into the other components that first year.

The main point is that most organizations cannot and probably should not try to build a full-service succession process in year 1. Focus resources on the components that provide the greatest near-term value. At the same time, do not completely ignore the other components altogether. Components that may not be critical in year 1 often become more critical over time. For example, when a company starts to get really good at doing talent reviews, managers and employees may start asking that more resources be put into candidate identification prior to the reviews and development programs to support follow-up actions after the

Table B.1
Succession Management Process Components

Component	Basic Level	High Performance Level
Succession framework	Succession calendar established and communicated showing when key actions take place for talent identification, review, development, staffing, and reporting.	Succession calendar is integrated with strategic and financial planning calendars; talent data influence strategic planning and vice versa.
	Process is largely static; does not change dynamically based on business needs.	Standard succession calendar is augmented by talent reviews addressing immediate business needs.
	Succession data are not shared widely across talent processes; succession is mainly a stand-alone exercise.	Succession events are tightly coupled with workforce planning, compensation, staffing, and development activities; data are automatically shared across talent processes.
Critical roles	Succession primarily focuses on typical critical roles such as senior leaders.	Succession focuses on key roles across the company where access to high-performing talent has a significant impact on business operations.
	Critical roles are identified based on leaders' subjective opinions.	Clear metrics and criteria are used to define what roles are critical.
		Critical roles are identified using a mixture of leader input and analysis of internal workforce data and external recruiting marketing data.

Candidate identification	Succession candidates are primarily nominated based on opinions of their manager or using organizational chart reporting relationships. Initial evaluations of potential and readiness are based on subjective ratings based on a few simple definitions.	Analysis of workforce planning and employee profile data is used to recommend candidates and augment manager opinions. Methods are established to support movement of candidates across organizational functions and departments to avoid talent silos. Evaluations of potential and readiness are based on a well-defined mix of objective and subjective assessment data; managers are fully trained on the differences among readiness, potential, and performance.
Talent reviews	Talent reviews occur only annually. Meetings are facilitated by HR business partners as part of their general duties. Identification criteria are outlined in advance and reinforced in discussions. Managers arrive at the review with basic employee profile information about current performance, career goals, and potential. Reviews are largely a systematic review of talent identified on succession plans. Majority of review focuses on assessing talent; little discussion of talent development actions.	Talent reviews occur in different forms throughout the year based on business needs. Facilitated by succession experts working in collaboration with HR business partners. Managers arrive at the review with extensive information on the potential, performance, and career development of candidates, including data collected through the use of rigorous assessments. Reviews start with discussion of key business and talent objectives and then dynamically focus on the candidates most critical to those objectives. Much of the review is spent talking about how talent is being developed, and not just focusing on talent assessment

(Continued)

Component	Basic Level	High Performance Level
Development programs	Basic career development plans in place for employees.	Data from talent reviews feed directly into talent development processes.
	Succession candidates are assigned development objectives based on talent reviews.	Creation of extensive leadership universities that provide multiple courses and resources to support development.
	High-potential employees are formally recognized by the organization, and efforts are made to address their unique career interests to encourage retention.	Job rotation programs used to provide succession candidates with critical skills and experiences.
		Managers are rewarded for attracting, developing, and promoting high-potential talent through their departments and into other areas of the business.
		The company provides high-potential talent with assessment centers, 360 development feedback, mentors, and other resources to help them realize their full potential.
		Discussing development planning is a major component of talent reviews.
		Employees' records of previous development influence decisions about their future potential.
		Development support may extend to outside roles, including board activities and nonprofit work.
		Creation of differentiated engagement programs that identify early-career high potentials and actively address their unique interests across multiple years or decades.
		Leveraging senior high-potential leaders in the mentoring and development of more junior high-potential candidates.

Staffing and pay decisions	No formal connection between succession and staffing and pay processes. Managers are not held accountable for linking succession assessments to tangible actions related to staffing or pay.	Data from talent reviews feed directly into staffing processes. Managers are held accountable for driving retention and development of high-potential candidates. The company actively tracks how many staffing decisions are in alignment with succession recommendations. Compensation strategies are developed to support retention of high-potential employees. Workforce analytics are used to identify optimal staffing strategies and career paths. Discussing staffing is a major component of talent reviews.
Succession resources	Succession process overseen by HR as part of general talent management; no dedicated succession function. Talent reviews are facilitated by HR business partners with limited support from corporate HR. Succession is viewed mainly as an annual event. Line managers are not held directly accountable for retention and promotion of high-potential talent.	Company has a dedicated succession center of excellence (COE) that oversees multiple talent pipelines across the company; integrated team has experience in talent assessment, development, staffing, and workforce planning. Succession data are a key feature of business operations meetings; line-of-business leaders meet monthly or quarterly with succession COE members to discuss talent and bench strength. HR business partners are trained and certified on methods used to support succession in their units. Operations managers are measured and rewarded based on retention, development, and promotion of key talent. Succession COE includes resources skilled in talent analytics associated with predicting promotion potential and employee retention.

reviews. This is one of the advantages of succession management. Getting better at one component of succession management creates pressure and encouragement within the company to invest in the others.

SUCCESSION MANAGEMENT MATURITY PATHS

To illustrate what building out a succession process over time might look like, we look at three succession management scenarios and how they could be addressed. These scenarios are intended to help you picture what the implementation of succession management might look like in your company. They are not considered best practices since what approach is best will vary considerably depending on what a company wants to achieve from succession management and the types of resources it has available.

Starting from Nothing with Nothing

This scenario describes a company that is starting succession management with little to no dedicated succession staff, limited HR technology, no strong history of succession management, and rudimentary leadership development and staffing functions. Because the company has little to build on in terms of existing processes or resources, it is important to create engagement among line managers early on so they will support future actions required to get succession off the ground:

- *Year 1:* Invest in establishing basic levels of functionality for most of the components except talent reviews. Use the talent review to educate managers on the importance of succession management. If done right, talent review conversations can get managers to realize the value of succession management and create a pull for more focus in this area. They will also lay the groundwork needed for managers to effectively distinguish high performers from high potentials. Also be sure to invest enough in succession management resources to build technology so the succession process can be done easily and efficiently without creating a lot of administrative burden on managers or HR.

- *Year 2:* Build out methods for defining critical roles and identifying talent. Use the talent reviews conducted in year 1 as a source of information for what criteria should go into these areas. Leverage the foundation created in year 1 to help managers more effectively identify and develop high-potential employees. Invest in succession management resources to create tools and technology that keep these new methods swift and efficient.

- *Year 3:* Focus on building out a stronger succession framework that creates more formal links between succession and development programs, and staffing and pay decisions. The organization may want to invest in creating differentiated engagement programs specifically for high potentials that encourage retention and accelerate their career development. Also continue building out the staff and technology succession resources that will allow taking succession management to higher levels of maturity.

A Few Standard Tools

This describes a company that has some history of doing succession at higher levels but limited staff focused specifically on succession. The company has a fairly strong HR technology platform but only basic resources to support development programs and staffing and pay decisions. In this scenario, succession management can help drive higher levels of maturity across multiple HR processes. This is done by creating more effective candidate identification and talent review methods that raise awareness among managers regarding the value of having better methods for staffing positions and developing high potential talent:

- *Year 1:* Focus on building out tools and succession resources to support better candidate identification. Use the information provided by these tools to create more productive talent reviews. Highlight the value of building staffing and development processes around the same criteria used for identifying high-potential talent.

- *Year 2:* Invest in technology and resources that support the integration of succession management with staffing and development actions. Create a succession framework that ties together activities related to setting business strategies, defining workforce needs to support these strategies, and identifying and developing talent to support these needs.

- *Year 3:* Take talent reviews to the next level so they go beyond simply reviewing succession candidates to actively discussing how to integrate business needs with talent management activities.

Rounding Out the Talent Function

This scenario describes a company that recently added staff specifically dedicated to building out succession management methods across the organization. The company has solid HR technology, strong development programs, and a strong staffing function. It has practiced succession management in the past, but only at a very basic level limited to senior executives and their direct reports. In this scenario, the company will leverage synergies created by tying succession to development and staffing activities so employees and managers perceive HR as an integrated function rather than a collection of disparate processes. This sets the stage for implementation of leading-edge workforce planning and analytics methods combined with aggressive talent development activities in year 3:

- *Year 1:* Focus is placed on consolidating staff and technology to support wider use of succession management. The company also leverages information from development and staffing programs to build stronger methods for identifying candidates based on key competencies and skills. This information is used to support more effective talent reviews.

- *Year 2:* Focus is placed on creating a stronger succession framework that more fully integrates defining critical roles, identifying candidates, talent reviews, and talent development and staffing.

- *Year 3:* Data and processes used for succession are leveraged to support use of workforce planning and analytics to guide business decisions. The value received from having a more effective, fully integrated succession management process justifies an increased investment in succession resources that will allow the company to conduct more frequent, operationally focused talent reviews.

In Summary

These three scenarios illustrate the myriad ways companies can build out succession management (see table B.2 for a summary). The main points to remember are these:

1. There is no one best way to build a succession management process. What approach is best depends on your company's business needs, available resources, and existing processes.

2. Although you do not need to fully invest in all seven succession components in year 1, it is important to make some investment in each component every year to ensure you do not build a process that ends up missing key components. To use an analogy, building succession management is somewhat akin to building a large house over multiple years. You may focus on building out the kitchen before you work on the garage. But it is important

Table B.2
Three Succession Management Scenarios

	Succession Framework	Defining Critical Roles	Identifying Candidates	Talent Reviews	Development Programs	Staffing and Pay Decisions	Succession Resources
Starting from nothing							
Year 1	Basic	Basic	Basic	*Standard*	Basic	Basic	*Standard*
Year 2	Basic	*Standard*	*Standard*	Standard	Basic	Basic	Standard
Year 3	*Standard*	Standard	Standard	Standard	*Standard*	*Standard*	Advanced
Few standard tools							
Year 1	Basic	Basic	*Standard*	*Standard*	Basic	Basic	Basic
Year 2	*Standard*	*Standard*	Standard	Standard	*Standard*	*Standard*	*Standard*
Year 3	Advanced	Standard	Standard	*Advanced*	Standard	Standard	Advanced
Rounding out talent function							
Year 1	Basic	Basic	*Standard*	*Standard*	Basic	Standard	*Standard*
Year 2	*Standard*	*Standard*	Standard	Standard	*Advanced*	*Advanced*	Standard
Year 3	Advanced	*Advanced*	Standard	Standard	*Advanced*	Advanced	*Advanced*

Note: The labels indicate the maturity level of the component to achieve by the end of the year. The italicized terms indicate the areas of focus for that year.

to know how the kitchen will ultimately connect to the garage. The location it may be important so it will be easy to take groceries out of the car and get them into the house. It is also very important to use technology for each component that supports integration over time. To continue with the house analogy, HR technology plays a similar role in succession management to that of electrical wiring in a house. You may not hook up everything in every room right away, but you want to frame the house with the right set of wiring so when the time comes to build out the master bedroom suite, you do not need to install a new electrical system.

3. The better you get at any one aspect of succession, the more value and pressure you will get from the organization to address the others. This is most noticeable when comparing talent reviews to candidate identification and development resources. If managers know they are going to have to discuss their teams in a rigorous talent review, they will welcome guidance that will allow them to more effectively identify and assess candidates in advance of the reviews. Similarly, employees will be much more favorably disposed toward talent reviews if they know the outcome is not just about talent evaluation but also about talent development.

The best way to create a world-class succession management process is to (1) prioritize the most immediate and valuable benefits the company can get from better succession management, (2) use this to determine which components of succession management will provide the greatest short-term value, and (3) implement actions to build out those components that take into account the eventual need to build out other components over time. If you carefully define and effectively execute these first steps in year 1, then the remaining steps in subsequent years will become easier, faster, and much more obvious.

GLOSSARY OF COMMON STRATEGIC HUMAN RESOURCE TERMS

The definitions that follow are based on what is considered to be common use of terms, although there is not clear agreement within the field on the definition of several terms. Definitions are limited to high-level descriptions of what a term represents, with minimal effort to describe the mathematical or theoretical aspects of terms that are associated with the scientific design of certain strategic HR tools and methods such as staffing assessments or employee surveys. Similarly, this glossary provides only general descriptive information about legal terms pertaining to strategic HR methods; it is not intended for formal legal guidance. Readers seeking such advice should consult legal counsel. Italicized words within a definition represent terms defined elsewhere in this glossary.

Ability, Abilities   Refers to mental capabilities and skills that influence the performance of specific job tasks. Many abilities are influenced by genetics, but learning and experience significantly increase performance levels with regard to most types of ability. Examples of common work-related abilities are verbal ability, numerical ability, spatial ability, and general cognitive ability.

Ability Tests   Tests that have been specifically designed to measure work-related *abilities*. These are often referred to as cognitive ability tests, critical thinking tests, problem-solving tests, reasoning tests, or intelligence tests.

Achievement Test   A test that measures acquired knowledge or skills, usually as the result of previous instruction and education. Examples are a test measuring a person's knowledge of foreign language or a test measuring familiarity and understanding of accounting rules and regulations. Achievement tests are often contrasted with *aptitude tests*, which are designed to measure individual characteristics that depend more on innate traits and abilities as opposed to prior learning and experience.

Active versus Passive Candidates   Distinction made between candidates who are actively looking for work and those who may be interested in job opportunities but are not actively seeking a job; for example, a person who is unemployed and looking for work is an active candidate. In contrast, a person who is already employed and is not actively looking for a new job, but whose attributes make him or her a good candidate for a position a company is seeking to fill, would be considered a passive candidate.

Adverse Impact   A situation in which the use of a specific HR methods results in members of a legally *protected class* receiving treatment that is not proportional to the treatment given to other employees or job candidates. Common examples of HR methods displaying adverse impact include staffing methods that disproportionately screen out members of a certain ethnic group or compensation or promotion methods that favor one gender over another. Adverse impact is not necessarily illegal if it can be proven that the HR method in question is clearly and directly related to job performance. Despite this, adverse impact is a major obstacle to workforce *diversity* and should be avoided whenever possible.

Americans with Disabilities Act (ADA)   Legislation passed by the US government that protects the employment rights of individuals with mental and physical disabilities. The ADA places significant restrictions on methods used to hire, promote, compensate, and terminate employees with certain physical or mental disabilities. The ADA and *Civil Rights Act of 1964* are considered to be the two most influential pieces of legislation affecting the use of HR methods, particularly those used for staffing, promotion, compensation, and termination.

Applicant Tracking System (ATS)   A software application designed to automate a company's *staffing* processes. Systems may provide support for a wide range of staffing activities including creating job requisitions, placing job postings on the web, communicating with candidates and hiring managers, receiving and processing job applications, screening and scheduling candidates, and enrolling newly hired employees into a company's payroll system or *HRIS*.

Aptitude Test   Assessments designed to measures a person's underlying potential for performing certain kinds of tasks. Most assessments labeled as aptitude tests represent different types of *ability tests* or *personality measures*. Aptitude tests are often contrasted against achievement tests, which focus more on learned skills and knowledge gained through prior education and experience.

Assessment Center   A set of activities meant to provide an assessment of an individual's key work-related attitudes, behaviors, competencies, and abilities. These are usually measured by activities that include *ability tests, personality measures, structured interviews*, and *work samples*. Assessment centers tend to be very expensive and most commonly are used for assessing the developmental needs of current employees at managerial levels and above. Companies often use assessment centers as a component of *succession management* or *leadership development*. Assessment centers used for employee selection purposes usually only when filling high-level leadership positions for which there are few candidates.

Assessment Delivery Systems   The system used to deliver assessment content to a candidate. Many assessment delivery systems are web based. Assessments can also be delivered using paper, phone, in person, kiosks, or wireless devices.

Attribute (Candidate or Employee)   Refers to characteristics possessed by individuals that influence their fit with different jobs. *Development assessments* and *staffing assessments* work by measuring attributes that either influence job performance or are requirements for employment. There are many different types of potential job-relevant attributes, including experience, education, credentials, knowledge, skills, abilities, interests, personality traits, and physical capabilities.

Average Length of Service   Data indicating the average amount of time employees remain in jobs or organizations after they have been hired. Average length of service is commonly used as a criterion for evaluating the impact of *strategic HR* methods used to predict or increase employee *retention*.

Background Investigations   A term that covers the checking and verification of different types of information about a job candidate. These investigations are important because they can help reduce the risk of employee theft and other *counterproductive work behaviors*. Background investigations usually consist of credit checks, criminal record checks, verification of citizenship, employment history or educational qualifications, and checks of motor vehicle records.

Balanced Scorecard   A method for setting and aligning goals based on a theory that a well-run organization needs to fundamentally focus on four types of activities: supporting external customers, achieving financial goals, supporting internal employees, and increasing operational efficiency. The method encourages organizations and employees to set specific goals supporting each of these four categories.

(BARS) Behaviorally Anchored Rating Scales   Rating method typically used with *structured interviews* or *performance ratings* to facilitate collection of accurate evaluations of a candidate or employee's attributes or behavior. BARS provide behavioral definitions associated with different rating values used to evaluate a person's attributes or performance. For example, customer service ratings might indicate that employees should get a 1 if they "avoid talking to customers," a 2 if they "ask customers if they have any questions," and a 3 if they "proactively engage customers in conversation about products and services and ask them if they have any specific questions." By associating specific, observable behaviors with different ratings, BARS help reduce subjectivity across raters when making evaluations.

Base Pay   A compensation term that refers to the primary salary given to an employee, not including *variable pay* or *incentive pay* such as bonuses or stock options. Some companies calculate base pay solely using salary, while other companies include salary plus the financial cost of benefits such as health care. The base pay for employees paid an hourly wage is often based on the number of hours they are expected to work, not including overtime wages.

Basic Skills Test   Assessments of competencies in basic skills that are widely required in training and employment settings (e.g., reading, writing, simple mathematics).

Behavioral Interview, Behaviorally Based Interview   An interview in which candidates are asked questions about work-related behaviors they have displayed in the past. The rationale behind this interviewing method is that past behaviors are the best predictor of future behaviors. Behavioral interviews are most often created by collecting information from job incumbents about the best and worst way to handle specific situations related to a given competency. This information is then made into questions and a set of rating scales that can be used to evaluate each question.

Bench Strength   A term used to refer to *talent pools* for different positions in an organization. The term comes from sports, where coaches refer to the strength of substitute players sitting on the bench who can fill in for other players if necessary.

(BFOQ) Bona Fide Occupational Qualification A candidate characteristic that can provide a legitimate reason for excluding a person from consideration for a job, even if it results in creating adverse impact. For instance, being a male is likely to be a BFOQ for the job of men's room attendant. It is legal to not hire women applying for this position since being male is a key job requirement.

Biodata A *self-report measure* that evaluates an applicant's suitability for a job based on his or her past experiences. Biodata can be used to assess aspects of a candidate's *personality, knowledge, ability, skills,* or interests.

Business Execution The ability of an organization to develop and use its workforce to accomplish business goals. It is often contrasted with business strategy and business assets. Business strategy defines what a company must accomplish to be successful. Business assets provide the tools and resources needed to achieve the strategy. Business execution is the process of getting the company's workforce to use its business assets to carry out its business strategy.

Business Execution Driver The six primary factors that influence a company's business execution capability: alignment, productivity, efficiency, sustainability, scalability, and governance. The importance of different business execution drivers changes depending on a company's business strategies, market environment, and workforce characteristics. Business execution drivers have a major influence on the design of *strategic HR processes.*

Calibration Methods used to ensure decisions about employee performance, pay, and potential are based on a common standard. Calibration methods involve comparing employees against a common standard of performance or basing performance on comparing employees against one another. Examples of calibration methods include *behavioral anchored rating scales, forced ranking,* and *expected distributions.*

Calibration Sessions A method of *calibration* that involves bringing together multiple managers or other individuals to discuss and agree on the performance, compensation, or potential levels of employees. Also see *talent reviews.*

Candidate Pool A group of people who are being considered for potential employment in a job or organization. Candidate pools can include internal employees, external *active candidates,* and external *passive candidates.* Candidate pools are similar in concept to *talent pools* and *bench strength.* The difference is that candidate pools usually refer to people being actively considered for a current position, whereas the other terms tend to refer to future possible candidates in general.

Candidate Profiles   Information that summarizes an individual's suitability for a job relative to specific job requirements. Candidate profiles often contain a graphical representation of a candidate's traits compared to the ideal range of these traits in terms of effective job performance. Many candidate profiles also contain detailed narrative information about a candidate's strengths and weaknesses relative to job performance requirements. Many companies use *employee profiles* as a way to create candidate profiles for existing employees to encourage *internal talent mobility*.

Career Development   Processes used to help employees determine how to improve their performance in their current jobs or build capabilities that will allow them to achieve their long-term career goals, including possibly moving into new roles within the organization.

Career Development Plan   Online tools or paper-based documents that define an employee's short- or long-term *learning objectives* and strategies and tactics to achieve them.

Career Interest Inventory   An assessment that focuses on helping people identify careers that match their interests. These assessments are useful for helping persons contemplating a career change to understand the type of work that is of intrinsic interest to them.

Career Portal, Career Site   The careers section of a corporation's web site. A wide range of functions and services is associated with these portals. Portals may include detailed information about a company's values, information and testimonials for current employees, interactive games or other activities that provide information about the company and its culture. Typically the most important section of a career site are tools people can use to search and apply for jobs possibly including links to assessments used to evaluate job candidates.

Civil Rights Act of 1964   A key piece of legislation that places severe restrictions on the use of selection methods and assessments that may have an *adverse impact* on candidates from certain demographic groups. This act led to the creation of the federal *Equal Employment Opportunity Commission (EEOC)*.

Closed-Loop Validation   *Criteria validation* methods that use data collected from employees after they are hired to optimize the relationships between prehiring assessment data and posthiring performance criteria.

Cloud Applications, Cloud Technology A term used to describe software solutions that are delivered to companies through the Internet but run on a vendor's computer hardware. Cloud technology is often contrasted with on-premise applications that are run on a company's own systems. Cloud technology has had a major impact on the availability and development of HR technology systems in general.

Cognitive Abilities Unique mental skills and capabilities associated with solving problems and processing data—for example, the ability to make decisions under time pressure, the ability to solve problems through the use of logic and reasoning, and the ability to track multiple types of information simultaneously (multitasking).

Commitments, Outcomes, Deliverables (COD) A method for defining job goals that encourages employees to think of goals in terms of three characteristics: the overall commitment the employee is making to the organization, measurable outcomes that will result from fulfilling the commitment, and specific deliverables that the employee will meet in order to fulfill their commitment. The COD method is an alternative goal-setting technique to the more widely used *SMART* method.

Compensation The salary, hourly pay, bonuses, company stock, health care benefits, and other rewards provided to employees in exchange for their service to the organization. It is often used to refer specifically to financial rewards, although companies are increasingly incorporating other financial benefits such as health care benefits and career development resources into the definition. Broader definitions of compensation are sometimes referred to as *total rewards* packages.

Competency A term often used in a variety of ways. The most common definition is "a set of behaviors that influence organizational performance. For example, "building relationships" and "planning and organizing" are competencies that influence performance in many jobs.

Competency Library A document, book, or website containing a list of different competencies such as the one provided in appendix A of this book. Competency libraries often include additional materials that support the use of competencies such as *structured interview* questions, *behavioral anchored rating scales*, or *career development* tips and suggestions. Competency libraries enable companies to create *competency models* taking advantage of predefined content, which is typically much easier than having to create entirely new competencies.

Competency Model   A set of *competencies* shown through *job analysis* to influence performance for a specific job or *job family*.

Core Competencies   *Competencies* that are considered to be critical across a wide range of jobs or an entire organization. Core competencies often reflect a company's fundamental *values* and *culture*.

Cost per Hire   The amount of money that must be spent to make each hiring decision. Can be computed using this simple formula: Cost per hire = Recruiting costs/number of positions.

Counterproductive Work Behavior   Work-related behaviors that are damaging to the employer. It usually refers to highly incompetent or intentionally damaging behaviors such as theft, fraud, absenteeism, violence, sexual harassment, or on-the-job substance abuse that negatively affect organizational performance.

Criteria Validity, Criteria Validation Study   A statistical technique used to demonstrate how well a staffing assessment predicts job performance. This technique usually involves the correlation of assessment scores of job applicants or existing employees with subjective *criteria* such as supervisory measures of job performance gathered using a *performance rating form*, or objective criteria such as attendance, sales productivity, or tenure. Criteria validity provides strong evidence of an assessment instrument's job relevance.

Critical Roles, Critical Positions   Jobs that are necessary to maintaining key company operations and where there is a significant shortage of talent. Examples are nurses in health care companies and maintenance specialists in utility companies. Also see *development roles*; *pivotal roles*.

Culture, Culture Fit   The match between the values and interests of an individual and the general work environment, norms, and career opportunities found in a company or functional work area of that company. Culture fit does not necessarily influence job performance, but often it influences other outcomes, such as job satisfaction, organizational commitment, and turnover.

Culture and Work Environment Fit Inventories   Assessments created to measure *culture fit* between an applicant and an employer. Many of these are based on the use of scales that measure personality, work values, and work preferences.

Dashboard Reporting   A feature found in many HR *technology platforms* that provides decision makers with comprehensive information about multiple employees and job candidates. Most dashboard systems use layered reporting in which high-level information about multiple employees or candidates is presented in initial screens that provide access to other screens containing more detailed information. For example, a dashboard might present overall employee turnover levels across the company and then allow users to drill down to look at turnover by department or division.

Development Assessments   Tools and methods used to provide employees with resources to support their career development. Common development assessments are *360 surveys*, and *career interest inventories*.

Development Objective   See *learning objective*.

Development Roles, Development Positions   Jobs that are viewed as feeder positions for providing employees with the skills and experiences needed to move into *critical* or *pivotal roles*. For example, many retail companies view assistant store manager positions as critical development roles for creating future store managers.

Development Strategies   In the context of *strategic HR*, usually refers to the plans and objectives an employee has created to build his or her capabilities, improve his or her performance, and advance his or her career.

Direct Reports   The employees who formally report to a manager. In most companies, managers have responsibility for hiring, managing performance, and making pay and staffing decisions for their direct reports.

Diversity   Refers to the demographic, ethnic, and cultural makeup of a company's workforce or applicant population. Most companies strive to have the *diversity* of their workforce reflect the diversity of their community and customers. HR methods that display *adverse impact* can decrease a company's diversity and may be illegal if they are not *job relevant*.

Drug Screen   Refers to a variety of assessment methods that chemically test for the presence of specific drugs in a person's metabolism.

EEO/Equal Employment Opportunity   The concept that individuals should have equal treatment in all employment-related situations. The term *EEO* usually refers to legal requirements and guidelines such as those provided by the federal *Equal Employment Opportunity Commission (EEOC)*.

EEOC/Equal Employment Opportunity Commission   The federal agency responsible for enforcing the *Civil Rights Act of 1964*, the *Americans with Disabilities Act*, and other key pieces of *EEO*-related legislation.

Employee Profile   A form, document, or web page containing job-relevant information about an employee such as skills, career interests, job title, job responsibilities, and career potential. Access to certain aspects of an employee profile are typically restricted based on someone's role. For example, everyone in the company may be able to see any employee's job title on his or her employee profile, but access to information about salary and performance levels will usually be limited to the employee's manager and other people who have a clear need to know this information.

Employment Brand   The message an organization sends to candidates regarding what the company is like as an employer. Creating effective employment brands is a major component of candidate *recruiting*.

Expected Distributions   A method of *calibration* where managers are told that their ratings of performance should generally conform to a certain preset distribution—for example, telling managers that roughly 10 percent of employees should be rated as "high performers" and roughly 5 percent are expected to be classified as "low performers." Expected distributions are different from *forced ranking* or *forced distributions* because employees are not required to make ratings conform to the distribution. But they may be asked to explain and justify why their ratings do not match the expected distribution.

Forced Ranking, Forced Distribution   A method of *calibration* where managers are required to place certain numbers of employees in different performance categories. For example, requiring managers to identify 10 percent of their employees as "poor performers." Forced ranking is the most extreme form of forced distribution as it requires managers to rank every employee in order from best to worst performance. Forced distributions can be effective in some situations provided they are done correctly, but they can significantly damage company performance if they are done in the wrong setting or in the wrong way.

Full-Time Equivalent/FTE   *Workforce planning* term used to indicate the level of staffing resources required for a position. One person working full time is considered to be an FTE, as are two employees working 50 percent time each. If a position required only one person to work half-time, it would be said to require .5 FTE.

Functional Competencies   *Competencies* that influence performance of jobs within a certain function or department. For example, financial planning might be a functional competency required for jobs in the accounting department but not required for jobs in the engineering department. Functional competencies are often contrasted with *core competencies*, which are required for all jobs in a company.

Hard Skills   An informal term that refers to specific technical abilities or solid factual knowledge required to do a job. It is sometimes said to reflect "what you know" as opposed to "how you use it," which is more a reflection of *soft skills*. For example, the ability to replace a flat tire might be considered a hard skill for an auto mechanic, while the ability to interact and build effective relationships with auto owners might be considered a soft skill for them. When the term *skills* is used by itself, it is usually referring to hard skills.

High-Volume Staffing   Staffing positions for which there are many openings to fill and many applicants applying for those openings. Entry-level customer service, retail, food service, and call center representative positions are examples of positions that often have high staffing volumes.

Human Capital   The people a company employs. It can refer to the number of employees a company has or needs to support its strategies, the capabilities of these employees, the financial resources required to employ these people, or all three.

   Human Resources (HR) Jobs and departments in an organization that are focused on ensuring the company is able to effectively hire, employ, manage, and develop the people needed to execute on company strategies.

Human Resource Information System (HRIS)   Software systems designed to support management of human resource data and administrative HR processes (e.g., payroll, job title, employee contact information).

Human Resource Management, Human Capital Management (HCM)   Processes, technology, and methods used to manage, support, develop and leverage *human capital* to support a company's business strategies.

Incentive System, Incentivize   Processes and technology systems used to administer *compensation* to employees. *Incentivize* refers to the act of tying compensation to certain employee actions or accomplishments.

Incumbents   Existing employees in a job.

Internal Staffing   Moving employees into different jobs within the company; includes both promotions and job transfers of existing employees.

Internal Talent Mobility   Movement of employees between different jobs across a company. Many companies seek to increase internal talent mobility through creating better *career development* and *internal staffing* processes. Internal talent mobility allows companies to maximize employee capabilities by moving people into jobs where they can provide the most value.

Interviews Assessments where candidate are evaluated based on how they answer questions posed to them by a person. Most interviews used open-ended questions. See also *behavioral interview; situational interview; structured interview*.

Job Analysis A systematic process for describing the behaviors that influence performance in a job. The results of job analysis can be used to guide development of *staffing assessment* instruments, *competency models, compensation* plans, and *development strategies*. Job analysis typically involves having consultants spend one or more days observing a job, interviewing subject matter experts, and collecting data from job incumbents and supervisors using structured questionnaires or focus groups.

Job Application A paper form or online process used to collect information from individuals interested in being considered as candidates for a specific job. Applications typically collect information such as a candidate's name, address, and work interests. They are often required to include material informing candidates of their legal rights and may also collect information relevant to *EEO* legislation.

Job Board A website or part of a website that allows job seekers to view available jobs posted by a variety of organizations. Once applicants have identified a job that they are interested in applying for, the job board provides them with a way to send critical job-related information such as a résumé to the employer. Many job boards also have a variety of additional services to help job seekers manage their careers and their ongoing job search process.

Job Family A grouping of jobs sharing similar characteristics (e.g., a typist, a receptionist, and an administrative assistant could all fall under the clerical job family). Things such as *competency models, staffing assessments*, and *talent pools* are often tied to job families.

Job Posting A notice advertising a job to candidates. Job postings can be placed in a wide range of locations, including online on company's *career portal* or on a *job board*, or as print ads run in newspapers or placed in store windows.

Job Relevance Term used to describe whether the *attributes* or *competencies* used for *staffing, performance management,* or *compensation* truly influence job performance or reflect actual *job requirements*. A key factor in evaluating the legal defensibility of an HR process is demonstrating its job relevance.

Job Requirement An *attribute* that is essential for being hired into a given job. Job requirements can be grouped into two general categories: requirements that are a necessary condition or *BFOQ* that candidates must meet in order to be hired into the job (e.g., possession of legally required licenses or certifications) and requirements in terms of candidate *attributes* that are determined to be critical for successful job performance based on a *job analysis* (e.g., possessing a certain level of job-relevant knowledge, skill, or ability).

Job Requisition   An internal document used in organizations to indicate a hiring need. Most companies do not start recruiting for a job until after a job requisition has been formally approved.

Knowledge   A body of information (conceptual, factual, or procedural) that can be applied directly to the performance of specific job-related tasks. For example, knowledge of the Java computer programming language is a type of knowledge relevant to performing certain information technology jobs.

Knowledge and Skills Tests   Tests of skills or job-specific knowledge. Examples include tests to assess a person's ability to use certain software programs or evaluate his or her understanding of specific technical terminology related to his or her profession (e.g., accounting tests).

Knowledge, Skills, Abilities, and Other Requirements (KSAOs)   *KSAO* is often used to describe the *attributes* identified through a *job analysis* as being critical for job performance. Information about a job's KSAOs can be used for a wide variety of HR functions, including selection, training and development, performance management, and compensation.

Leadership Development   Processes and tools focused on building leadership capabilities. Leadership development programs are typically a key component of *succession management.*

Learning Objective   A set of skills, capabilities, qualifications, or experiences employees want to acquire to improve the their current performance or advance their career. The purpose of most training and development programs is to help employees achieve learning objectives. *Career development plans* are used to define strategies to help employees achieve learning objectives. Learning objectives are also referred to as *developmental objectives.*

Learning Management, Learning Management Systems (LMS)   Processes and technology used to manage the delivery of training and development resources to employees. Major components of many of these systems are tools allowing companies to create, deliver, and track whether employees have completed specified online and classroom-based training courses.

Legally Defensible, Legal Defensibility (as applied to staffing and compensation methods)   Providing sufficient evidence to demonstrate job relevance and appropriate nature of an *HR* process according to relevant government laws, regulations, and guidelines. See also *Americans with Disabilities Act; Civil Rights Act of 1964; EEOC.*

Level-Specific Competencies   Competencies describing behaviors that influence the performance of jobs at different levels of the organization. For example, a company might have specific competencies for individual contributor, manager, and senior leader positions. Level-specific competencies are often contrasted with *functional competencies* and *core competencies.*

Merit Pay   *Compensation* provided to employees in recognition of their performance. Merit pay increases are usually based on a percentage of the employee's current salary. For example, a high-performing employee might be given a merit pay raise equivalent to 8 percent of his or her current salary. Merit pay is usually based on overall performance ratings and results in a permanent adjustment to someone's salary. It can be compared to *variable pay*, which is usually provided as a one-time award based on achieving annual, quarterly, or monthly performance targets.

Motivational Fit   Degree to which a person's interest and preference for working in certain types of jobs and environments match the characteristics and environment associated with a specific position or organization. Motivational fit is similar to *culture fit*, but focuses on a person's match with a specific job as opposed to a match with the broader organization or work group.

Multiple Hurdles   An approach that requires a job candidate to pass a series of assessments in order to progress in the selection process. Multiple hurdle assessment processes involve administering assessments at different points in the staffing process. Candidates must pass certain assessments early in the process before they are asked to take additional assessments later in the process—for example, requiring that candidates pass a *prescreening questionnaire* before they are allowed to participate in a *structured interview.*

Multirater, Multirater Assessment   Performance management method where information or ratings, or both, are collected from several people who work with the employee as part of the appraisal process. For example, a manager's performance evaluation might incorporate multirater input provided by the manager's supervisor and the manager's *direct reports.*

Networking, Social Networking   In the framework of *strategic HR*, networking typically refers to actions that help employees build relationships with other members of the organization. Networking is also used in the context of staffing to refer to actions taken by recruiting and hiring managers to build relationships with current or potential job candidates. The specific term *social networking* is usually used in the context of *social technology* systems that allow people to develop and maintain relationships with professional colleagues, coworkers, and friends.

Nine Box   A method commonly used in *succession management talent reviews* to evaluate employees based on their performance and potential. A nine box is a three-by-three grid where one axis is used to categorize employees according to three levels of performance and the other axis is used to categorize employees based on three levels of potential. The most valuable employees are those who appear in the upper-right corner since they have the highest levels of both performance and potential. Most companies use three-by-three nine boxes, although some companies create similar boxes with four-by-four grids (referred to as a "sixteen box") or other combinations. Some companies use a nine-box framework to evaluate employee performance where one axis corresponds to ratings of "what employees accomplished/ goals" and the other axis corresponds to "how they accomplished it/ competencies."

Normative   Processes that compare employees against one another based on their performance or potential. Many *calibration* methods emphasize normative performance comparisons.

Norm Groups   A group of individuals whose assessment scores are used to calculate *norms* for an assessment. This process is often called "norming an assessment." Norm groups might consist of existing employees, candidates applying for a particular job in an organization, or groups of people applying for the same type of jobs across several organizations.

Norms   Databases that can be used to calculate average scores on an assessment for a particular group of candidates or employees. Norms are often used to guide decisions about how to interpret assessment scores. For example, norms would be required to determine if a candidate's assessment score is above the fiftieth percentile relative to other candidates applying for similar jobs. Norms can also be used for *calibration*.

Onboarding A *transition management* program focused on helping employees adjust to new jobs or organizations. Most onboarding programs focus on newly hired employees, although onboarding programs can also be used to support internal transfers.

Operating Cost Refers to the financial resources required to run a company, department, or process. The majority of operating costs for most companies is tied to employee *compensation*.

Passive Candidate See *active versus passive candidates.*

Pay for Performance Processes designed so employees receive different amounts of compensation based on their level of job performance. It is rooted in a belief that people will be more productive if they are paid for their results. Pay for performance, however, works only if (1) employees understand the expectations for their performance, (2) employees see the rewards as adequate incentive for pursuing these expectations, (3) employees feel they are capable of meeting the expectations, and (4) the methods employees use to achieve these expectations truly support the needs of the business.

Performance Feedback Information provided back to employees that provides them with guidance on what they need to start, stop, or continue doing to improve or maintain their performance level. People cannot effectively improve their performance if they do not receive accurate and meaningful performance feedback.

Performance Management Processes used to communicate job expectations to employees, evaluate employees against those expectations, and use these evaluations to guide talent management decisions related to compensation, staffing, and development. Performance management encompasses a variety of activities including *talent reviews, calibration, pay-for-performance plans, performance feedback*, and other methods that measure employees based on the degree to which their actions and accomplishments align with the expectations and objectives of the company.

Performance Rating Forms, Criteria Ratings A form that used in a *criteria validation study* to measure employee performance. Managers or supervisors typically use performance rating forms to rate the performance of subordinates based on a set of specific job-related criteria. The ratings made using these forms are then correlated with an employee's test scores in order to provide statistical evidence of the relationship between the test and job performance. Collecting accurate performance ratings requires the use of well-designed forms, clearly communicating to raters that the ratings will be used only for assessment validation and will not be shared with the people being rated or any others in the organization and providing detailed instruction on how to appropriately measure and evaluate employee behavior.

Performance Variance   Indicates the difference in financial value associated with high- versus low-performing employees. It can be thought of as the difference between the value of a great employee and the cost of a bad employee. Performance variance is a function of both the value of good performance and the cost of bad performance. The higher the performance variance in a job is, the more value there is in hiring the best possible candidates for the job and actively managing and developing the performance of employees after they are hired.

Personality, Personality Traits   Attributes that reflect a person's behavioral tendencies, habits, and preferences. Personality is often referred to as a reflection of person's "typical performance" over time, as opposed to *abilities*, which are said to reflect a person's maximal performance when working on specific mentally or physically challenging tasks for a relatively limited amount of time. See also *soft skills* (which primarily reflect personality and interests) and *hard skills* (which primarily reflect *knowledge* and *abilities*).

Personality Measures   Assessments that measure *personality traits*. To avoid the clinical connotations associated with the term *personality*, many assessment vendors call their personality measures by other names, such as "workstyle assessments" or "talent measures."

Personnel Selection   The components of a staffing process used to determine whether to make a job offer to a candidate.

Pivotal Roles, Pivotal Positions   Jobs where small differences in performance have a significant impact on company profitability. This includes strategic leadership roles but may also include key operational roles such as plant managers in manufacturing companies or technical experts in software and biomedical research companies. It may also refer to roles that include very large numbers of people, such that small changes in performance have big impacts on profitability (e.g., frontline jobs in a retail organization). Also see *critical roles; development roles*.

Posthiring Development and Training Systems   Systems created to help new employees adapt to the job and reach maximum performance as quickly as possible. Typically involves providing employees with some form of developmental feedback on their strengths and weaknesses related to their new job. It may also include materials and tasks designed to help orient new employees to the organization and build social relationships with their new coworkers.

Prescreening   The evaluation of candidate qualifications early on in the staffing process. Prescreening is typically used early in the hiring process to rank or remove applicants based on their job *qualifications*. This frees up resources to be focused on gathering more in-depth information from qualified applicants.

Prescreening Questionnaire   An assessment tool that asks candidates to answer a set of predefined questions about job *qualifications* and *requirements*. The term *prescreening* is used to describe these questionnaires because they are commonly used to eliminate unqualified candidates early on in the selection process.

Protected Group, Protected Class   Refers to the groups of individuals protected by *EEO* legislation. The classifications for protected status include race, gender, religion, color, national origin, age, disability, and veteran status. Employers may not refuse to hire or discharge anyone on the basis of the protected classifications.

Psychometrics   Statistical processes and metrics that are often used during the construction of assessments and performance measures. The quality of an assessment or other measure of employee performance and potential can be evaluated based on its psychometric properties. Various psychometric techniques can be used during assessment development to help ensure the assessment's *reliability* and *validity*.

Qualified Candidate   A candidate who meets the minimum requirements to be eligible for a position. Regulations set forth by the *EEOC* require that companies track the demographic characteristics of qualified candidates to document potential *adverse impact* of selection methods. Specific information is available from the federal government that is intended to legally define when a candidate is considered to be a qualified candidate.

Qualifications   Specific candidate characteristics or attributes that influence their eligibility for a job. Common qualifications include previous work experience, educational background, and job relevant skills and knowledge. See also *requirements*.

Qualifications Screens   See *prescreening*.

Recruiting Functions associated with finding and bringing new talent into an organization. The term recruiting is largely synonymous with *staffing*. Some people use the term *recruiting* when referring to elements of staffing focused on *sourcing* candidates as opposed to *selection* of candidates.

Recruiting Marketing A specialized area of *recruiting* focused specifically on techniques used to advertise and market jobs to potential candidates. Recruiting marketing often emphasizes the use of Internet websites, search engines, and job postings combined with *workforce analytics* to determine what sources provide the greatest numbers of qualified candidates with the least cost.

Reliability Reliability reflects the stability of an assessment or measure. The more reliable an assessment is, the more a person's score on the assessment will remain the same over time. Reliability provides a sense of how much difference in assessment scores is due to stable differences between candidates or employees and how much of these differences are due purely to error of measurement (i.e., chance). Reliability is typically reported in the form of reliability coefficients that range from 0 to 1. Reliability coefficients for most well-designed assessments are above .6. It is important not to confuse reliability coefficients with *validity coefficients*.

Requirements Characteristics applicants must possess to be considered for employment in a job. Common requirements include minimum levels of previous job experience or education, licensure or citizenships requirements, and willingness to perform specific job tasks (e.g., willingness to work certain shift schedules). Requirements differ from *qualifications* in the sense that candidates either do or do not meet a job's requirements but may differ by degrees in terms of the level of qualifications they have for a job. See also *bona fide occupational requirements (BFOQ)*.

Requisition See *job requisition*.

Retention Refers to the length of time employees remain with a company or organization after they have been hired. Many assessments are designed to help increase employee retention. Retention is most effectively measured using statistics that reflect *average length of service*.

Road Map, Strategic HR Road Map Refers to a company's long-term plan for implementing and enhancing the methods used to support HR processes. A good strategic HR road map defines when different programs are going to be implemented, how they relate to each other, the general level of resources they require, and how they support the company's business execution needs.

Most road maps define projects through at least three years, with the recognition that long-term plans are likely to be modified if business needs shift.

(ROI) Return on Investment Refers to the financial value associated with the use of an HR method or any other type of organizational action or intervention. ROI is calculated by dividing the dollar value gained by the intervention by the costs associated with the intervention. See also *utility analysis*.

Screening Typically used to refer to assessment processes designed to remove applicants who do not meet minimum *requirements* or lack key job *qualifications* from the *candidate pool*. Screening methods typically focus on removing candidates who do not fit the job, in contrast to *selection* methods, which typically focus on identifying the candidates with the greatest potential for job success. Screening typically occurs early in the hiring process, while *selection* occurs later in the process.

Selection Typically used to refer to assessment processes that are designed to identify applicants in a *candidate pool* who possess *attributes* that suggest they have a high potential for job success. Selection may include the step of making a job offer to applicants who are considered eligible for hiring. Selection methods can be contrasted with *screening* methods, which typically focus on removing candidates who do not fit the job.

Selection Ratio Statistic indicating the number of applicants who pass a staffing assessment compared to the number of applicants who complete it. For example, if ten applicants completed an assessment but only five were considered to have passed the assessment, the selection ratio of the assessment would be 50 percent (5 divided by 10 = .50). Although it is not always the case, often the lower the selection ratio is for an assessment the more likely the assessment is to display *adverse impact.*

Self-Report Measures Assessments that ask applicants to describe themselves by indicating their interests, preferences, beliefs, and history. Examples of self-report questions including asking candidates if they agree with statements such as "I prefer to work alone," asking candidates about previous life experiences ("Have you ever quit a job?"), or asking them to evaluate their capabilities ("How skilled are you as a project manager?"). Many forms of assessments are self-report measures, including *personality measures*, *biodata* measures, and *prescreening questionnaires*. The phrase *self-report measures* typically describes assessments that use multiple choice questions to collect information from candidates, although technically an *interview* could also be considered a type of self-report measures.

Simulations, Job Simulations   Assessment tools that measure candidate skills by having them respond to a variety of situations designed to simulate actual job tasks. Simulations vary from low-fidelity paper-and-pencil description of different job scenarios, to high-fidelity simulations that use people to act out the roles of hypothetical customer or coworkers.

Situational Interview   A type of interview that asks candidates to discuss how they might respond in a specific work-related situation. An example is an interviewer asking a candidate, "What would you do if you were faced by an irate customer?" These questions differ from *behavioral interviews*, which focus on asking questions about specific behaviors that have already occurred, while situational interviews focus on presenting hypothetical work related situations.

Skills   Refers to a person's knowledge or physical capabilities related to perform a particular task or closely related set of tasks. Proficiency in a skill depends on a mix of natural talents and abilities, as well as experience and practice. Skills are often contrasted with behavioral *competencies* using the statement that "the skills define what you know how to do, and competencies describe how you apply your skills to achieve job goals."

Skilled Jobs, Skilled Labor   Skilled jobs are positions that require fairly extensive specialized skills, knowledge, expertise, and *qualifications* to perform. Nurses, mechanics, accountants, lawyers, and engineers all hold skilled jobs. In contrast, the jobs of retail clerks and fast food workers are not considered to be skilled since a company typically teaches employees any specialized skills and knowledge they need to perform the work. Skilled labor refers to people who possess the specialized skills needed to perform skilled jobs.

SMART Goals   Goals that meet the criteria of being specific, measurable, achievable, relevant, and time bound. The SMART goal framework is one of the most widely used techniques to ensure employees are given well-defined and appropriate goals. Although it is not the only framework for doing this (see *COD* goals).

Social Technology, Social Networking Technology   Technology designed to help people develop, build, and maintain relationships with others. The most common generally available social technology systems as this book is being written are probably Facebook, LinkedIn, and Twitter. In addition to these public systems, many organizations provide employees with access to social technology systems designed specifically to support social networking within the context of specific jobs or organizations.

Soft Skills   An informal term used to describe personal, interpersonal, and attitudinal behaviors that influence job performance. Frequently contrasted with *hard skills*, which are associated with technical knowledge and performance (e.g., what a person knows), soft skills describe aspects of job performance that reflect how people interact with others and manage themselves when faced with challenges and problems (e.g., how a person uses his or her knowledge).

Sourcing   The act of finding candidates to apply for a job opening. Sourcing can be active or passive. In active sourcing, recruiters search databases and job boards to look for and identify qualified candidates. Passive sourcing uses resources such as print advertisements, career pages, or job boards to help applicants find out about available job openings and compel them to apply. See also *active versus passive candidates*.

Staffing   The process of acquiring, deploying, and retaining a workforce of sufficient quantity and quality to create positive impacts on the organization's effectiveness. The process used to hire new employees into an organization. This term tends to be used somewhat synonymously with *recruiting*.

Staffing Assessment   Any tool or system that collects information from job candidates for the purpose of aiding hiring decisions. Examples include tests, questionnaires, and simulation exercises used to measure an individual's employment-related qualifications or characteristics (skills, knowledge, aptitudes). The information collected is used to influence or guide subsequent staffing or personnel decisions.

Staffing Assessment Administration System, Assessment Platform   An electronic system, usually online, that allows staffing professionals to configure and administer staffing assessments. These systems allow users to accomplish tasks such as scheduling candidates for assessments, attaching links to assessments to *job postings*, tracking a candidate's progress in the selection process, and sorting and searching assessment results.

Staffing Metrics   Statistical information about aspects of the staffing process—for example, staffing efficiency, time to fill a position, selection ratio, test or selection system validity, and cost per person hired.

Strategic HR, Strategic HR Processes   The methods and processes used to ensure a company's workforce delivers on its business strategies. It is often described as "getting the right people in the right jobs doing the right things and in a way that supports the right development for what we want people to do tomorrow."

Structured Interview A set of procedures used to ensure standardization in the interview process. Structured interviews use a set of standardized questions that are asked of all applicants. Applicant responses to these questions are scored using structured rating scales such as *BARS* that provide the ability to demonstrate the relevance of each answer to specific dimensions of job performance. These interviews provide significantly higher levels of validity then do traditional, unstructured interviews. The two most common types of structured interviews are *behavioral interviews* and *situational interviews*.

Subject Matter Expert (SME) Term used to refer to people who possess in-depth information about the nature of a job, work environment, or employee performance. SMEs play a critical role in providing the information needed to perform a *job analysis*. Typical SMEs include human resource personnel, hiring managers, and current employees.

Success Profile A poorly defined term that is used to refer to *competency models, candidate profiles*, or *employee profiles*.

Succession Management Methods used to ensure a steady supply of qualified talent for critical job roles. Historically, succession management focused on figuring out who would replace top executives. Organizations now use succession management for roles across the company, including key individual contributor positions. Many tools have been created specifically to support succession management (e.g., *nine box* talent reviews), but much of succession management is about coordinating other talent processes such as *workforce planning, staffing*, and *career development* to forecast, identify, develop, and place talent in critical positions.

Talent Management People use this term both broadly and narrowly. When used broadly, talent management is basically synonymous with *strategic HR*. When used narrowly, it refers more specifically to actions associated with *succession management, leadership development*, and *career development*.

Talent Pools Identified groups of internal employees or external candidates considered to be potential candidates for future jobs in the organization. Talent pools often include *active candidates* and *passive candidates*. One of the purposes of *workforce planning* is ensuring companies maintain large enough talent pools to support their future business needs.

Talent Reviews Meetings conducted to review and discuss the level of talent found within a company or department. These reviews typically involve bringing together several managers from within a company to discuss the performance and potential of employees in their groups. Most talent reviews are facilitated by a *strategic HR* professional. Talent reviews are frequently used to support *calibration* and *succession management.*

Technology Platform The technology system used to deliver, score, and manage HR processes. See also applicant tracking systems (ATS), *learning management systems (LMS),* and *human resource information systems (HRIS).*

Tenure The amount of time someone has spent in a specific job or organization. See also *average length of service; retention.*

Test Another term for *assessment.* The term *test* is usually applied when assessments are used to place people into categories as being eligible or ineligible for a job. This is in contrast to assessments that are used to provide information about candidates but do not actually classify them as being qualified or unqualified for a job.

360 Degree Survey A performance feedback survey designed primarily as a performance development tool. These surveys collect information from an employee's peers, supervisor, and direct reports regarding the employee's effectiveness in terms of critical work-related behaviors and *competencies.*

Total Rewards A term used in *compensation* to refer to the total benefits that employees receive from a company: salary, bonuses, health care, educational reimbursement, and any other financial rewards. The term *total rewards* is used to ensure that employees recognize the full range of rewards and resources they are receiving from the company.

Transfer of Training The degree to which employees effectively use skills acquired in one setting to address business challenges encountered in a different setting—for example, applying knowledge learned through a class on customer service to actually solve customer service challenges encountered at work. Transfer of training is a critical factor important to the effectiveness of development programs.

Transition Management Development programs focused on helping employees transition into a new job or move from one position to another within the organization. Also see *onboarding.*

Turnover The percentage of employees who leave a job or organization within a set amount of time. For example, annual turnover in a job is calculated by dividing the number of employees who left the job in a given year by the total number of employees in the job that same year. Turnover is typically divided into two categories: voluntary turnover, reflecting employees who chose to quit a job for various reasons, and involuntary turnover, reflecting employees who were fired or otherwise let go from their jobs. Turnover statistics are often used to evaluate the impact that *strategic HR* processes have on employee *retention*. However for statistical reasons, *average length of service* is considered to be a superior measure of *retention* than turnover.

Uniform Guidelines on Employee Selection A set of guidelines and regulations issued by the *EEOC* that describe how to create legally compliant and defensible staffing practices.

Unskilled Labor Employees or job candidates who do not possess specialized skills or capabilities. A major employment challenge facing many companies is they have jobs that require *skilled labor* but much of the available workforce is unskilled labor.

Utility Analysis Financial methods used to identify the costs, benefits, and *ROI* associated with HR methods, particularly *staffing*. Utility analyses help demonstrate the value added by estimating past or projected financial gains captured from using a specific HR process.

Validation The process of establishing the validity of a personnel selection assessment. See also *validity*.

Validity The extent to which an assessment truly measures what it is purported to measure. It indicates the degree of accuracy of predictions or inferences based on assessment results. See also *criteria validity*.

Values The term values can be interpreted two ways in the context of strategic HR. First, it can refer to interests and beliefs that influence what one chooses to do. In an assessment setting, values typically refer to preferences about the kind of work people want to do and the organizational environment they want to work in. Values are often used in assessments designed to predict *culture fit* and *motivational fit*. Second, it can be used to describe behaviors and norms employees are expected to display within a company. A company's values are often used to define its *core competencies*.

Variable Pay *Compensation* consisting of one-time bonuses and other financial rewards given to employees in recognition for work accomplishments. Variable pay is typically closely tied to performance against goals, in contrast to *merit pay*, which is often focused more on performance against *competencies.*

Vendor Any organization that makes *strategic HR* tools or technology available for sale to members of the general public or to qualified consultants. Vendors tend to fall into different categories (e.g., HR technology vendor, training vendor, staffing assessment).

Virtual Workforces, Virtual Employees Workforces and employees who do not work in an office owned and operated by the company. Most virtual employees work from their homes. Many employees work virtually or from home a few days a week, although more and more companies are employing full-time virtual employees.

Work Environment The place where a job is performed.

Work Environment Fit The match between a person's interests, *skills*, and preferences and characteristics of the work environment. Similar to *motivational fit.*

Work Samples *Job simulation* assessments that require applicants to perform tasks highly similar or identical to tasks actually performed on the job.

Work Style Describes personality and work values that influence job performance. See *personality measures.*

Workforce Analytics Tools and processes used to evaluate the financial impact staffing and workforce management actions have on company performance. Data for workforce analytics are often provided by *learning management, human resource information systems*, and *applicant tracking systems*, which collect information across multiple candidates, positions, and assessments. Workforce analytics data are often used to examine the business impact and *validity* of HR methods and practices.

Workforce Planning Processes and methods used to forecast future staffing needs. Workforce planning is used to predict the types of *talent pools* companies will need in order to support future business operations, taking into account the size of the current workforce, employee *turnover* and *average length of service*, and increasing or decreasing demand for different types of jobs. Workforce planning is used to guide *staffing* strategies and *development strategies.*

ABOUT THE AUTHOR

Steven Hunt is vice president of Customer Research at SuccessFactors, an SAP company, where he guides development and implementation of strategic HR solutions to maximize workforce engagement and productivity. Hunt has more than twenty years of experience designing human resource applications supporting a range of areas including performance management, staffing, career development, executive coaching, leadership development, organizational culture, employee engagement, workforce transformation, and succession management. A recognized expert in the design and deployment of technology-enabled talent management solutions, Hunt has assisted in implementation of systems that have improved the performance of millions of employees working for hundreds of companies ranging from small start-up organizations to many of the largest employers in the world. He has worked with organizations across a variety of industries including but not limited to retail, health care, manufacturing, finance, information technology, energy, transportation, and the public sector. His work has taken him to almost every continent on the globe. He has written articles for trade and academic journals ranging from the *Wall Street Journal* to the *International Journal of Selection & Assessment*, and authored a previous book on the applied use of staffing assessment methods entitled *Hiring success: The art and science of staffing assessment and employee selection* (2007, Pfeiffer). Steve regularly presents at customer events as well as industry and academic conferences. He holds a PhD in industrial-organizational psychology from The Ohio State University, a BA in applied mathematics from the University of California, San Diego, certification as a Strategic Professional of Human Resources (SPHR) from the Society of Human Resource Management, and serves on advisory boards for the Society of Human Resource Management, the Society of Industrial Organizational Psychology, the Workforce Institute, the *Journal of Management*, and several other talent management organizations.

INDEX

Page references followed by *fig* indicate an illustrated figure; followed by *t* indicate a table.

objectives using, 261–263; development method of, 253t, 256; integrated with other development methods, 260fig; mapping roles, relationships, and resources to, 262t; metrics used for, 290t

CEOs (chief execution officers): defining strategy role of, 28; endorsing, enforcing, and exhibiting change by, 347; hypothetical conversation on strategic HR processes between CHRO and, 39–40

Change: defining how you will create and measure, 308, 319–323; defining requirements for, 334–337; defining what it will look like, 308, 314–319; endorsing, enforcing, and exhibiting, 346fig–347; enlisting line leadership to drive, 345–347; identifying what you want to, 308, 309–313; operationalizing the, 323–327; providing tools and training to support, 337–345; stakeholders in HR process for, 335fig–337; the two basics of strategic HR to create and sustain, 351–352; why most initiatives take three years to reach full effectiveness, 313

Change creation metrics: description of, 308, 319; questions to ask about, 319–320; of strategic HR process impact, 321t–322t

Change definition: description of, 308, 314; distinguishing between process automation and business transformation, 314–316t; examples of transformation events associated with HR processes, 317t–318t

Change identification: of critical actions for business execution, 308, 309; steps taken for, 309–312; talent process maturity grid for, 310t–311t

Change management traits potential, 277

Change operationalization: achieve perfection through application, 324; cross-functional steering team to help with, 323; description of, 308, 323; enlisting line leadership to drive, 345–347; move

from a push to a pull for, 325; pace the change, 324–325; providing tools and training to support, 337–345; technology used to support, 324

Change tools: branding HR processes as, 344–345; how technology works as a, 337–344

Cherniss, C., 334

CHRO (chief human resource officer), 39–40

Circuit City: bad management and demise of, 1–2; examining the HR success and failures of, 7

COACH Method: creating consequences, 239; establish credibility, 238; increasing awareness, 238–239; increasing employee performance using the, 237–239; providing help and support to employees, 239; set objectives, 238

Coaching: competencies in context of, 173–174; to increase workforce alignment and productivity, 160; replacing performance evaluation with performance, 155–156; year-round performance, 188

Coaching feedback, 338fig

COD goal model: on commitments, outcomes, and deliverables, 117–118, 119–120; evaluating goals using the, 131; guidelines on how to apply, 118–120; implementing goal cascading using the, 129–131

Coffman, C., 107

Cognitive traits potential, 276

Commitment: COD goal model on, 117–118, 119; example of a goal written using COD format of, 119; how to ensure employees feel a sense of, 120–123; "what I'm doing" answered through, 119

Common interest groups, 142

Communication: using goals as tool for, 123; of pay and staffing decisions based on performance evaluation, 204fig, 210; strategies for coordination goals to foster, 141–142. See also Feedback

ods used by, 216; Jack Welch's effective leadership of, 6–7, 216

research on performance evaluation impact on, 153–155; strategic HR impact on, 349–350

Organizational values: goal importance is determined by, 138; pay and promotion as expressions of, 55–56

Organizations: "goal-driven," 104–107; proactive recruiting, 70, 73–74; reactive recruiting, 70; three kinds of transformation by, 314–315

Outcomes: COD goal model on, 118, 119; example of a goal written using COD format of, 120; metrics used for, 292; "why I'm doing it" answered through, 119

P

Pacing change, 324–325

Participative goal setting, 120–122

Pay bonuses, 223–224

Pay-for-performance programs: aligning business results with, 22–23; limitations of, 23; scenarios illustrating possible outcomes of, 221–222

Pay/salary. See Compensation

Performance: defining effective, 168–183; how performance management impacts organizational, 159; research on performance evaluation impact on organizational, 153–155; strategic HR impact on, 349–350. See also Job performance; Productivity

Performance calibration, 214

Performance coaching, 155–156

Performance evaluation steps: A: integrate objective data, 204fig, 205–206; B: employee self-assessment, 204fig, 206; C: coworker and customer input, 204fig, 206–207; D: manager's initial assessment, 204fig, 208; E: manager and employee review, 204fig, 208; F: manager's overall assessment, 204fig, 208; G: manager's manager review, 204fig, 209; H: process administrator review, 204fig, 209; I: talent review and calibration sessions, 209; J: final assessment,

204fig, 210; K: providing employee feedback, 204fig, 210; L: communicating pay and staffing decisions, 204fig, 210; M: performance improvement plan (if needed), 211

Performance evaluations: avoid tying them to employment anniversary dates, 189; calibrating, 211–220; for classification versus development, 162–165; compensation decisions based on, 220–224fig; debate over the use of, 155–156; deciding on the purpose of, 191–192; designing rating scales to use for, 192–200; designing the process and steps of, 200–201, 202–207, 208–211; development decisions on, 226–228; increasing process maturity of, 242–244; justice and fairness issues of, 241; keep compensation and staffing decisions distinct from, 189–190; making decisions about content of, 190–191; separated into descriptive assessment and normative evaluation, 189; staffing decisions based on, 224–226; understanding the benefits of, 153–155; workforce management decisions based on, 228–230. See also Evaluation; Job performance

Performance improvement plan, 204fig, 211

Performance management: anxiety by HR professionals over rigorous, 230–233; anxiety by managers over rigorous, 236–237, 239–240; balancing the conflicting goals of, 159–161; changes affecting manager and employee adoption of, 234t–235t; description of, 151; difficulty of, 152–153, 156–157; employees' use of, 240–242; examining how to increase productivity using, 151–152; negative mind-set of employees regarding, 344–345; 120 survey process for, 207–208; process objectives, elements, and trade-offs, 166t–167t; role of competencies in, 173–174; two sides of, 163fig; why we need, 158–159. See also Managers; Right way

Performance management cycle: guidelines for structuring your, 186–190; illustration of a, 184*fig*; linking business operations, employee effectiveness, and workforce management, 187–188; managing business operations, 185; managing employees effectiveness, 185–187; managing workforce resources, 187

Performance management design questions: deciding how to use the performance evaluation data, 220–230; how do you define effective performance?, 168–183; how to structure performance management cycle?, 183–190; how will you calibrate performance evaluations?, 211–220; how will you evaluate performance?, 190–211; listed, 161; what are your primary objectives?, 162–167*t*; what training and incentives to use?, 230–242

Performance rating scales: avoiding overly complicating performance weights, 196–197; base ratings on well-defined performance criteria, 196; descriptive labels used for, 194*t*–196; five-point versus seven-point, 193–194; inadvisable of using overall performance, 197–199; issues to consider when designing, 192–193

Personality questionnaires, 92*t*, 257

Peterson, S. J., 23

Physical ability tests, 90*t*

Pivotal jobs, 68, 69*t*, 75

Predefined goal plans, 125–126

Prescreening questionnaires, 92*t*

Proactive recruiting organizations, 70, 73–74

Procedural justice, 241

Productivity: assessing capacity for sustaining performance and, 37; attracting, developing, and retraining high-performing employees, 16; coaching to increase, 160; distinguishing between alignment and, 32–33; examining how performance management is used to increase, 151–152; how to get newly hired employees up to full, 93–94; identifying and addressing low-performing employees, 16; limitations of pay-for-performance programs to increase, 23; linking different HR processes to, 41*fig*, 42; maximizing workforce, 15–16; performance management process objectives, elements, and trade-offs for, 166*t*; strategic human resources (HR) purpose of facilitating, 16–17. *See also* Performance

Professional recruiting, 85*t*, 87

Promotion: decision-making related to, 55–56; establishing guidelines for internal, 225; performance management to facilitate decisions on, 160; relationship between goal accomplishment and, 133–135

Purpose-driven employees, 135–136

Q

QWERTY keyboard, 12

R

Rating scales. *See* Performance rating scales

Reactive recruiting organizations, 70

Recruiters: hiring process role of the, 79–83*t*; time-to-hire metric for performance evaluation of, 70–73

Recruiting: changing role of, 61; generational differences that may impact, 88–89; getting hiring managers to take seriously, 62–64; hiring manager involvement in, 65–66; how to improve success and processes of, 94–96; prehiring and posthiring metrics, 95*t*–96; proactive, 70, 73–74; process maturity levels, 96*fig*–97; reactive, 70; to support business execution, 60–61; time-to-hire metric for performance evaluation of, 70–73; workforce planning and job design components of, 67. *See also* Hiring; Job candidates

line leadership to drive the change, 329, 345–347; establishing HR leadership credibility, 329, 330–334; providing tools and training to support change, 329, 337–345

Strategic human resources (HR) process maturity: examples of transformation events associated with HR processes, 317*t*–318*t*; goal management, 145–147; performance management, 242–244; recruiting process, 96*fig*–97; right development, 44*fig*, 46; right people, 44*fig*; right things, 44*fig*, 45; right way, 44*fig*, 45; talent process maturity grid for determining critical actions, 310*t*–311*t*

Strategic human resources (HR) processes: business execution and, 27–57; change supported by branding, 344–345; fundamental, 17–20; increasing maturity of, 43–46; relationship to specific business executive driver, 41*fig*; role of goals in an integrated, 107–110; sailing small boat analogy for design of, 352; to support business executive, 39–41; supporting business executive drivers by implementing key, 57; understanding employee performance factors for effective, 24. *See also* 4R model; Integrating strategic HR processes

Strategy: analogy of weight loss, 28; business execution requirement of defining, 27; CEO role in defining, 28

Structured interview guides, 89–90, 91*t*

Stupidus Maximus Award, 1

Succession calibration, 215

Succession management: achieving learning objectives using, 261–263; development method of, 253*t*, 255–256; integrated with other development methods, 260*fig*; mapping roles, relationships, and resources to, 262*t*; metrics used for, 290*t*

Sustainability: as business execution driver, 34; definition of, 34; linking different HR processes to, 41*fig*, 42; performance management process objectives, elements, and trade-offs for, 167*t*

T

Tactical transformation, 314, 315

Talent management: balancing internal versus external hiring, 66–67; building talent pools, 84*t*, 86; changing focus from quantity to quality hiring, 59–60; development addressing specific talent requirements, 267–270; HR technology (2001 to 2010) supporting, 30–31; performance management to facilitate decisions of, 160; problems with using ROI to justify, 332; strategies for integrated, 66–67; workforce planning and job design, 67. *See also* Hiring

Talent poaching concept, 297–298

Tasks: description of, 115; distinguishing between goals and, 115; job, 179

Technical onboarding, 93

Technology: change operationalization and supporting, 324; development program, 285*t*–286*t*; how change is enabled by, 337–344; learning management systems (LMS), 256; social, 85*t*, 87, 142, 201–202. *See also* HR technology

360 survey: assessment using, 256; lesson on misguided development using a, 251; metrics used for, 291*t*; 120 survey versus, 207–208

Time-to-fill, 71, 72, 73

Time-to-hire, 70–73

Time-to-start, 71, 73

Toegel, G., 251

Top-down development, 303–304

Training resources: achieving learning objectives using, 261–263; development method of, 253*t*, 256; integrating with other development methods, 260*fig*; mapping roles, relationships, and resources to, 262*t*; metrics used for, 290*t*

Transactionally driven employees, 136, 137

CPSIA information can be obtained
at www.ICGtesting.com
Printed in the USA
JSHW050909040623
42632JS00007B/150